Cinema and Brexit

Cinema and Society Series
General Editor: Jeffrey Richards

Acting for the Silent Screen: Film Actors and Aspiration between the Wars
Chris O'Rourke

The Age of the Dream Palace: Cinema and Society in 1930s Britain
Jeffrey Richards

Banned in the USA: British Films in the United States and their Censorship, 1933–1960
Anthony Slide

Best of British: Cinema and Society from 1930 to the Present
Anthony Aldgate & Jeffrey Richards

Beyond a Joke: Parody in English Film and Television Comedy
Neil Archer

Brigadoon, Braveheart and the Scots: Distortions of Scotland in Hollywood Cinema
Colin McArthur

Britain Can Take It: British Cinema in the Second World War
Tony Aldgate & Jeffrey Richards

The British at War: Cinema, State and Propaganda, 1939–1945
James Chapman

British Children's Cinema: From the Thief of Bagdad to Wallace and Gromit
Noel Brown

British Cinema and the Cold War: The State, Propaganda and Consensus
Tony Shaw

British Film Design: A History
Laurie N. Ede

Children, Cinema and Censorship: From Dracula to the Dead End Kids
Sarah J. Smith

China and the Chinese in Popular Film: From Fu Manchu to Charlie Chan
Jeffrey Richards

Christmas at the Movies: Images of Christmas in American, British and European Cinema
Edited by Mark Connelly

The Classic French Cinema 1930–1960
Colin Crisp

The Crowded Prairie: American National Identity in the Hollywood Western
Michael Coyne

The Death Penalty in American Cinema: Criminality and Retribution in Hollywood Film
Yvonne Kozlovsky-Golan

Distorted Images: British National Identity and Film in the 1920s
Kenton Bamford

The Euro-Western: Reframing Gender, Race and the 'Other' in Film
Lee Broughton

An Everyday Magic: Cinema and Cultural Memory
Annette Kuhn

Family Films in Global Cinema: The World Beyond Disney
Edited by Noel Brown and Bruce Babington

Femininity in the Frame: Women and 1950s British Popular Cinema
Melanie Bell

Film and Community in Britain and France: From La Règle du jeu to Room at the Top
Margaret Butler

Film Propaganda: Soviet Russia and Nazi Germany
Richard Taylor

The Finest Years: British Cinema of the 1940s
Charles Drazin

Frank Capra's Eastern Horizons: American Identity and the Cinema of International Relations
Elizabeth Rawitsch

From Moscow to Madrid: European Cities, Postmodern Cinema
Ewa Mazierska & Laura Rascaroli

From Steam to Screen: Cinema, the Railways and Modernity
Rebecca Harrison

Hollywood and the Americanization of Britain: From the 1920s to the Present
Mark Glancy

The Hollywood Family Film: A History, from Shirley Temple to Harry Potter
Noel Brown

Hollywood Genres and Postwar America: Masculinity, Family and Nation in Popular Movies and Film Noir
Mike Chopra-Gant

Hollywood Riots: Violent Crowds and Progressive Politics in American Film
Doug Dibbern

Hollywood's History Films
David Eldridge

Hollywood's New Radicalism: War, Globalisation and the Movies from Reagan to George W. Bush
Ben Dickenson

Licence to Thrill: A Cultural History of the James Bond Films
James Chapman

The New Scottish Cinema
Jonathan Murray

Past and Present: National Identity and the British Historical Film
James Chapman

Powell and Pressburger: A Cinema of Magic Spaces
Andrew Moor

Projecting Tomorrow: Science Fiction and Popular Cinema
James Chapman & Nicholas J. Cull

Propaganda and the German Cinema, 1933–1945
David Welch

Shooting the Civil War: Cinema, History and American National Identity
Jenny Barrett

Spaghetti Westerns: Cowboys and Europeans from Karl May to Sergio Leone
Christopher Frayling

Spectacular Narratives: Hollywood in the Age of the Blockbuster
Geoff King

Typical Men: The Representation of Masculinity in Popular British Cinema
Andrew Spicer

The Unknown 1930s: An Alternative History of the British Cinema, 1929–1939
Edited by Jeffrey Richards

Withnail and Us: Cult Films and Film Cults in British Cinema
Justin Smith

Believing in Film: Christianity and Classic European Cinema
Mark Le Fanu

The Lost Worlds of John Ford: Beyond the Western
Jeffrey Richards

Cinema and Brexit

The Politics of Popular English Film

Neil Archer

BLOOMSBURY ACADEMIC
LONDON • NEW YORK • OXFORD • NEW DELHI • SYDNEY

BLOOMSBURY ACADEMIC
Bloomsbury Publishing Plc
50 Bedford Square, London, WC1B 3DP, UK
1385 Broadway, New York, NY 10018, USA
29 Earlsfort Terrace, Dublin 2, Ireland

BLOOMSBURY, BLOOMSBURY ACADEMIC and the Diana logo are
trademarks of Bloomsbury Publishing Plc

First published in Great Britain 2021
This paperback edition published in 2022

Copyright © Neil Archer, 2021

Neil Archer has asserted his right under the Copyright, Designs and Patents Act,
1988, to be identified as Author of this work.

For legal purposes the Acknowledgements on p. x constitute an
extension of this copyright page.

Cover design: Charlotte Daniels
Cover image: Daniel Craig in Skyfall (2012) directed by Sam Mendes
(© Sony Pictures / Collection Christophel / ArenaPAL)

All rights reserved. No part of this publication may be reproduced or
transmitted in any form or by any means, electronic or mechanical, including
photocopying, recording, or any information storage or retrieval system,
without prior permission in writing from the publishers.

Bloomsbury Publishing Plc does not have any control over, or responsibility for,
any third-party websites referred to or in this book. All internet addresses given
in this book were correct at the time of going to press. The author and publisher
regret any inconvenience caused if addresses have changed or sites have
ceased to exist, but can accept no responsibility for any such changes.

A catalogue record for this book is available from the British Library.

Library of Congress Cataloging-in-Publication Data
Names: Archer, Neil, 1971- author.
Title: Cinema and Brexit : the politics of popular English film / Neil Archer.
Description: London ; New York : Bloomsbury Academic 2020. | Series: Cinema
and society | Includes bibliographical references and index. |
Identifiers: LCCN 2020019127 (print) | LCCN 2020019128 (ebook) | ISBN
9781501351334 (hardback) | ISBN 9781350104488 (epub) | ISBN
9781350104495 (pdf) | ISBN 9781350104501
Subjects: LCSH: Motion pictures–Great Britain–History–21st century. |
National characteristics, British, in motion pictures. | Motion pictures–Political
aspects–Great Britain. | Motion pictures–Social aspects–Great Britain.
Classification: LCC PN1993.5.G7 A835 2020 (print) | LCC PN1993.5.G7
(ebook) | DDC 791.43/658–dc23
LC record available at https://lccn.loc.gov/2020019127
LC ebook record available at https://lccn.loc.gov/2020019128

ISBN: HB: 978-1-5013-5133-4
        PB: 978-1-3502-7434-1
        ePDF: 978-1-3501-0449-5
        eBook: 978-1-3501-0448-8

Series: Cinema and Society

Typeset by Integra Software Services Pvt. Ltd.

To find out more about our authors and books visit www.bloomsbury.com
and sign up for our newsletters

Contents

List of illustrations	viii
Acknowledgements	x
General Editor's Introduction	xi
Introduction: Film through the looking glass	1
1 Film politics: Brexit, brand Britain and soft power	37
2 Comedians and sunscreen: The English holiday film and the idea of Europe	59
3 'Not to Yield': Globalization, nation and the epic imagination of English cinema	99
4 Genius of Britain: The English scientist film and other science fictions	139
5 Through a screen, darkly: Austerity genres, Brexit topographies and the precarity of national cinema	171
6 Just follow the bear? StudioCanal, transnational franchises and a European English cinema	203
Conclusion: Longing for yesterday?	229
Notes	237
Bibliography	267
Index	282

List of illustrations

1.1 The conjunction of the (media) stars: James Bond (Daniel Craig) and Queen Elizabeth II in *Happy and Glorious*, made for the 2012 London Olympic Games opening ceremony. Directed by Danny Boyle © BBC 2012. All rights reserved   43

1.2 Made in London: *Harry Potter and the Deathly Hallows: Part One* (2011), a flagship film used as publicity for the GREAT Britain campaign. Directed by David Yates © Warner Bros. Pictures 2011. All rights reserved   55

2.1 Welcome to 'Europe'! Arrival, and the introduction of a dead cat, in *The Inbetweeners Movie* (2011). Directed by Ben Palmer © Film4 2011. All rights reserved   70

2.2 'Europe' as an advertising aesthetic: Eddy and Patsy's imagined Riviera in *Absolutely Fabulous: The Movie*. Directed by Mandie Fletcher © Fox Searchlight Pictures 2016. All rights reserved   73

2.3 'Budget Wings': The 'experience economy' runs up against economy airlines in *Absolutely Fabulous: The Movie*. Directed by Mandie Fletcher © Fox Searchlight Pictures 2016. All rights reserved   76

2.4 Celebrating itself as a model of 'European cinema': Singing on the *Croisette* at the end of *Mr. Bean's Holiday*. Directed by Steve Bendelack © Universal Pictures 2007. All rights reserved   86

2.5 A Room with a Distant View: Ironies of the 'authentic' tourist experience in *The Trip to Italy*. Directed by Michael Winterbottom © BBC 2014. All rights reserved   90

3.1 Stages in the (Epic) Hero's Journey: Churchill, alone amongst men, endures his *Darkest Hour*. Directed by Joe Wright © Focus Features/Universal Pictures 2017. All rights reserved   112

3.2 The *Skyfall* of the Gods: Bond, Q and Turner's *The Fighting Temeraire*. Directed by Sam Mendes © Sony Pictures Releasing 2012. All rights reserved   114

3.3	Resurgence and renewal: Turner, referenced and re-worked, in the conclusion of *Skyfall*. Directed by Sam Mendes © Sony Pictures Releasing 2012. All rights reserved	116
3.4	Muscular diplomacy: The authority of a populist King Arthur, acknowledged by the Vikings, at the end of *King Arthur: Legend of the Sword*. Directed by Guy Ritchie © Warner Bros. Pictures 2017. All rights reserved	125
3.5	Optimism of youth: The schoolboy sword-bearer, and his Round Table, in *The Kid Who Would Be King*. Directed by Joe Cornish © 20th Century Fox 2019. All rights reserved	126
3.6	The connotations of the 'European' game: Dug's 'English' side faces 'Real Bronzio' in *Early Man*. Directed by Nick Park © StudioCanal UK 2018. All rights reserved	132
4.1	'Heritage' space as the Futures of Britain: Jane Wilde, Stephen Hawking and Cambridge University in *The Theory of Everything*. Directed by James Marsh © Focus Features/Universal Pictures 2014. All rights reserved	152
4.2	Dev Patel as Srinivasa Ramanujan in *The Man Who Knew Infinity*: critical history and institutional promotion combine. Directed by Matthew Brown © Warner Bros./IFC Films 2015. All rights reserved	155
4.3	The computer, situated futuristically within a 'natural' mise-en-scène, in *The Imitation Game*. Directed by Morten Tyldum © The Weinstein Company 2014. All rights reserved	159
5.1	Continuity and revision: Transatlantic casting in austerity contexts – Anne Hathaway in *One Day*. Directed by Lone Sherfig © Focus Features 2011. All rights reserved	184
5.2	'New Survey Suggests Happier Britain': A troubled view from Conservative England in *The World's End*. Directed by Edgar Wright © Focus Features/Universal Pictures 2013. All rights reserved	192
5.3	A laughing matter? Chris and Tina turn their gaze on the viewer towards the end of *Sightseers*. Directed by Ben Wheatley © StudioCanal UK 2012. All rights reserved	201
6.1	London's European city as a port in a storm: Mr Gruber remembers the *Kindertransport* in *Paddington*. Directed by Paul King © StudioCanal 2014. All rights reserved	219

Acknowledgements

The research for large parts of this book was undertaken thanks to a BA/Leverhulme Small Research Grant, which enabled me to make invaluable visits to the BFI in London and to the Cinémathèque Française in Paris. I am especially grateful to the British Academy for this award.

Many thanks to Rebecca Barden and everyone at Bloomsbury, along with the Cinema and Society series editor Jeffrey Richards, for encouraging this project and seeing it through to publication. The book's readers also provided insightful advice at an earlier stage of its development: the finished product owes a lot to their excellent suggestions.

I'm indebted to Keele University for supporting and hosting the Film and Television Studies after Brexit workshop held in April 2017, and from which many of the ideas and arguments in this book emerged. I am especially obliged to all those who gave talks and participated in the discussions that day: Owen Evans, Beth Johnson, James Leggott, Jonathan Murray, Julian Petley, David Forrest and Clive Nwonka.

My thanks as usual to colleagues at Keele. Special thanks, above all, to Helen Parr and Gavin Bailey for being such good neighbours.

Big shout out to Jacqueline Wilson and Michelle Obama for the literary company during the early months of 2020. And to Jürgen Klopp: maximum respect. *There can be only one!*

As ever, my love to Giulia Miller and Noa Archer for reminding me what's really going on.

And of course, a big salute to all the NHS doctors, nurses and staff for their unstinting commitment: a lesson to all of us.

Finally, whatever the rights and wrongs of Brexit, its impacts are most likely to be felt by those who, for reasons of birth or age, were not permitted a say on the future of the country in which they live or will grow up. For what it's worth, this book is dedicated to them.

General Editor's Introduction

There has rarely been in recent years a time when the question of national identity has been so urgent and contested. The referendum on Britain's membership of the European Union split the country more bitterly than almost any ideological conflict since the English Civil War. It divided families, communities and political parties. It re-energized the demand in Scotland for independence and in Ireland the desire for reunification. Coming in the midst of all this turmoil, the Windrush scandal exacerbated the questions of immigration and race which were also fundamental to the Brexit debate.

Neil Archer argues that popular English cinema does not directly reflect an agreed national identity but should rather be read as 'a site of contradictions, erasure and myth'. His concentration on English rather than British cinema is amply justified by the fact that it was English votes that determined Britain's exit from the European Union. Archer's idea of Englishness is one that emphasizes its difference from the prevailing characters of both European culture and Hollywood cinema. He explores his theory through the study of specific film genres: the holiday film, the scientist biopic and the epic. During the course of this he not only analyses some of the key English films of recent times, but also their production context. A running theme of the book is the future of English cinema in a globalized world. Stimulating and thought-provoking, *Cinema and Brexit* puts Neil Archer's book in the vanguard of the rapidly emerging new discipline of Brexit Studies.

Jeffrey Richards

Introduction: Film through the looking glass

On the morning of 24 June 2016, I was walking to school with my five-year-old daughter, having left back at home, all over the news, the alternately ashen and beaming faces of the men who had instigated, lost and won Britain's referendum on EU membership. Whichever way you looked at it, the country was now a different place, though life carried on as normally as it possibly could. Some celebrated; others mourned. Children went to school, people went to work, the buses continued to run – more or less on time.

Glancing at the number 25 that passed me on the school run that morning, the mental image of those middle-aged men was replaced by that of two well-preserved, if not slightly pickled, middle-aged women. This was an advertisement for *Absolutely Fabulous: The Movie* (2016), the first big-screen outing for Jennifer Saunders and Joanna Lumley's comic duo, derived from the long-running BBC series of the same name. The advert showed Saunders and Lumley balanced on an over-sized, spraying bottle of Bollinger champagne: an invitation to join Edina and Patsy on the first British cinematic adventure of the summer. Released the following week, *Absolutely Fabulous* would turn out to be the first British film of the post-referendum era. This, I now recognize, was where this book first took shape. Welcome to Brexit cinema![1]

It may seem facetious to begin a book on cinema and Brexit with *Absolutely Fabulous*, and its paean to political indifference and champagne-soaked hedonism. Its inclusion here, though (and I will discuss the film in a later chapter), is entirely serious, and exemplifies the approach this book will take. As I will suggest here, in investigating cinema within the contexts of Brexit, if we *don't* look at a film like *Absolutely Fabulous*, what exactly *are* we looking at?

Future accounts of film in the Britain of 2016 may highlight a number of things. As we will see later, discussions of British cinema's successes may focus on big-budget blockbuster franchises that, while made in Britain, may for some have nothing to do with 'British' cinema at all. Others may point to the popularity of revamped television comedy or returning rom-com properties, in the form of *Absolutely Fabulous*, the *Dad's Army* film or *Bridget Jones's Baby*. Others may reasonably ignore these altogether, and hold up as the most significant British film of the year *I, Daniel Blake*, winner of Cannes' coveted Palme D'Or. Ken Loach's characteristically excoriating tale of failings in the British welfare system, on the face of it, would suggest by comparison how relatively unimportant other films were to an understanding of the nation's contemporary contexts and divisions. With no disrespect intended to Loach's film, I argue in this book that this is not the case. To make an inevitably simplistic but relevant comparison: Which film, in the contexts of the EU referendum, tells us more about modern Britain, and its relationship to Europe? A film shot in England, feted at Cannes and seen by twice as many people in France as in its own country? Or a film shot partly in Cannes, feted by no one in particular and which reaped $20m at the UK box-office – almost five times as much as Loach's film?

Such comparisons, to use the old adage, are odious. The evaluation of film is hardly reducible to such statistics. Moreover, in analysing such differences in viewing habits, we also need to take into account the asymmetric practices of distribution and exhibition that privilege one film, as in this instance, over another. From one perspective, more people in Britain went to see *Absolutely Fabulous* simply because it was on more screens. But in turn – and this lies at the heart of this book's aims – we need to ask what informs these circumstances. We need to make sense of what, for want of a better word, we will call such 'popular' cinema, if we are to get the fullest sense of how a national audience sees its films, and, in turn, sees itself. Uneven processes of production and screening are never just blunt or random industrial facts, as they tell us precisely how a national *industry* sees itself and its productions. They tell us about the kinds of films, in other words, it wants to make, for constituencies of viewers it has in mind.

The case of British film in this respect – and, as I will clarify later, for particular reasons I am realistically referring in this book to *English* film – is a significant one. As Andrew Higson has explored in his book *Film England*, referring to what he calls 'culturally English filmmaking' in the 1990s and 2000s, 'British' cinema is perennially constructed with an eye towards specific markets, whether these be global or local. A long-standing tradition of 'low-budget, more independently made ... indigenous films' persists, more often than not 'concentrat[ing] on local places, characters and identities'.[2] These films have frequently focused on 'ethnic minority communities' or 'the working classes and the post-industrial underclasses'.[3] *I, Daniel Blake* is clearly in this category. Such smaller cost films rarely aspire to sizeable domestic or export distribution, the assumption being that their style and subject matter cannot hold wide appeal. For a number of linguistic or cultural reasons, meanwhile, another tradition of British cinema has been able to capitalize on the global appeal of Britishness – or as Higson specifies, 'Englishness' – giving rise to the popular success of certain 'culturally English' cinematic forms. These include, though are not limited to, the rom-com, genre parodies, the literary adaptation or franchises such as *Harry Potter*. In this book I will add some other film types to the list: 'holiday' films and biopics, road movies, 'epic' films and sports movies. Exactly how these films in narrative and aesthetic terms can be said to represent and above all 'reflect' the contexts of contemporary national life is a complex question. The point I will make, though, is that they clearly both represent and reflect an *idea* of the nation that is amenable to both domestic and often global audiences. It is a cinema that recent traditions of English-centred film production have chosen as a means of representing England, as/and Britain, both at home and abroad, for good or ill. These films form the subjects of analysis in this book. Identifying the relevance of these films for our understanding of Brexit, and indeed the relevance of Brexit for these films, is one of its main tasks.

How can we talk about cinema and Brexit? What this book is (and isn't) about

In setting this task, we need firstly to ask how we make sense of the correlation – if it exists at all – between a body of films and the discourses around Brexit. As I outline below, while I argue for the work of films to construct particular narratives of nation, and to inscribe notions of identity, this book does *not* argue that cinema has played any obvious instrumental role in the ideological contexts underpinning the 2016 EU referendum, even though it may have played an incidental role in the wider subsequent discussions. It is quite possible of course that these films *indirectly*, or in specific cases, directly contributed to the ideas and viewpoints sustaining both sides of the EU debate. There are already a number of studies investigating if, and how, mass- or social media may have contributed to the populist or nativist sentiments informing much of the Leave agenda in the run-up to the referendum.[4] For reasons I set out below, to make similar claims for film would be problematic. There is potential scope for some sort of audience analysis, looking at the ways in which varied viewers respond to particular ideas and representations in cinema. Such a project, though, for it to say anything substantial, would be a vast one. As it would be based mostly on how audiences respond to given films, which might be in entirely different or even antithetical ways, such a project would have significant sociological impact. But as much as it might tell us about the viewers and what they bring to films, it would in itself tell us very little about the films themselves, in terms of how they are made, where they are coming from and why.

Making assumptions, then, about what circumstances films may be seen to reflect, is not my focus here; though as I will explain, this is also largely for methodological reasons. As a work of film and cultural studies, moreover, it is not my concern here to fathom why Britain voted to leave the EU. Nor is my own opinion on Brexit especially relevant here. At points I will highlight what lessons recent and contemporary films have to offer in terms of a meaningful response to Brexit, on the part of a British film industry that is already globalized and transnational. I will also focus on some of the paradoxes inherent to the ways we might view the 'national' cinema, in light of the more isolationist agenda around Britain's place in, and out of, the EU. This is not, though, to take a particular ideological or divisive line on my part, but rather to make a point about the interconnected nature of so-called 'British' film and its exhibition and reception abroad. It is quite possible that, for reasons of political opinion, some readers might take issue with the arguments I set out. As I argue in Chapter 1, though, one of the critical issues in popular cinema during the last decade or so is that it has so consistently failed to engage representationally with an audience (or at least, a particular imagined audience) that is, in turn, at once culturally and socially excluded. A responsibility of both cinema production and British cinema studies is to identify this omission. This book therefore holds that the drive towards Brexit cannot nor should not be wished away by a desire to return to some good-old pre-referendum days – if only for the reason that those old days evidently weren't so 'good' at all, as Brexit subsequently demonstrated.

It is also important to stress that, for the purposes of this book, 'Brexit' is identified not so much, narrowly, in terms of Britain's actual exit from the EU, but in terms of the broader contexts of the EU referendum. It is striking the extent to which even the process of *discussing* Britain's withdrawal from the EU could define a whole period; a protracted and largely fruitless process of diplomatic impasses between the UK and European counterparts, and one with significant impacts for the future of the UK as such (especially in terms of the so-called 'Irish backstop' and its role in the exit negotiations). Forcing the issue of Brexit, in dictating the terms of how and when Britain should leave, has even crossed the lines of democratic and lawful constitutional action, in terms of Boris Johnson's legally overturned decision to 'prorogue' parliament in 2019. The mere idea of Brexit, it turns out, began to paralyse and divide as soon as the vote for Leave was cast, if not before. From a cultural and ideological point of view, moreover, we can say that Brexit already happened on 24 June 2016. More to the point, the EU referendum confirmed the already ideologically divided nature of Great Britain (and above all England), and its fractious, in many cases hostile, attitude towards the EU (or 'Europe' and 'Europeans' in general), stemming most systematically from Europhobic voices within the ruling political class. If some people either failed or did not wish to take account either of these circumstances, or the real possibility of a Leave vote, it is partly a consequence of the ways culture, including film, also failed to acknowledge these issues. To an extent, the most obvious argument in this book for cinema's contribution to Brexit is to suggest that it ignored its very possibility.

Inevitably, given the limited timeframe since 2016, only some of the films under discussion here were released after the EU referendum, and of these, most went into production before June 2016. There will no doubt be more concrete cinematic responses to the post-referendum climate, and plenty of academic responses to these films and contexts. This book's particular contribution, specifically, is to investigate popular film output during a period leading up to, and in the three years beyond, the referendum. This is a period only latterly defined by Brexit as such. Yet it represents a longer period of significant political and social transformations that contributed, in various ways, to the discussions around EU membership: discussions which, in effect, have been going on since the end of the Second World War, when the idea of a more federally united Europe was first broached. The more recent period that forms the main subject of this book encompasses the last years of Tony Blair's premiership, and the end of the New Labour project in 2010, when the Conservative and Liberal Democrat parties formed their coalition government. New Labour, though, would have a belated send-off in the form of the London 2012 Olympics: an event planned and awarded under Blair's government in 2005, though eventually overseen by the new premier, David Cameron. These Games, like the ones that followed in the referendum year, would see Britain emerge as a perhaps unlikely sporting superpower, at the same time as grassroots participation and public sporting infrastructure declined. Such decline can be linked to the austerity policies introduced by Cameron and his Chancellor, George Osborne, in 2010; policies that bit hardest into the budgets of public services and local councils, while seemingly leaving highest income earners and the financial drivers of the City unaffected. This was ironic, since austerity itself was a legacy of the 2008 global economic crisis; the impacts of, and responses to which, exemplified the Western world's seeming dependency on economic globalization and neoliberal capitalism, whose theories and effects may be insufficiently understood, but most significantly felt, by those on whom they impact the hardest. It was many of these economically disenfranchised (though far from exclusively these) that, in June 2016, would vote to leave the EU; driven by austerity, some analysts argue, towards the populist, anti-globalization rhetoric of Nigel Farage and the UK Independence Party (UKIP).[5]

While it often does, popular cinema, it should be noted, has no *necessary* or inevitable remit to remind us of these circumstances. The bigger argument of this book, though, is that this is precisely why we should study it: not because of what it 'mirrors', but because of what it often refracts, misrepresents or simply doesn't show. This is not necessarily due to any political intent as such on the part of the film's producers and creators, which for the most part remains unknowable and irrelevant as far as viewers are concerned; nor to any assumed political opinions on the part of the audiences to whom these films are directed. More realistically, and more concretely for this present study, it is a condition of the kinds of frameworks of expectation established, both through the recent reception history of British film and through industrial policies, for what films about Britain and the British do, be it for domestic or global audiences. Whatever their imaginary links to the circumstances that produced Brexit, I argue in this book that these films work to construct a narrative and historical *imaginary of Britishness*; or perhaps more accurately, *Englishness* (as Britishness); one that proves both revealing and at points problematic in the light of recent circumstances.

One important note to make, then, is that this book does not specifically consider films 'about' Brexit, for the main reason that we are only, if at all, just starting to see them. A key objective throughout the chapters, though, is to highlight the ways in which a narrative of the nation, a particular *projection* of national image, but also a *protection of national interests*, is enacted through film policy and production. Interweaving these analyses through the discussion of varied cultural contexts, I will highlight the significance of popular cinema during this time in cultural, economic and political terms. The overarching understanding of these films, and this period of filmmaking, is that they offer a certain narrative of the nation, and a narrative about its cinema, that is at once consistent with and problematically disjointed from its actual contexts. Even, then, when my case studies do not focus on Brexit more specifically, they are always about Brexit *implicitly*, since they are effectively about where – according to the films, anyway – we think we are at in Britain, or at least would like to be.

On this score, what might Brexit itself tell us about the country that, if only in terms of those allowed a voice in the debate, voted for it? Data on the EU referendum may not reveal everything about the national state of mind, or its precise relationship towards Europe, and, by inference, the world beyond British shores. Yet there are significant pointers. The Brexit vote was driven largely by older voters, who were not only the largest majority in favour of Leave, but were also the most significant age group with regard to turnout. Though sometimes generalized as a working-class 'protest' vote, Brexit is equally informed by Leave-voting middle classes, especially in the over-35 demographic. Nor, amongst the English vote at least, was it significantly differentiated in terms of region: there was, for instance, no major north–south divide informing the vote. Ethnically, white voters were considerably more likely to opt for Leave than BME voters, a considerable majority of which, though far from all, supported Remain. But overall, significantly, it was a genuinely *popular* vote, with a public turnout significantly higher than for local or even general elections.[6] In terms of what we can infer from such data, they suggest Brexit is the manifestation of a popular sentiment that goes across cultural and economic distinctions. Yet they also highlight some coherent factors driving the vote to detach from the EU: the significance, in this case, and feelings, of an ageing population; the sense that Brexit spoke less for an ethnically diverse nation, and more for a monocultural one (and, as I note later, a mostly *English* one); but also, the idea that Leaving the EU is not motivated obviously, or exclusively, by any sense of economic necessity or frustration, but rather by other political- or identity-based concerns. The films under discussion in this book are not necessarily *about* these contexts, though as I argue, many of the stories they tell, and the broader logic behind their production, are driven by similar ideas, beliefs and debates to those informing the discourses around Brexit.

In short, *Cinema and Brexit* is about the stories that a national cinema tells itself and its domestic and global audience. More particularly, this book is about what happens when contemporary circumstances oblige us to re-examine these stories. Admittedly, and as I will discuss shortly, without the contexts of Brexit we possibly would not be talking about these stories at all. Yet the stories, most of them made or envisaged before the EU referendum even happened, would still be there. This is all the more reason, I suggest, why we need to turn to them at this point in time.

What do we mean by 'popular' and 'national' cinemas (and why does it matter)?

The question of what constitutes a 'popular national cinema', which I am defining here as my main subject matter, is a less straightforward concept than it might initially appear. We can start though with two potential definitions. For some, it may identify a particular kind of cinema, associated broadly with an idea of *style*. This suggests a dominant aesthetic form, or certain genres: what we might typically call the 'commercial' or 'mainstream' cinema. Exactly what formal properties such a cinema has are not always so easy to define, though. In a most basic sense, and as a second definition, a popular cinema is the type of cinema most people see, or are at least presumed to see. In other words, a popular cinema is simply the most commercially successful cinema. We should not infer though that any particular style or genre leads to popularity, because, to a significant extent, we cannot either predict or presume what will constitute a 'successful' film in the first place. Nevertheless, by looking at clusters and patterns of film production, and the policies often informing this production, as this study does, we can gather a sense of what is *expected* to be successful.

As has been widely noted, the discussion of a popular cinema in the majority of national contexts needs to contend with the fact that the second definition – the films most people see – almost always describes Hollywood cinema. Higson has identified the problems and limitations inherent to defining a national cinema, especially when such definitions are restricted to political ideas around appropriate representation, or led by critical evaluation and judgement.[7] Such attempts to determine the national cinema, Higson suggests, paradoxically fail to deal with the popular forms that do not fit into critically preferred categories. In turn, the concept of 'national cinema' is very often 'used prescriptively rather than descriptively, citing what *ought* to be the national cinema, rather than describing the actual cinematic experience of popular audiences'.[8] This has long been overwhelmingly the case in Britain, where few independently made British films can ever compete commercially with the films made and distributed by Hollywood studios, and which continue to fill multiplex screens.

What in fact can we concretely say about a British national cinema, let alone a 'popular English cinema', in the contemporary context? While box-office receipts, as already noted, are only a partial measure of how we understand a popular film culture, they make for revealing reading in the case of British film audiences. A quick survey of 2018's and 2017's most popular films in Britain shows, unsurprisingly, the dominance of Hollywood product, with family and animated films (Disney's *The Incredibles 2*, and *Beauty and the Beast*, Universal's *Despicable Me 3* and Fox's *The Boss Baby*) lining up alongside the now-familiar superhero-franchise subjects (*Avengers: Infinity War*, *Black Panther*, *Guardians of the Galaxy Vol. 2*, *Spider-Man: Homecoming* and *Thor: Ragnarok*). More obviously local relevance comes in the form of Christopher Nolan's *Dunkirk*, sitting in second place in 2017, or Joe Wright's Churchill drama *Darkest Hour* (2017), sitting just outside the 2018 top ten. Like 2016's two most popular films (*Rogue One: A Star Wars Story* and *Fantastic Beasts and Where to Find Them*), *Dunkirk* qualifies as a 'British' production because of its use of British locations. *Dunkirk*'s production company (Syncopy, founded by Christopher Nolan with his wife and co-producer Emma Thomas) is also British. Like those two films from 2016, though, its main source of financing comes through the Hollywood studio with which it enjoys a distribution deal (Warner Bros., who, as holders of intellectual property rights for *Harry Potter*, also oversee *Fantastic Beasts*). Similarly, *Darkest Hour*, as a production of the British company Working Title, is financially sustained through the latter's deal with Universal Pictures, its parent company. We have to move quite far down the list before we find British productions that do not enjoy this significant 'inward investment' from Hollywood. In 2017, for example, it is the formidable Paddington Bear's second cinematic outing (*Paddington 2*), produced by David Heyman's Heyday Films and the Anglo-French company StudioCanal, that we find nuzzling its way into the top twenty. And in 2016, a little further down the list, we find *Absolutely Fabulous*.

This is not surprising. As I shall note in Chapter 1, the importance of inward investment films such as the *Fantastic Beasts* films, but also even the *Star Wars* series, seems in part to sustain a certain idea of British cinema and its continued health. This begs the question what, in the contemporary context, we might understand at all by the idea of a popular British or English cinema. A central argument in this book is that it persists, often as a kind of narrative or set of generic tropes, through many of the films made during these recent years. There is also a sense inscribed in these films, in terms of their narrative content and form, that they are very different creatures from the big studio productions that command most attention at the box-office, both in the UK and worldwide. Yet in many cases, as I will explore, the 'idea of Englishness' constructed through these films needs to be weighed alongside the various contexts – economic, political or otherwise – within which they are made and viewed. There is a self-assertiveness on display in these films, even in their most apparently self-effacing and jocular form. Yet this fact is in itself often ironic, given the uncertain, precarious and above all dependent relationship British cinema appears to have with Hollywood.

We cannot separate the 'national' of a national cinema from these alternately commercial and political concerns. Indeed, a reasonable question is why, and to what ends, we talk about 'British cinema' at all. A 'national cinema' is not so much a neutral descriptive category as a political one: a concept, from one viewpoint, 'mobilised as a strategy of cultural (and economic) resistance; a means of asserting national autonomy in the face of (usually) Hollywood's international domination'.[9] The renewed, albeit slightly reworked significance of this last sentence in light of Brexit hardly needs stressing. The vote to leave the EU, and the protracted process of Britain's extrication from it, brings the idea of the national firmly into play. Underpinning much of the vote itself and the subsequent debates around EU withdrawal in Parliament, and shaping many of the attitudes towards the EU in exit negotiations, is an idea of British self-sufficiency. This is mingled with an assumption that it can still influence European decisions or even enjoy similar benefits to remaining EU members. In the most hard-line formulation of some of its proponents, a 'no-deal' Brexit, representing a decisive break from both the EU and the European Economic Area, is a desired option. Yet this, as proponents of such a 'hard' Brexit have often emphasized, is in the aim of attracting lucrative global partnerships beyond Europe. Ironically, given that the Leave vote was informed by the mantra of control and sovereignty, its most extreme implications are the reliance on trade deals with economically more powerful countries, such as the United States. A similar dependency, as this book notes at various points, to the one underpinning much 'British' cinema in the twenty-first century.

As this book explores, this problematic and questionable sense of national difference and autonomy, both from Europe and even from Hollywood, is a defining feature of much recent English film production, shaping an idea of popular English film for the years before, and following the referendum. The relevance of a popular national cinema in light of Brexit, then, is that it has already embodied so many of the same assumptions underlying British withdrawal from the EU. Equally, British cinema's wider reliance on US economic investment is a perennial reminder of the real economic order of things during these contexts.

We also need to work out what kind of audience we are referring to when we use the word *popular*, given the ambiguities of such a term. Any tendency to discuss the films here in terms of a 'popular national cinema' confronts the fact that they can only represent a national body in a very limited sense of the term. Most films are made within a nexus of industrial practices and already-globalized strategies of production and marketing. The everyday business of film production, and in many instances the films' narratives themselves, operate in a cultural, geographical and economic framework disassociated from the everyday realities of much national life. This in turn raises the possibility of a third, and more etymologically exact, idea of a popular cinema, in terms of it being a cinema 'of the people'. But is this ever possible? As Richard Dyer and Ginette Vincendeau argue, our efforts to construe a popular national cinema in these terms run up against blunt economic factors. The production and exhibition of film, largely because of its costly nature, can never 'belong' to any people as such. As Dyer and Vincendeau put it, in discussing cinema, this 'pure' notion of the popular 'is wholly untenable. It may even be that there can be no understanding of popular film without reference to the market, because popular cinema has only existed in a market economy'.[10]

At first glance, and taken out of context, such arguments might smack of a rather vague and totalizing assertion, to the extent that *all* cinema is imbricated in market forces and economic concerns. Such an extreme viewpoint would collapse two films as apparently antithetical as *I, Daniel Blake* and *Absolutely Fabulous* into equally competitive categories of market product, albeit targeted at different audiences and serving the commercial interests of different producers. This is not entirely untrue: produced as it (in fact) is by an array of European companies with vested interests in the film's exhibition, *I, Daniel Blake*, like most of Ken Loach's films since the 1990s, is not an exception to the general rule.[11] Yet such a broad viewpoint hardly does justice to the different representational and narrative commitments across films, or the range of ways such films are received and discussed by viewers. The subtle and important inflection in Dyer and Vincendeau's argument, though, is that cinema as a medium remains difficult to separate from the networks and aesthetics of a 'mass' culture: one with which a popular cinema can, depending on one's definition, either be equated, or to which it can be opposed. The distinction made here is one between a commercially driven and industrially produced culture, associated with what Theodor Adorno and Max Horkheimer provocatively termed the 'culture industry', and (to use the more Anglo-Germanic term for the popular) a 'folk' culture that is 'artisanally, locally produced and consumed'.[12] Even the most ardent attempts to posit such a 'folk' cinema in European national contexts, though, have had to confront the fact that the kind of forms and iconographies around which such cinemas work is almost always affected by broader global influences and images. Cinema is already far too economically globalized, and too culturally global in its points of reference. As Dyer and Vincendeau conclude, as far as cinema is concerned, 'There can be no search for a pure folk popularity in a material situation so fundamentally complex.'[13]

To make one thing clear at this point: it is not the aim of this book to deny the possibility or existence of such an 'artisanal' or 'locally produced and consumed' filmmaking; nor to deny the existence of films outside the type of circuits I am discussing here. Exactly what Brexit may represent and imply in terms of production opportunities, funding structures and filmmaking diversity is already a keen subject of discussion within European academic contexts, as well as a number of industry and government-led reports, and I would draw the reader's attention to these recent developments.[14] Equally, the British Film Institute (BFI), which since 2010 has been the funded body responsible for driving British film policy and promotion, has taken significant account of what Brexit would mean for independent and regional filmmaking; both in a commissioned report on Brexit and the screen industries, and in its most recent five-year policy plan (and I will turn to these later in the book).[15] Much of this discussion, though, inevitably involves speculation about the future. As this is beyond my remit, I have chosen to look at these particular films within a specific time frame, because they best encapsulate the 'complex material situation' in which popular national cinemas find themselves, straddled between their bid to speak to the popular audience, while at the same time shaped and informed by globalized cultural and economic forces.

The point in my initial comparison between *I, Daniel Blake* and *Absolutely Fabulous* was to highlight the difficulty of reconciling competing conceptions of both the popular and the national. But it is ultimately my contention that *Absolutely Fabulous* is, in this instance, an equally important case study: not so much because of its level of popularity, but because it also exemplifies the 'material situation' of the national cinema at this moment. *I, Daniel Blake* is an unusual case of a film that found an audience in excess of its typical expectations, yet, for all the critical and media attention the film received, this audience remains relatively prescribed. Looking at it in the light of Brexit, it is also a very pertinent example of how a genuinely 'European' British cinema – as a film made with the help of diverse European production and distribution partners – remains a marginal cinema within its specific national contexts.[16] It is an inevitable aspect of a folk culture's emphasis on locality that only with difficulty can it encompass the representational demands of a greater constituency or diversity – or, indeed, 'nation'. Whether we like it or not, at some level the otherwise competing terms of the popular (as both 'mass' and 'folk' culture) accede to each other when it comes to describing a popular national cinema, as films that are widely inaccessible to audiences and the broader public cannot so easily take their place here. *Absolutely Fabulous*, even if just by virtue of its coverage, can lay greater claim to popular representation.

What this overview suggests is that the popular in any popular cinema is a more fraught and contested notion than it may at first appear. The problem of reconciling the antithetical notions of mass and folk cultures is itself reflected in the way so many of the films discussed in this book are addressing a domestic national audience, yet one already situated within a global film economy. This economy is itself doubly focused; both in local terms (making films for a British audience familiar with the forms of Hollywood cinema) and global ones (making these same films with an *international* audience in mind). Yet popular English cinema, in what I call a process of *managed contradiction*, is frequently striving to differentiate itself from these same formal qualities that inform it in the first place. This idea that a popular English cinema is 'not like Hollywood' is something I explored at length in a previous book, *Beyond a Joke*, where amongst other things I looked at recent genre parodies, such as *Wallace and Gromit: The Curse of the Were-Rabbit* (2005), *The Hitchhiker's Guide to the Galaxy* (2005) and *Hot Fuzz* (2007). The difference there was that this assertion of difference existed as part of a reflexive and ultimately generous dialogue with Hollywood cinema. In this case, the above films both identified the influence of Hollywood and incorporated its narrative and aesthetic tendencies into their 'English' settings. Such films, in other words, acknowledged their indebtedness to a Hollywood imaginary that has significantly influenced both them and their audience. As such, they are transnational films by default – as also befitted their transatlantic production contexts. It is in turn no accident that, within the 'little England' frameworks of films like *The Curse of the Were-Rabbit* or *Hot Fuzz*, these latter films are so inherently derisive of such enclosed and limiting worldviews.[17] Indeed, their satirical targets are precisely the exclusionist, ageing and essentialist mindsets of a Middle England that eventually proved important to the success of the Leave campaign in 2016 (a point to which I return in a later chapter).

The main argument in *Beyond a Joke*, then, was that certain modes of comic English film, and parody in particular, functioned to differentiate English film within a competitive global and globalized market it recognized in the same process. A film like *A Hitchhiker's Guide to the Galaxy*, for example, based on Douglas Adams's cult radio show, television series and novel, could mark its comic distinctiveness from mainstream sci-fi cinema, yet also acknowledge the influence of this cinema through its parodied aesthetics and points of reference.[18] Not to do so would in fact be hypocritical, as well as strategically off the mark, given that the film was a $50m CGI-driven movie distributed worldwide by Disney, and therefore required global-scale returns on its economic investment. One of the things that consequently interests me about many of the films looked at in this book is that they work to disavow such influence, while actually still operating within highly generic structures, or employing mainstream cinema norms. Appropriations of the epic film and the sports movie, for instance (both discussed in Chapter 3), illustrate some of the peculiar tensions at work in these films: films which often make use of a Hollywood generic syntax, while at the same time strive to indicate through narrative content and context (especially the reliance on the 'unlikely' hero, or the opposition to 'unsporting' foreign opponents) how distinctively English they really are. But this also proves another indicator of the slippery character of the popular in a national context: the point, here, where an already globalized mass-cultural form (genre film) is appropriated in the service of a speculative 'folk' or 'people', in distinction from the globalized mass culture. As I argued in the previous book, a popular English cinema can make use of such globalized forms in the pursuit both of domestic and international success, using them to construct versions of Englishness; versions, though, that are rooted in incongruity and irony, and an awareness of Englishness precisely as an always contingent, and often ridiculous, *idea*. But when the interplay of other film forms and cultures is disavowed, we abandon play and self-awareness for the potent but dangerous charms of *myth*.

Myths of England and their conveyance through culture have been mobilized at historical junctures to reinforce national, and sometimes nationalist, sentiment. The notion of British sovereignty and the country's sense of entitled distinction from mainland Europe, for instance, is a narrative that goes back as far at least to the Arthurian legends: legends that, in fact, have seen the light again since the EU vote (as I discuss, again, in Chapter 3).[19] The charm, in turn, of a film such as *Monty Python and the Holy Grail* (1975), lies in the way it both embraces and then emphatically undermines the grammar and semiotics of such myths, through forms of linguistic and cinematic parody. Our capacity to recognize parody, though, and its effectiveness, depends fundamentally on the power of myth and of cinematic genres in the first place. Indeed, myth and genre cinema go so neatly together because both work at some profound level through what psychologists call 'heuristics': short-cut, fast-track mental processes that make sense because they 'feel right', even if (or because) they are supported by conscious or unconscious biases and prejudices. This accounts for their shortcomings in political discourses, but also their potential appeal to divisive political voices. These are the 'instinctive' truths we frequently follow or even live by, not because we have arrived at them through patient deliberation and reasoning, but because they are quicker and easier to come up with and retain.[20] Heuristics underpin our snap judgements about people (especially strangers), and perceived threats that do not, when thought through, hold up to scrutiny. They also shape our capacity to form quick and often unexplained allegiances to, or antipathies towards, certain individuals in position of power.

The success of ideologues such as Nigel Farage, the former UKIP leader and subsequent co-founder of the Brexit Party, is to foster popular sentiment largely through the construction of myth, frequently reduced to broad or even one-word categories: 'immigration'; 'Brussels'; 'the Establishment'; and 'sovereignty'. The insistent call to 'take back control' ran through Farage's appeal to the so-called 'People's Army' he exhorted the British public to join in the run up to June 2016.[21] It is not at all my aim to argue in this book that some of the more extreme aspects of Farage's right-wing agenda, and his appeal to a kind of popul*ist* revolt, find their way into popul*ar* cinematic form (though we should be interested to see if any arguments emerge elsewhere along these lines). I should also stress that, while discussing some of the potential meanings and connotations within these films, there is no link implied here to any intentions or opinions on the part of those involved with the films' production: links which, unless otherwise noted, are most likely inadvertent, especially within the more extended terms of the films' production histories.

As Ian Jack has argued, though, even if the links of films like *Darkest Hour* or *Dunkirk* to Brexit are inadvertent, the way they have been received by anti-European commentators and proponents, and in turn their very availability as films for such popular response, is significant and revealing. Especially in some of their more patriotic or populist manipulations of history, Jack suggests, films such as the above feed into the sense of 'an England congratulating itself on its past – an idealised past, shorn of inconvenient fact'.[22] What we can therefore pursue is the possibility that an English cinema of this period, for whatever motive, is playing some part in the construction and maintenance of long-standing national myths, founded in self-perceptions of entitlement, self-sufficiency and distinction, especially from the European mainland. As I explore at a later point, in fact, these myths are not necessarily operating from a position of extreme Europhobic antipathy. Rather, it is an attitude embedded in varied constituencies of English life and culture, and even – counter-intuitively – in its apparently more 'Europhile' aspects; so much so that it is structured into a great deal of English cinematic production in often banal ways. An *idea* of Brexit, in other words, is already cultivated and sustained within popular English film production during the years preceding the EU referendum, and in films that have come out shortly after it.

'Film Politics'

It is useful at this point to clarify the methodological approach of this book. Isn't there, we might ask, an intrinsic problem in suggesting that film plays a role in the construction of popular myths, and at the same time, is tied up in the 'fundamentally complex' realities of global production practices? Within these 'complex' terms, how can it have any meaningful connection to actual circumstances? I have already made the point that narrative cinema has no obvious *necessary* reason to engage with, or be discussed in light of, social and political contexts. How, if this is the case, can we realistically discuss the contexts of Brexit as manifested through cinema? What, if at all, guarantees any correlation between the largely commercial interests of a globalized British film industry and the representation of contemporary social, political and cultural concerns?

This is the perennial issue with what is sometimes called the 'reflectionist' critical approach, which primarily sees film as holding a mirror up to its contemporary social and political contexts. As I will note below and at later points in this book, a number of films released since the referendum have been reviewed by the press in relationship to Brexit, with questionable historical and methodological legitimacy. Inferring social context from contemporary film in this way is often, as David Bordwell suggests, 'the last refuge of journalists writing to deadline'.[23] Seeing films as allegories for defining political contexts makes good copy, and also makes for a neat story. But such stories are often fictions. The capacity of these films to say anything about Brexit is questionable, for the simple reason that they went into pre-production years before the referendum took place, or was even confirmed (following David Cameron's general election victory in 2015). The tendency towards reflectionism in film analysis, then, as Bordwell summarizes, is one that relies on 'loose and intuitive connections between film and society ... [and] on spurious and far-fetched correlations between films and social or political events'.[24] This is not to say, of course, that we should not aim to understand films within the varied social contexts in which they are produced; merely that we need to be very careful in our justification of such an approach, or what our findings are. Working out exactly how and why a given work is significant within social contexts becomes, then, the first challenge facing the analyst of these films.

This problem was raised in September 2017 during an interview, at the Toronto International Film Festival, between *The Guardian* film critic Peter Bradshaw, and Eric Fellner and Tim Bevan, the founders of Working Title, Britain's most successful film production company.[25] Responding in particular to the imminent release of the company's *Victoria and Abdul* (2017), about the later life of Queen Victoria, and more specifically *Darkest Hour*, which focuses on Winston Churchill's role in the early part of the Second World War, Bradshaw asked Fellner and Bevan whether they saw any continuities between the recent socio-political circumstances of Britain and their films. Bradshaw's question may have been informed by the appearance within the same year of several other films revisiting the period (such as *Churchill*, *Their Finest* and *Dunkirk*); or indeed, the prominence of Churchill as a character in the first season of Peter Morgan's Netflix series *The Crown* (2016–). The congruence of these films at this time, and their occasional tendencies towards nostalgic patriotism, has not been lost on other commentators looking to understand the ties between Brexit and popular culture.[26] Yet the idea that Working Title had responded to these contexts was one that Fellner robustly deflected, reminding us that any film in the company's schedule is usually in development for several years before it is even produced, let alone comes to the screen. The cultural *Zeitgeist*, he suggested rather enigmatically, 'comes to the films'. From his company's perspective, the only thing that concerned them was 'telling good stories'. Bordwell's similar point is that what we understand by the *Zeitgeist* is more realistically an effect proceeding from the films themselves, rather than anything to which the films respond. How, in fact, do we identify a 'spirit of the times' in the first place? For Bordwell, it is more accurate to say that the *Zeitgeist* is constructed through popular cultural representations, such as films, which is why the effort to infer a *Zeitgeist* from them tends towards circularity: 'All popular films reflect social attitudes. How do we learn what the social attitudes are? Just look at the films!'[27]

To elaborate on Bordwell's point, popular film is also inevitably leading in terms of its capacity to reflect the times. As it happens, a lot of people in Britain during 2017 and 2018 saw *Dunkirk* and *Darkest Hour*, for whatever particular reasons, and whatever side of the political or Brexit spectrum they might be coming from. When viewers consistently and disproportionately attend certain films over others, it may tell us a few things about audience's particular preferences (as I discuss later, with reference to the James Bond movie *Skyfall* [2012]). But in the most literal sense, the fact that a higher proportion of viewers in Britain saw *Darkest Hour* than some other film only really tells us that viewers preferred the former over the latter. But also, as noted earlier, they saw this film because it was available to see. Audience attendance and response may affirm the viability of certain films or genres, but they do not in and of themselves conjure them out of the air. Film it and they will come: but if you don't film it, there won't be a ghostly space marking its absence. Audiences will just have chosen other things offered to them, defining an altogether different *Zeitgeist*.

In one respect, then, while this book makes a claim for the significance of popular cinema for understanding recent times, it is also in part a cautionary work about the shortcomings of using film to discuss contemporary social and political themes. Or at least, we need to be more specific in identifying what it is films *actually* represent. As an event that somehow demands an explanation, or a story, Brexit can send us hurrying to look for its incipient 'signs' in prior and contemporary cultural production. But *had Brexit never happened* – if there had been a 2 per cent swing in the voting on 23 June 2016 – what would we be looking for? The limitation to looking at these films as representations or reflections of Brexit is that such literalist readings proceed largely from the *contexts of reception*, not the films themselves. *Dunkirk, Darkest Hour, Absolutely Fabulous, Paddington 2* and *Early Man* (2018), the latter a particularly ripe target for post-referendum readings, would have seen the light of day regardless or not of the EU referendum decision. In our alternative film-historical universe, would we now be scouring the last few years of film production to find reflections of how and why the UK voted to *remain* in the EU? No doubt, as an interpretive game, we could find such evidence – indicating in the process the pitfalls of reading too much socio-political relevance into popular fiction films.

And yet: as much as we should be wary of constructing a too-literal and ahistorical causality between social contexts and films, we can still think about films in terms of patterns and groups of meaning. Something interesting is inevitably going on when, within a small space of time, we experience a cluster of films with similar narratives and themes being produced and screened. This suggests more than just an arbitrary or coincidental occurrence. As noted above, a national film culture at any particular historical juncture is largely determined by the films that are exhibited for audiences to see: But *why these films* and not others? Given that all film production is a high-risk economic venture, there need to be conditions and motivations for particular films like *Darkest Hour* or *Early Man* to be produced in the first place. Their existence points, in fact, to a more long-term and persistent *imaginary* of Englishness or Britishness; one that is seen to appeal to both domestic and, as often as not, international audiences. In rejecting a simplistically reflectionist view of film and Brexit, then, I am actually arguing for something at once wider in popular English cinema, but also more mythical and important. It is important precisely because it is not always so obvious in its cultural or political relevance; yet it both precedes and exists alongside, and also in spite of, the contexts of the EU referendum and its aftermath. In this respect, I question Jack's conclusion that, without Brexit, films like *Darkest Hour* would simply exist as a 'harmless elegy', since it is the supposedly 'harmless' qualities of such films that might otherwise blind us to their mythic and ideological work.[28]

Central to this approach is to see the films, in terms of their inception, their aesthetics and their narratives, as manifestations of particular film *policies*. To an extent, as I will discuss throughout this book, this relates to specific policy-making on the part of government, or of government-sanctioned bodies overseeing film production and its promotion. In this instance, we cannot separate wider policy, and indeed policy towards Europe and the rest of the world, from the production of films. As I note in the following chapter, for example, film policy in the 1990s, and Britain's production relationship with the European mainland, was directly effected by governmental ambivalence towards Europe (leading, for instance, to the UK being withdrawn from the Eurimages scheme in 1996). Equally, to take another example, the dominant inclination towards inward investment and Anglo-American production since the 2000s, and especially in more recent discussion, highlights the broader political and economic leanings towards the United States, both as a vital trade partner and as a market for Britain's creative-industries output.

But in talking about policies, I am also referring to the strategic production decisions made by film companies not necessarily dependent on, or constrained by, governmental policy. To go back to the example of Working Title, Fellner's suggestion that the *Zeitgeist* 'comes to the films' is an astute one (not to mention self-validating from the perspective of his company), identifying as it does the ways that films can become the often unwitting subjects of, or magnets for, a broader cultural discussion. And yet, the notion that a well-established and successful company like Working Title is only interested in 'telling good stories' feels disingenuous. This is because such statements underplay the process of selection and brand-reinforcing at work in the company's films, but also the importance of identifying cultural relevance as a significant commercial strategy.[29] In a general sense, we can see these in terms of Working Title's inclination towards certain genres, iconographies and casting, most prominently from its cycle of romantic comedies, to its more recent literary adaptations, and now, perhaps, to historical dramas like *Victoria and Abdul* or *Darkest Hour*; as well as middle-brow biopics such as *The Danish Girl* (2015) and *The Theory of Everything* (2014) (the subject of a later chapter here).[30] These tendencies have for the most part both informed and fed on a globally marketable idea of Englishness in the form of the country's comedic, literary and historical traditions.[31] But is it, we might ask, totally irrelevant that *Darkest*

Hour was green-lit just a few months after the publication of Boris Johnson's popular 2014 biography, *The Churchill Factor*? Whatever *Darkest Hour* may actually say about the time and place in which it is viewed, it certainly chimes with wider contexts of cultural production, in Britain at least.

Indeed, in terms of popular English cinema's managed contradiction, cultivating mythic and generic forms for domestic and international consumption is of paramount importance, bolstering the idea that this national cinema is in rude health, and above all, in control of its own destiny. Higson's opening argument in *Film England* is that a culturally English cinema has, through the 1990s and early 2000s, sustained itself in economic and critical terms. A similar argument is made in Geoffrey Macnab's more recent *Stairways to Heaven: Rebuilding the British Film Industry*, which opens with the strong claim that, in contrast to the 'prolonged slump' of the late 1980s, this national industry is now 'booming'.[32] This shows a reversal of the gloomier prognoses of the 1980s – when government funding of the national film industry dwindled – which predicted 'little room for small-scale national production' within the predominance of 'the global media entertainment business'.[33] Higson nevertheless situates relative contemporary prosperity within the terms of 'precarious and unstable' times, and an industry that remains 'undercapitalised … without a large enough domestic market to allow it to develop substantially, and lacking the scale of infrastructure that characterises Hollywood'.[34] There nevertheless remains the insistence that having a *globally* competitive and influential film industry is both desirable and possible. But given the infrastructural contexts Higson describes, this comes, as I have already suggested, with particular negotiations between national cinema and a global audience. As Nick Roddick remarked some time ago, the fact that English is spoken in Britain may be as much a hindrance as a help to its film industry, allowing as it does a steady flow of non-dubbed and non-subtitled Hollywood product to assume cultural centrality. This in turn diminishes the 'cultural imperative' to make local films: something that becomes more applicable, for instance, in other European countries.[35] But having a large North American audience for English (language) films has also provided the British film industry with a mutually informed cultural and economic incentive, in terms of the possibilities for exporting film as cultural goods. A popular English cinema, defined in this respect as one that aspires to production scales and global cultural reach in the Hollywood vein, will always – as Higson contends – be working through ideas and images of Englishness that are as much imaginary projections or fantasies of the latter, as they are attempts to 'represent' in any strict sense.

National film policy in this regard refers to various strategies, in terms of aesthetics, filmmaking practices and wider discourses, along with economic incentives, used to promote the production and visibility of a cinema in the given country, but also beyond. In Britain, such policy has been alternately and often mutually shaped around cultural interest and industrial concerns, though what runs throughout this history as a constant aspect are 'the strategies designed [by filmmakers] to attract sufficient funding for … films to be made'.[36] The promotion of a certain *type* of cinema (such as 'culturally English cinema') has predominated over recent decades, most often combining cultural conceptions of 'Englishness' with a pragmatic approach to domestic and global audience expectations. Film policy as set out and approved by government has undergone a variety of changes over the century of cinema's existence as a popular medium and also industry (I shall touch on some of these in Chapter 1). As implied above, though, the perennial tension within film policy-making has been how to weigh up issues of culture with purely financial questions of film's value to the national economy. As John Hill has in turn noted, film in the UK is something of a cultural exception in relation to other aspects of governmental arts policy, in that policies around cinema have mostly been 'concerned with the preservation and support of commercial filmmaking', rather than with the preservation of a particular aesthetic or cultural criterion.[37] The national cinema supported by policy, in other words, is most often the cinema that is expected to draw the biggest audience, domestically and/or overseas, with whatever kind of narrative and aesthetic content that entails.

The recognition that, in this century, national film policies are largely in place to aid films operating in a commercial, free-market system, is an important one for the studies in this book. This is because it turns our attention to the more systematic, strategic approaches on the part of film producers to make use of national motifs or myths to reach wider domestic and often international audiences. In terms of policy as an aspect, etymologically and practically speaking, of *politics*, this has frequently played out with film as part of a nexus of government-sanctioned interests that we can summarize as the national 'brand' (or, as I touch on in Chapter 1, within the terms of a 'creative industries' remit on the part of government). Film in this sense, as both an attractor of industry and a marker of specific national character internationally (what I discuss later in terms of its 'soft power'), always has a political function, even if not obviously *about* politics as such.

The bottom line for this book, then, is that we need to consider not just films that seem to be 'about' Brexit, but also the films, and the film policies and strategies informing them, that don't seem to be about Brexit at all; films that, in fact, seem to promote the idea that *there is no problem*. These films may be, if not necessarily part of an actual problem, cultural manifestations of a broader and incipient issue. Much of the discussion in this book focuses on cultures of filmmaking that, if not obviously having contributed to the popular vote to leave the EU, have nevertheless played a role in representing or naturalizing particular attitudes towards Europe, and in turn, Britain's significance vis-à-vis the European mainland. This is especially the case with some of the 'holiday films' I discuss in Chapter 2, as well the epic films and sports movies I analyse in Chapter 3. As I also argue in that chapter and the one that follows it, other tendencies in film production during this period have developed particular mythologies of national character and achievement. While such films often celebrate specific British figures and successes, their work of representation needs to be set against the broader social, economic and political contexts in which they emerge, and which their narratives often disavow. Again, these films do not explicitly contend with the contexts around Brexit. Yet they are significant for the ways that many of the circumstances informing Brexit, and those being brought to light by it – social disenfranchisement, economic inequality, a disillusionment with government and elite institutions – should focus our attention on the discrepancies between popular representation and actual circumstances.

But it is also important to note that any cinema which is active in its *resistance* to exploring social contexts is inherently *about* these contexts, if only by virtue of their omission. The pressing case for this particular book, and its partial return at points to some of the arguments I have made previously, is that a popular cinema that denies or simply does not identify any problem is in some respects contributing to the very problem it directly or inadvertently avoids. Comedy, the subject of my previous study, is in this regard a prominent case in point, because of the way its mode of discourse specifically calls upon certain constituencies of viewers to identify with its jokes. As I will show in Chapters 2 and 3, creating humour based around the difference between the English and 'Europeans' is a potent tactic in popular genre film. Such films drift towards a type of politically 'incorrect' comic discourse; the capacity of which to speak both for, and to, populist or nativist attitudes has been widely discussed. As Andy Medhurst has argued, for example, the comedian Roy 'Chubby' Brown's career of profane humour, one that frequently targets minority and marginalized constituencies, has strong appeals to its audience's sense of place and shared culture.[38] Medhurst no doubt challenges some readers' limits of acceptability by asking us to engage empathetically with a comic whose act, at one stage-show he recounts, included telling any asylum seekers in the audience to 'fuck off home'.[39] But most humour, from whatever political position it comes from, is always implicitly telling *someone* to fuck off, since it is established around a shared culture or belief, and therefore a prescribed framework of recognition.[40] It may never occur to us, subsequently, that there is anything intrinsically violent in sharing laughter. It is just 'common sense'. But Medhurst's comparative point about Chubby Brown's fans is that they feel exactly the same.

Just as we need to take a critical approach to more notionally 'correct' representations in film, then, we also need to be prepared, as I noted previously, to engage meaningfully with more 'incorrect' examples. This is hardly a radical position to take, of course; and like any book this one also excludes a great number of films that warrant analysis and consideration. In the aim of going forward, though, I believe that film studies focusing on British, and especially English, cinemas in the light of Brexit needs to be prepared to contend with a diverse and often-antagonistic range of representations. Cherry-picking our way through a critically or academically approved body of films, highlighting those works that fit with a preferred idea both of the nation and of cinema as an art form, has an important advocatory purpose. I have done this often enough, and in some of the conclusions I arrive at here, this present study will no doubt do much the same thing. Understanding Brexit, though, means trying to understand various sides of the discussion. I am not sure that fashioning a preferred narrative of a national cinema, exemplary as the films might be, is not just telling each other, in a closed circle, the stories we would like to hear about ourselves – and, in some respects, ignoring other stories that equally need to be heard and understood. Delimiting the discussion in a political sense, ironically, can end up constructing the same kind of limits and barriers such discourses, and the films they describe, often strive to challenge. No doubt there are readers who would both challenge this view and take issue with my own (inevitably prescribed) choice of films here. Others may argue that my analyses do not go far enough. All for the better, if it takes the discussion in new directions! This book makes no claims for completeness: rather, it is an early intervention in what, I hope, will become a wider body of study. I hope, at least, that readers will understand where I am coming from, and what I am trying to do across the chapters of this book.

On 'Englishness': The scope of this book

While this book's subtitle highlights its focus on 'popular English cinema', it is of course implicitly addressing 'British cinema' as its main subject, if only through its conflation with 'Brexit' as a 'British' exit from the EU. This is potentially problematic for a number of reasons. First and foremost, the vote for Brexit was largely an English one. Over 15 million of the votes for Leave, out of the majority total of 17.4 million votes overall, were cast in England. This was not in itself sufficient for a majority, which came via the combined votes cast for Leave in Wales, Northern Ireland and Scotland. Yet of those three countries, only Wales (at 52.5 per cent, just below England's 53.4 per cent) showed a majority for Leave. While Scotland's 2014 referendum on independence had ultimately seen a significant backing for the country to remain in the UK, the 2016 referendum revealed it to have the most overwhelming support for continued EU membership, at 62 per cent of the vote (every Scottish council, in fact, returned votes in favour of Remain).

The very neologism 'Brexit', therefore, manifests another example of Britishness being absorbed by England, to the point where England and Britain become – if only in the former's greater interests – the same thing. As Julian Petley has cogently summarized in a recent essay, one of the revealing things about individual national identities within the UK is that, historically speaking, they have generally been something only the 'other' home countries have.[41] Scottishness and Welshness have been long asserted as distinctive identities within, or sometimes against, Britain, or at least against England. But until fairly recently, 'Englishness' has been an identity in search of a place, so much has England assumed its role *as* Great Britain: a historical fact that makes the recent rise of an exclusionist English nationalism (in form, for instance, of the English Defence League, as well as the mainly English support for UKIP) so striking, but also telling of more incipient tensions. As Richard Weight argues, for instance, the strong emergence of a specifically English national sentiment, and the relatively recent embracing of the Saint George's Cross as the English symbol, coincides with Scottish and Welsh parliamentary devolution in the late 1990s, alongside perennial antipathy to the EU.[42] Petley, following in this vein, identifies the emergence of 'the English question' around this same time: the growing sense that the biggest country in the UK was not, to quote one particular Englishman, 'get[ting] a fair suck of the sauce bottle'.[43]

Looking then at cinema, Petley shows that the same casual association of England with Britain runs through a sizeable history of film criticism.[44] Raymond Durgnat's seminal 1971 work of socially and politically inflected film history, *A Mirror for England* (the title of which is deliberately misappropriated by this introduction), is a prime suspect here, given that its subtitle is *British Movies from Austerity to Affluence*.[45] Alexander Walker's *Hollywood, England: The British Film Industry in the 1960s* is a similar case in point.[46] Walker's book is a bit more nuanced than its title suggests, though, inasmuch as it focuses largely on the ways that a mostly English, and eventually a specifically *metropolitan* England, came to stand in for 'Britain' more generally in the eyes of Hollywood studios investing in the country's filmmaking infrastructure and cultural capital (a point I also highlight, with reference to more recent films).

In light of these points, one of the main observations Petley makes about Higson's *Film England*, drawing on a critical review of the latter by Claire Monk, is that its focus is quite narrow. Two of Higson's eight chapters, for instance, look exclusively at Jane Austen films while others explore broadly similar areas, such as the literary adaptation and the period drama. As Petley suggests, whatever the particular intentions behind such studies, they may tend to reiterate a predominantly English view of Britain, prescribing a certain type of cinematic identity rather than challenging it, and failing to expand the otherwise narrow scope to look at films beyond 'big-budget Englishness for export' movies.[47] The broader point of a study like Higson's *Film England*, nevertheless, is that an idea of British film production and its reception around the world has tended to focus on 'culturally English' elements above all else, and it is the nature of, and reasons for, these circumstances that are his main object of study. While I engage with different subject matter and contexts, I am not going to pretend that this present book greatly challenges this broader framework, which mostly remains the dominant circumstance in which so-called 'British films' are made and received. It is fair to say that, to borrow Monk's corrective phrase, what I am really discussing is mostly 'Institutionally British filmmaking', and not the much broader type of culturally English cinema for which she argues.[48] But neither is it the purview of this book to endorse this cinema, nor to suggest acquiescently that it is without problems. In fact, the limitations of this cinema in terms of political representation, and the assumptions of Britishness as Englishness often manifest within it, are key subjects of critical analysis throughout these chapters. Furthermore, I actually make a case for those films all too easily reducible, otherwise, to more generalized categories. In my final chapter, for instance, where I look at more transnationally European productions of 'British' film, I extend the discussion beyond the limits of such 'institutional' thinking; arguing, in fact, that popular franchise film does not necessarily devolve to the idea of a 'British' movie 'made-in-Hollywood', but can in fact reinvigorate and challenge conceptions of national identity and cinema.

Nevertheless, what all of this means is that, on the whole, I will not be looking in much detail at filmmaking cultures and practices that depart from this framework. I do not, for example, give specific consideration to distinctive or contesting tendencies of Scottish, Welsh or Northern Irish cinemas. I hope the reader understands that, in omitting such works, I am not for a moment indicating that we should not look at them. Obviously, we should. A pre-eminently popular 'British' movie like *T2 Trainspotting* (2017), for instance, while its pre-Brexit production contexts mitigate against its direct narrative treatment of this theme, clearly invites discussion with regard to Scotland's contemporary position vis-à-vis England, and its own identification with Europe, especially in light of a popular resurgence of Scottish nationalism and support for devolution. If I do not consider such films in this present study, it is largely because the subject lies too far outside my own areas of knowledge, as well as the central argument of this particular book.[49] Similarly, exploring the types of films Monk suggests we ought to do within the terms of culturally English cinema – lower budget films, ones exploring different, under-represented regions and stories – would be a rich and valuable study. But whether or not I could undertake it (and here, by way of response, I again defer to other writers better qualified to do so), my specific argument in this book, as already noted, demands different kinds of subject matter.[50]

Admittedly, there is always the risk that in doing this, I am only further collapsing the idea of 'British cinema' into a set of mainly English preoccupations and archetypes. In response, I ask the reader to acknowledge the critical view with which I view both these circumstances and the films it produces. Indeed, the point that Petley makes is that Englishness is naturalized *as* Britishness, to the extent that one is assumed to represent the other. This notion of Englishness as it were 'speaking for' Britain is central to many of the issues I engage with, critically, in this book. By contrast, a film like *T2*, like its predecessor *Trainspotting* (1996), is a more 'culturally Scottish' film that engages critically with Scotland's relationship to England, in a way that is much less common in 'English' films: films that often assume a coherent and consensual Britain. This indicates another way that the focus on 'English' films in this study is not an arbitrarily prescribed one, as in many respects I am concerning myself with a very distinct ideological viewpoint vis-à-vis 'the nation'. Moreover, and more pragmatically, talking about 'English' cinema as a category of film production is hardly specious, since it makes a clear distinction between English-produced and -centred films, and those made more concretely in Scotland, Wales or Northern Ireland. Notably, the question of devolution, especially in Scotland, has hardly gone away since the latter's 2014 referendum. The subsequent EU vote, in fact, only refocused attention on the future of the UK after Brexit, and in particular, the future of Scotland as the most pro-European nation. In terms of the implications for cinema, Jonathan Murray has already pointed out the extent to which Scottish film production, in further distinction to that south of the border, has looked towards its nearer Scandinavian neighbours as more obvious film-production partners.[51] In a more fully devolutionary context, it is entirely probable that the discussion of 'British cinema' would, by definition, largely be confined to 'English' productions, so it is reasonable to concentrate on this category here.

Another related risk, though, is that in producing this book itself, I am actually contributing to the maintenance of narrow geopolitical and conceptual frameworks, precisely by limiting my study to the analysis of

'English' or even 'British' cinema in the first place. When the environmental activist Greta Thunberg, in a 2019 speech to European political leaders, chided them for 'hold[ing] three emergency Brexit summits' whilst, in global climate terms, 'our house was falling apart', she was rhetorically targeting the overevaluation given to comparatively minor matters of national identity within a globally connected and interdependent world.[52] In terms of an analytical and critical practice, the late Ulrich Beck has discussed this in terms of what he calls 'methodological nationalism'. For Beck, this refers to the practice of limiting theories of culture, identity and politics to state-bounded terms: 'Methodological nationalism ... imposes a *territorial* understanding of society based upon state-constructed and state-controlled borders.'[53] As a *methodology*, this is understood not just in terms of a quasi-mythical nation existing outside of the frameworks of analysis, ready to be discerned and described: more specifically, it also refers to the limitations of academic practice itself, once it delimits its view of cultural output and importance to this 'state-constructed' framework. Is writing a book concerning Brexit, one might ask, even in addressing concerns *about* Brexit, merely to reiterate once more the spurious and mythic nationalist methodology lurking behind such discussion?

To such potential criticism, I offer two responses. Firstly, as I note above, an overarching question within this book is what we actually mean by 'British' or 'English' cinema anyway, given its largely transnational condition and dependence. If I use these terms at all, it is often to highlight their limitations or paradoxes, arguing, as I ultimately do, for a more 'cosmopolitan' view of English cinema; or even, as I explore in the final chapter, an understanding of popular English cinema as *already European*. Secondly, I feel the focus is justified, inasmuch as one of my key aims is to identify the attitudes and policies that underpin and reinforce methodological nationalism itself. Brexit, as a very idea, epitomizes a state-limited understanding of people, culture and politics, and can be seen as a popular reaction precisely to the types of cosmopolitan identity championed by pro-European thinkers like Beck. It is founded on the idea that imagined entities such as 'nations' or 'Britons' actually exist, and should inform the bordered geopolitical organization of the world. If we are going to make sense of Brexit and the role of culture in discourses around it, this inevitably means honing in on its own very specific and delimited perspectives.

It is also important that the reader understands my specific use of terms in this book to describe particular filmmaking practices and discourses. For the reasons I have touched on above, I concur with the view that 'British cinema' has often been misleadingly discussed in terms of 'English cinema'. I am focusing on similar films that, for good or ill, have tended to represent British filmmaking on a wide, often global scale. To discuss these films in terms of 'British cinema' is, accordingly, misrepresentative of other national filmmaking practices and cultures within the UK. For the most part, then, unless indicated otherwise, I will mostly use the terms 'English' and 'Englishness' in my discussions – with the frequent use of quotation marks an indication that I see even these more specific terms in an incomplete or discursive sense. Again, one of the main points in this book is that the transnational nexus of economic and cultural interests informing popular film production makes describing movies as, say, merely 'English', an almost impossible and misinformed task. Hopefully, then, the reader will understand that my use of such terms is critical, rather than indicating a desire to make any particular claims for 'English films' over and above any others.

The chapters of this book

While the discussion of British cinema often focuses on its capacity to embody or even promote ideas of nationhood, this is often carried out in an interpretive way that fails to consider the contexts of film production or specific actions of film policy at an industrial or governmental level. As my first chapter investigates, can we make clear connections between what we see in film representations, and specific intentions on the part of policy-makers, towards the promotion of a country? Or going further still, can we identify a political agenda in works of popular fiction filmmaking? In this instance, it is not in any 'indications' of Brexit that we can view the recent cinematic past, but rather in the *positive* representations of a 'global' and post-imperial country, peaking during the era of New Labour and finding their greatest public manifestation in the 2012 Olympic ceremony. Looking back at this ceremony from a renewed perspective, and expanding on the conclusions to some of my previous work, I consider the specificity of its featured media figures (James Bond, Mr. Bean, Harry Potter), and how the uses of these figures articulate potent, yet in other respects narrow and prescribed, conceptions of twenty-first-century Britain: conceptions that are not 'universal', but in fact correspond to very specific political agendas in the promotion of Britain both commercially (as 'Brand Britain') and politically (in terms of Britain's investment in global 'soft power').

It is of course essential that in a book about film and Brexit, we consider the way Europe is represented on the English screen. The second chapter therefore argues that the under-explored and critically overlooked form of the English 'holiday film' offers up important reflections on the construction of national identity, especially in terms of the positioning of Europe within such films. As I explore, with reference to recent films such as *The Inbetweeners Movie* (2011) and *Absolutely Fabulous*, and their link to an earlier tradition of films such as *Carry on Abroad* (1972), the English holiday film is characterized by a contradictory pull: that between a comic performance of Englishness that is resistant to its European setting, yet at the same time one dependent on this setting as the constituent part of its very English utopia. I consequently highlight the problematically divisive nature of the comic holiday film that sees 'Europe' (the mainland) as at once a rightful space of freedom and play, yet is at the same time the site through which the inflexibility of Englishness, and a resistance to the very idea of 'being European', is made manifest.

I go on to consider the ways in which, through films ranging from Morecambe and Wise's *That Riviera Touch* (1967) to *Mr Bean's Holiday* (2007), a similar idea of European as 'cinematic' is explored. As I show in my analysis of the latter film, with reference also to *The Trip to Italy* (2014), the English holiday film has both acknowledged and resisted the idea of a 'European cinema' as a defined concept beyond the popular mainstream or the types of international franchise films typified by *Mr Bean's Holiday*. I end the chapter nevertheless with some remarks on the capacity for self-reflexivity in the holiday film, looking at the wider *Trip* series of films (2010–17) as examples of how the genre can reflect the contexts of Brexit, but also be a means of challenging the latter's ideological bases of British independence and significance.

Like the holiday film, the epic is an intermittently produced and under-explored genre in the English context. Its significance to the national cinema lies in its mobilization of specific mythic archetypes or legends, often linked to broader narratives of 'nation building'. This, I discuss in Chapter 3, is particularly the case with recent films exploring the King Arthur myth across varied contexts

(*King Arthur: Legend of the Sword* [2017] and *The Kid Who Would Be King* [2019]), as well as derivatives of this same myth, such as Aardman's sports/epic film *Early Man*. My analysis of these films focuses on their specific, and in this case differentiated, engagement with tropes of nation and adversity, and their particular construction of a type of popular community. I nevertheless highlight how the commercial reception of these films draws attention to the limits of the 'epic' register in English filmmaking, within the wider global contexts of film production. As I argue, then, the 'problem' of the epic in popular English terms is in part the overestimation of culturally English themes as global selling points; and, most saliently in the contexts of Brexit, a hubristic notion of national significance. I also look at the way period films such as *Darkest Hour* draw on similar mythic archetypes to evoke, along with various other contemporary films, the contexts of the Second World War. Linking this discussion with a detailed analysis of the 2012 James Bond film *Skyfall*, I consider the potent ways in which a national narrative of resilience and return is structured into these films, forming in the process a kind of cinematic origin story. As I discuss, these focal choices, in the case of *Skyfall* especially, proved particularly powerful in the domestic market, yet indicated an unusually inward-looking, and also combative, representation of national identity as far as the series was concerned. Both *Skyfall* and *Darkest Hour*, in this fashion, play a significant mythic role in shaping a national imaginary of self-sufficiency and exceptionality.

In the same way that Chapter 3 highlights the mythic construction of the English or British sportsperson in the contexts of the twenty-first century, Chapter 4 considers how, with a particular focus on two recent biographical films – *The Theory of Everything* (2014) and *The Imitation Game* (2014) – the scientist figure is shaped to specific ends. If still slightly mad, the scientist in these films is neither quite so bad nor as dangerous as some of their earlier counterparts.[54] What remains interesting here, though, is the way the English scientist figure is mobilized within cinematic images of, and in turn cinematic discourses around, the past. What is it, I ask in response, which encourages the framing of science and technology in these cinematic terms? And what can it ultimately tell us about perspectives on and around science in contemporary English culture? As I argue, the recourse to an aesthetic of heritage in the scientist film both romanticizes and naturalizes scientific discourse and the institutions that sustain it (or are, in turn, sustained by it).

As I suggest, the persuasively 'natural' evocation of science in these films works to generate myths of science and nation, eliding some of the more critical and interrogatory questions around science and technology in Britain. At the same time, such films, with their generic recourse to images and narratives of the past, can also function as critical *revisions* of national history, working indeed to debunk reductive – and from an ideological point of view, more convenient – narratives around Englishness and technology. As I discuss with reference to *The Imitation Game*, this is especially significant, with regard to the much disavowed importance of technology to military application, and Britain's actual nature as a 'warfare state'.[55]

My fifth chapter looks at recent and emerging tendencies in popular English cinema with particular emphasis on representations of economic context, space and identity in genre films. The analysis takes its initial cue here from the coverage of films in *Beyond a Joke*, which paid particular attention to comic cinema of the New Labour era, epitomized by Working Title's line in transatlantic romantic comedy and genre parody. As this chapter explores, recalling my discussions in Chapter 1, modes of genre parody, but also aspects of romantic comedy, have for some time been assuming a less culturally confident and less positive tone; as noted in the geographical contexts, more pessimistic narratives, and more critical engagements with the recent past on display in films like *The World's End* (2013), *One Day* (2011) and *About Time* (2013). This comes to an even more troubling head in films such as *Sightseers* (2012). Ostensibly a comic road movie, the parody trappings of this flim only faintly conceals its tale of disenchantment and a failed English romanticism and of a violently exclusionist and xenophobic retreat into the protected enclaves of national heritage and nostalgia. Looking at the production contexts of these films, I consider how, as with the 'epic' film of Chapter 3, representational shifts in these films owe much to the transformed status of British cinema globally, and the changing contexts of global film production and culture. At the same time, the chapter focuses on the way these films nuance established frameworks for transnational exhibition, shifting from the outdated modes of metro-centric 'underdog' comedy, towards more self-reflexively critical and ironic takes on Englishness in a globalized world.

Leading on from the previous chapter, the sixth and final chapter of this book considers the contemporary and possible future contexts of popular

English cinema, offering a detailed look at representations within, and the reception of, Aardman/StudioCanal's *Early Man*, and above all StudioCanal's *Paddington* (2014) and *Paddington 2*. Looking at these examples of the prevailingly dominant 'family film' genre, I examine the significance of the transnational production contexts and StudioCanal's industrial ambitions to the success of the latter two films. Analysing the *Paddington* films in more detail, I also make a case for their capacity to signify as both English *and* European films – or rather, as *European English* films – through their narrative, aesthetic and representational strategies, and their forms of distribution. Addressing some of the concerns already raised towards the end of this introduction, in this chapter I discuss and critique the tendency to historicize cinema in discretely national terms, as an example of methodological nationalism. I in turn use Beck's 'cosmopolitan' model to think about identity in the StudioCanal project, and the *Paddington* films especially. As I conclude, these Anglo-French films offer an important nuance within the established frameworks of popular English cinema, and also provide evidence of the vitality of transnational European production for what we might otherwise call 'British cinema'. Above all, in both their narratives and their production and reception case histories, the *Paddington* series demonstrates the self-defeating nature of isolationist national approaches, and the varied, mutual benefits of thinking of Britain in European terms.

1

Film politics: Brexit, brand Britain and soft power

Both film policy and industrial strategies rely on certain ideas about, expectations of, and indeed promotions of, a cinema for and of a 'nation'. In practice and reality this representation of and for the national body excludes as much as it may notionally include. It is also as much directed towards *global* perceptions of Englishness or Britishness as it is aimed at any domestic audience.[1] Far from reflecting social realities, there may be a profound disconnect between cinematic representation and what it purports to represent. This inevitably raises questions about why, but also *for whom*, a national cinema exists and operates.

This chapter engages, then, with the sometimes under-explored question of what we really mean by the analysis of a 'national cinema'. Rather than rely on a consensual idea that 'British' or 'English' cinema exists, and that it constitutes a subject of study, in this chapter, I want firstly to identify what is *at stake* both in its institutional and critical construction. In this chapter, I work with the idea that a 'British' cinema, which in this case is more accurately an English cinema, while in some senses a diffuse descriptive category, can also be applied to the particular mobilization of certain cinematic motifs. In this case, this mobilization plays an active role in the promotion of a British cinematic 'brand'. One of the questions I ask here, then, is what an idea of 'British cinema' is actually *for*, rather than just taking it as a given. In asking this question, this chapter suggests that we think clearly about how and why filmmaking policy and practice interrelate. In this instance, it is to create specific images and meanings not so much for the nation (such as it exists), but as political manifestations of the nation and the national at a global and geopolitical level.

Film policy, promotion and propaganda

As John Hill has pointed out, conceptions of a national film culture in terms of policy have not always been economic in their focus, but have perennially been informed by conceptions of film and its cultural value, including its value as a national product.[2] Ideas around a 'culturally British' film industry have been reinforced in this century by various initiatives, such as the distribution of National Lottery funding by the former UK Film Council, or the 'cultural test' as a means to promote British production through tax relief.[3] In effect, these initiatives conflate cultural and economic concerns in their combined emphasis on sustainability of production and appropriate representation. The complexities of this model, in terms of what it actually means for British film production and culture, have been discussed at length elsewhere.[4] For the present purposes of this chapter, I am interested more in what is often mentioned only in passing, or at least in less quantifiable terms, within the discussion of British cinema. As Hill states, film policy in the UK has also 'depended upon cultural assumptions about the significance of film for the projection of "national culture" at home and abroad'.[5] He goes on to add that 'while government film policy has sometimes been promoted as a hard-headed commercial industrial strategy it has rarely turned out to be so straightforwardly the case.'[6]

My interest here in this 'projection of national culture' responds to a slight vagueness or limitation in its wider discussion. Jack Newsinger summarizes the strategic position of New Labour film policy earlier in this century, in terms of its promoting 'cultural and social aims … but only in so far as they could be justified in terms of training, infrastructure development, tourism and so on'.[7] The final unresolved 'tourism and so on', while situated within the context of Newsinger's broader, nuanced discussion, only highlights how tricky it is to pin down the relationship between film production and the supposed promotion of a national brand. That this relationship exists, though, is axiomatic to most recent discussion of British film. From the perspective of British cinema's international exposure, key production tendencies, for instance, such as the literary adaptation or period costume drama, given the global viability of these particular motifs, can be linked to the touristic promotion of national 'heritage' to viewers at both an international and national level.[8] Typically this involves the perpetuation of a tourist industry around certain authors (Jane Austen, the Brontë sisters), or more recently, the promotion of Warner Bros.' *Harry Potter* studio tour in Leavesden.[9] The 'Paddington Trail', feeding explicitly on the popularity of the 2014 and 2017 films, and devoted to the metropolitan history of Michael Bond's popular creation, is another recent manifestation of these tendencies.[10] The economic benefits of such ventures are obvious. Speaking at a House of Commons committee session shortly after the dismantling of the UK Film Council, where she was asked to justify British film's 'value for money' in the contexts of public spending cuts, British Film Institute CEO Amanda Nevill spoke of those benefits existing alongside 'the hard industry edge': in this case, 'the way in which [film] promotes Britain as a place to come to – the tourism benefits'.[11] Nevill's point though, from one perspective, is equally 'hard' in its focus on these peripheral or contingent economic benefits. Unless, that is, she is talking about something else: the cultural, or even *political*, dimension of film tourism. Less frequently considered in these discussions, in general, are the more intangible assets that cannot simply be reduced to the 'hard-headed commercial' logic of film export or publicity for tourist sites. At this point the commodity logic of film policy elides into the strategically political use of film imagery. Beyond any assumed economic use, what is *politically* in play in this 'projection of "national culture" ... abroad', and how can we identify it?

This is briefly addressed by Newsinger, reflecting on the success of *The King's Speech* (2010), and in Christopher McMillan's recent essay on *Skyfall* (2012). These articles refer to the two films, respectively, as 'a piece of royalist/tourist propaganda'[12] and 'to some extent, an expensive promo for Britain'.[13] These assessments of the films are easier to state than to prove, though, as well as indicating on face value a rather simplistic reflectionism. *The King's Speech* may indeed elide some of the more problematic aspects of George VI's reign, letting that particular monarch off the hook by drawing on Colin Firth's affable star persona.[14] Equally, *Skyfall*'s eventual reconstitution of Bond as a nostalgic figure, harking back to the start of the 007 series, appears to turn back 'the uncertainty surrounding the future of Britain'[15] in the era of post-imperialism and possible devolution (I will return to this in Chapter 3). Undoubtedly, the films can be interpreted or used in this way. However, to speak of such films' narratives as active forms of national propaganda or promotion relies on an almost conspiratorial link between governmental policy and, in these cases, commercial cinematic forms. Specifying intention behind film, or showing how this intention is made visible, is a difficult task, especially with regard to political meanings.

Once we start focusing, as David Bordwell suggests we do, on the 'specific causal processes' underpinning film production, we get an even stronger sense of the dislocations between film's apparent political representation and production contexts.[16] These are telling in this instance, given that the 'national' influence on these films at the level of production is only ever partial. Though much touted as one of the great achievements of the UK Film Council, for example, *The King's Speech* actually sits within a fairly familiar nexus of transnational production and exhibition parties, including the Weinstein Company and the distributors FilmNation. And as much as the UK basis of Eon Productions guarantees a certain British status for the Bond movies, their continued existence is only ever relative to the health of the Hollywood corporations that fund and distribute them (the production lull between *Quantum of Solace* [2008] and *Skyfall*, on account of MGM's filing for bankruptcy, being illustrative of this point).

Rather than look at individual films out of context as somehow conveying political intent, the more pointed political concern here is to identify in what degree films like *The King's Speech* or *Skyfall* exemplify the types or scales of British filmmaking that are, in the first instance, privileged by broader film policy. As Paul Dave has suggested, one of the peculiar but potent aspects of British cinema as an industry is that it is able to draw on cultural elements as its own form of commodity and promotion. For Dave, this cinema relies on the 'historic hyper-visibility [of] Englishness' as its most 'exploitable' aspect: a 'mythic and globally recognized culture ... with all its abstract, idealized and marketable characteristics'. This is a 'legacy' that, for Dave, represents 'both a problem and an opportunity' in terms of cultural policy.[17] Dave's view points to the idea, then, that popular English cinema (as 'British' cinema) is inherently driving cultural ideas around Britishness on a global scale – a process that is at the same time a political one – within the same process of marketization. And as Dave also intimates, this inevitably involves a narrowing of the parameters through which Britishness is understood.

2012: History, parody, spectacle

To explore this further, I want to look at a British event motivated and defined precisely by its role as a projection of the national culture for a mass international audience; one which also drew significantly on the global currency of cinematic and other media figures. In deploying both the figure of James Bond and Queen Elizabeth II within its programme, the London Olympics opening ceremony of July 2012 tapped into the same national iconography that supposedly informed the success of films such as *The King's Speech* and *Skyfall*. This is overdetermined by the form and expectations of such events, as the obligation to address a mediated global audience has been structured into the planning and delivery of the Games since Moscow in 1980.[18] Given the inflated costs involved in both bidding for and producing such events (the London ceremony alone cost £27m), they have frequently been seen in economically promotional terms, with the staging of the Games itself once viewed as 'part of a whole development strategy for a city'.[19] This idea only goes so far, though. In the historical contexts of then emerging or re-emerging global cities such as Seoul (1988), Barcelona (1992) or even Beijing (2008), 'development strategy' makes sense. But it is less obviously relevant to the already-established 'world city' of London in 2012: a city that had not only enjoyed decades of global cultural and touristic recognition, but was also the financial hub of contemporary Europe.

From this point of view the Olympic Games were *specifically* political in their inception: part of a broader attempt on the part of the New Labour government, as Robert Hewison argues, to erase memories of the earlier Millennium Dome – an economic and public relations fiasco – as well as its disastrous intervention in the Iraq War, which began in 2003.[20] The Department of Culture, Media and Sport (DCMS) (formerly the Department of National Heritage) played the energizing role in preparing the Olympic bid in 2005, with its public body, the Olympic Delivery Authority, vowing to manage the games and its varied physical and symbolic legacies. As stated on its official website homepage, among the aims of the DCMS are 'to drive growth, enrich lives and promote Britain abroad, and highlight … Britain as a fantastic place to visit. We help to give the UK a unique advantage on the global stage, striving for economic success'.[21] The Olympic Games and its legacies were also a key focal point of the GREAT Britain campaign, a wide-scale initiative drawing on the work of the British Council, the Foreign and Commonwealth Office, UK Trade and Investment, Cabinet Office, the Department for Business, Innovation and Skills, and Visit Britain. According to its mission statement, the GREAT Britain campaign aims to 'showcase … the best of what the UK has to offer to inspire the world and encourage people to visit, do business, invest and study'; emphasizing in turn the country's 'global leader' status in 'industries like music, fashion, design and film'.[22] As McMillan notes, the same campaign ran a short film in conjunction with promotional drive for *Skyfall*.[23] In the video, brief moments from various Bond movies, including the upcoming film, were match-edited into various shots, showing, for instance, fly-by images of British landscapes or views of London, interspersed with various words splashed in capitals (EXCITING ... INSPIRING ... TIMELESS ...). The film ends with the slogan 'BOND IS GREAT BRITAIN' across a shot of Daniel Craig's 007, in one of the last images from *Skyfall*, looking out across the rooftops of central London.

The importance of cinematic and more broadly media archetypes was hardly lost on the producers of the 2012 opening ceremony, coordinated by film and theatre directors Danny Boyle and Stephen Daldry, along with writer Frank Cottrell-Boyce. But it was also a specific inflection on the use of these media figures that distinguished the event. As I have argued elsewhere, the strategically parodic use of generic Bond motifs, as the Queen – within a short inserted film – leapt from her own helicopter strapped into a Union Jack parachute, suggested a self-reflexive and ironic relationship to the national iconography that is already hinted at in the James Bond GREAT Britain advert (Figure 1.1). If part of an opening ceremony's 'galvanising function' is to 'forge a national narrative [and] sense of an "imagined community",'[24] the London event showed a canny sense of the way this community, such as it may exist, operates through media images (whether fictional or actual). This status of the images was underscored by their incorporation into an eclectic bricolage (integrating, in the case of the above short film, fictional and actual figures), and a parodic juxtaposition of incongruous elements.[25] The later introduction of Rowan Atkinson's Mr. Bean persona, playing the one-note synthesizer part in the theme from *Chariots of Fire* (1981), only underscored this idea further. The fact that Atkinson's daydreaming persona here lampooned the opening sequence of this Oscar-winning film, one so tied up with discourses around nostalgia and heritage, emphasized the ceremony's often self-deprecating and irreverent reflection on its national past. This 'domestic' focus was at the same time strategically global, inasmuch as these media figures are also significant international exports. The *Mr. Bean* series (Thames Television/Central Independent Television, 1990–5), for example, enjoys the status as one

Figure 1.1 The conjunction of the (media) stars: James Bond (Daniel Craig) and Queen Elizabeth II in *Happy and Glorious*, made for the 2012 London Olympic Games opening ceremony. Directed by Danny Boyle © BBC 2012. All rights reserved.

of the UK's most widely exported shows; a fact that underpinned the export production logic of the two Bean movies (*Bean* [1997] and *Mr. Bean's Holiday* [2007], both produced by Working Title).

These images are here mobilized within the terms of a mass-media event for which such figures, *because*, rather than in spite of their capacity for ironic self-reflection, serve as benchmarks for the kind of creative and cultural output the ceremony, and the broader remit of the DCMS and GREAT Britain campaign, wanted to promote. Laughing at a certain idea of oneself, in short, can be a good strategy for attracting an audience, investors and visitors. Such images, I have suggested, constituted 'a parody of Englishness that was also, in its same gesture, a confident expression of what Englishness means in a global media context'.[26] It may though have been an incautiously limited approach on my part to make too strong a claim for this ironized 'expression of Englishness', failing as it did to account for broader political ramifications. Whatever ways it mobilized it, this aspect of the event drew quite narrowly on a popular cultural face of Englishness, perhaps to the exclusion of more diverse contexts.

My previous study emphasized how specifically twisted, post-imperial and typically post-Conservative versions of national heritage (made, as they were, within the New Labour era) proffered a critical comic vision of contemporary

England. I did not dwell, however, on the possibility that such representations were themselves shaped by the concerns and worldviews of specific, and in themselves quite limited, constituencies and agendas. In a prescient essay on the transformations of European national cinemas within the contexts of economic and cultural globalization, Thomas Elsaesser notes how the national has paradoxically re-emerged in the contexts of a Europe that is at once expanding in scope, and shrinking in terms of border permeability and access. Like Elsaesser, my interest was mainly on the non-aggressive nature of this new mediated type of 'soft' nationalism, and the possibilities for an ironic mode of representation that served to re-purpose the national as a form of global branding tool.[27] In taking this as its own end, though, I did not develop at length what Elsaesser himself more hints at than defines; namely the 'political power' of such an approach.[28] It is vital to stress that such comparatively soft use of the national and its archetypes is far from disinterested in its political aims.

Contesting the idea that the self-effacing aspects of the ceremony were sufficiently progressive in themselves, we should note that the emphasis on *formal* qualities of a given text (in this instance, parody) does not in itself adequately confront *content*, in terms of the centrality of the subjects themselves (the dominant media figures of James Bond, The Queen and Mr. Bean). As parody theorist Dan Harries has argued, within an ironic postmodern culture, parody no longer establishes a critical position vis-à-vis its target texts.[29] If anything, it participates in the maintenance or 'resuscitation' of dominant media forms in an ironized though still self-proliferating circuit. In this case, the effects of parody are subordinate to the predominance of these 'culturally British' archetypes – or more specifically, culturally *English-as-British*, and therefore its own type of erasure – that represent a limited perspective for understanding film and media culture. The emphasis on an ironic or comic logic to national self-projection gets around the problem of an assertive national (or nationalist) projection, one often associated with events such as the Olympic ceremony, and in particular, the previous ceremony of Beijing 2008. Boyle, Daldry and Boyce's conception managed to enjoy its display of British cultural history without ever seeming to veer into jingoism. Yet the ceremony still remained an energetic and purposeful global statement, employing motifs carefully selected for their capacity to speak broadly across the domestic and international contexts.

The comic fusion here of Bond, the Queen and Bean, in the latter case (via *Chariots of Fire*) relocated to late-imperial contexts, implicitly addressed the idea of a British Empire, yet in the same process it consigned it humorously to the past. But inasmuch as English film culture insists on the historical traces of empire and the national past as its subject, even if critically to revise or deride them, this imperial imaginary seems impossible to shift. English film production through 2017, for instance, saw the release of *Their Finest*, *Dunkirk* and *Darkest Hour*, all focusing on the Second World War, and *Victoria and Abdul*, about the later years of Queen Victoria. The online giant Netflix, meanwhile, invested $100m dollars in the first season of Peter Morgan and Stephen Daldry's *The Crown* (2016–), chronicling the ups and downs of Winston Churchill and the House of Windsor in the immediate post-war years. Merely looking at the subject matter here is to be reminded that the insistence of and on the past, however comic, critical or revisionist this return might be, is at the same time another instance of how this past is reiterated and reified as a form of nationally specific spectacle: what Andrew Higson describes as English cinema's 'surprisingly resilient national stereotypes'.[30] The Olympic ceremony was, in Hewison's words, an attempt to 'rewrit[e] the traditional national story', and to 'free [this story] from the grasp of the institutions that define official culture': something inscribed in its own focus on certain national institutions (such as the NHS sequence), and its mass use of volunteer performers.[31] And yet, it still set itself up to criticism, inevitably, by using a history of exclusion as its backdrop and narrative core: the history of Imperialist Britain, conveyed through the focus on Britain's Industrial Revolution.[32]

London, Britain, the world: Universality, or exclusion?

Irony and parody, then, do not guarantee inclusivity. Looking at these earlier contexts from the post-referendum perspective, it is clearer that the economic and cultural disparities pre-existing at the social level are, to a significant extent, reiterated at the level of cultural policy and production, in terms of selective inclusion and the erasures this involves. There is in some sense an overlap here between the conception of the London Olympics as a project and implications of recent film policy. As someone who has grown up in England, with strong personal and familial ties to its capital city, I acknowledge the pride and pleasure I took from the Games as an event. But from a cooler perspective, in terms of its initial conception, I also found myself asking what the London Olympic Games were for. Both the precise economic benefit to the region of East London where the Games took place (the so-called 'Olympic Legacy') and the impact of holding them remain something of an enigma to analysts. Some studies of such events indicate that any notable 'profit' made from the Olympic Games is meaningful not in terms of tangible economic benefit to the host nation, which is at best temporary.[33] More significant are the aims in terms of the soft effects of prestige, international exposure and presence; the 'feel-good' factor for participants, visitors and viewers.[34] This view can be further supported with reference to the budgetary policies underpinning UK sporting development and attainment, which focused, in this instance, on medal potential at the expense of wider participation and representation. The cycle of increased British Olympic achievement through consecutive Games in the 2000s (Sydney in 2000, Athens in 2004 and Beijing in 2008) reached a high point in London, where the Great Britain team won twenty-eight gold medals, putting them third on the medal table behind only the United States and China (I will return to these contexts in Chapter 3).

Expenditure on film production is different from that on sport, as, unlike the funding given to elite athletes, it notionally comes with the expectation of financial returns. Yet the logic of UK film policy in this regard – at least in terms of what we might call the *national* good – is uncertain. It is doubly significant that the Mr. Bean skit in the 2012 Games should use *Chariots of Fire* as a subject for parody, given that the latter was mobilized prematurely in the early 1980s as a flagship film for British cinema production. As a film enjoying a degree of US-derived inward investment, it was also a model for a type of cinematic practice that has a legacy precisely in films like Working Title's *Bean* films, which, like much of the company's output, enjoys a financing and distribution deal with Universal Pictures. The ideological debate surrounding *Chariots of Fire*, especially its supposed narrative links to Thatcherite values of individualism, tends to overwhelm the film's significant (but equally Thatcherite) economic pointers to the national film industry: the idea, in James Chapman's words, that 'private investment rather than government subsidy was the way forward', with all the attendant economic insecurity this entailed.³⁵ In other words, a British film industry would be best served by the production of a certain type of 'quality' film competing within the global free-market economy.³⁶ Or as Margaret Dickinson and Sarah Street summarized in 1985, writing in the contexts of Conservative-led privatization of the film industry, such changes would 'almost certainly lead to a decline in all film activity not promoted by major commercial interests'.³⁷

It is notable within these contexts that the Chair of the UK Film Council at the time of its closure, in 2010, was Tim Bevan, the Co-Chairman of Working Title. Unsurprisingly, given his company's production practices, inward investment was the policy Bevan saw as most advantageous to the UK Film Council tax-credit model.³⁸ Speaking at the aforementioned post-UK Film Council House of Commons session, alongside Nevill, Bevan's opening response in defence of the film industry was to highlight the £1bn brought into the UK economy every year through investment in film production. This, at least in the order of things, was prioritized over the incentives towards diversifying low- to medium-budget British production (a strategy that, at least from the point of view of government, had been seen to produce more commercial failures than successes).³⁹ What Hill describes as the 'Janus-faced' character of British film production under New Labour, and the Film Council, is characterized by this movement between the encouragement of local production and the economic pragmatism of getting films made in the UK which 'would otherwise be made "abroad" (and thus ... might be said to be only potentially "British")'.⁴⁰

It was the New Labour Culture Secretary Chris Smith, in his arts manifesto *Creative Britain* (1998), who gave shape to this economically driven perspective; one frequently discussed, as per the title of Smith's book, in terms of a shift from 'cultural industries' policy to one focusing on the *creative industries*.⁴¹ Smith highlights the 'unprecedented market share' of 'British made' films in the year New Labour came to office (1997), with *The Full Monty* and *Bean* at the top of the UK lists, and asserts his commitment to doubling this share for British films.⁴² Elsewhere, in a speech originally given in Los Angeles, Smith highlights plans to siphon National Lottery funding into the production of small- to medium-budget films; though not before stating that Britain should be a hub for 'all aspects of the industry ... [and] a bridge, geographically, culturally and economically, between Europe and the United States'.⁴³ Indeed, it is the attractiveness of the UK as a place for inward investment that forms the top and tail of Smith's Los Angeles address. Instigated by the new government, the Film Policy Review Group's 1998 report, *A Bigger Picture*, in its assessment and prognosis for the British industry, joins up many of the dots in Smith's book. As the report notes, Britain's 'fragmented' production culture lagged behind the 'distribution-led, integrated structures' of the American industry.[44] Britain produced 'risky and low-budget' films that the bigger market in the United States neither needed nor wanted. To increase British cinema's export potential, the report summarized, but also to appeal to a domestic audience apparently averse to risk and too much realism, the emphasis should be on creating 'a more consistent supply of entertaining films with broad audience appeal'.[45] The report consequently cites what was then Working Title-Polygram's *Four Weddings and a Funeral* (1995) as an exemplary film within this model: 'immensely enjoyable and quintessentially British, [with] universal appeal'.[46]

As *Sight & Sound*'s Nick Roddick argued in a response to the report, its limitation was in overlooking the economies of scale that made such ambition a challenge. In the efforts to compete on this 'bigger' scale, British cinema turns itself into a commodity, which is then a brand. Such approaches, Roddick suggests, tend towards conservatism: 'You can only brand what already exists, and to do so is no blueprint for future action.'[47] It is possible to view Working Title's subsequent signature cycle of romantic comedies (including *Notting Hill* [1999] and *Love Actually* [2003]) within these branded terms. Yet it is also notable how these films happen to chime with both Smith's and the Film Policy Review Group's cultural and economic vision for UK cinema at the turn of the millennium. This is achieved largely in their construction of a particular idea of national identity, represented mostly by metropolitan London, as a spacious and economically amenable place, with a trans-European and transatlantic citizenship.[48]

The capacity of these films to project an image of London's creative and friendly world city is arguably their most significant political dimension, in terms of their capacity to generate and enhance Britain's global 'soft power': in political theorist Joseph Nye's terms, the ability to obtain international strategic goals through attraction rather than coercion, especially through the promotion of culture, political ideals and policies.[49] As I have argued, the London Olympics performed a similar role, through its genial, playful and self-effacing (but no less assertive) display of Great British archetypes. In the

2015 report on its annual 'Soft Power 30' index, Portland Communications, a consultancy agency that undertakes and produces this list, placed the UK at the top (above Germany, the United States and France). The report identified as main engines of British soft power entities such as the BBC World Service and the Foreign and Commonwealth Office; while in its concluding sections, it also identified the importance of the GREAT Britain campaign and the 2012 Olympics at its focal centre.[50]

To what ends is this power exercised? A pre-Olympics report by the Foreign and Commonwealth Office (FCO) stated that the games should play a role in 'promot[ing] the refinement of the UK's image' globally.[51] At the same time, however, scepticism towards the potential cultural and economic benefit of the Olympics to the wider UK, beyond London's somewhat detached 'world city', was detectable within government opinion itself.[52] The Olympics as a broader project has itself been critically analysed in terms of its exclusivity, from the perspective of both class and global geopolitics. Far from a 'universal' event, the Olympic Games (both summer and winter versions) tend to privilege elite sports (and, in turn, socio-economically privileged competitors), while also being dominated, at a representational level, by First World/Global North countries. This is seen both in terms of the proportion of medals won and with regard to hosting: no African or South Asian country, for instance, has ever hosted the summer Games, and it has only once been to South America (Rio in 2016).[53] In this respect the Olympics is already implicated in, and to an extent promoting, an imbalanced view of the world order that concentrates 'symbolic power' in already-dominant global centres and cities.[54] But, as already noted, this concentration of symbolic power through the 2012 Olympics also tended to focus mostly on London, rather than Britain more broadly, and even then, with question marks around its local regenerative promises. Indeed, beyond the more ephemeral legacy of the 2012 Games, the mainstays of British soft power have been – or were already being – undermined at the broader level of government policy and spending at that time. The declining investment in public sports facilities (though not, as already noted, elite performance) needs to be weighed alongside other cuts, made in then Chancellor George Osborne's Comprehensive Spending Review of 2010. One commitment was to cut the budget of the British Council, and another, to stop direct funding of the BBC World Service – those same institutions, ironically, identified as major sources of British soft power.

But it is also unclear what, if anything, the 2012 Games was actually 'selling'. As a London School of Economics report identifies, the symbolic import of the London ceremony, which traced a narrative from the Industrial Revolution through progressive stages in pop culture, building up to the arrival of the internet, was to emphasize the UK's transformation 'from a manufacturing stalwart into a major exporter of services'.[55] The global perception at stake in the ceremony was, therefore, that of a Britain whose 'comparative advantage had little to do anymore with manufacturing', but rather one which 'benefited from a distinctive capability in media and entertainment': the promotion, in other words, of a creative industries agenda.[56] As the same study observes, though, film's major contribution to the development of British soft power is not commensurate with its industrial presence or its contribution to national GDP, which in fact remains comparatively small.[57] To some extent, then, studying the history of British national cinema, at least in terms of propaganda, is an attempt to explain the gap between film's 'perceived importance' and its actual market contribution.[58] What stands out in 2012, as a culmination of a New Labour-driven cultural–political project, is a sense of disconnect between the kinds of film at the forefront of this project, and their connection to a broader and inclusive sense of the popular. Like the films, to a large extent, these were images of how 'Britain' would like to be seen, from an early twenty-first-century global, or maybe 'global city', perspective.

That was then. Four years on from the London Olympics, and just a few months after the EU referendum, watching a film like *Bridget Jones's Baby* (2016) offered ample evidence of the renewed contexts for viewing and understanding the kinds of movies privileged and facilitated by policy. This third film in the *Bridget Jones* series is already inherently nostalgic for the New Labour years in its links to the previous two films made fifteen and twelve years previously (*Bridget Jones's Diary* [2001] and *Bridget Jones: The Edge of Reason* [2004]). Made prior to the referendum, but released just after it (and not unlike *Absolutely Fabulous* [2016], which it in many respects resembles), *Bridget Jones's Baby* is a time-warping film, inviting us to hang on to a past that is clearly faded: an oscillation marked in the latter film by its frequent insertion of footage from the earlier instalments. But what is also striking is how much *Bridget Jones's Baby* insists on a view of its almost exclusively *metropolitan* milieu that is mostly unchanged, even if it incorporates new trends along the way. The film's script has fun deriving satirical laughs at the expense of youthful media-industry hipsters with 'ironic beards' (and, we might also add, Northern accents), and revels in the comic reference to leisure-industry fads, or, when Bridget is taken off to a Glastonbury-style event, music-festival culture. But these are still variations within an imagined London topography and cast that more or less assumes affluence and participation in the media and creative industries within which Bridget, showing no obvious talent or ability, operates. This metropolis is one in which TV news producers run into internet dating billionaires while 'glamping' in customized yurts, and where the backdrop switches between organic food markets, glass-fronted media centres and City of London skyscrapers. Its composited dream of the city inevitably subsumes, or at best delimits, any ambitions the film might otherwise have to contemporary social relevance. And from my personal experience of watching this film (a rather melancholy one, I should say), Brexit has only helped to make this dislocation abundantly clear.

This latter reading further informs my central argument that we need to look closely at the films in the years prior to and around the EU referendum to understand some of the latter's contexts. From the viewpoint of Remainers, the memory of the 2012 Games may be a bitter-sweet one, as the event encapsulated the high moment of London's world-city status; a status that Brexit, London's mostly pro-Remain vote notwithstanding, has subsequently tarnished. From another perspective, of course, the success of London 2012 could be seen as demonstrable evidence of Britain's resilience and prowess, extending in this case – as I explore later – to the results in the actual Games. London 2012 might from this perspective be a final glorious bow in Britain's pre-Brexit global era. But it may also have been an indicator – and not entirely an innocent one – of well-established tensions, divisions and omissions that would surface visibly four years later.

Asking, then, as the final part of this chapter will do, what the potential opportunities are for British soft power in the post-referendum contexts, is possibly beside the point. The more pertinent question would be whether or not the pursuit of soft power, the need for abiding global influence, as vague as this may be, is part of the problem. Looking for ways to enhance British soft power is by its own nature another way of working within a *national* mentality – as opposed, for instance, to a more 'cosmopolitan' view of inter-relationship and influence.[59] Nor can the perceived values of soft power be separated from the political philosophies and geopolitical agendas underpinning it. The playing field for soft power, like Olympic sports, is asymmetrical, both at a domestic and global level. London is a truly global place, but not just in the sense of its diverse citizenry, and its status as a hub for a plethora of mobile denizens. It is also a global city in Saskia Sassen's influential definition, in terms of its concentration of financial services, stock exchanges and multinational company headquarters, making it a 'node … in the global economic system' with a 'reach and reference … beyond a single nation'.[60] As Johan Andersson and Lawrence Webb note, like the indexes of soft power, the kind of league-table of global super-cities is also rigged, as it is often these same extra-national financial consultancies, misappropriating Sassen's critical methods, who compile them.[61] By a similar token, the ability to attract and influence requires first and foremost that the influencing state wields the necessary level of material resources, international partnerships and 'hard' power influence for it to be 'attractive' in the first place.

The exercising of soft power therefore operates in an already 'hierarchical international system' that is biased in favour of dominant First World powers; but also, as this implies, the global systems and networks that benefit them and help maintain the dominant hierarchies.[62] The sense of dislocation and disenfranchisement from these same global world systems and orders, as already noted in my introduction, was viewed as a key factor in motivating the popular vote against Britain's EU membership. The London Olympic year was one that, in many respects, appeared to have brought the nation 'together'. The subsequent referendum vote was a clear demonstration of how no mass-media event, or the ideas around it, could really speak for such a vast and contested political body.

What next?

Reiterating Dickinson and Street's pessimistic prognosis for a national cinema shaped by commercial interests, Hill argued in 1992 for a national cinema that offered 'a more varied and representative range of film and media output than the current political economy of the communications industries allows'.[63] The inference here is that it is governmental initiatives that can productively orient representation. But as Higson responds, why should we necessarily expect such forms of cultural work to proceed from state funding?[64] What this immediately suggests is that diverse discourses and cultural representations around Brexit are potentially in the hands of those same private and transnational creative constituencies that, hitherto, have called into question the idea of a 'national cinema' in terms of inclusivity and diversity. This chapter has already indicated that this is a potentially awkward fit. As was quickly mooted after the EU referendum, Britain's post-Brexit, declining-currency destiny as an affordable studio facility for American production, appealing as this may be to some, offers little hope for a genuinely inclusive, diverse or dissenting British cinema; a cinema that some saw as already jeopardized by former Film Council policy at its most economically pragmatic.

As already noted, the references in the Olympic ceremony to Bond, Mr Bean and, via an effigy of Lord Voldemort in one of its sequences, Harry Potter, only emphasize that local productions with significant inward investment from Hollywood have largely represented 'British cinema' for many viewers both domestically and globally. A British Film Institute (BFI) report at the end of January 2017, indeed, trumpeted the success of 2016 as a successful year for 'the UK film industry', noting the record-breaking investment of £1.6bn on British film production, and UK box-office figures indicating a 27.5 per cent share for 'UK-made films'.[65] Predictably, this expenditure and market share reflected the dominant impact of inward investment films, made in the UK with UK crews, such as *Rogue One: A Star Wars Story* (2016) and *Fantastic Beasts and Where to Find Them* (2016), or of Working Title productions such as *Bridget Jones's Baby*. This reflects many of the aims previously put forward in the BFI's 2012 policy documents. These stress the pursuit of inward investment, especially from the United States in its role as the United Kingdom's 'most significant inward investment client'.[66] The BFI's 2012 international strategy paper is from its outset very clear in its emphasis on 'UK film's continued success and growth' being dependent 'entirely on its ability to maintain a strong global position', pointing as its primary statistic to the average £1bn a year production investment, of which 70 per cent comes from the United States.[67] In its stated intent to work within the aims of the GREAT Britain campaign, 'both to seek ways in which film can contribute to GREAT, and to use GREAT to maximise international commercial opportunities for UK film',[68] BFI international policy converges to some extent with the broader aims of the British Film Commission, whose 2016 magazine, alongside profiles of UK creative talent, highlighted the location potential and post-production facilities upon which international production can call.[69]

Coming as it does soon after the referendum, the language in the 2017 BFI annual report is both pointed and telling, above all in its across-the-board intention to downplay the negative consequences of Brexit and promote the UK to international investors. Hence, the Minister of State for Digital and Culture, Matt Hancock, asserted that such record-breaking statistics 'demonstrate that the UK's world-leading film sector continues to thrive and that Britain *remains open for business*'; a point echoed by Nevill, for whom the statistics 'show that UK film *is open for business*'; while Adrian Wootton, from the British Film Commission, strikes a slightly more cautionary though equally positive note, calling upon industry and government 'to ensure the UK *remains a competitive destination* and a compelling offer for international production'.[70] The rather obvious emphasis here on the *remaining* strengths of UK production, its implicit rebuff to the idea that the country may in fact be 'closed' (or that it *has left*), underscores an obvious anxiety on the part of a film industry and film policy-makers contending with the potential economic impact of Brexit. This is not just with regard to European co-production, but also in terms of Britain's continued appeal post-EU to potentially fickle Hollywood investors. But there is also underlying the discussion a concern with the UK's ability to generate soft power within the more negative frameworks of Brexit.

In light of the productions it references, the extending hand in the recent report is across the Atlantic first and foremost, rather than over the Channel. It shows a continuation of the same incentivizing privileged in the GREAT Britain campaign, which in its promotion used a flagship film of inward investment transatlantic co-production: a poster image from *Harry Potter and the Deathly Hallows: Part One* (2011), inscribed with the invitation to 'make your next film in the UK', benefitting from the country's 'thousands of iconic locations and world-class talent' (while the image of Tower Bridge in the poster somewhat misrepresents the film, London figures prominently in *Deathly Hallows*, when Harry, Ron and Hermione apparate into Shaftsbury Avenue, at the heart of tourist London [Figure 1.2]).[71] As Higson points out, the efforts on the part

Figure 1.2 Made in London: *Harry Potter and the Deathly Hallows: Part One* (2011), a flagship film used as publicity for the GREAT Britain campaign. Directed by David Yates © Warner Bros. Pictures 2011. All rights reserved.

of bodies such as the British Film Commission to get the Harry Potter films made in Britain, which ultimately proved successful, might have been carried out in the cultural aim of protecting a celebrated national property, but such efforts were also economic, ensuring a decade of production and investment in an English studio.[72] They also hardly represented a blow to Warner Bros., who could consequently keep overall costs lower and – eventually – buy up the Leavesden studio for lucrative public tours.

Despite its proximity to Britain – and the rather more obvious point that Britain had been a member of the EU and its earlier manifestations since 1973 – Europe had for some time prior to the EU referendum been the less attractive target for British film policy, especially during the years of the UK Film Council. Andrew Spicer has recently commented on the way Britain's 'broader Euroscepticism' is manifest at the level of UK film policy from the end of the 1990s.[73] Spicer identifies in particular the governmental decision, in 1996, to leave Eurimages, the Council of Europe film fund, and the fact that the UK did not re-join under the new government and the new UK Film Council. For Simon Perry, the CEO of the Film Council's predecessor, British Screen, these moves made the UK 'the coproduction partner-of-last-choice within Europe': retrospectively, in fact, Perry suggests that in film policy terms British producers 'Brexited in 2000'.[74]

It is not clear that the immediate post-UK Film Council environment was significantly different. In the same Olympic year of 2012, the BFI released as part of its five-year plan the proposal *New Horizons for UK Film*. As Higson notes, within this plan 'there was not one single mention of Europe' as either a key audience target or a production partner. Rather, the bigger and large emerging markets of China, Brazil and the United States were identified as the British film industry's 'key priorities'.[75] These priorities, Higson goes on to suggest, only further support the industry's case for inward investment films. The similar cinematic reference points at work in the London ceremony, from this perspective, were in tune with more contemporary circumstances of British film production, but only within these same prescribed terms: the terms, specifically, of the earlier New Labour/UK Film Council agenda.[76]

There is also the small print, as it were, to consider. Beyond the attention-grabbing headlines in the BFI report, the picture for 'independent' British cinema – those films not made with major inward investment, or Hollywood distribution deals – is less impressive, indicating only a 1.2 per cent share for such films worldwide. A recent report from the European Audiovisual Observatory (the survey operated through the European Commission), focusing on the potential impacts of Brexit to European film and television, highlights that UK co-productions dominate EU markets, but predominantly in terms of those films made with US investment (28 per cent of UK film output).[77] The economic contexts here consequentially acquire cultural implications. Any discussion of Brexit and the immanent futures of British film must also take into consideration the findings of the 2017 report by the Screen Sector Task Force, convened by the BFI, which looked into the combined cultural and economic impacts of leaving the EU and also the European Economic Area (EEA).[78] From the view of this report, the potential benefits to the UK film industry were clearly in terms of increased inward investment, with foreign studios benefitting from the weaker pound and the loosening of EU regulations (though as the film industry analyst Stephen Follows has noted, this cheerful solution would make the British industry precariously sensitive to currency fluctuations[79]). The potential negatives, meanwhile, are numerous; from the impacts to cast and crew mobility, to the loss of training funds, and the reduced funding and distribution opportunities for British-produced film supplied by the Creative Europe scheme. All of these would hit the independent sector the hardest.

These realities are reflected in *BFI2022*, the BFI's 2017 five-year plan, which is clear from the outset on the national industry's need to 'up its game' in the 'post-referendum world', in order to 'sustain and grow further the UK's position'.⁸⁰ Notably, though, *BFI2022* seems strategically aimed less at courting big investment opportunities, and more towards building diversity into national film production. The introduction of Regional Development Funds, for instance, is highlighted as part of a broader incentive to 'support … the growth of independent film production beyond London'.⁸¹ The language of the plan as a whole suggests that the perception of the film industry, and by inference that of the 'creative industries', is that it is too consolidated around the capital city, at the costs of more meaningful social inclusion and a wider talent base. As stated: 'For the sector to really flourish, we need to recognise and promote the wealth of talent and creativity from across the whole of the UK, in addition to London'; 'We can be proud of the internationally recognised expertise in our capital city. But when voices from all the regions and Nations of the UK are not properly represented, that is detrimental to UK film as a whole.'⁸² Or elsewhere: 'Under-representation across the board needs to be addressed, along with the persistent imbalance of filmmakers and producers based in London and the South East, and the broader socio-economic factors inhibiting access for talent and audiences.'⁸³ We cannot say with any certainty whether or not such a reiterated move away from London, at least in intent, is any specific response to the regional disparities of the referendum vote, which to a large extent only underlined the sense of dislocation between metropolitan viewpoints and the rest of the country. Or, indeed (in the plan's specific reference to the 'Nations of the UK'), whether it responds to the perception of a predominantly 'English' cultural representation of the UK as a whole, to the expense of Scotland, Wales and Northern Ireland. And yet, the conciliatory, reflexive tone of the plan certainly reads like an attempt to redress the 'imbalance' within the country's cultural representation: one that the plan, as noted above, admits is evident.

In terms of Europe, meanwhile, *BFI2022* acknowledges the types of evidence outlined above, noting 'the value that the UK screen sectors bring to the rest of Europe', and the significance of the UK staying within the Creative Europe (formerly the MEDIA) programme.⁸⁴ At the same time, the plan highlights the need to 'flourish in markets outside the EU' as a specific response to the EU referendum result and its repercussions. As Spicer points out, while the BFI has made a case for remaining within the European Convention on Cinematographic Co-production, like its Film Council predecessor, it has argued against re-joining Eurimages.⁸⁵

Seeing how the *BFI2022* plan pans out is, inevitably, the subject of another, much wider study. My more limited aim in this first chapter was to outline some of the factors both shaping and shaped by UK film policy in the years preceding, and then just after, the EU referendum. As I have discussed, policy during this period is determined largely by a global, creative-industries agenda: one that blends commerce, culture and politics, mobilizing potent, commercially appealing cultural ideas of Englishness. The broader political implications of this cinema can be understood in terms of its limits and its narrowness. As other commentators have discussed, these limitations should be seen mostly in terms of policy's failure to engage meaningfully with domestic contexts of social exclusion: issues which, as I have noted, informed the 2016 EU referendum in important ways.

But as I have also discussed here, another implication of policy at this time is its apparent reluctance to engage with Europe. If the British film industry can, as noted earlier, assume a certain presence in European markets – largely on the back of the types of inward investment films discussed in this chapter – even prior to the EU referendum, Europe does not seem to have been a significant point of focus for British films. I will return in more detail, in the final chapter, to the contexts of British film policy and Europe, and above all, to the importance of cross-Channel collaboration in film production. As a preface to this, though – and, in many respects, a preface to the rest of this book as a whole – I would like to turn to this question of Europe and its role, both historically and recently, in popular English film. The next chapter therefore considers the ways Europe has figured, both as a geographical and imaginary space, in several recent films. Viewed above all in light of recent political developments, this cinematic relationship with the European mainland proves to be a revealing one.

2

Comedians and sunscreen: The English holiday film and the idea of Europe

As I noted in the introduction, an important aspect of discussing a national cinema is to work out *whose* 'national cinema' we are talking about. In political respects, this is an important question, touching as it does on proprietorial and political questions of how audiences relate to, and identify with, films. But it also raises questions about the discursive ways in which film scholarship can both dictate and delimit the field of study, sometimes in problematic and misrepresentative ways.

As a graduate student, giving my first proper lecture on the subject of 'French national cinema', I turned – as my film education up to that point led me to do – towards a canonical diet of *auteur* film, avant-garde and oppositional cinema theory. My lecture would go on to present a role call of familiar director figures, from Jean Renoir and Jean-Luc Godard to Clair Denis and Agnès Varda. On reflection, my overview, shaped though it was by a keen awareness of the critical frameworks surrounding French film production, was absurdly narrow. As a colleague at that time suggested to me, in identifying this as 'national' cinema, are we only doing so in wilful disregard, even ignorance, of a *popular* cinema: a cinema 'of the people', that in more concrete terms represents the national film-going body, and the 'imagined communities' of nation? One that is reflective of the nation in ways that art and auteur cinema, equated with 'national' cinema mainly by film critics and academics, has never really been? In other words: in our pursuit of the 'correct' object of analysis, do we overlook the less obvious, and therefore more challenging and important object of study: in this case, the 'bad' and the 'despised' film? Or simply, the film deemed too unimportant to analyse (and therefore, my colleague would suggest, the first film to which we should turn our attention)?

The holiday film – one of the main examples my colleague would suggest – is not unique to English cinema culture, and is in fact more developed as a genre elsewhere. In Italy, for instance, it was for nearly thirty years a Christmas institution; hence the generic name of the *cinepanettone* ('Christmas-cake film') given to such films. These include titles such as *Christmas on the Nile* (2002), *Christmas in India* (2003) and *Christmas in Miami* (2005). As Alan O'Leary notes, these broadly comic and formulaic films, typified by the presence of characters frequently expressing prejudicial and racist views, are regarded with embarrassment and scorn by particular sections of Italian society and cultural commentators.[1] As their titles suggest, the films are based around various holiday destinations, and feature often crude representations of race and culture, and equally stereotyping responses on the part of the film's protagonists to their temporary host countries. As I will explore in this chapter, while not as consistently developed as a genre in English film culture, the English holiday film makes use of comparable social and cultural contexts, and an often similar set of ideological frameworks to the *cinepanettone*, in its popular narratives and representations.

As I have already noted with reference to my previous study of parody, we can praise comedy for its critical intent, yet at the same time, can mistakenly assume that jokes stand for a universal viewpoint. Rather, they may simply stand for the attitudes and concerns of particular cultural, political and even economic constituencies. Comedy cuts both ways: humour, from whatever ideological position, works in a constructive and divisive sense across identity boundaries. 'Humour, in short', argues the philosopher Noël Carroll, 'maintain[s] what we might call an *Us* – the *us* that abides by the pertinent norms. But where there is an *us*, there is typically also a *Them*, against whom the rest of us define ourselves'.[2] These norms, continues Carroll, constitute both the parameters of a culture and in turn of what can be considered humorous, with obvious implications for the construction and maintenance of our imagined communities:

> What humour does, for the most part, is … to reinforce our command of these norms – to rehearse and perhaps sometimes to refine our access to the pertinent norms and deviations from them … Comic laughter in concert with like-minded and like-feeling revellers confirms, reinforces and celebrates our membership in a community defined by our infectious laughter, [and] of our converging norms.[3]

Humour is a powerful means of identification for its harmonizing potential, but frequently depends upon us laughing at others in the same process. As we will see in this chapter, the English holiday film is in a privileged position to express these notions of converging norms. It does this through its mobilization of a collective holidaying unit situated at once within and at a remove from a cultural and physical otherness, in the form of the holiday destination.

Looking specifically at the significance of racial and ethnic humour, Andrew Stott echoes Carroll in his assertion that such joking 'helps to establish group identity by demarcating the line between "us" and "them"' (his example is the mockery of different ethnic types in Shakespeare's *The Merchant of Venice*).[4] Yet as Stott subtly notes, by its own violent nature such humour 'also acknowledg[es] the *anxiety* induced by racial difference, which it seeks *to mitigate* through laughter'.[5] Humour directed at the racial or ethnic other, in other words, includes within its own construction a sense of the other's potential superiority, which laughter strives to negate. As I show in this chapter, some of these films betray a similarly ambivalent relationship between the implicit 'us' and 'them'; an ambiguity that highlights the uncertain history of England (more specifically, in this case, than 'Britain') vis-à-vis Europe as a physical, cultural and political entity. On the one hand, then, the films under discussion here reiterate or reinforce a particular imaginary of England and its fractious historical relationship to the European mainland. At the same time, this chapter goes on to make a claim for the more reflexive, political potential of the holiday film, to articulate the complex relationship both the English tourist and English film have with continental Europe and, as an extension of its culture, European cinemas.

An abiding image for me of the immediate post-referendum contexts, as I noted at the very beginning of this book, was that of Jennifer Saunders and Joanna Lumley, reprising here their television roles of Eddy and Patsy in *Absolutely Fabulous: The Movie* (2016). Whether or not the immediate post-referendum release was strategic, *Absolutely Fabulous* found itself dropped into a UK more openly divided than it had been for years. For the Bollinger-spraying comedy of *Absolutely Fabulous*, it was perhaps the worst of times – and therefore, perhaps, the best of times. Whether its title, in the contexts of its release, is viewed as a bitter irony or a statement of fact depends on the individual viewer. In terms of its geographies, however, *Absolutely Fabulous* was a distinctly ironic first release for Britain's post-referendum era. If not strictly a tale of two cities, it is at least a tale of one expensive city and an even more expensive European destination, split as it is between its first half in London and its second on the French Riviera. This is the destination to which Eddy and Patsy flee, in an effort to escape the attentions of the British police, but also in pursuit of their particular idea of the good life.

From one very literal perspective, *Absolutely Fabulous* offers its British viewers forms of material escape from their island in an already escapist form of comic fantasy (the plot of the film, it is worth remembering, revolves around Eddy accidentally drowning supermodel Kate Moss). By its own terms, the comic holiday film, a category in which I would locate *Absolutely Fabulous*, is also a cinematic hiatus from the spaces, routines and logic of everyday life. Like cinema itself, it is its own type of *heterotopia*: a space and time existing both within and beyond the actual world and everyday experience. In its heterotopian sense, to bracket such a film off as merely fantastic overlooks the very specific contexts and connotations of its destination: one that is at once imagined *and* actual, both unimaginable *and* compensatory. As I will go on to explore with regard to this film, its idea of escape is embedded within a very specific history and continuity of English culture and its idea of Europe.

At home, away: British holidays and Europe, in brief

The 2016 referendum vote to leave the EU only manifests in a concrete and decisive way the uncertainty with which 'Europe', as a political entity, cultural concept and physical space, has been discussed historically in the UK. There had, it is worth recalling, already been a referendum on membership in 1975, only two years after Edward Heath had taken the country into what was then the EEC (European Economic Community). Dominic Sandbrook's willingness to treat the referendum as something of a comedy relates in part to the fact that it was overseen by a Labour Prime Minister, Harold Wilson, who had never seemed that interested in Europe, to protect the European membership negotiated by an ardently pro-European Conservative, Edward Heath, whose government Wilson had ousted a year previously.[6] But what is also striking about the 1975 referendum is that its debates seemed to exist in isolation from (mainland) Europe itself, or at least from an idea of what it might mean to be 'European', and wholly hinged around what was in it for Britain. A media and opinion-poll backdrop of the time, for instance, indicated little interest in the future of Europe as a factor, and much more concern with the country's dreadful inflation figures.[7]

Viewed in this light, the referendum reversals of 2016 cannot really be seen as a public volte-face around European identity, since this 'identity' already was, for the most part, negligible. As Hugo Young points out in *This Blessed Plot*, his study of Europe as a site of contestation within post-war British politics, Heath was the champion and architect for a certain idea of Europe that was beyond the material or imaginative scope of many fellow Conservatives – let alone most Labour politicians and supporters suspicious of 'continental' ways.[8] In a way that would not be repeated at Prime Ministerial level until the premiership of Tony Blair, who was never afraid to show off his French, Heath was very much a man 'of Europe': well-travelled, close to continental colleagues, versed in their culture, and linguistically conversant (if not always fluent). But this put Heath significantly out of step with a much less-travelled public, many of whom, in the early 1970s, had no more than a slight grasp of what 'Europe' was actually like.

What *can* be ascertained from this period, to an extent, is the degree to which some idea of Europe starts to seep into the popular national culture; in a similar way that, most predominantly, American pop culture had informed British life in the 1950s and 1960s. But the connotations are different here. If, to again look through Sandbrook's slightly ironized view, this popular 'European' infiltration of the early 1970s was encapsulated by Swedish pop stars singing in English, from Abba's 'Waterloo' to Sylvia Vrethammar's 'Y Viva España' (both from 1974), this particular idea of Europe suggested an exoticism, even a sensual strangeness: one, though, tempered by its accommodation to Britain's detached worldview via the use of English as its language.[9] The continentalism evoked here seems largely a token one, and yet, for the narrowness of its parameters, it is a conception that takes hold. It does this mostly at the level of everyday culture and habits, and above all, holidays.

The main distinction here from American-influenced pop culture is that Vrethammar's song, however weird and refracted in terms of what it actually represents, has a more experiential reference point in terms of the growth of

Mediterranean, and especially Spanish, package holidays during this period. Shaped in part both by the demise of the British resort as the dominant UK holiday destination from the 1960s and by what John Urry and Jonas Larsen call the 'internationalisation' of travel around the same period – including, in this case, General Franco's pragmatic decision to rework and promote much of Spain as a tourist haven – the UK was a more active country than most in forging links between emerging domestic tour operators and new Spanish resorts.[10] The sun-seeking British tourist would henceforth, from this time, benefit from early innovations in air travel, computerized booking systems, and the cheap prices that integrated tour companies were able to offer.[11] That the idea of the foreign holiday was, by the 1970s, establishing itself as a defining part of the British imaginary was further indicated by the appearance of dedicated television shows such as the BBC's *Holiday* programme (launched in 1969) and ITV's *Wish You Were Here* (in 1974).[12] Though the country was let in quite late to the European party, the continental European holiday would soon become a British institution, and an integral aspect of the popular British imagination.

A 2017 annual report from the Association of British Travel Agents (ABTA) confirmed that, despite the implications of Brexit, European countries remain, after the UK, a preferred destination for the majority of British holidaymakers (with 63 per cent of survey respondents identifying this choice).[13] A 2017 report in the *Economist* corroborated the view that Britons, amongst European citizens, are most likely to choose other mainland European countries as their holiday destination.[14] At the same time, statistics from Eurobarometer, the European Commission's public opinion monitor, identified that 'only 33% of Britons defined themselves as "European" to a greater or lesser degree – the lowest level of any EU member state'.[15] As an object of cultural analysis, therefore, which brings into focus issues of identity and nation, the English holiday film, and English holiday culture more broadly, throw up an array of paradoxes. Focusing specifically on the type of Mediterranean holiday formerly associated with working-class tourists, but subsequently with a more affluent and younger ('18–30') demographic, commentators have noted the extent to which much English travel abroad has been little informed by types of romantic perspective, or the desire to see new countries and cultures. Instead, the holiday offers difference allied to familiarity. The English tourist epitomizing such pursuit is one characterized less by a sense of adventure or exploration, than by the minimizing of risk;[16] while his or her dominant choices in terms of consumption, both culinary and cultural, are shaped not by the desire for something new, but by the need to reassert their native identity.[17]

Though somewhat stereotypical, it is important to note that this idea of a (certain type of) English tourist, one enjoying the home comforts of English Premier League football on satellite TV, accompanied by a steady diet of 'bacon, beans and sausages', also contains its own contradictions.[18] As Hazel Andrews argues, on the back of fieldwork in resorts such as Mallorca, national identity is not so much assumed but is in effect re-inscribed and 'compounded' by these same acts of consumption.[19] But it only does this because such acts take place in a removed and distinct context. Consuming 'British' in a foreign context is therefore tantamount to what Michael Billig calls a manifestation of 'banal nationalism': a process wherein the consumer-tourist identifies as national not through aggressive assertion, but more through the feeling of difference in the everyday practices of holidaymaking.[20]

This is an important inflection, as it brings into focus the intrinsic paradoxes of the tourist experience: the capacity, but also the desire, to be at once home *and* away; the extent to which the nationalistic habits of the English traveller abroad involve in some ways a peculiar negotiation between two spaces. The same happens with the English holiday film once it makes the move overseas. When the twenty-fourth outing for the domestically popular *Carry On* series, *Carry on Abroad* (1972), turned its attention to the European mainland, it indicated the increasing prevalence in national culture of the cut-price Mediterranean package holiday, which as we have seen, had been pioneered by British tour operators since the mid-1960s.[21] Actually shot in Slough, *Carry on Abroad* is set in the fictional resort of 'Elsbels': a supposed paradise island of unfinished hotels, terrible plumbing, womanizing locals and dubious law enforcement. The film ends, significantly, with the cheap hotel disintegrating in a rainstorm, and the guests eventually decamping to the domestic comforts of their local London pub.

Despite its apparent derision of the package-holiday experience, though, *Carry on Abroad*'s peculiarity is that it operates not at a remove from, but in lockstep with the increased prominence of British travel to Mediterranean resorts. The film encapsulates the cultural importance for popular cinema of the time to 'entrench' its audience in 'representations of recognisable British life'.²² As a popular cinematic institution spanning two decades, the appeal of the *Carry On* films to historians, of film or otherwise, is their presumed capacity to reflect, in some sense, aspects of the contemporary social, cultural and political life to which the series ran in parallel. This is an idea substantiated by the series' changing reference points and, in the case of *Carry on Abroad*, transformations in class mobility, as its assumed audience finds itself able to take its holidays cheaply in Spanish resorts. Within this logic, a film like *Carry on Abroad*, that lampoons British Mediterranean holidaymaking, can only make sense within the terms of a popular audience sold on, and actively participating in, this same experience. It is an experience that is therefore at once celebrated *and* mocked.

The allusion here to *Carry on Abroad* may be limiting in terms of its specific time and place, and the assumed audience it addresses. A surprising thing about some of the films discussed in this chapter, though, is the way they consistently reinforce a similar idea of Europe beyond and across any particular social contexts. Both in May 2016 and then in the early summer of 2019, the English entertainment news media was briefly abuzz with the word that new *Carry On* movies might be in the pipeline.²³ This turned out to be a misleading rumour; but when the fuss died down, what remained overlooked was that the series hadn't really gone away: it had merely been adapted to new contexts and, as I shall discuss, gentrified. *Carry on Abroad*'s dynamic of celebration-and-derision persists into, say, *The Inbetweeners Movie* (2011), based on the popular Channel 4 show about four boys in their final years at school. Yet the film itself (of which more below) appears to reassert its holiday-abroad ritual experience for the benefit of an audience – younger, here, and notably no longer so clearly prescribed by economic brackets or class – that the film identifies, and whose experience it reflects.

Looking at the English European holiday film allows us, then, to work through the particular types of projections and negotiations made between English culture, the emerging globalization of the tourist experience and the increasing significance of continental Europe within it. But an added and vital question here is why, in the English instance, this negotiation so often takes the form of the *comic* film; or even more specifically, one that effectively inserts or relocates pre-established and familiar comic personae into the holiday setting. This is either, as in *Carry on Abroad*, through the adaptation of a familiar franchise, cast and formulaic narrative. Or beyond this – in *Absolutely Fabulous*, but also *The Inbetweeners Movie*, and the slightly earlier *Mr. Bean's Holiday* (2007), going back as far as the TV comedy duo Eric Morecambe and Ernie Wise in *That Riviera Touch* (1966) – variations on that oft-despised British form, the big-screen sitcom adaptation. Examining this reiterated mode of relocating the familiar and domestic, and the consistency of a certain type of comic approach in these films, we can go some way to establishing an idea of Europe within this popular cinematic imaginary.

Travels to an English Utopia: The comedian and the holiday film

Film comedy, as Geoff King highlights, 'often involves the display of negative qualities such as failure, incapacity ... inadequacy and sheer bad luck'.[24] These qualities are literally incarnated in the body and performance of the comic actor at the film's centre. We nevertheless need to understand the contradictions of this comic body within the holiday film. In these instances, notions of the body's inadequacy or incompetence need to be seen in light of what its *opposite* terms represent; for example, the anxiety-inducing ethnic and racial 'other'. The 'failure' of this comic body can also make it an object of resistance, as well as derision. Looking at various comedian-actors such as Steve Coogan, Jacques Tati and Roberto Benigni (and I would add to this list other specifically English stars like Rowan Atkinson and Simon Pegg), King highlights the way such performers 'are often distinguished on [appearance] grounds from straight romantic or action-based heroes'.[25] As a result, such performers 'might offer a more plausible basis for identification or allegiance'.[26] This capacity for identification is based on the 'smaller gulf ... between the kinds of world they inhabit [or] in which they find themselves, and those of the typical spectator'.[27] Broader traditions of English comedy film, especially in its referential dialogue with Hollywood (for instance, Simon Pegg's genre parodies, *Shaun of the Dead* [2004] and *Hot Fuzz* [2007]) have similarly worked to juxtapose national contexts with Hollywood's aesthetic norms, constructing a cinematic idea of Englishness-as-smallness.[28] Yet, to reiterate King's point, this is a smallness we might more readily recognize or believe in because of its comparative and comic difference from Hollywood norms. This greater proximity of the comic 'everyman' figure, typically emerging in non-Hollywood national contexts, assumes significance when seen in relationship to its notionally dominant, but in turn less sympathetic, other.

The importance of the comedian to the holiday film is forged through the comedian's low, often chaotic or anarchic persistence, and their presence within a physical and cultural landscape that is, or at least threatens to be, uncomfortably different. Within such a context, the comedian-protagonist cannot really undergo transformation within the narrative – but this is part of his or her charm. Discussing, for instance, the comic personae elaborated through the films in the *Carry On* series, Andy Medhurst highlights the importance to these films of repetition and predictability in terms of situation and performance style. Above all (borrowing a phrase from J.B. Priestley), Medhurst notes that the performers in question hardly ever deviate from 'the droll chunk of personality' with which they are synonymous.[29] In the English film tradition especially, as is the case with all of the films discussed in this chapter, the comic film actor has often moved, sometimes only temporarily, onto the big screen from pre-established televisual contexts. In many respects, then, their cinematic excursions, predicated as they are on the TV shows' popularity, insist on established expectations that make the predictable comic persona a central part of the films' narrative dynamics.[30] When the holiday film is transposed from an original sitcom, moreover, the film inevitably brings with it connotations from this prior text; and in the sitcom's case, these connotations are typically of stasis and perennial return. The sitcom thrives on, and is defined by, the repetition of a given circumstance within which the protagonists are typically constrained.[31] So, while the sitcom film adaptation is frequently premised on its characters going somewhere different, and therefore breaking this routine (as is the case in the films discussed here), the inherent conservatism of the broader comic situation is always pulling them back to the familiar and known.

It is in this level of predictability that such texts develop 'a sense of audience communality [and] a "common knowledge" circulating between audience and film-makers'.[32] A scene from Morecambe and Wise's *That Riviera Touch* exemplifies this process. Here, as 'Eric' and 'Ernest', the characters' names reiterate the duo's familiar TV identity ('Eric and Ernie') from their ITV show *Two of a Kind* (1961–8). The pair visit a casino, at the invitation of a glamorous French woman met earlier that day on the beach. From a narrative point of view we are in a superior position, unaware as they are that their charming female host is using them as stooges in an elaborate jewel theft. Yet within this set-up the pair can still exert a measure of control through comic performance. As Ernest works his way through plates of snails and frog's legs, his frontal positioning within the mise-en-scène allows him to register – with a repertoire of facial contortions – his marked cultural discomfort, leading him eventually to deposit the offending items in the wine-bottle basket (with predictable results once the waiter comes over to pour). Meanwhile, Eric searches forlornly for the same girl by the roulette table, where his failure to communicate is misinterpreted as a desire to play. In this case, his insistence that his friend is 'about 25' and that she would be here 'around nine' are taken as betting instructions, leading to him winning a fortune without knowing why. While one of the film's presumed selling points is its glamorously exotic location, Morecambe and Wise's resolutely English and monolingual personae, familiar from their television work, is transposed wholesale into the setting. The effect here is to mitigate through their interactions and reactions the possible discomforts of cultural and linguistic displacement (the coup de grâce here being that Eric's ignorance makes him rich).

For Medhurst, it is precisely this 'eliciting of complicity' in such series as the *Carry On* films that defines them as pre-eminently popular.[33] But as I have stressed, this popular complicity can also be divisive. Comedy, from whatever viewpoint it emerges, can be used to 'firm up the lines that separate', whether these be in league with or against prejudice.[34] The laughter that comedy elicits, even if a consolatory fiction, offers what Medhurst calls 'a moment of unity … a haven against insecurity [and] a point of wholeness'.[35] Comedy's popular capacity to generate complicity inevitably takes on ideological aspects once it becomes a 'haven' in the face of a *foreign* other, or the other's corollary in the form of actual or figurative boundaries. It is also the stubborn insistence on sameness and inflexibility, *even if* this is seen to 'fail', that marks the type of discursive work such comedy can perform in the holiday film. This is because, in narrative terms, we here so frequently see the English tourist placed in positions of social, cultural and often physical inferiority, be this through economic exploitation, linguistic insufficiency or (perhaps above all) sexual inadequacy.

Living 'The Dream': Uses of Europe in *The Inbetweeners Movie* and *Absolutely Fabulous: The Movie*

Like *Carry on Abroad*, *The Inbetweeners Movie*, filmed on location in the Mediterranean resorts of Malia and Magaluf, is in thrall to the same tropes of difference and denial, while also reiterating a specific holiday ritual. Much of its comic intent derives from a series of already well-rehearsed narrative cues, and an ensuing set of confirmed expectations extensively detailed in the promotional material for the film, such as the trailer and DVD packaging. The four boys, embarking on their first holiday after finishing school, will subsequently be faced with shoddy holiday accommodation, run by an insanitary proprietor (Figure 2.1). Confusion as to the true nature of what they assume to be the 'child's toilet' in the bathroom, and the inevitably gross pay-off, clearly works around the assumption that the film's viewers know what a *bidet* is, even if the cultural bemusement it provokes is shared. Hopeful attempts at holiday sexual conquest, meanwhile, will at first be thwarted: on the part of Simon Bird's nerdish Will, in particular, it will be opposed by the physically more prepossessing form of Greek barman Nikos – one of the few non-English characters in the film – whose subsequent revelation as a two-timing beach lothario confirms his cultural

Figure 2.1 Welcome to 'Europe'! Arrival, and the introduction of a dead cat, in *The Inbetweeners Movie* (2011). Directed by Ben Palmer © Film4 2011. All rights reserved.

and moral separation from the group. Beyond this, *The Inbetweeners Movie* revels in a litany of dysfunctional holiday traits that culminate in the group remarking how literally 'shit' the experience is: from the discomforts of package holiday travel, to the general filth of their hotel, to their capacity to lose nearly all their money by the end of their first night on the town. And yet, this particular film still manages to end with the boys revelling on a yacht, enjoying this terrible experience to the full, having dealt with various obstacles and found a set of like-minded female holidaymakers with which to partner up.

Like the earlier *Carry on Abroad*, then, *The Inbetweeners Movie* seeks to mine an abject and in some senses derisive type of compensatory humour from the foreign holiday experience. The peculiarity here is that the lamentable fiasco of the cinematic overseas holiday runs up against the film's effort to represent the realities and ritual of the *actual* holiday experience, presumably for much of the audience on whose own experiences the narrative is premised. The film's form in fact trades on this sense of identification and participation. Within the film's episodic structure, *The Inbetweeners Movie* returns perennially to the beach-front nightlife in a ritualistic fashion throughout the film, here in lurid and intoxicated sequences of Mediterranean sights and sounds, cued to thumping dance anthems, with repetitious montages of alcohol consumption and shots of the jostling tourists along the strip.

From the perspective of a national cinematic rite of sorts, these tensions can be reconciled, inasmuch as the film enables a somatic and ritualistic rehashing of, or even preparation for, the presumed pleasures of the Mediterranean holiday. At the same time, the film ensures that such intoxication never threatens the boundaries defining one's national self. Any culturally distinctive aspects of the holiday experience are consequently bracketed off from their existence in any specific social, cultural and political space: Will's initial bookish interest in seeing local historical sights, for example, is quickly rebuffed by his friends, and the group consequently never move beyond the resort. Those things that in turn make the holiday experience 'different', then, are precisely those familiar but domestically less obtainable entities: sunshine, sea, available sex and freedom from family or work. There is a form of protective layer at work in these films, a kind of cultural sunscreen: a deprecatory and ironic force-field that allows the wider world in, while also keeping it at bay.

Within these terms, the package holiday offers a form of utopian experience, but a utopia that needs to be carefully defined. Etymologically, from the Greek, a utopia is a 'happy place' (*eu-topos*), but it is also a 'no-place' that does not exist at all (*ou-topos*). The utopia is in this sense an ideal place that cannot exist. Yet it persists in the *hetero*topian idea of a space that is there and not there, both here and elsewhere: the peculiar experience of being 'in but not in, of but not of, home but not home, neither here nor there'.[36] In terms of the contradictions inherent to the English holiday film, its paradoxes suggest a utopia that is culturally England, only situated anywhere else *but* England (the 'best of both worlds', in this respect). It seems hardly accidental that the tourist demographic of *The Inbetweeners*' Greek island resort, and the crowd who end the film partying out in the Med, is almost uniformly English – not to mention predominantly white and heterosexual – existing to all intents and purposes in its own cultural and geographical bubble.

There is a similar utopian movement in *Absolutely Fabulous: The Movie*, in which the French Riviera takes on the connotations of both a narrative point of escape and also a type of suspended fantasy space. And while focusing on a very different demographic, there is a similar emphasis to *The Inbetweeners Movie* on entirely English, and almost exclusively white, enclaves, with any locals once more limited to mostly functional narrative roles. The broader goal of Eddy and Patsy's flight to the Riviera is to pursue Patsy's old flame Charlie, a millionaire now residing in Saint Tropez. Eddy and Patsy's aim is in turn to have Patsy finally accept the marriage proposal made to her four decades previously, reaping the financial benefits in order to live out what they repeatedly call 'The Dream': in this case, a soft-lit, slow-motion montage of sea, sand and Campari; an advertising-style montage from an earlier decade, cued to the retro strains of Peter Sarstedt's faux-French 1969 hit, 'Where Do You Go To (My Lovely)?' (Figure 2.2).

Since the original 1990 publication of John Urry's *The Tourist Gaze*, the idea that many tourists pursue a romanticized and prefabricated 'idea' of the visited tourist site has become axiomatic in mobility studies and beyond. Tourism involves the creation and pursuit of 'myths' that precede travel in the prior mediated forms.[37] Such mediated myths become important for tourists looking to maximize the unique experience of their often-expensive holiday, while mitigating the potential for risk, failure and anxiety.[38] It is very easy

Figure 2.2 'Europe' as an advertising aesthetic: Eddy and Patsy's imagined Riviera in *Absolutely Fabulous: The Movie*. Directed by Mandie Fletcher © Fox Searchlight Pictures 2016. All rights reserved.

within these terms to deride Eddy and Patsy's 'dream' of the Riviera for what it so palpably and aesthetically is: a pastiche, constructed through re-purposed advertising style (languorous dissolves, dewy backlighting, composite images of exotic backdrops and glasses being filled); along with the musical accompaniment of a British pop song enumerating all things vaguely French, from an English perspective, *c.* 1969 (Sacha Distel, the Boulevard Saint-Michel, Napoleon Brandy).

Because of this foregrounding of the tourist gaze *Absolutely Fabulous* opens itself up to the possibility of a satirical reading. As King argues, types of 'fish-out-of-water' comic narratives, while at one level appealing to our sense of solidarity and empathy, can also become the object of derision, as the omniscient viewer observes the protagonists with 'a pleasurable sense of superiority'.[39] In this case, the sense of 'pertinent norms' identified by Carroll is more slippery, falling potentially on the side of a viewer and expelling the protagonists. As Stott argues, the original television version of *Absolutely Fabulous* (BBC, 1992–2012) worked through the display of its protagonists' 'grotesque physicality', an outcome of the 'contradictory' demands placed on them by their fashion ideals.[40] In the film, similarly, Eddy and Patsy become the unwitting victims of the comedy, by virtue of the disparity opening up between their perception (The Dream) and reality (their material incapacity to bring this dream into being). Indeed, we consequently see that they have no ready money available to fund their consumption, turning instead to credit cards, the function of which they barely understand. The film has in fact been here before, in a manner of speaking, as it revisits the 'France' episode from the first series of the television show. In this episode, Eddy and Patsy decide to take some time out in a rustic Provencal cottage. The comic aspect of their ensuing misadventures derives once more from a viewer's ability to separate real circumstances from the duo's limited perception. In this case, while squirreling away free drinks on the aeroplane, Eddy and Patsy's failure to understand French finds them asking for mini-bottles of '*le parfum*' and '*la poubelle*'. Later, they consistently ignore the old local who turns up several times at their door, to tell them that the simple cottage they are staying in is the wrong place, and that the staff are waiting for them in the château a few miles down the road.

Since these jokes targeted at English monolingualism remain mostly non-translated, without, for example, the evidence of subtitles, the register and direction of humour in the show remains dependent on the particular viewer. If not understood, the capacity for a more critical type of humour is undermined. This makes the 'France' episode of *Absolutely Fabulous* highly ambiguous with regard to its titular subject matter, though in this regard it is largely consistent with the contexts of English travel by which it seems inspired. The episode was made three years after English writer Peter Mayle's book *A Year in Provence* (1989) had captured the appeal of French second homes or relocation to the affluent classes. By the turn of the millennium, beyond the huge numbers of UK tourists entering France via the Channel Tunnel, low-cost ferry and air travel, it was estimated that 600,000 houses in France, many of them in the Midi, and in the rural areas of Languedoc and Gascony, had British owners.[41] Mayle's stated devotion to going native notwithstanding, both the more caustic observations of some French commentators and the stated intentions of many long-stay tourists and ex-pats suggested the move across *La Manche* was less to do with any specific engagement with France or French-ness, but more a pragmatic choice of 'lifestyle'. 'Owning a corner of France, and making it a second or even a first home, came to embody the Arcadian dream close to British hearts, but unobtainable at home at a reasonable cost.'[42]

The language here, in Robert and Isabelle Tombs's study of Anglo-French relations, is pointed, emphasizing the way the 'Arcadia' of the European second home is routed in a *domestic* notion of ideal, yet unobtainable, accommodation. In the Riviera retreat of *Absolutely Fabulous*, similarly, the emphasis is on conspicuous consumption rather than the cultural attractions or difference of the places they visit or reside in. The film benefitted financially from the French 'TRIP' (Tax Rebate for International Production) scheme, designed to incentivize foreign film production in France, ensure the employment of French personnel, though also – in this case – encourage the touristic promotion of its resort locations.[43] This again indicates the actual fluidity and transnational nature of such films, while also highlighting the discrepancy between these filmmaking cooperations, and the symbolically national ends to which they can be employed in the films' narratives. Urry and Larsen point towards the way questions of 'lifestyle' in holiday-planning and foreign relocation encapsulate the tendencies of a (post)modern 'experience economy', and the move towards what they call 'corporeal travel'.[44] Within this view, the 'time space compression' ushered in by the globalization of travel and communications has transformed our experience of 'the globe' itself, not just with regard to temporality and distance, but in terms of the way borders and differences between formerly differentiated spaces have collapsed. Tourism and everyday practices of consumption within this view conflate, thanks in no small part to the accessibility of global destinations via low-cost air travel.

As globalized forms of consumption and tourism come together, then, geographical and cultural 'place' is overwhelmed by the consumer's heterotopian creation of individuated 'space'. As both *The Inbetweeners* and *Absolutely Fabulous* illustrate, the most basic and obvious manifestation of this tendency is the absorption of the holiday destination by the everyday habits and practices of the visiting or relocated culture. Within these contexts, *Absolutely Fabulous* becomes ambiguous in terms of its satirical dimension, inasmuch as its content, in an amended way to the earlier episode about France, largely reflects similar consumer experiences to its popular audience. On their way to the French south, the women find themselves not in their anticipated space of complimentary champagne and nibbles, but in the confined and very uncomplimentary world of low-cost airlines (Budget Wings: 'We're Winging It!'). The gateway to Eddy and Patsy's getaway dream is in turn tempered by the cloying proximity of other travellers, indifferent and sarcastic flight attendants, and over-priced pre-packed sandwiches (Figure 2.3). In terms of the film's own intra-textual relationship to the earlier television episode,

Figure 2.3 'Budget Wings': The 'experience economy' runs up against economy airlines in *Absolutely Fabulous: The Movie*. Directed by Mandie Fletcher © Fox Searchlight Pictures 2016. All rights reserved.

where they enjoyed all the perks, this represents a marked downgrading in their expectations of overseas travel. Yet the pair's recourse to low-cost air travel, just like that of the boys in *The Inbetweeners*, permits an echo both of the popular accessibility of such trips, and in turn the relative democratization of such consumerist experiences. These experiences are potentially shared by the film's own audience: an audience who can themselves, in turn, live 'The Dream'. Indeed, as Urry and Larson show, budget airlines, which the UK, along with the cheap package holiday, did more than any country to bring about and advance, were the very motor of the contemporary tourist economy, rather than just one of its effects.

Absolutely Fabulous, then, becomes another text poised between celebrating and deriding the holiday experience, marked as it is by this tension between promotional display and a profound anxiety with regard to its own fantasies. Eddy and Patsy's downgrading is here just one manifestation of their dwindling financial expectations, linked to their simultaneous demise in cultural, and eventually sexual, currency, as the duo struggle to maintain their already brittle influence in a changing fashion world and economy. It is not so much the pursuit of a lifestyle 'experience', as it is the pursuit of the means to live it, that is the film's narrative motor, as we first see Eddy trying unsuccessfully to sell her autobiography to a prospective publisher, then desperately and disastrously vying for the attentions of Kate Moss. Using Patsy, effectively as millionaire bait, as a means towards economic self-sufficiency, is a last resort in this instance.

The balance of *Absolutely Fabulous* is in turn awkward, pitched as it is between a parody of, *and* publicity for, a tourist experience that is both democratized *and* inaccessible. By highlighting the delusions and discomforts of popular modern tourism, like *The Inbetweeners*, *Absolutely Fabulous* perpetuates the nationally specific image of English incongruity overseas, in turn constructing and reinforcing its own idea of Englishness in the face of continental Europe. At the same time, the film's own allusion to the increased possibilities of such trips for British tourists, along with its formal properties of publicity and display, accentuates its own complicity with this reductive and Anglocentric tourist gaze. This is one in which, again, the European continent operates as a fantasy or utopian extension of England (or more specifically in this case, metropolitan London) itself.

The undiscovered country: (Not) looking at European cinema in *Mr. Bean's Holiday* and *The Trip to Italy*

The use of Cannes on the part of *Absolutely Fabulous* is, it should be noted, hardly unusual in the wider contexts of European filmmaking. Mariana Liz has discussed what she calls the 'cinematic postcard' tendencies of contemporary European film, with its privileging of internationally familiar locations, acting as forms of cinematic tourist attraction.[45] The particularity that Liz notices here, looking at films such as Woody Allen's *Match Point* (2005) and *Midnight in Paris* (2010), Pedro Almodóvar's *Todo sobre mi madre/All about My Mother* (1999) and Cédric Klapisch's *Auberge Espagnole/Pot Luck* (2002), is that their varied uses of European cities (London and Paris, Barcelona in the latter two films) are allied to specific conceptions of European culture, and even politics. Allen's London and Paris, for instance, are marked by historical and cultural landmarks (opera houses; museums) and the iconographies of twentieth-century painting, music and literature while Klapisch's take on Barcelona, focusing on the relationship between a group of Erasmus students, sees it as a utopian meeting point not just for European travellers, but for the European project itself and its cosmopolitan philosophy.[46]

This begs the question why, for instance, British films make less use of these destinations, and when they do, why they make very different uses of them.

Klapisch's *Pot Luck*, for instance, is based around underlying assumptions of global mobility within education. While the UK participates in the Erasmus scheme, it is unusual to see any British film that depicts this same kind of culture. This might suggest that such films are prescribed by specific domestic contexts of class and economics, and the confines of their linguistic and cultural outlook. However, while this sense of culturally domestic isolation is structured into the narrative of many of these films, it consistently runs up against the paradox of *geographical* movement in the films, which contradicts it. The idea, moreover, that the educational expectations of these English films' audiences preclude the types of European cultural exchange we see in, say, *Pot Luck* does not ring true. *The Inbetweeners* film, for instance, is rooted in the ordinary expectations of a sixth-form and most likely higher education, with a number of the protagonists making references to their eventual passage through university. In distinction even to their parents' generation, higher education in general is more of an assumption on the part of much contemporary British youth, than it is a particular marker of elite academic achievement or social privilege. If this is true, it would seem to suggest that European cultural aspirations and meeting points are not unrealizable aspects of the English tourist experience, or of a film like *The Inbetweeners*. It suggests, rather, that the films, and their 'ideal' intended audiences, are simply not interested in engaging with this possibility. Rather than an inevitable or given aspect of the English holiday film, then, the resistance to moving beyond its prescribed idea of Europe naturalizes what is, in reality, a particular isolationist framework.

Whatever European aspirations there are – or rather are not – in the English holiday film also correlate to national attitudes to cinema. Though a significant historical consumer of Hollywood film Britain is less receptive than most European countries to other European films. As the recent European Audiovisual Observatory report on Brexit and film noted, the UK's cinematic relationship to the rest of the EU, just like its touristic one, is marked by intense contradiction. UK co-productions are among the most widely screened across the EU28 countries, yet the number of non-British EU films released in the UK lags behind the EU average. The EU represents a quarter of the global market for the UK's box-office revenue; yet for films by the other EU28 countries, the UK represents just 1.8 per cent of their admissions. Notably, in terms of averages across the rest of the EU, national productions are the minority in terms of European films screened in any one country: the inverse of what happens in the UK.[47]

The engagement with European film in the UK context is, such statistics suggest, a more limited one than in other EU countries. The somewhat tiered exhibition in the UK, meanwhile, which tends to showcase Hollywood and British films at the multiplexes, while consigning European film mostly to independent and specialist screens, is a further way in which non-Anglophone film is marginalized. The fact that so many popular English films discussed here focus not so much on metropolitan cities like Paris or Barcelona, but rather on the French Riviera or island resorts (we can also in this respect include the *Mamma Mia!* films [2008, 2018]), would also suggest the prevalence of a defining and popular Mediterranean myth of Europe, rather than one based specifically around European art and culture, its cinema included. The origin of this image is to some extent an already globalized post-war film culture, typified in part – and ironically, given for what it notionally stands – by the Cannes Festival, which since the 1950s has been, amongst other things, a showcase for international film glamour and stars. This image is also suggested by Hollywood's post-war 'runaway' productions in France and Italy, such as the romance films involving love affairs between American women and European men (*Three Coins in the Fountain* [1954], *Summertime* [1955]), though at other points the reverse (*Roman Holiday* [1953]). The 1950s and early 1960s also saw the importance of landmark European destinations, such as Paris and the French/Italian Riviera, in English-language musical and dramatic films. These included *An American in Paris* (1952), *Lili* (1953), *Funny Face* (1957) and *Bonjour Tristesse* (1958), and various, frequently comic 'caper' movies, from *To Catch a Thief* (1954) and *Charade* (1960) to *The Pink Panther* (1963) and *Bedtime Story* (1964). The Cannes Festival, on its way to becoming one of 'the most mediated event[s] on the planet',[48] in the formative era of the 1950s, would play a role in the promotion of many of these films. These were often, at the same time, global advertisements for the region, promoted through the already-transnational vehicle of the Hollywood runaway production. Or as Jean Cocteau put it in 1953, there was 'this [strange] Côte d'Azur seen in Technicolor by the Americans'.[49]

Cannes, indeed, was always about consumption. Kieron Corless and Chris Darke's account of Cannes's rise in the 1950s and beyond enumerates the very same images that will later be used to signify the magnetism of the Côte d'Azur in *Absolutely Fabulous* – 'palm trees, the beach, the gently winding Croisette, expensive yachts bobbing in the harbour'.⁵⁰ Cannes also becomes celebrated for the conspicuousness of luxury fashion items that 'consolidat[e] France's international reputation for luxury': the glimpse, on the famous Cannes red carpet, of 'Bulgari earrings, maybe, or a Louis Vuitton bag, or a couture dress'.⁵¹ It is therefore a further particularity of these popular English films' uncertain relationship to Europe that, in a film like *Absolutely Fabulous*, we see only the most vaguely 'cinematic' idea of Cannes, without the film evincing any obvious interest in the festival's espoused ideals of cinematic art.

This question of cinema is political in itself, especially in terms of understanding Britain's relationship with Europe. Cinema has been seen as significant to Europe and a European 'project' more broadly, yet has been less recognized as such within the UK. As both Liz's study and another recent volume on European cinema note, the formation of the EU as an entity is founded not merely on economic and political bases, but also on a commitment to the correlative idea of 'cultural integration', and to a 'cultural idea of Europe'.⁵² One of the key questions engaging historians and theorists of European cinema in recent years has consequently been what kind of initiatives have linked this European idea with actual cultural production. We can enumerate various production incentives, for instance, such as the EU's MEDIA scheme, or the Council of Europe's Eurimages: the scheme, as I noted in the previous chapter, from which Britain rather inexplicably withdrew in 1996.

While the definition or even existence of a 'European cinema' remains elusive, the extent to which English productions engage or not with some of these tendencies offers some reflection on the idea of Europe they espouse or reject. Indeed, just as *Absolutely Fabulous* engages with a cinematic idea of Cannes that excludes cinema, *Mr. Bean's Holiday* actually seeks to refashion festivals like Cannes in its own image. The film depicts the eponymous protagonist's chance win of an all-paid Riviera holiday, and his floundering efforts to reach his destination following various incidents and blunders. During Bean's journey, on boarding the TGV at Paris, he accidentally separates a young Russian boy and his father: the latter, it turns out, being a jury member of the Cannes Festival. When Bean, handicapped by monolingualism and incompetence, attempts without success to return the boy to his parent, he loses his money and tickets, obliging him in turn to improvise his way to the coast. He is helped in this instance by the generous attentions of an aspiring young French actress, Sabine, who eventually drives him to Cannes, where she is due to appear in a film being screened. As the watching Sabine finds out her small part has been cut, Bean gets the attention of the audience by finding a way to run the images of his own holiday movie (that he has been filming on a handheld DV camera), featuring both the boy and Sabine, over the soundtrack of the film. The boy is reunited with his father, and this new 'edit' of the movie is received with rapture by a hitherto indifferent audience, converting Sabine into the festival starlet du jour and saving the reputation of the film's pretentious director. As Bean's young travelling companion is reunited with his father, the English holidaymaker crosses the *Croisette* by climbing over the tops of trucks and cars, before finally reaching the longed-for Mediterranean waters.

As this outline highlights, *Mr. Bean's Holiday* is more generous than other popular English films to a certain idea of Europe, and a kind of cultural entente cordiale between Britain and France. This is strategically unsurprising. Atkinson's Bean persona, as already noted in Chapter 1, is a major cultural export; a fact already reflected in the film's production and distribution contexts, overseen as the film is by Working Title and the European studio StudioCanal. The film accordingly indicates its debt to a certain idea of Frenchness that is rooted in its cinema. It does this materially, through its locations, and to a sporadic use of veteran or young French stars, such as Jean Rochefort and Emma de Caunes. It also does this intertextually, in the titular allusions to the comic actor Jacques Tati's own classic holiday film (*Les Vacances de Monsieur Hulot/Monsieur Hulot's Holiday* [1953]). The accordion that infuses Howard Goodall's score when Bean arrives at Paris's Gare du Nord may also conjure recent memories both of the setting and of Yann Tiersen's infectious music, for the French-language crossover hit *Le Fabuleux destin d'Amélie Poulain /Amélie* (2001). Beyond this, though, the acknowledgement of French cinematic influence is slight, and its Euro-cinematic points of reference remain, at least for Anglo-American audiences, broad. Indeed, the only obvious filmic quotation in the film, in which a hitchhiking Bean waits – and waits – for the arrival from afar of a Provencal *paysan* on a motorized bicycle, alludes to Omar Sharif's desert appearance in David Lean's *Lawrence of Arabia* (1963).

Where exactly is *Mr. Bean's Holiday* coming from then? As a joint production venture between Working Title and StudioCanal, it indicates the pragmatism of transnational co-production and distribution, catering for diverse reception contexts. Speaking from the English perspective, it is more Francophile in its content and points of reference than many films. But the nature of this Francophilia is very specific in its concerns for particular, exclusive and even stereotypical images of France. These are 'cinematic postcards', to again use Liz's phrase, from Paris's Grande Arche de La Défense down to the Cannes beachfront, via the already sleek and cinematic vehicle of the TGV (*Train à Grande Vitesse*); the vehicle for which, like the French locations themselves, the film acts as something of an advertisement. The film is unusual, though, in specifically identifying the most celebrated symbol of a French, and more broadly European, cinematic heritage. In these respects at least, *Mr. Bean's Holiday* has much the feeling of film that views France and its cinema as an alluring object of desire, drawing on impressions of France and Frenchness that have already become exotic and specialized in the transitional contexts of film distribution across borders.[53]

The most striking aspect of *Mr. Bean's Holiday*, however, is its highly ambivalent relationship to the Cannes Festival. This is the film's narrative endpoint and, implicitly, an event celebrated by the film. Yet at the same time, it is also its most evident target of parody. Whatever its other influences, the official remit of Cannes, since its conception and eventual consolidation of critical outlook, has been to promote an *auteurist* conception of cinema. Central to Cannes's traditions has also been the idea that cinema can act as a form of political expression that challenges dominant ideologies (a look through the recipients of the coveted *Palme d'Or*, since the 1970s especially, testifies to this, including works such as Costa-Gavras's *Missing* [1982], Chen Kaige's *Farewell, My Concubine* [1993], Emir Kusturica's *Underground* [1995], Theo Angelopoulos's *Eternity and a Day* [1998] and Michael Moore's documentary *Fahrenheit 9/11* [2004]). Exactly how this conception plays out in terms of a legacy of *European* auteur cinema is encapsulated well by Corless and Darke's account of Michelangelo Antonioni's controversial screening of *L'Avventura*, which ended up winning the special Jury Prize, in 1960. *L'Avventura* revolves around the disappearance of a young woman on a volcanic island, and a resulting pursuit that is neither resolved nor, in terms of the woman's disappearance, explained. This approach to storytelling, along with 'the film's leisurely rhythm, its "dead times" and lingering expressive shots of landscape and environment' led to it being deemed, by those who did not jeer at it, 'a revolutionary work'.[54] However we might view both this kind of film and the rather leading type of discourse that subtends it, it is a fairly undisputed fact that these tendencies in European film gave rise to the notion of Cannes as 'promoter of a "certain idea of cinema"', shaped around the often wilfully enigmatic figure, and often challenging output, of the auteur superstar.[55]

Mr. Bean's Holiday was poorly received by British film critics, though one of the more surprising positive responses came from the BFI's *Sight & Sound*: typically, the magazine most supportive in its editorial remit of auteur filmmaking and the film festival network. One of the qualities highlighted by *Sight & Sound* reviewer was the film's joke at the expense of 'arthouse filmmaking';[56] the way, as Tobias Hochscherf and James Leggott describe it, the film 'mock[s] the pretentiousness of the European festival circus'.[57] In *Mr. Bean's Holiday* this satirical aspect centres on the film-within-the-film screened at the festival, only to be disrupted by Bean's home video. Entitled *Playback Time*, this example of the 'Cannes' film is (in actual fact) an acutely funny parody of auteurist excess and narcissism. As the film opens, we see the face of its director-writer-star, Carson Clay (played with conviction by a game Willem Dafoe), looking directly into the camera as he moves up an escalator, the background reeling slowly behind him. The credits list Clay's multiple creative inputs before the title is revealed and the film rewinds backward – a technique employed at the start of Michael Haneke's French arthouse hit *Caché/Hidden* (2006), released a year before *Mr. Bean's Holiday* – only to start the same shot all over again. What we see of the film carries on mostly in this vein, as Clay's endless monologue meanders on in voiceover, the action seemingly going nowhere as the camera lingers enigmatically over its star's sculptured features.

As with any parody, Clay's film-within-the-film exemplifies the ambivalent position the parody text has with regard to its subject, bringing in this case a finely judged sense of the tonal peculiarities and excesses of cinema at its most wilfully obscure and self-absorbed. *Playback Time* might hark back jokily to the era of films like *L'Avventura* or Alain Resnais's opaquely cryptic *Last Year at Marienbad* (1960), or the provocative festival showmanship of auteurs like Lars von Trier. Perhaps needless to say, though, Clay's film, of which the screening audience – Clay aside – are bored silly until Bean's intervention, is hardly representative of a 'typical' Cannes competition film. Three of the Palme d'Or winners from the years just prior to *Mr. Bean's Holiday* are anything but obscure or even formally challenging. *The Son's Room* (2001) is a fairly straightforward tale of middle-class family bereavement; *The Child* (2005), like the Dardennes brother's earlier *Rosetta* (1999), blends social-realist content with a classically driven narrative; while Ken Loach's *The Wind That Shakes the Barley* (2006) locates the director's familiar political and historical sensibilities within a mostly classical structure, narrating a young man's entry into the Irish Republican cause.

It is more accurate to say, then, that the idea of auteur cinema derided in *Mr. Bean's Holiday* suits the aims of the film, in terms of setting up a contrast for Atkinson's type of ingenuous English character-comedy. But this does not prevent the film using the festival to set up its own idea(l) of a European cinema. As noted in the previous chapter, it is important to see Mr. Bean within the terms of a confidently global and transnational set of cultural strategies that chimed with New Labour's aspirational and Europhile worldview, as well as its 'creative industries' remit. This confidence underpins the rhetoric of *Mr. Bean's Holiday*, in line with its transnational production basis: the film as a jaunty vision of cross-Channel collaboration, one that, moreover, can happily dispense with the hoarier and 'difficult' tendencies of 'European cinema', in favour of something that is collectively amenable while still 'European'. As Hochscherf and Leggott perceptively note, the dominant critical emphasis on Working Title as constructing globally appealing images of Englishness, or inflections on the Anglo-American relationship, obscures its specifically European strategy, underpinned by its twenty-first-century distribution deal with StudioCanal:

> The success of [Working Title] needs … to be placed … within the broader framework of a cross-continental trend for production companies that seek to challenge the American market strategy by way of Hollywood strategies themselves … It was this dual orientation towards American and European financiers that resulted in co-productions that have as much claim to international as mid-Atlantic status.[58]

The characteristically naive and aggressively calculated intrusion of Mr. Bean into the contexts of Cannes seems very pointed in its efforts to undermine the cultural authority – even credibility – of the arthouse film. But it also puts forward, in the form of *Mr. Bean's Holiday* itself, a viable mode of cross-continental production that is an alternative to both the festival-type film *and* Hollywood's market-dominant juggernauts. And inasmuch as the film achieved significant returns on its quite modest budget – $230m against $25m – the film achieved exactly what it set out to do.

This comes very much to the fore against the backdrop of a stridently globalized Hollywood, against which notions of a 'European cinema' seem poised between a desire to play Hollywood at its own game, or to retrench within the terms of artistic and cultural specificity. Cannes has in fact been a key site for this tension. By 2007, Cannes, under the directorship of Thierry Frémaux, had let Hollywood re-emerge as one of its constituent parts, with new 'tentpole' movies such as *The Matrix Reloaded* (2003) and *Star Wars Episode III: Revenge of the Sith* (2005) being revealed in high-profile out-of-competition screenings.[59] To this extent events like Cannes continue to be ambivalently positioned between a vaguely begrudging acknowledgement of popular global film culture, and its insistence, via its official competitions, that these big films do not belong to the 'critical, aesthetic, historical and cinematic' continuities that it prefers to reward with prizes.[60] Indeed, though it was not screened at Cannes, *Mr. Bean's Holiday* used the location with the Festival's blessing, with crew snatching footage of the actors on the famous red carpet, and shooting the screening sequence in the Palais des Festivals et des Congrès, the main exhibition site for the festival.[61]

This is then the playful context from which *Mr. Bean's Holiday* draws its narrative. The film bears many of the hallmarks of the Working Title comedy, in its mixture of boldness and *faux-naiveté*. It also shows remarkable chutzpah in concluding with Bean leading a beach-front sing-along to Charles Trenet's classic piece of French *chanson*, 'La Mer' (Figure 2.4). The film's intent to surf on the distant waves of Jacques Tati places *Mr. Bean's Holiday* within the contexts, not so much of the *cinéma moderne* exemplified, for European cinephiles, by the innovations of Antonioni and the like, but of a postmodern and intertextual cinema that is happy to pursue artistic credentials, but also global audiences, largely through forms of quotation, pastiche and parody. The result here is a form of cinema astute in its acknowledgement of Europe and assertive in its intent to proffer a commercial scale of filmmaking that is, at the same time, distinctive from the dominant American cinema.

Figure 2.4 Celebrating itself as a model of 'European cinema': Singing on the *Croisette* at the end of *Mr. Bean's Holiday*. Directed by Steve Bendelack © Universal Pictures 2007. All rights reserved.

In terms of the points made previously, though, *Mr. Bean's Holiday* also fits within the particular conception of a 'European' British film that is confident in its continental export value, without, at the same time, seeing any specific need to engage with or even recognize other European cinemas in any detailed way. From one perspective, then, the film's gesture to a type of cosmopolitanism betrays its intrinsically monocultural position: that of a popular English film arbitrating its own idea of Europe and European cinema.

Michael Winterbottom's film/television series *The Trip to Italy* (2014/BBC, 2014) takes a slightly different approach to these same contexts: in this instance, by concealing its cinematic high-modernist reference points within a comic tale of failed recognition.[62] The result is not so much a rejection of the European auteur tradition as an enquiry into what such traditions can actually mean in the postmodern contexts of reproduction and tourism. This is achieved via the narrative conceit of two British travellers on the European cultural trail: these are played by actors Steve Coogan and Rob Brydon, playing fictionalized versions of themselves (these characters henceforth identified here simply as 'Steve' and 'Rob'). This slightly episodic, road-movie and mock-documentary format is also a form self-consciously tailored towards the expectations of an 'Italian' trip for English-speaking audiences. This altogether makes *The Trip to Italy* a particularly apt work in terms of the relationship Britain has to the European mainland.

The importance of cinema to this continental trip, after the north-western England settings of its predecessor *The Trip* (BBC, 2010), is immediately underscored by its title; an alternative translation of the 1954 film *Viaggio in Italia/Journey to Italy*. This is a film about another trip made by two English-speaking travellers, so the acknowledgement of Roberto Rossellini's film on Winterbottom's part is neither accidental nor surprising. In fact, the lingering shots of Pompeii's ash-preserved figures, shown when Steve and Rob visit the ancient site, are quoted almost directly from this earlier work. Alongside Steve's efforts here at seriousness, musing on mortality over the ossified body of a victim, Rob shifts the register more towards parody, as he converses with the body using his much-peddled 'small man in a box' voice (in the earlier film, by contrast, the sight of a man and a woman's bodies being revealed by archaeologists reduces Ingrid Bergman, confronting divorce from her travelling partner George Sanders, to a fit of weeping). In Winterbottom's film, an interconnecting montage of the bodies behind glass, cued to the strains of Richard Strauss's 'Im Abendrot' (which we hear frequently over the course of the film) reiterates the more elegiac tone of *Journey to Italy*, whose couple walk around Pompeii for the most part without speaking. Linked by the music as a sound bridge, this brief sequence is followed by a long rear-angle shot of Steve and Rob wandering down a path (a very similar one, it seems, to the path viewed at one point behind Bergman and Sanders in the 1954 film). In this instance, though, the sound track is overwhelmed by the two comics describing the volcanic 'blanket of death' descending on the city, in the mannered vocal style of Frankie Howerd, star of the BBC comedy series *Up Pompeii!* (1970). Not for the first time in the film, the narration plays off broader points of reference against the apparent ignorance of the travelling pair, placed within a cinematic history they (or rather, the characters they play) cannot acknowledge or recognize.

The Trip to Italy, to follow the terms of road-movie historian David Laderman, exemplifies or at least highlights the inevitable fate of the road movie in its postmodern contexts, doomed to become 'a commercialized, or depoliticized, repackaging of modernist aesthetics'.[63] As the Pompeii sequence of *The Trip to Italy* suggests, though, there is something slightly different at work here, as there is an obvious and ironic disconnect between the 'modernist aesthetics' the film acknowledges, and the deliberate failure of its characters to play their allotted roles within the point of reference.

In the final section of the film, for example, aboard a boat in Capri, Steve's assistant Emma spots on a boat trip the Villa Malaparte Jean-Luc Godard used as a setting in his film *Le Mépris/Contempt* (1963); a building we subsequently see, from a distance, in a point-of-view shot from the boat. In the same way that Emma earlier notes the fascination of Pompeii to fans of *Journey to Italy*, her reference to *Contempt*, in some ways Godard's own take on Rossellini's film, forms another part of *The Trip to Italy*'s network of associations. Taken on face value, then, the specific reference to *Contempt* in *The Trip to Italy* asserts the latter's kinship with Godard's film. Yet the particular nature of the allusion in Winterbottom's film complicates this notion. When the Euro-cinephile Emma identifies the house from *Contempt*, this moment has no obvious narrative or affective dimension, but is simply something else to look at. Once more, it is processed within the privileged and consumerist terms of high-end tourism, on the way to another largely exclusive dining experience. As with her previous mention of Ingrid Bergman in *Journey to Italy*, in fact, Emma's auteurist references barely register with either Steve or Rob (the former quips facetiously that *Contempt*'s plot – sexy beginning with a tragic ending – sounds like 'the opposite of a massage'). Whatever might be at work originally in *Journey to Italy* or *Contempt* is therefore subordinated to such films' new status as tourist sites/sights, fragments of cultural history to be consumed alongside other forms of destination.

Quotation of auteur cinema here, therefore, is merely one reference among others, flattened of its evaluative meaning, or even its signification. There is of course a paradox here. As Bruce Bennett observes, regarding a similar piece of ignored intertextuality in Winterbottom's earlier *A Cock and Bull Story* (2005), such comic undermining of European art cinema seems to indicate a 'fear of intellectual pretentiousness', and yet its humour relies on 'an informed cine-literate audience' who would identify the points of reference being purposely ignored.[64] In *The Trip to Italy*, the characters' obliviousness to such allusions within the setting itself imposes – depending on your viewing position – either an ironic gap between them and the film's wider narrative address, or a shared sense of miscomprehension. But whether or not we get the joke, and even if we enjoy it within the parodic context of *The Trip to Italy*, we are effectively allowing such auteurist references to exist 'blankly' at the same comic register as anything else. What, in other words, does the concept of auteur cinema actually mean when it can be so easily mobilized to incongruous, comic effect? *The Trip to Italy* is sold in part on the appeal of its two stars as gifted impersonators. The film is in turn peppered with voices and allusions from an array of (principally) Anglo-American film and media contexts. What the film implicitly asks, then, and what Emma's own touristic 'quotation' of both *Journey to Italy* and *Contempt* invites us to consider, is where the difference lies between a comedian's Roger Moore impression and an intertextual cinematic nod to Rossellini and Godard. Why would the latter mean anything different? Why, in fact, would they not merely devolve to another set of cinematic postcards, to go with the rest?

We need at this point, though, to bring the discussion back to the main argument of this chapter. This comic meditation on the value of European art cinema within a culture of quotation and reproduction does not specifically need the contexts of an *English* holiday film for it to work. The cultural specificity and significance of *The Trip to Italy*, nevertheless, lie in the way the film very consciously contributes to the longer and culturally specific history of English tourist mediations of the host country. These extend at least as far as the travels of Byron and Shelley – the two poets whose journey through Italy is the primary point of emulation on Steve and Rob's part – and the aristocratic, educative traditions of the so-called Grand Tour. But it is ultimately in the way the film enters the circulation of Anglo-centric cinematic projections of Europe that its cultural points are most clearly made. Drinking on a balcony in Rome, for example, not far from the Spanish Steps, Steve remarks contemptuously that the city has too many tourists. Steve echoes here the same complaint made by his character's literary hero, Byron, two centuries previously. Rob pulls his co-traveller up on this, pointing out that they are themselves only adding to this inflation of tourists; and that, in fact, right at that moment they are reiterating precisely what E.M. Forster chronicled a hundred years before: the romanticization of Europe on the part of English tourists in *A Room with a View* (1908). Rob's reference, though – via an uncharacteristically poor impersonation of Daniel Day-Lewis – is specifically to the 1986 film adaptation of Forster's novel, set and filmed partly in Tuscany. *The Trip to Italy* thereby forms part of a continuity that includes Rossellini and Godard; but in a global cinematic culture in which representation is so many palimpsestic layers, its Italy is also one filtered through an already transnationally mediated popular vision. With

A Room with a View, made by the Anglo-American producer-director team of Ismail Merchant and James Ivory, we have another English vision of the continent re-packaged mostly for domestic and transatlantic audiences.

This experience, already pre-packaged in Forster's time by Baedeker guides, and increasingly mediated by the time we get to Winterbottom's film, balances 'authenticity' with a necessary *distance*. Forster's title, *A Room with a View*, slyly alludes to the expectations of visual consumption, but also the physical remove required, in the 'real' tourist experience so longed for by his protagonists. The protagonists of the film, in turn, can never get *too* close. This is an idea that the marketing of both the 1986 film and also *The Trip to Italy* in fact reassert. Original poster images for *A Room with a View*, as well as the packaging for more recent DVD issues, have the film's two young stars, Helena Bonham Carter and Julian Sands, seated at a window with the sunlit rooftops of Florence behind them (an image extrapolated from the film's concluding scene). Equivalent publicity for Winterbottom's film has Coogan and Brydon posing at a dining table, with the distant view of the Italian coast in the background. One of the latter's key visual motifs, in fact, inevitably motivated by the contexts of privileged travel within which Steve and Rob operate, is the distant, downward gaze from a series of physical vantage points (Figure 2.5): whether these be hotel-room windows and balconies, or – as in the same sequence described above – elevated restaurant terraces.

Figure 2.5 A Room with a Distant View: Ironies of the 'authentic' tourist experience in *The Trip to Italy*. Directed by Michael Winterbottom © BBC 2014. All rights reserved.

It is in this referential and ironic dimension, then, that *The Trip to Italy* establishes its own peculiarly English space. Though distinctive in its referential and formal connections to the European auteur tradition, just like the Cannes of both *Absolutely Fabulous* or *Mr. Bean's Holiday*, *The Trip to Italy* purposely imposes its own cultural barrier between a European cinematic and cultural history, and both our and the protagonists' potential to engage with it. It is at this point – where the comedy of the English abroad becomes the tragicomedy of failed, even impossible comprehension – that the film exceeds the restricted confines of its predecessors and antecedents, while at the same time, drawing attention to the national confines those other films only feign to transcend. As I will conclude below, this potentially makes *The Trip to Italy* a progressive and importantly forward-thinking work within the traditions of the English holiday film, as much as it is also an astute reflection on the latter's history.

Funhouse mirrors: Brexit, bilateralism and irony in the holiday film

I have of course been dealing here with representations and fictional constructions. How the films' actual *audiences* may engage with Europe, culturally or politically, is beyond the scope of this study. My point here is not that these films can be used to say anything specifically about how their viewers understand or feel about the European continent or the presence, or otherwise, of Britain in the EU. What such films do 'reflect', though, if we measure them in terms of producers' expectations of their audiences, and how these films have consequently performed, is the strangely conflicted and ambivalent relationship that Britain, and England more specifically, has had to Europe since the end of the Second World War. As discussed at the beginning of the chapter, the political and popular relationship to Europe has always been uncertain, even at times, like in 1975, when we officially said 'Yes' to Europe. Yet alongside all this, the European continent itself retains a guardedly utopian function in English film culture; at once a sun-splashed haven for its English visitors, while at the same time maintained at a cultural distance. But it is a haven to which the English have perennially returned, in cinema as in real life. Brexit suggests, in the widest sense, that the nation doesn't want Europe; yet culturally at least, or in terms of the pleasures and experiences Britons expect and crave, it seems the nation can't do without it.

Discussing the 'idea of Europe' in these films is more accurately to ask *which* Europe, or rather, what *type* of Europe it is that such films project or promote. This contested idea is, as the Brexit debates and vote showed, deeply embedded in both the history and recent contexts of its politics. With some significant exceptions, Hugo Young argues, the British governing class is too intellectually, culturally and geographically removed from mainland Europe to ever properly be part of it. (Post-)imperial assumptions around Britain's global Empire or its Commonwealth, combined with a lingering sense of post-war superiority, together with the lack of physical borders with the mainland, have sustained this imaginary distance. The origins of what became the EEC, and subsequently the EU, were built on trade agreements between formerly warring nations, largely to ensure that recent history would not repeat itself. The economic impact of this arrangement would be felt by the UK before its successful entry in 1973, but the underlying political foundations of UK membership would lack the urgency and historical proximities of, say, the Franco-German relationship: one that remains crucial to the European project. Young's conclusion points to the ways that, up at least to the Blair government in 1997, practical, economic and environmental benefits of EU membership were rarely acknowledged, and national prosperity usually attributed to the kind of questionable domestic strengths that would later underpin the claims of Brexiteers. If Britain has consistently had trouble identifying itself as a European country, it does not necessarily mean its political elites do not acknowledge 'Europe' at all; but as Young suggests, the mistake they have consistently made is in subscribing to 'the notion that the EU did not constitute "Europe"'.[65] The vague language of former Prime Minister Theresa May post-referendum, especially in her official letter of withdrawal from the EU, re-inscribed this oversight, with its insistence that we are leaving the EU while 'not leaving Europe'. What does this mean?

While May's successor, Boris Johnson, was the main Conservative driver for the Leave vote, his uncharacteristically reticent televised speech the morning after the EU referendum hinted at the confusion in his own position:

> We cannot turn our backs on Europe. We are part of Europe, our children and our grandchildren will continue to have a wonderful future as Europeans, travelling to the continent, understanding the languages and the cultures that make up our common European civilization ... But there is simply no need in the 21st century to be part of a federal government in Brussels that is imitated nowhere else on Earth.[66]

Johnson in this way relied, at this moment of rupture, on a long-standing idea of continental Europe as an extension of England, through which it is the Englishman's pleasure to wander as he sees fit; though without, it seems, needing to take responsibility for it or help maintain its upkeep (needless to say, Johnson is also speaking from a position of considerable social and economic privilege, rather than from the 'popular' position he has claimed to represent since the referendum campaign). In this same gesture, Johnson also fails to account for the fact that, as Young suggests, modern 'Europe' cannot be separated from the practical realities of the EU. Similarly, the rhetoric of the Leave campaign failed to acknowledge that the mobility and economic liberties enjoyed by the UK in the early twenty-first century cannot be detached from four decades of EU membership – or more precisely: that the UK, in dire economic straits, joined the EEC in the first place in order to enjoy these greater opportunities and liberties. Equally, the English holiday film displays an ambivalent, or at least thoroughly mediated, relationship to an extremely limited conception of Europe, but one that works tacitly around the *historical assumptions* of English presence overseas. What remains to be seen is how this might change within the contexts of Brexit: when, like Johnson's imagined children and grandchildren, Brits are still opting to take their holidays in Europe, but when the wait at passport control is suddenly that bit longer, and when the pound stretches that bit less further – as has mostly been the case, in fact, since the summer of 2016.

A central sticking point in the fruitless exit negotiations between the UK and the EU in the wake of the referendum was the idea that the UK post-Brexit could still enjoy access to the benefits of the EU (such as free trade), without needing to reciprocate in kind (for instance, allowing free movement of people across the UK border). We can characterize this highly undiplomatic approach in terms of a *unilateralist* relationship to the European mainland on the part of its supporters and promoters. Analysis of the films under discussion in this chapter has suggested the similar relationship popular English film has with Europe: one in which the benefits to the British interest exclusively predominate over any benefits to the host countries. We can see this once more in terms of the inherent contradiction relating to the holiday film. It is notable that both *The Inbetweeners* and *Absolutely Fabulous* were in box-office terms the most successful independent British films (i.e. films not benefitting from Hollywood's inward investment) in 2011 and 2016 respectively. As a rare example of a small-scale domestic production viably competing with Hollywood, *The Inbetweeners* (with a budget of £3.5m) was something of a phenomenon. At the UK box-office in 2011 it was outperformed only by *The King's Speech* and *Harry Potter and the Deathly Hallows: Part Two*, and its eventual DVD went on to become one of the fastest selling units ever in the UK. And yet, some very mild impact on the wider English-language market aside, *The Inbetweeners*, like *Absolutely Fabulous*, was neither extensively screened nor viewed on the European mainland. Presumably, this is because the films would be considered too culturally specific – or narrow – and therefore incomprehensible or unappealing to foreign audiences. It is consequently telling when this insular exhibition logic is applied to films such as *The Inbetweeners* or *Absolutely Fabulous*, seemingly *because*, not in spite of, their nominal engagement with continental Europe. The further these films go in narrative terms, the less well they travel.

As touched on in the previous section of this chapter, though, this type of unilateral relationship or reductively Anglo-centric view of Europe is not exclusive to those films that focus on British enclaves, or to those limited to domestic exhibition. Ginette Vincendeau, in a perceptive essay on British depictions of France, identifies *Mr. Bean's Holiday* within a continuity that comprises both sitcoms such as *'Allo 'Allo!* (BBC, 1982–92) and heritage-style literary adaptations like *Charlotte Gray* (2001). These films and shows, argues Vincendeau, tend to appropriate idealized and often de-contextualized images in order to create a favourable but highly problematic vision of France. The contribution of Mayle's *A Year in Provence*, which as we have seen informs the earlier TV episode of *Absolutely Fabulous*, has gone some way to reinforcing the longer historical image of France as 'countrified … especially compared to urbanized Britain'.[67] Indeed, once *Mr. Bean's Holiday* leaves Paris, with its Mitterand-era paeans to modern French architecture and engineering, it is the gilded lavender fields of Provence that predominate in its mise-en-scène. This romanticization has the implicit effect of re-framing Britain as economically and intellectually dominant: while by comparison, the idealized construction of France as 'pre-industrial' risks 'foregrounding a backward image, divorced from any factual evidence about the achievements of French technology in areas such as … medicine, nuclear energy and transport'.[68] Vincendeau's observation, then, subtly addresses the point that particular conceptions of Europe are not simply divisible across pro- or anti-European constituencies, or the guarded territories of the 'Leave' and 'Remain' camps. Even the most well-intended tourist impulse can play into long-standing English conceptions of national superiority over its neighbour.

Like many of these films, the fantasy of free European movement within EU withdrawal casts its consumerist gaze across the Channel while erecting barriers on the home front. There are, however, cracks in the walls that suggest the possible potency of the holiday genre, in addressing both historical and our new contemporary contexts, since the instabilities and ambiguities built into such films allow them potentially to work in complex ways. We have seen that even within the rather crude comic strategies of *That Riviera Touch*, Eric (Morecambe)'s failure to understand the rudimentary nuances of both French and roulette may work in his financial favour: But is this necessarily at the expense of the French hosts, or of a potential French audience? The absence of subtitles here allows complex and varied responses. The monolingual Morecambe persona may embody the 'typical' English viewer similarly excluded by language, but the scene also allows for the bilingual possibility that we assume a more omniscient view of the joke, thereby exercising our own more *bilateral* perspective on the film in general. Indeed, as much as Eric profits from his ignorance, he only does so because the casino staff can interpret his English; something he fails to do for their French. Granted, the assumption of universal comprehension is tied up with a unilateral English fantasy of Europe as a place where everyone, naturally, 'speaks the language'. Yet the film here offers at least the possibility of an alternate viewing position from the other side, as it were. Similarly, as already observed with reference to the 'France' episode of *Absolutely Fabulous*, much of the humour is mined from the pair's linguistic incapacity to decipher French. More explicitly, though, the understanding of such jokes relies here *entirely* on a familiarity with French which itself runs against the show's only superficial monolingualism. To the extent, in fact, that full comprehension of the show depends upon a cross-cultural familiarity and linguistic ease that is significantly beyond its gauche protagonists.

Equally, when the old French food gags from *That Riviera Touch* are reprised in *Mr. Bean's Holiday* – where the protagonist fails to digest a plate of oysters (depositing them in the bag of a neighbouring diner), and then contrives to eat his plate of shrimp, shells and all, to predictable aural and visual results – is our laughter here at the absurdity of eating *escargots* and *crevettes*, or rather, at this untravelled Englishman's gastronomic ignorance? Just as the Provencal jaunt of *Absolutely Fabulous* reflects the increasing accessibility of such trips for affluent Brits, Mr. Bean's journey by Eurostar only mirrors the same trips made in great number by British visitors, who are by now far from bewildered by the culinary habits of our French neighbours. *Mr. Bean's Holiday* in this sense embeds a comic tale about lack of sophistication within a film that assumes a level of cross-Channel sophistication on the part of its audiences. Our potential laughter here is in turn the comfortable one of a cultural worldliness that Bean, as an entirely regressive figure of Englishness, contravenes.

And as noted previously, albeit an astute means of exercising soft power influence, Bean's parodic Englishness is also an effective mode through which the national can be accommodated in diverse international contexts – as the film's solid European box-office clearly shows. One of the quirky things about *Mr. Bean's Holiday*, in fact, is that the central character's monolingualism, relocated to France, only accentuates his essentially silent nature further. Indeed, it is evidently one of the advantages and underlying strategies of Mr. Bean as a televisual and cinematic concept that his muteness renders him so easily transferable across cultural contexts. While, then, *Mr. Bean's Holiday* might embody a certain form of pseudo-cosmopolitanism (as noted above), it is also a kind of model for a genuinely transnational production. As I will also discuss in the final chapter, the kind of co-production strategies exemplified by *Mr. Bean's Holiday* serve as ways to generate cultural, as well as purely economic, benefits and relationships across the European countries in which they play. The ironies that I have outlined with regard to *The Trip to Italy* also work through a simultaneous movement between a viewer's ability to understand the cinematic reference point, and the recognition that the characters have failed to do so. This is a strategy that at least allows for the possibility of recognition, on the viewer's part, of the tourist's lack of knowledge and gaps in cultural competence. Such representations may be part of a representational strategy that is both canny in its deliberate *mis*representation of English insufficiency and being implicitly exclusive in its address to specific contexts of consumers and cinematic production. Yet it also offers the potential for a type of domestic and exportable film comedy that, crucially, looks towards decentring Englishness from its cinematic vantage point.

In other words: when both the assumptions and deficiencies of Englishness in Europe (cultural, linguistic, sexual) are exposed, the English tourist in Europe becomes his or her own subject of comedy, and in turn – an important possibility in light of Brexit – a self-critical figure amenable to audiences both within Britain, and, optimistically, beyond. Appropriately enough for a journey that sees Steve and Rob returning again and again to impersonations of Roger Moore, who in his already ageing incarnation of James Bond was a campishly delusional image of English sexual and geopolitical prowess, *The Trip to Italy* perennially sees Steve ignored by the female figures he hopes to capture in his gaze. Arriving at their first hotel near Genoa, Steve and Rob walk to a terrace balcony, past two young couples chatting around a table. Steve glances back at one of the women on his way. When he consequently begins to chat about the couples with Rob, their conversation is inter-cut with close-ups of this same blond-haired girl. From a strictly formal sense the scene reiterates the symptomatic 'male gaze' of classical narrative cinema, the young woman captured within the distant and perusing observation of the two men. This is a gendered gaze that, from the girl's position as 'foreign', is also inscribed with the power-play of national identity (the 'right', in this case, of the English traveller to stare at foreign women). Steve's gaze, though, is highlighted here as ineffectual. Never returning it (there are no eye-line matches to indicate this), she appears happily unaware of his presence, chatting to her young male companion. Since we only hear Steve's voice and not hers, this further undermines the gaze and, if anything, flips it round derisively onto the on-looking men. Steve's narration of the non-existent exchange underscores this reversed relationship, acknowledging that now, as he enters middle-age, he can only be seen by such women as an ageing homosexual on holiday, or at best, 'a benevolent uncle'. The film in this regard dismantles the English tourist's gaze, not so much by resisting it, but through indifference; an indifference that returns the tourist to his position as such, stripped of any assumptions of privilege or mobility, returned to *his own* status as visitor, and as 'other'.

Conclusion: So close, so far … so close

As I have argued in this chapter, the holiday film, in both an older and now more recent English tradition, works through a contradiction; one in which the site and sights of otherness, European destinations in this case, become locations for a utopian Englishness. Innocently or otherwise, this cinematic process effectively removes 'Europe' from representation, beyond its status as an extension of 'national' space. The pursuit of different experiences that is fundamental to the modern English holiday experience enacts, in the same gesture, an erasure of much that might be perceived as different in cultural terms. As a national cinematic institution of sorts, the genre suggests at once the limitations of English space as site of pleasure and release; while at the same time, it is a genre that is enclosed unto itself. Above all, and for reasons that give these films their contemporary significance, such films frequently reveal how dependent this English utopia is on the European mainland.

The English holiday film has to this extent played a significant cultural and ideological role in underpinning the peculiarly ambivalent relationship of England to the European mainland, and in more explicitly political terms, to the European 'project' itself. As I have noted, the outcome of Britain's referendum on EU membership is an overt manifestation of this relationship, but also a point beyond which the English holiday film may need to rethink its parameters and possibilities. We shall see, and as I have argued above, the ambiguities and capacity for self-reflection within the genre offer plenty of possibilities for more critical and inclusive films. In the end, the key for the English holiday film is to get its head firmly from out of the Mediterranean sand, and to take a good look around. As this chapter has explored, what one might find, and the conclusions one might draw, are often surprising.

3

'Not to Yield': Globalization, nation and the epic imagination of English cinema

Introduction: The epic film at the intersection of the global and the national

This chapter examines a particular, and in many respects revealing, tendency in popular English cinema emerging in the years immediately following the EU referendum: what I am describing here as the English 'epic' film. Fitting into this category, I suggest, are a range of films including Guy Ritchie's *King Arthur: Legend of the Sword* (2017); Aardman's Bronze-Age underdog story *Early Man* (2018); the Churchill drama *Darkest Hour* (2018), which turns to the same contexts of Christopher Nolan's earlier *Dunkirk* (2017), viewed from Westminster; and most recently, Joe Cornish's *The Kid Who Would Be King* (2019), a modern return to the King Arthur story, from the perspective of teenagers in an English secondary school.

This is not unfamiliar territory for popular English cinema. A 1958 film produced by Ealing Studios, also called *Dunkirk*, had told the story of the evacuation; this film, meanwhile, was just one of literally dozens of British films that returned to the Second World War as a theme in the decades following it.[1] As recently as 2007, the event had also been memorably visualized, and played a central narrative role, in Joe Wright's film adaptation of Ian McEwan's novel *Atonement*. The King Arthur legend, meanwhile, even if sometimes (like Ritchie's film) made through the funding of Hollywood studios, has proved a perennial subject for both film (*Excalibur* [1981], *King Arthur* [2004]), and more recently, exportable British television (*Merlin* [BBC, 2008–12]). As James Chapman argues in his study of the British historical film – a study comprising films such as *Henry V* (1944), *Scott of the Antarctic* (1948), *Zulu*

(1964), *Chariots of Fire* (1981) and *Elizabeth* (1998) – such films are *popular* in the sense that they are generally made for broad-based audiences, not the 'professional historian'.[2] As a result they are more likely to further a 'version of the past that promotes dominant myths about the British historical experience'; 'myths', here, in the sense that such films 'tend to endorse narratives that accord with popular [British] views of history'.[3]

How and why there has been a re-engagement with the epic form is one of the questions I wish to ask in this chapter. In line with the rest of this book, I am above all concerned with the ways specific myths of Englishness are mobilized in the (presumed) interests of international, as well as domestic, appeal. I look in particular at how the Arthurian story weaves its ways through these various texts and intertexts – including, as I discuss here, in the important precedent of *Skyfall* (2012), one of the most commercially successful 'British' films of all time. Analysis of these films as a recent group is instructive, in terms of what it suggests about the currency of these myths; both in and as a national imaginary, but also, as an assumed archetype for contemporary English film in the global market. One of the things I will therefore consider will be the importance of particular narrative tropes in these films, and how they appeal – especially in a domestic context – to particular ideological and territorial ideas of national, and *popular*, identity. My analyses of the films here will therefore carry on much of the work of the previous chapter.

In looking at these films, though, it is important to note that they neither can nor should be considered outside the more material contexts of a globalized film industry and audience. Such contexts remind us that a popular English cinema exists, for the most part, not as some natural wellspring of native stories – whatever that might possibly be. Rather, it exists largely as a consequence of, or response to, particular cinematic trends or tendencies at the global level. As I have noted, this is a book about the stories a national cinema tells its audience: analysing this in the contexts of Brexit, this study inevitably touches on issues of national self-perception and projection, and of national global-standing. The epic, mythic form is well-suited to this task. And yet, in combining this with a more materialist approach, this chapter, and the ones that follow, also engage with the actual, global contexts of industry, and how this impacts upon the types of films being made.

This is a significant inflection, as it points to the ways that narratives and representations in a popular English cinema are, more accurately, negotiations between these dominant national myths, and industrial expectations of what, on an *international* level, these popular myths comprise. As usual, for example, in discussing a company like Working Title, we have to see their perennial return to the historical epic – from the highly successful *Elizabeth*, to its sequel, *Elizabeth: The Golden Age* (2007), to the more recent *Mary, Queen of Scots* (2018) – not entirely as attempts to engage with British history, but as attempts at sustaining an internationally appealing genre in the form of the historical film.[4] As I will go on to consider in Chapter 5, this means that such films are always contending with the vicissitudes of global film culture, and the always uncertain notion of what constitutes box-office appeal. While, then, as I will argue here, *Skyfall* provided the perception of both a powerful, self-sufficient Britain *and* a film industry to match, it is also notable that many of the other films discussed in this chapter were relative commercial failures. In the case especially of the two King Arthur films, as well as *Early Man*, these failures are in part indicative of a popular English cinema in thrall to, yet unable to negotiate or compete with, broader industry contexts. In other words, a globally targeting, popular English cinema within this time, and one that exploits the triumphalism of the epic form as its vehicle, reveals itself to be at the same time subservient to broader market trends. But it is also a form unable, in this instance, to sufficiently integrate domestic narratives within broader global cinematic frameworks. As such, these films are as significant to understanding the state of the national film industry as they are to understanding the state of the nation: and in many ways, I argue here, this amounts to much the same thing.

The epic has often been seen as playing a role in the shaping and defining of national identities, specifically because of its origins in oral traditions and, subsequently, in the form of literature. The 'modern' epic – Shakespeare's history plays, the writings of 'Ossian' the Scots bard, the Finnish tale-cycle *Kalevala*, the 'Celtic twilight' poetry of W.B. Yeats – is a constructed and largely fantastical form, exploiting myth's interplay of fiction and history.[5] More recent writers like J.R.R. Tolkien, to take the most prominent example, used the trappings of fantasy fiction to shape their own epic mythos, itself drawing on Anglo-Saxon histories, to fabricate a kind of ersatz origin story for England.

The epic in this foundational literary or dramatic form has only recently (Tolkien's work being a good example here) extended beyond its more national confines. Understanding the epic in a *cinematic* context, though, requires a further shift in thinking. The film epic shares with its literary predecessors many parallel features: a frequent focus on mythical time in the form of a history 'before history'; an emphasis on scale, of setting, on high emotion and narrative stakes; an equivalent stylistic emphasis on grandeur and dramatic power, or what Vivian Sobchack has evocatively called the genre's 'surge and splendor'.[6] But there are important differences, which relate as much to the economics and logistics of film production as to issues of aesthetics and narrative. As Robert Burgoyne notes, in his introduction to *The Epic Film in World Culture*, the genre is shaped by a 'central paradox', namely

> the contradiction between the traditional messages embedded within epic form – the birth of a nation, the emergence of a people, the fulfilment of a heroic destiny – and the long history of the epic film as an international, global narrative apparatus not bound by nation or ethnicity.[7]

As Burgoyne and many of the contributors to his book note, while the epic film *can* still be mobilized in the service of particular national cultural or political agenda, more pragmatically, the scales of such production mitigate against their capacity to work in purely domestic contexts. Increasingly, the box-office dividends for such films, made both within and beyond Hollywood, are in wider international markets.[8] As Burgoyne remarks in his study of *Gladiator*, the 2000 film often viewed as having kick-started the genre's revival, the 'economic dimension of epic films … make international coproductions and multinational distribution and exhibition arrangements a necessity … Epic films need to appeal to an international audience in order to recoup their investment'.[9] Epic films are, in this respect, precariously balanced: they are at once called on to evoke specifically national contexts, while relying on more globally identifiable forms; they may wish to appeal to a specifically national cultural identity, while existing at the intersection of varied international production contexts and economic demands.

As this suggests, exploiting the epic as a vehicle for narratives of nation, above all within the contexts of smaller producing industries, is fraught with tension. At once the most strident of forms, it is also one of the most vulnerable to the fashions and fortunes of the cinematic market. The rest of this chapter explores how these recent films have tried to negotiate these tensions.

Skyfall and *Darkest Hour*: Epic heroes and the (national) origin story

Skyfall, the twenty-third film in the James Bond series, is a remarkable example of the epic imaginary at work in popular cinema. In terms of its significant, even unprecedented, domestic appeal in the UK, the film invites consideration for its deft manipulation of epic form. Its power as a film, as I discuss here, lies in its ability to rework the James Bond movie as a form of national myth. While acknowledging its continuity with the rest of the series (2012 was also the fiftieth anniversary of *Dr. No*, the first Bond film), *Skyfall* constructed for itself an unusually strong sense of independence and renewal. This was also, and in a previously unforeseen way, constructed in terms of a peculiarly British, or rather *English* narrative. This, I argue, is a factor behind the film's unusual domestic success. But it is also, in the process, a potent work of disavowal: both of the contemporary global contexts the film purports, with a significant degree of realism, to depict; and also, of the globalized economic contexts for the film's existence in the first place. While the film predates the main debates around the EU referendum, then, its engagement with and imagining of the place of Britain on the global stage, and the popular reception of the film, make it central to any discussion of cinema and the ideologies and discourses around Brexit.

Darkest Hour, as already noted in the introduction, is a Working Title production, made within that British company's long-standing deal with Universal Pictures. Directed by Joe Wright, it was written and co-produced by Anthony McCarten, who also scripted Working Title's earlier biopic *The Theory of Everything* (2014). As discussed earlier, *Darkest Hour*, which dramatizes Churchill's selection as prime minister in May 1940, and the critical weeks leading up to the Dunkirk evacuation, was both discussed and appropriated by various viewers within the terms of Brexit. I have already suggested that such appropriations are problematic, from a historical point of view, given the film's longer gestation. Speaking informally as one of the film's viewers, I suggest its potency lies in its capacity to be read according to whatever political position you might bring to it. In this way, its narrative of native British endurance and determination, in the face of overwhelming German aggression, appeals to ideas of nationhood, independence and strength (and it helps, of course, that we know how the story ultimately plays out). Whether we see any allegorical link in the film regarding the relationship of Britain to the EU in the twenty-first century is, I would suggest, a moot point at best. Yet it is abundantly clear that Joe Wright's film, as with Nolan's *Dunkirk*, lent itself to a particular Brexiteer narrative of heroic resolve and independence.[10]

By the same token, *Darkest Hour*'s dramatic focus on the conflict between Churchill and his political adversary, Lord Halifax, one of the main proponents of appeasement in the face of the Nazi war machine, strongly contrasts the former's ebullience with the latter's craven desire to protect what might remain of British interests and possessions. The agitating, unctuous presence of Halifax throughout the film, often lurking in the shadows of the War Cabinet room, clearly marks this figure as the villain of the piece; yet any link here to the present is open to interpretation, depending on whether one might see the vote to Leave as itself a craven act, turning away from the complexities, allegiances, and indeed the moral responsibility, of being part of a Union, rather than the brave leap it is depicted as by its supporters. As the writer Alan Bennett remarked in his diaries the day after the EU referendum, the vote to Leave evoked for him an image of Munich in 1938, and Neville Chamberlain's claim of 'peace in our time': a sense of 'half the nation rejoicing at a supposed deliverance, the other half stunned by the country's self-serving cowardice'.[11]

This openness to interpretation indicates the difficulty of trying to pin down something as slippery as contemporary relevance with regard to historical film, even leaving aside more concrete historical factors such as production contexts. But as I have also previously noted, *Darkest Hour* does not exist in a cultural vacuum, but was produced at a similar time to several other high-profile works dealing with similar contexts. Part of my point in this chapter, in fact, is that the Churchill myth already operates powerfully in *Skyfall*, to the extent even that the latter establishes a template of sorts for future productions. This particular myth is also already circulating in other cultural forms; not least of which being Boris Johnson's 2014 biography of Churchill, published a few months before *Darkest Hour* went into development. We know where *that* appropriation of the Churchill narrative ultimately leads, with Johnson's successful 2019 campaign to become prime minister, his bullish commitment to whatever-the-cost Brexit and his insistence that compromise or further delay would be a form of national 'defeat'. But Johnson is evidently not alone in turning to such mythologizing, either as a form of self-identification, or as an archetype and narrative mobilized for political, or – in the case of *Darkest Hour* – cinematic ends.

The more pertinent broader point here involves the way a specific type of narrative form, allied in this instance to a specific English individual or archetype, is perennially mobilized in the interests of a (British) national cinema. English cultural archetypes, as discussed in the first chapter, are seen as the British cinema's global currency. In a soft-power sense, they are often the country's political currency as well. Consequently, we need to consider the significance to this cinema's wider image of these particular myths. One of the questions I will raise here, in fact, is to what extent these recent films are indicative of a cultural turn *inward*; or at least, indicate a reconfigured attempt to negotiate the global reach and expectations of popular English cinema.

As I will suggest, this turn is largely problematic, whichever way you look at it: either in terms of its entrenched, but itself also limited, national focus; or equally, in terms of its assumptions around the universality of these English narratives, for the global audience to which they are, in fact, largely directed as mid- to high-budget Anglo-American productions. The epic as a form, and as appropriated in both *Skyfall* and *Darkest Hour*, relies on narrative tropes that often dwell on the suffering of the protagonist, who, through force of will and character, transcends physical and emotional pain, or public opprobrium, in order to realize their historical destiny.[12] In the traditions of the epic, this is a destiny frequently tied up with the birth, or re-birth, of *the nation* as a 'body'. One of the aims of this chapter, both in this first section and in the following one on the King Arthur films, will be to explore how this is achieved, through structural and stylistic means.

Epic cinema and the paradoxes of decline

To read much of the academic discussion around *Skyfall* is to be struck by the tone of threat, gloom and imminent national collapse the film apparently evokes. 'In *Skyfall*', writes Christopher McMillan, 'Bond, the embodiment of

Britain, is in decline'.¹³ The 2012 film showed the hero as 'older' and 'frailer' than many of his incarnations, especially in the two previous films starring Daniel Craig as 007.¹⁴ The Britain it represented, meanwhile, was an equally weakened and vulnerable one.¹⁵ Marouf Hasian, seeing *Skyfall* as illustrating the new and intangible perils of the contemporary world, contrasts it with earlier films in the series, approvingly quoting another commentator to the effect that 'this isn't your grandfather's James Bond'.¹⁶ As Terence McSweeney sums up, Craig's Bond in *Skyfall* 'struck a chord with new millennial audiences because [Craig] was a more human figure [whose] on-screen failures ... far outweigh his successes'.¹⁷

If we were to leave the discussion there, *Skyfall*'s appeal to these 'new millennial audiences' would appear to rest on its realistic, unsparing reflection of difficult times. Such an approach, though, in relation to a film like *Skyfall*, is questionable. Viewed in this most literal and descriptive way, *Skyfall* does not make sense. There are many more direct, less costly and potentially more affecting ways of illustrating national decline and our twenty-first-century vulnerabilities than a $200m Bond movie; just as there are plenty of films dealing more explicitly with these contexts that failed to command a fraction of that attention. But on the whole, British viewers at least did not go to see those alternatives: they saw *Skyfall*.

Darkest Hour is a similar case in point. Wright's film opens with documentary image of German war preparations and a map indicating the inexorable movement across Europe of the Nazis. Its title, while obviously referencing one of Churchill's most famous speeches from 1940, could also be a knowing joke about the 'darkest moment' prioritized in many screenplay theory conventions, usually at the end of the long second act.¹⁸ In *Darkest Hour*, this is the point at which the prime minister, confronted by the likely decimation of retreating British forces, and the subsequent inevitability of German sea-borne invasion, accedes to the entreaties of Halifax and offers to pursue terms for peace. In other words, *Darkest Hour* dangles the spectre of an alternate British history of military catastrophe, invasion and surrender: a historical trajectory deflected only by the fortune of Dunkirk's Operation Dynamo. A dark hour indeed, though not so dark that it put off domestic audiences, who helped make *Darkest Hour* one of the most popular British films of 2018.

If we are to avoid making merely generalized assessments around *Skyfall*, it is important to be attuned to both its paradoxes as a film and the contexts in which it came out. As McSweeney observes, this is the same period that produced the expanding Marvel franchise and 2012's *Avengers Assemble!*, a film similarly shaped, supposedly, by the legacy of 9/11, as well as that year's *The Dark Knight Rises*, the third film in Christopher Nolan's Batman trilogy. One of the things that consequently makes *Skyfall* so significant is that it is something of a series *outlier*, rather than a continuation; but also, that it is largely out of step with the otherwise dominant superhero-film syndrome. It has not been lost on *Skyfall*'s commentators that the film is steeped in iconographies both of Englishness (and ultimately, as McMillan notes, a political negotiation of Scottishness) and of Bond's own cinematic past, from the views of a grey and drizzly Westminster and M's Churchillian bulldog paperweight, to the silver and sleek Aston Martin DB5, the iconic car from *Goldfinger* (1964), to which Bond here returns. Unlike in the previous instalment, *Quantum of Solace* (2008), the 007 of *Skyfall* shirks collaboration with American colleagues, vaunts his technologically anachronistic character in the face of Ben Whishaw's young and condescending Q, and prefers to drive his vintage car rather than the latest product-placed model. But from the most basic evidence, the film worked *because of*, not in spite of, these specific moves *against* the current of the contemporary blockbuster film.

One way then in which Bond, via *Skyfall*, has been rethought for the contemporary era is through the specific appeal of his vulnerable body, seen here to quite literally represent the *national* body. We already know that, on the surface at least, the world of Craig's Bond pays lip service to the challenging global contexts of British security and intelligence in the 2000s and 2010s. The catalyst for *Skyfall*'s narrative is when a bomb rips into London's MI6 building, triggered by Javier Bardem's Silva, an estranged former agent and now a virtuoso in cyber-terrorism. Yet as Klaus Dodds argues, Craig's battered agent serves as a physical locus through which a narrative of (national) resilience, or even a *fantasy* of it, can be worked. Locating *Skyfall* within the terms of London and the UK's vulnerability to terrorism, and as the first film in the series to show the city responding to such attacks, Dodds suggests that the film offers the imaginary reassurance of London history, and an assertiveness in the face of adversity most clearly formed through the experience of the Second World

War. The film's status as a reflection of vulnerability gives way here, then, to its appeal as 'a form of resilience that ultimately rewards both a flag-waving belligerence (demonstrating resolve) and a sense of restraint (not acting like the terrorists and killing indiscriminately, for example)'.[19] Like *Darkest Hour*, then, it also appeals to the contexts of a prior, nationally defining war and an attendant sense of moral high-ground over the adversary.

Nobody does it better: Englishness and the middlebrow epic

An essential point to make about *Skyfall*, as with *Darkest Hour* in many respects, is that it appears to be doing something different when, in many respects, it does not. This perception of difference is what matters, though. Such a discussion needs to focus then on ideas and discourses of 'quality' in *Skyfall*, and how these in turn mark and distinguish this film from some of its predecessors, while still maintaining (or, just as pertinently in this case, re-establishing) continuity with series traditions. These issues are important from this book's perspective, inasmuch as ideas of artistic quality foster notions of cultural distinction and exclusivity. But it is also because, in this distinction from the popular mainstream, the perception of quality can also work to generate a higher sense of realism, and hence belief. As already noted, part of *Skyfall*'s outlier status relates to its sense of difference from the same blockbuster contexts in which it is situated. The film's remarkable achievement as a culturally English film is to do all these things, yet for an audience substantially *in excess*, in terms of numbers, even of most 'mainstream' cinematic output. *Skyfall*, in fact, forces us to change the way we understand 'popular' contemporary cinema.

Sally Faulkner's recent study of so-called 'middlebrow' cinema is a useful intervention in this regard, highlighting as it does the flexibility of this elusive but cogent term. Often associated with a certain type of filmmaking aesthetic thought to appeal to viewers wary of the commercial mainstream – some of its main examples being the historical film, the biopic or the literary adaptation – the middlebrow has also been considered in terms of a certain kind of audience. This audience, it is supposed, is inclined both to particular kinds of films and to the particular spaces in which they are shown. This presumed audience is usually one that is middle-aged, middle-class and educated (or at least aspirational with regard to the latter two), and in turn tending towards the art-house screen rather than the multiplex. As Faulkner notes, though, these mid-scale conditions for most quality films do not preclude the possibility of large-scale popular success for the films in question; nor, in a similar way, the possibility that films not fitting the evident aesthetic bill may be taken up by audiences designated as middlebrow.[20] As Faulkner argues, this is what happened with Oscar-winning 'genre' movies such as *Titanic* (1997), and *The Lord of the Rings: Return of the King* (2003), which transcended the divide between quality cinema and the blockbuster.[21]

This suggests the middlebrow is more contingent than prescribed; although as Faulkner highlights, quoting Tim Bergfelder, there is in these instances always some act of consecration at stake which implies 'aspirations relating both to the films themselves and their audiences'.[22] Bergfelder, like Jim Collins in an earlier study, points to the pictorial and literary-derived modes of 'heritage' cinema as one example of this middlebrow aspiration.[23] As Bergfelder adds, cinematic forms and genres can themselves adapt to middlebrow aesthetics for strategic reasons of domestic and international exhibition and prestige. Quality genres such as the biopic or the epic film have endured across international cinematic contexts, revealing the way popular genres can appropriate and thrive on middlebrow connotations while not necessarily conforming to many of the typical expectations of the term.[24]

In this collapsing of erstwhile cinematic distinctions, high-profile films like the Bond series now pursue directorial talent in a way that bolsters both the film's profile and the commercial and cultural status of the filmmaker. Christopher Nolan's association with the Batman series is perhaps the best example of this synergy between producer rationale and creative talent. Equally, though, the decision on *Skyfall* to bring in Sam Mendes, whose CV includes an Oscar for *American Beauty* (1999) and a lustrous career as an innovative British theatre director, imported artistic kudos into a studio franchise. Craig's physically fatigued, terse performance style adds further weight to the film's suppositions of quality, in this respect with regard to its 'authenticity'. Steely and chilly cinematography by Roger Deakins, meanwhile, which drains London of colour while preserving its drizzly charm, adds to this middlebrow mix.

Certainly, the aspects of realism identified in the film in critical and academic reception acknowledges some aspiration in the film towards more serious aesthetics and content. But the specific appeal of *Skyfall* to British audiences is also underlined by its record-breaking box-office status, the first 'British' movie to take in £100m at the domestic box-office. Most importantly, though, this was a *middlebrow* audience. Statistical figures on UK audience demographics in 2012 point revealingly to a significant drop in attendances on the part of cinema's presumed 'core' demographic of 15–24-year olds (the 'millennial' blockbuster audience).[25] While these made up only 25 per cent of the UK box-office in 2012, compared to almost 40 per cent in 2009 and 2010, the upper-end of the over-45s emerges as the dominant demographic, representing 36 per cent of tickets sold. This might be ascribed simplistically to the popularity of period films or more demographically targeted films from that year such as *The Best Exotic Marigold Hotel, War Horse* or *The Iron Lady*. Yet the true prominence of these three films at the UK box-office – they took in £20m, £18m and £9m, respectively – suggests that they could not have had such a significant impact on the shifting demographic sands. When we then take into account that *Skyfall* accounted for 9 per cent of *all* UK box-office income in 2012, we may reasonably deduce that the film drew a considerable chunk of its theatrical audience from that older, emerging demographic within popular cinema culture. Indeed, when we get more specific results for the next Bond film, 2015's *Spectre*, we find that it was among the films to draw above-average audience percentages in the older demographic, in a year which saw the 45+ audience increase even further. In all, 36 per cent of *Spectre*'s audience came from this group – 23 per cent of it in fact from viewers aged 55 and over. 'Not your grandfather's James Bond'? Evidence suggests, in fact, that grandfathers, or at least older parents, were a key part of its box-office success.

The other earlier-quoted suggestion that *Skyfall* 'struck a chord with millennial audiences', then, requires some qualification, as it is less obvious that millennials were the main audience for the film, at least in the UK. While *Skyfall* at a global level merely rubbed shoulders with its franchise peers, in *domestic* contexts *Skyfall* did *double* the business of any of the established franchise movies released that same year; a clear indication that the film, to its 'local' audience, was something more than Just Another Blockbuster. It suggests that its popularity relied strongly both on its appeal to viewers beyond the assumed Hollywood demographic and to some idea of national filmmaking identity.

What then, does *Skyfall* say about this nation, and how might it appeal? The main point to make here is that this film, more than any previous Bond outing, is unusually focused around modes of national self-reliance, here as a response to national vulnerability. As Tobias Hochscherf writes with reference to *Quantum of Solace*, the 2008 film was unusual in its implication that the British secret service was so dependent on its US counterparts, personified in this film for the second successive outing by Jeffrey Wright's Felix Leiter. At the same time, any suggestion that this depicted a renewal of the Cold War 'special relationship' would be to simplistically reduce the complexities and imbalances of this relationship in the post-9/11 era, and to overlook the fact that Bond is acting now 'in a globalised world with volatile markets, powerful global corporations and ephemeral political, economic and military alliances'.[26] This in turn is what *Skyfall* both acknowledges and then resists, reasserting Bond's fundamental Britishness. The film pays visual lip service to the expansive new frontiers of modern 'Europe' (Istanbul, in the pre-credit sequence), the bewildering sites of modern global capital (here, the neon-dappled skyscrapers of Shanghai), and to the new elusive anxieties and stateless threats of the twenty-first century (cyber-terrorism). Yet it does this only as a prelude to the film entrenching itself for its second half firstly in London, and finally, to Bond's ancestral home of Scotland. Americans, strikingly, are nowhere to be seen in this film. Whatever the status of the 'special relationship', there is no sense in *Skyfall* that it is anything worth investing in. Cinematic *inward investment* is of course a different matter, and precisely that which makes a film like this possible; but the strong national emphasis in *Skyfall* obscures this material aspect to the film.

The intelligence services in *Skyfall* have also gone underground, after MI6's Thames-side building is attacked: a move that blatantly – since we're told the new temporary headquarters are repurposed Second World War premises – links the film's narrative to Churchillian contexts. *Darkest Hour* in fact takes this idea of the underground to more expressive and thematic depths. The prime minister is frequently filmed in the narrow confines of the war rooms, or walking down tunnels. At other times, at heightened moments of crisis, Churchill is viewed through narrow gaps or windows that contain him even further within the frame: at one point when he makes his futile plea to an ineffective Franklin Roosevelt, he is even filmed in the toilet, the composition

Figure 3.1 Stages in the (epic) hero's journey: Churchill, alone amongst men, endures his *Darkest Hour*. Directed by Joe Wright © Focus Features/Universal Pictures 2017. All rights reserved.

literally confining him in despairing isolation (Figure 3.1). Like *Skyfall*, which also takes its hero to figurative lower depths – having him presumed dead and out of action – *Darkest Hour* revels in the abjection of its hero before his, and consequently the nation's, moment of renewal.

While *Skyfall*, then, maps its central character's frailty into the film's mostly grey mise-en-scène, this approach strategically serves as a base and catalyst for the film's overarching tale of resilience. It is not how Bond begins, but his capacity to 'bounce back' from adversity that is key, as a symbolic indication of 'political resilience'.[27] A sequence at a climactic point in the film shows Craig's Bond, still weary but ready again for active duty, running through the London streets in a bid to intercept Silva, who is on his way to kill Judi Dench's M at a government hearing. The sight of massed police cars and fire engines conveys a sense of emergency, partly through evoking images from the 7 July 2005 bombings: the coordinated series of attacks on the London Underground and bus network that nearly paralysed the city. In a powerfully emotive montage, underscored by Thomas Newman's music, the image of Bond running is overlaid with M's speech to the committee. Speaking firstly of fear, and of the unknown, 'opaque' threats hiding 'in the shadows', M concludes by citing the final lines of Alfred Tennyson's poem *Ulysses*: 'We are not now that strength which in old days / Moved earth and heaven; that which we are, we are; /

One equal temper of heroic hearts, / Made weak by time and fate, but strong in will / To strive, to seek, to find, and not to yield.' The film's integration of Tennyson's poem here has a potent twofold effect: both to reassert the film's claims to cultural distinction, in its use of nineteenth-century verse, and also to situate 007 within a broader and richer mythological context, one with strong connotations of national formation and re-birth: Bond, in fact, as Britain's Once and Future King. As McMillan elaborates:

> The use of Tennyson's *Ulysses*, in addition to symbolising the fading glory of both Britain and Bond, provides a link to the Arthurian legend set down by Thomas Malory in *Le Morte d'Arthur* (1485) which Tennyson retold in *Idylls of the King* (1859-85). Interestingly, the new M [at the film's conclusion] is called Malory. Furthermore, the title sequence of *Skyfall* has Bond fall into water, where he is clutched by a woman's hand. Much like Arthur, Bond dies but is fated to return messianically when Britain needs him most.[28]

As spoken by Judi Dench's M, whose bulldog statuette is the one object to survive the terror attack, there is a clear effort in her speech to evoke a Churchillian moment. This narrative of national re-birth, centred around the symbolic resurgence of an individual hero, is also a key aspect of *Darkest Hour*, though here with an even more overtly 'popular' inflection. Churchill's return from the wilderness of surrender and appeasement comes when, surveying the London citizens from the vantage point of his car, and viewed in a slow-motion tracking shot, he gets out and decides to take the underground. The fictionalized scene that follows allows the erstwhile mental landscape of Churchill's mind (represented, as noted above, by enclosed spaces and tunnels) to be inhabited, *populated*, precisely by the 'ordinary' British people who until that point do not have an active role in the drama. Here, we find a cluster of 'ordinary' commuters from varied parts of the UK, as well as the former British Empire, in the form of a young Caribbean man, who recognizes and then completes Churchill's quotation from Lord Macaulay's epic poem 'Horatius'; notably, another appropriation of nineteenth-century verse within genre-film form. The commuters encourage the prime minister not to yield to German aggression, cementing his resolve to resist the line of appeasement. This highly sentimentalized sequence has attracted derision from some commentators for its historical fabrication, and its tokenistic embrace of racial diversity.[29] Yet, to recall James Chapman's point, historical accuracy in such films is secondary to a *mythic* function, which is here to provide a broader popular image of this same 'underground' resistance epitomized by the film's Churchill: in this instance, in the form of a cross-sectional representation of the British public – and the modern *viewing* public – itself.

Skyfall offers a similar narrative of resurgence and renewal, drawing in this instance not on poetry, but on British fine arts. An early scene in the film, in London's National Gallery, has Bond introduced to his new, young quartermaster (Figure 3.2). Incarnated now as an almost archetypical geek barely out of his teens, Q meets 007 in front of J. M. W. Turner's *The Fighting Temeraire*: the 1839 painting that depicts the last moments of one of the warships employed in the Battle of Trafalgar. Looking at the painting, Q lightly teases Bond: 'It always makes me a little melancholy, a grand old warship being hauled away ignominiously for scrap.' Q's implicit allusion to Bond's declining state and status is underlined by his assertion that he can do more damage with his laptop before his 'first cup of Earl Grey' than Bond ever could out in the field. The evident reflection here on both the character of Bond and the remains of the British Empire is heavily marked. Turner's late-Romantic aesthetic intertwines here with the connotations of the film's enigmatic title, with its echoes of a Wagnerian *Götterdämmerung*; the downfall of the Gods.

The limitation though is in thinking that the scene's *allegorical* dimension equates to what *Skyfall* is ultimately saying, in terms of its narrative development and conclusions. Whatever associations may be drawn between Bond and

Figure 3.2 The *Skyfall* of the Gods: Bond, Q and Turner's *The Fighting Temeraire*. Directed by Sam Mendes © Sony Pictures Releasing 2012. All rights reserved.

Turner's ship, more important are the inflections that the film eventually offers on this image. Coincidentally or otherwise, the concluding lines from Tennyson's *Ulysses* were also found on the Antarctic memorial cross dedicated to Captain Scott, seen in the final shot of 1948's *Scott of the Antarctic*.[30] *Skyfall* shares that latter film's focus on endurance, but not so much its commemoration of dignified failure. As Dina Iordanova reminds us, the epic as a long-standing narrative form coheres around 'a tragic protagonist whose historical mission puts him at odds with the limitations of the era'.[31] Bond's resilience, as already seen, plays a vital role in terms of the way *Skyfall* enacts its narrative of national, as well as individual, endurance and return. The idea of Bond as a protagonist out of step with his times, yet able to work and overcome the 'limitations of the era' in order to fulfil a national historical role, only reinforces this epic dimension to his character and the film. The 'tragic protagonist' of the epic is of course a figure whose role in the shaping of history is overdetermined, either by our knowledge of history itself, or from the historical reiterations of the narrative. *Darkest Hour* allows us to plumb the depths of national capitulation and a Nazi-occupied future not because it entertains this future or imminent prospect, but because this future did not happen. Churchill is fated to transcend 'the limitations of his era' because we know how things turn out for him and for the country. Within the contexts of the Bond series' longevity and perpetual recycling of itself, meanwhile, this idea of historical destiny is influenced by our expectations around the series and the end of such films: that Bond will, inevitably, 'not yield', but will succeed and endure.

Bond's role in history, his agency as the epic protagonist, is reasserted towards the conclusion of *Skyfall*. In painting *The Fighting Temeraire*, Turner altered the geography of the Thames by having the ship pulled west, in order to capture the setting sun. The shot of 007 looking over the London rooftops near the end of *Skyfall* reiterates the composition of Turner's painting, in effect situating Craig's Bond in the same physical space as the warship (Figure 3.3). But Bond is here facing a sun that is rising, not setting. In such a move, in fact, *Skyfall* draws not only on Turner but on a wider tradition of Romantic painting (most notably Caspar David Friedrich's image of *The Wanderer* [1818] that places the lone individual within or before a sublime landscape). And, needless to say, because of the shot construction here, Bond serves as a possible textual proxy for a viewer's own physical and ideological perspective.

Figure 3.3 Resurgence and renewal: Turner, referenced and re-worked, in the conclusion of *Skyfall*. Directed by Sam Mendes © Sony Pictures Releasing 2012. All rights reserved.

To complete Adele's lyric from the film's theme song, we will, as a body, 'stand tall', and 'face it all together'.

But face *what* exactly? Like most myths, *Skyfall* does not appeal to a rational or actual sense of things as they are. As Dan Hassler-Forest suggests, this is part of the contemporary appeal of franchise films like Nolan's contemporaneous Batman series, with their well-worked, traumatic origin stories. They are, Hassler-Forest argues, indicative of a postmodern moment in which the sphere of culture takes over from reality, and where myths become nature: in Roland Barthes's words, the point at which myth 'organizes a world … without depth, a world wide open [where] *things appear to mean something by themselves*'.[32] *Skyfall's* conclusion brilliantly obviates any broader geopolitical, devolutionary or other post-imperial contexts to which the film otherwise alludes, precisely through its powerful aesthetic appeal to a sense of Englishness or Britishness (or even, 'Bondness'): a sense of strength and resilience that is effectively beyond words. But there is the problematic sense here that this is an essentially empty appeal: not unlike the so-called 'War on Terror' itself – or even Brexit, from one perspective – a narrative of resilience along ideological lines, without a really defined or coherent target.

This is especially so here, as *Skyfall's* re-birthing story is steeped not so much in the historical past, but in the *cinematic* past. Andrew Higson's suggestion that, within the postmodern, a historical heritage culture offers a 'flat, depthless pastiche' of the past, in part as a way of bolstering against the uncertainties of the present, lends itself to our understanding of *Skyfall* and its peculiar national appeal.[33] The qualification here is that *Skyfall* is on the surface neither an obvious retreat into the past, nor one that is flat and depthless in the pictorial way that Higson, for example, sees heritage cinema. Rather, the film offers the spectacle of a re-tooled cinematic continuity with its own brand. We see this through the eventual and confident rejection of Q's new digital world, the revival of its most celebrated artefacts (such as Bond's old car) or the eventual return to a pared-down, post-imperially revisionist headquarters, with the new M receiving him through a leather-backed door, and a new (black) Miss Moneypenny, played by Naomi Harris, greeting him on the other side. I have speculated, though with some suggestive evidence, that *Skyfall* attracted back to the cinema an ageing generation previously ostracized by recent Hollywood production. We should nevertheless recall that this demographic was younger once, and a lot of them grew up in the cinema watching Bond. *Skyfall* is a return for more than just its hero.

Very British blockbusters

In a versatile way, Skyfall can take in its range of global locations – including China, an emerging market for franchise movies like this one – without appearing beholden to any of them, such is Bond's solitary movement through this world. In its consequent progression homewards, towards its origin story, the film amply demonstrates the possibility, within the domestic market above all, that allying inward economic investment to an inward-looking *cultural* investment, during uncertain times – cinematically and otherwise – can pay financial and critical dividends.

In its movements between the global and the local, *Skyfall* is very effective in acknowledging and playing to its diverse production and exhibition frameworks (the film's global distribution was carried out by Sony; production funding came from both MGM and Columbia). At the same time, it manages to disavow this global aspect of the Bond franchise, by rooting itself in an apparently national narrative and mise-en-scène. It might be going too far to suggest, as has been the case, for example, in discussions of French historical epics, that *Skyfall* exemplifies a national cinematic 'response to globalization'.[34]

This would be awkward, for the simple reason that the very production of a film like *Skyfall* relies dually on the investment of multilateral production and distribution practices, and on the already globalized status of 007 as international export brand. Yet we can credit a considerable amount of the film's force to the way it draws on those same themes and iconographies – (cinematic) history, landscape, other native art works – that have, and not exclusively in the French context, worked to produce popular and often exportable genre films, marked by their difference from the global cinematic mainstream.

Much of *Skyfall*'s distinctiveness, then, resides in its capacity to be viewed not as a global genre film at all, but as an entirely national story. In this respect, *Skyfall*'s politics lies in its potential to repudiate, at an imaginary level, its own contexts of production, but also the (geo)political realities of a globalized and interconnected age that produces it and underpins the film's narrative. Attempting in turn to make any correlation between *Skyfall* and events of 2016 is problematic, of course, and any sense that the film informed the discussions around Brexit would be coincidental at best, and probably inadvertent. Yet its inherent emotional and mythic appeal relies strongly on notions of resilience and isolation in the face of wider threat. *Skyfall* is, above all, an emblematic film for the complex cultural, economic and political negotiations between the global and the local in this part of the twenty-first century.

Darkest Hour, as I have discussed here, can be viewed in a similar though somewhat differently inflected way. *Skyfall* works to make its cinematic, mythic figure the stuff of (cultural) history itself; while *Darkest Hour*, inverting this paradigm, seeks to make its actual historical protagonist the subject of cinematic myth. Bond's global appeal as an agent of British soft power is, from a logical or even definitive point of view, because he does not exist except at this cultural level. But what happens when, in the case of *Darkest Hour*, British cinema seeks global export value in its historical figures? There is little new here, in terms of a cinematic practice, as already noted. But in the contexts of Brexit above all, the investment in particular cinematic genres and typologies assumes a different and more political significance.

Assumptions around what constitutes a successful British film, either artistically or commercially, are very much linked to the contexts in which they are viewed and discussed. The supposed 'universality' of myth is often exposed by its discussion and reception outside national contexts. Surveying, for instance, the critical response to *Darkest Hour* in France – the one other country physically represented in the film, when Churchill flies there to exhort its leaders to repel the German invasion, only to be met by a form of resigned Gallic shrug – highlights the more sceptical response to these kinds of stories from other national perspectives. A mostly positive review of the film by Luc Chessel in the left-leaning *Libération*, for example, with an implicit acknowledgement of Brexit, pointedly asks '*why make this film now?*'[35] Recognizing that *Darkest Hour* is not so much a biopic as a 'demopic', an attempt to narrate the becoming of a people via the figure of Churchill – who comes to embody, in himself alone, 'the whole kingdom' – Chessel argues that the film rarely questions this mythic association, leaving the real significance for its time and place uncertain.[36] Nicolas Azalbert's mixed review in *Cahiers du cinéma*, meanwhile, is more direct in its emphasis on the film's ideological role in the immediate contexts of the Brexit 'crisis': 'what better than a return to the most fundamental values of the homeland, and to that quintessential figure of the most strident nationalism ... Churchill ... the flag-bearer and voice of England'.[37]

Such responses, implicitly, also hint towards native assumptions around national narratives and their global significance, since for the most part, the events around Dunkirk and Operation Dynamo are much less well known outside the UK. As Chapman nuances, Dunkirk is 'probably the most mythologized event of the Second World War', yet only 'from the British perspective'.[38] Nolan's *Dunkirk*, as already noted, already a remake of sorts, is steeped in a longer tradition of British wartime films, but this remains a mostly British fixation; and indeed, one character aside – a French soldier posing silently as English so he can join the evacuation – Nolan's film is not particularly invested in the fate of French troops. One French critic writing on Nolan's *Dunkirk*, in fact, revealingly refers to the evacuation as 'an obscure episode of the Second World War'.[39] Quoted in a 2017 review for his film in the French magazine *Les Inrockuptibles*, Nolan is at pains to indicate that the story of the Dunkirk evacuation is one 'that every English boy studies at school'.[40] Even within the British context, this is misleading in its universalist assumptions (I, to take one example, am Nolan's contemporary, but I don't recall learning about it), and is possibly more reflective of Nolan's particular schooling (at the private Haileybury and Imperial Service College). Above all, the fact that Nolan is at pains to explain the significance of his narrative subject matter, to journalists who often need to spell it out to their readers, reveals something about the limitations of these stories beyond British shores – but more importantly, the potential hubris in assuming that they might actually matter to others as much as they do to 'us'. The following section of this chapter highlights some of these problems in more detail.

Strong men, weak markets: Adventures and misadventures in the Arthurian epic

King Arthur: Legend of the Sword, like both *Darkest Hour* and especially *Skyfall*, operates in production contexts across this local–global framework, while also, like many Arthurian films, accommodating the simultaneous demands of history and fantasy. This is a film, after all, which opens with the dark mage Mordred leading a pack of massive armoured elephants (evoking the *mûmakil* from Peter Jackson's *The Lord of the Rings* series [2001–3]) against King Uther Pendragon, in a lavishly orchestrated, CGI-intensive battle sequence. A film like *Legend of the Sword*, because of the mixed generic demands placed on it as a globally aspiring blockbuster (of which more below), cannot cohere so easily within many of the forms and functions we might associate with historical or epic films. And yet, *Legend of the Sword*'s situation within a form of imagined national space, and recourse to a quasi-historical figure such as Arthur, enables it at least to 'establish an emotional connection to the past', and in turn, to issues of nation and national belonging.[41] Indeed, uncertainty as to Arthur's historical existence is to some extent an irrelevance, given his persistence in cinema and other forms as a *cultural* figure. As a recurring myth, it might tell us little about the past in strict historical terms, but it tells us a great deal about the kinds of stories to which we return in order to narrate an idea of nation. Quoting Mikhail Bakhtin's work on genres, Burgoyne's main claim for historical films as historical work is that they provide 'crystallized forms of social and cultural memory that embody the worldviews of the periods in which they originated, while carrying with them "the layered record of their changing use"'.[42] What is of significance here, therefore, is the specific 'use' of such films as a 'record' of particular cultural contexts and inflections.

As Chapman writes with reference to *Scott of the Antarctic*, that particular film helped cement the latter's thwarted Antarctic expedition as a defining national story. This, though, was notably a story about 'failure, but also [about] finding dignity in that failure'.[43] The Dunkirk evacuation itself, Chapman adds, reserves a special attraction in the British context not so much as a tale of triumph, but, like Scott's journey, in its combination of 'folly and … grandeur'.[44] As Nolan's film is keen to show, if Dunkirk was a success, it was a shambolic one; or at best, one that relied on a genuine sense of 'amateur' spirit, in the form of the generosity and courage of the civilian sailors who joined the evacuation fleet. As I will explore both later in this chapter and in the one that follows, like many myths, such depictions of noble failure and gallantry, though having evident cultural and political appeal, are as disavowing as they are actual representations of the national character. As I have hinted above, the most striking aspect of both *Skyfall* and *Darkest Hour* with regard to their exploitation of myth is their *resistance* to accepting failure, and ultimately, any suggestion of fragility, either in their narratives or in their depictions of the central protagonists. 'Not to yield': this emphasis on national *strength* under siege becomes a defining aspect of the more recent English epic, and its 'changing use' in these more recent contexts.

This is very much the case for *Legend of the Sword*, where the changing use involves re-working the Arthur story through the prism of Ritchie's familiar cinematic milieu, established through films such as *Lock, Stock and Two Smoking Barrels* (1998) and *Snatch* (2001): the terrain of 'mundane urban modernity', and specifically, a 'dark and dirty version' of London as a 'teeming … infernal metropolis'.[45] Ritchie's Arthur, at the end of the film's opening pre-credit sequence, is orphaned when his parents are murdered by his uncle, Jude Law's Vortigen, and is left to float Moses-like down the Thames, carried to the newly post-Roman city of Londinium. The film then accelerates through Arthur's childhood, as he is taken up by a group of women in a brothel. We quickly see Arthur's growth and entry into adulthood, repetitively showing his education into petty theft, fighting and the cruel ways of the world. *Legend of the Sword* integrates Ritchie's signature stylistic and narrative ticks: rapidly edited montage sequences, events told visually in flash-forward as one character describes a plan, or fight scenes that oscillate between extremes of speed, as the action is alternately frozen and then ramped. Throughout, we see the emergence of the low-life band of brothers from whom Arthur learns his life skills. They join him, as the film develops, in a popular rebellion to defeat the usurping Vortigen. These commoners, in turn, are established as the first Knights of the Round Table, seen being built at the end of the film.

As already noted, the epic is a narrative of dramatic proportions, in which charismatic individuals struggle against the repressive forces of their times, in order to realize their destiny: one that is here frequently linked, in the sense of a 'historical mission', to a wider *collective* destiny. The powerful body of the epic hero, then, effectively embodies the imaginary of a people, evoking through the past an anticipated present from which it is being viewed. This helps explain the potential appeal of epic in cinematic terms, but also the importance of the (typically) male body as the locus of a popular imaginary and desire. This underpins the collapsing of many epic films' titles into the names of their male protagonists, which become inextricable from the spectacular bodies of the actors who portray them: Kirk Douglas as *Spartacus*; Charlton Heston as *Ben Hur* and *El Cid*; Russell Crowe as (the) *Gladiator*; Colin Farrell as *Alexander*, and in Ritchie's film, Charlie Hunnam as *King Arthur*. It is, of course, not a big leap from the imaginary work of cinematic epic, to the more modern mobilization of 'epic' national struggle within the rhetoric of populist politicians: some of whom, indeed, have chosen to actualize the 'hard' masculine aesthetics of the epic protagonist, if not always in body, then at least in word and action. *Legend of the Sword* strives from its opening scenes to align itself in narrative and ideological terms with an assembled *populus*; one that, as noted above, exists in distinction from the more aristocratic and courtly connotations of earlier Arthurian films, such as *Camelot* (1967), *Excalibur* or *First Knight* (1995).

While striving for a popular local resonance, *Legend of the Sword* is also inevitably diverse in its efforts to negotiate the global contexts of its production and reception, above all, by mobilizing specific cinematic motifs and structures. It does these, however, to particular narrative ends that are at once problematic and even self-contradictory in the context of a British or English 'national cinema'. Taking inspiration from *Gladiator*, it is as much the idea of Rome, as one of Dark-Age Britain, that informs the film's aesthetics. In the aforementioned credit sequence, as Arthur's movement down river opens up onto a panoramic vista of the city, we see a slightly ruined gladiatorial arena dominating the background. The man who constitutes a father figure of sorts to Arthur is George, played by British-Chinese actor Tom Wu, who runs a fighting school in the city. The mixed-ethnicity casting around Arthur points towards its similar use in *Gladiator*, which, as Burgoyne suggests, figures the film's vision of a 'collective emergence … expressed through the solidarity of the gladiators'.[46] The link here is further established by the casting of the Beninese actor Djimon Hounsou, who played Juba to Russell Crowe's Maximus in the earlier film, as the loyal knight Sir Bedevere.

For Burgoyne, *Gladiator*'s capacity to exceed its parameters as a 'Hollywood' movie comes by virtue of this multi-ethnic collective it evokes. 'The gladiator-slaves here might be seen as a kind of counter-empire, a mongrel mixture of nomads and remnants … naming and dramatizing a force of resistance'.[47] In its consolidation of Arthur's band as the new Knights of the Round Table by the film's end, *Legend of the Sword* aspires to *Gladiator*-like depths, yet there are telling differences between the two films. At the conclusion to *Gladiator*, Maximus defeats the corrupt emperor Commodus, but dies himself in the process. The 'collective renewal' brought about in the arena in *Gladiator* is not through Maximus's victory or prowess in itself.[48] Rather, it is his eventual death that helps bring about historical change, in the form of a nascent democracy, since Maximus's death marks the end of the Roman arena as a site of struggle between the empire's slaves and its rulers. Maximus's ambiguous entry into the film, as the powerful but troubled general leading his armies into their final battle, emphasizes his epic narrative role as the tragic agent of historical change, bridging the violent past and a better future.[49] But this requires his own life be sacrificed in order to provide a cut-off point from this past.

As noted already with reference to *Skyfall*, though, the imagination of the contemporary English epic is not a tragic one. In contrast to *Gladiator*, *Legend of the Sword* allows for no ambiguity in its treatment of combat and eventual victory, with Arthur's army eventually overcoming Vortigen and returning to power in Camelot. Identifying these points of comparison also invites us to consider some of the pleasures they afford, and in particular, the specific, even if vicarious, appeal of mostly masculine forms of *virility* in these texts. Higson notes how often films about medieval England, with their frequent emphasis on political violence and machinations, and their 'dirty realist' aesthetics, appeal to an idea that the modern and the medieval are intertwined. Such films, then, 'suggest … that barbarism and a primitive sensibility have not disappeared, but live on in the present day world'.[50] Indeed, latent within Burgoyne's reading of *Gladiator* is the sense that its appeal is linked less to its evocation of history, and rather to its *contemporary* relevance and inspiration. It is striking that its abiding images of masculine strength, as well as its Roman military motto of 'Strength and Honor', figured prominently in memorial imagery and tattoos following the attacks of 9/11, and the 'crisis of national identity and modern social structures' this event catalysed.[51] For Higson, as much as the medieval film and the epic has the capacity to allegorize our contemporary political and social contexts, we evidently cannot rule out the more unruly way that such films, or epic series like HBO's *Game of Thrones* (2010–19), 'are in some ways a licensed space for representing the transgressive and the taboo'.[52] Higson is right to point out that, in many respects, cinema merely provides 'a legitimate and respectable space in which certain modes of behaviour can be played out, modes of behaviour that are currently considered unrespectable or decadent, outmoded or primitive'.[53] Yet Higson's reference to 'modes of behaviour' that are '*currently* considered unrespectable' is historically and culturally contingent. It implies a consensual view of the limits of acceptable behaviour that is intrinsically rational and, indeed, 'modern'. But how well-defined, in truth, are the boundaries, and how do we measure 'legitimate and respectable' viewing pleasures? Especially, we might add, when many of the pronouncements and actions of the world's leaders themselves, fully visible in the media, increasingly test these boundaries?

By the end of *Legend of the Sword*, after Arthur's popular army has defeated his usurping uncle, the new King is able to rebuff a band of Vikings come to claim the fee owed them by Vortigen. Notably, given the post-referendum contexts in which the film emerged, this fee from overseas is in the form of young Britons, demanded as slave labour. This conclusion draws on similar elements in canonical Arthurian narratives, such as Book V of Malory's *Le Morte D'Arthur*, and the entirety of the earlier English alliterative poem *Morte Arthure*, whose stories hinge on taxes demanded of Britain by the Holy Roman Empire.[54] In both of these works, these demands from the European mainland initiate a war fought less for money than for ideas of sovereignty and the right to live freely and civilly. In *Legend of the Sword*, no such war is necessary, and Arthur's power and charisma are enough. But this is specifically figured in terms of Arthur's aggressive determination *not to yield*. The final

Figure 3.4 Muscular diplomacy: The authority of a populist King Arthur, acknowledged by the Vikings, at the end of *King Arthur: Legend of the Sword*. Directed by Guy Ritchie © Warner Bros. Pictures 2017. All rights reserved.

images see the men from across the seas kneeling to Arthur, after the latter has demanded from them that they respect England and the Crown, and forgo their demands. Arthur's justification here, as he phrases it, is that it is better to have friends than enemies; yet here, these are only ensured through the veiled threat of physical response (Figure 3.4). It is here, in ideological terms, that the connections to *Gladiator* erode more fully: the post-imperial utopianism of the latter replaced, here, by a swaggering assertion of national cultural and political confidence, underpinned by the authority of the sword itself.

The Kid Who Would Be King, by contrast, is in many respects a counter-narrative to films like *Legend of the Sword*. Writer-director Joe Cornish opens his film with a quick re-telling of Malory's Arthur story, rendered in traditional 2D-animated style. This is a film steeped in a mythical idea of England, ranging across the ancient sites and lay-lines of the country, from Stonehenge to Tintagel to Glastonbury Tor. It is also most notable in its concentration on conflict less as something turned towards the external other, but as an *internal* rift in the national body. The film offers its putative villain in the form of Arthur's half-sister Morgana, rising from her prison below the earth to wreak havoc and enslave the land and its people. Yet in the contexts of the narrative Morgana seems more of a vague symbol of a greater, socio-political issue to which the film consistently makes reference: the notion, as voiced by Morgana early in the film, that the country is 'divided, fearful, leaderless'. It is the absence of proper national direction, rather than foreign threat, that provides the source of crisis. In this film, the sword ends up in the hands of twelve-year-old schoolboy Alexander, who rallies a band of Knights – and, refreshingly, Ladies – composed of his best friend, the two reformed school bullies, and eventually a horde of pupils from his comprehensive school.

This crisis is only very broadly sketched in *The Kid Who Would Be King*; yet its deliberate contemporary resonance, and perhaps accidental dialogue with *Legend of the Sword*, is clear. We hear, for instance, a radio bulletin at the start of the film describing the threat to world security posed by 'populist leaders'; while similar, apocalyptic headlines and warnings are shown splashed across newspaper front pages. While noting that (like *Legend of the Sword*) his film was in development for several years, Cornish has admitted that these loose references to the recent contexts of Brexit, Trump and other populist political contexts are 'half design, half coincidence'.[55] As he adds, the contemporary circumstances of Britain show that 'old resentments and evils … that we thought were in the past hav[e] re-emerged'; an observation that underpins his film's emphasis on 'the idea of people needing to be unified'.[56] In a similar way to Cornish's debut film *Attack the Block* (2011), which pitted a gang of inner-city youths against an alien invasion – another film in which, significantly, adult males are either hostile authority figures, or absent altogether – *The Kid Who Would Be King*'s main gambit is to tell this story almost entirely through the perspective of young teenagers (Figure 3.5). While dictated by the 'family film' genre within which it coheres (on which more below), this choice is also political, explicitly focusing

Figure 3.5 Optimism of youth: The schoolboy sword-bearer, and his Round Table, in *The Kid Who Would Be King*. Directed by Joe Cornish © 20th Century Fox 2019. All rights reserved.

on a younger generation at once marginalized by, and at the same time energized in response to, the reactionary politics of an older generation; with regard to its relationship to both the European Union and, increasingly, climate policies.[57] As Merlin, in his older form (played by Patrick Stewart), tells the group at the film's conclusion: 'A land is only as good as its leaders – and you will be *excellent* leaders.' In this case, Merlin's comment refers to the group's ability to overcome division and work collaboratively, in the service of a greater good rather than personal interest. But the comment is also a pointed one in its identification of youth as the future, and a source of optimism.

Legend of the Sword and *The Kid Who Would Be King*, then, show two very different uses of a particular myth to very distinct ideological ends. Perhaps, though, the more telling lesson here is what links both these films: a sense, in this instance, that a market for such national myths is questionable. Partly because of its extensive use of CGI, *The Kid Who Would Be King* was a significantly more expensive film than Cornish's earlier, lo-fi *Attack the Block*. It turned out to be a major financial disappointment for its producers (Working Title) and distributors (20th Century Fox), failing to make a return on its $60m budget. Given its subject matter and origin, its performance in the UK seemed surprisingly poor, reaping less than $5m from its theatrical run. The film also failed to make a significant impression in mainland European countries, where it had been expected to perform better.[58] *Legend of the Sword*, meanwhile, was originally planned by its Hollywood producer, Warner Bros., as the first film in a possible Arthurian franchise. Ritchie's co-producer and co-writer on the film was Lionel Wigram, a Warner Bros. veteran who was a producer on the *Harry Potter* series and now the *Fantastic Beasts* films; and like those films, Ritchie's was also shot in the Warner Bros. studio at Leavesden. Yet, at least with regard to its inflated production budget, *Legend of the Sword* proved to be one of 2017's biggest flops, undoing plans for any further instalments.[59]

Both these films, in this respect, highlight the difficult negotiations between national culture and global contexts of production and reception. As various scholars have observed, erstwhile conceptions of a genre such as 'children's film' or 'family film' have adapted to, and been driven by, film-industrial shifts, and in particular, the tendencies towards franchizing on the part of conglomerate Hollywood studios.[60] Taking into consideration the costs of both producing and marketing contemporary film, the pursuit of sufficient financial return means that family films have tended to become 'globally-oriented mass media that target the broadest possible demographic and ethnographic cross-section'.⁶¹ Classification categories such as 'PG-13', meanwhile, or 12A in the UK, have also encouraged studios to produce more 'mature' films that are nevertheless accessible to younger audiences, with even 'YA' (Young Adult) series such as *Twilight* (2008–12) and *The Hunger Games* (2012–14) being stretched to accommodate multiple-demographic interest.⁶² To this extent, Noel Brown argues, the 'family film' has 'developed to the point where it transcends cinematic typology'.⁶³ In the form, for example, of franchises such as *Star Wars* or the Marvel Cinematic Universe – both of which, alongside Pixar Animation's films, are overseen by Disney – it has simply become the dominant form of twenty-first-century cinematic product.⁶⁴ All family films in the current cinematic marketplace contend with these releases, with all the publicity and distribution power from which they benefit, plus the much valued 'pre-awareness' they enjoy as commodities.

Cornish has acknowledged his debt to the Hollywood family movies he grew up watching, such as *E.T.: The Extra Terrestrial* (1982), *The Goonies* (1985) and *Stand by Me* (1986). Allusions to these films in *The Kid Who Would Be King* are plentiful – the suburban settings, the absence of strong father figures, and of course, the idea of children banding together to defeat evil. If anything, Cornish's film is self-conscious in its efforts to locate itself in a pop-cultural landscape, with Alexander and his best friend Bedders invoking both Luke Skywalker and Harry Potter as narrative precedents for their own quest (and *The Kid Who Would Be King*, though in a slightly different way from *Legend of the Sword*, most likely trusted in a wider audience generosity towards films about boy wizards). The main problem, though, in attempting to situate this nostalgic film into the contemporary cinematic context is that, by its own nature, this time has passed. *The Kid Who Would Be King* also owes something to a series like *Stranger Things* (2016–), which itself pastiches a Spielbergian cinematic world of suburban 1980s culture. *Stranger Things*, though, has achieved success in the very different narrative and economic contexts of Netflix. As *movies*, the very texts this latter series evokes – the same ones that inspired Cornish's film – would be outliers within the contemporary cinematic landscape. Cornish's efforts to root his film in a very English pre-modern and contemporary vernacular, it should be added, along with his focus on youth, marks the film as a novel intervention within its broader cinematic contexts, exemplifying a culturally English cinema in the much more democratic and inclusive potential of the term. Yet this national focus also marks some of its limitations, at least in terms of its bid for a wider reception and impact.

Similarly, its politics aside, Ritchie's effort in *Legend of the Sword* to construct a studio tent-pole property in his very specific stylistic and linguistic vernacular is impressive. Yet it is also limited in its expectations, or at least hopes, with regard to what constitutes a commercially viable franchise property. Series such as the *Harry Potter* films, and Peter Jackson's two Tolkien trilogies (2001–3, 2012–14), have contributed to the idea that 'culturally English' cinema has an important currency in contemporary film industries and cultures. This is true, though as qualified in Higson's own use of the term, it describes an idea of Englishness that is quite diffuse in its application and appropriation, often by film-makers and producers with no connection at all to the UK or to its film industry (the case, for instance, with Jackson's New Zealand-based films).[65] But more importantly, the global prominence of particular British intellectual properties, such as Harry Potter, risks luring us into the mistaken assumption that it is Englishness *in itself* that sells. Rather, especially in the case of the *Harry Potter* adaptations, it is the situation of such characters and stories, as already globalized commodities, circulating through world popular cultures, that allows them to become franchisable film properties. As I will explore in more detail in Chapter 5, the wider prominence of culturally English film is also highly contingent. In focusing too casually on the impact of the *Harry Potter* films in twenty-first-century global cinema, we might overlook the number of abortive culturally English franchises made in their ilk, and which failed to reach a presumably expected audience. The attempt, for example, to film Philip Pullman's *His Dark Materials* trilogy, restricted to just one film (2007's *The Golden Compass*), is an operative case in point here; as is the more recent, critically and commercially disastrous film adaptation of *Mortal Engines* (2018), produced by Jackson, based on the first in the popular four-book series by English YA author Philip Reeve.

Seen in this way, then, the contrasting political content of both *Legend of the Sword* and *The Kid Who Would Be King*, so far as they might tell us anything about the films' reception, are partly beside the point. It is hardly my interest to act here as a sounding board for film-industry speculators, but rather to indicate some of the recent contexts in which popular English cinema seeks, and fails, to exert an influence it may assume it has, based on outlier global phenomena such as *Harry Potter*. Box-office data do not represent a film's meaning for its audiences; yet in this instance, looking at the kinds of investment levels in these culturally English properties, and subsequently, the levels of return they expect to generate, provides a strong indication of what is hoped by producers and filmmakers to work on both a domestic and a global level. From a generous perspective, the relative failures of both films lie outside their control. Yet from another, more critical perspective, the scale of investment in these mythic English tales suggests a belief, again, in the 'universality' of such stories. The reality, at least in this particular instance, is one of significantly diminished expectations. Ritchie's cinematic Arthur, in the story fashioned for him, may be able to command respect from overseas; but Ritchie's film doing the same proves a more daunting proposition. Cornish's politically significant film, meanwhile, invests in a very different idea of near-future England. The more melancholy aspect of its reception, though, is that *The Kid Who Would Be King* is ultimately a minor film, without the reach or relevance to which it aspires. All of which is a shame, but also a more realistic reflection of what, at this point in time, we might understand English cinema, or even 'culturally English cinema', to be.

'It's Coming Home': The epic deceptions, and prospects, of the English sports film

A similar issue of what we might call misplaced universality concerns *Early Man*, from Aardman Animations and director Nick Park, creator of the *Wallace and Gromit* films. Unsurprisingly, its narrative of an insular 'English' Stone-Age tribe working together to defeat an avaricious 'foreign' invader accumulated a degree of post-referendum attention; *The Guardian*'s reviewer going so far as to ask if the film was a 'Brexit-for-juniors commentary'.[66] When these analogies with Brexit were put to Park in a *Financial Times* interview, the director (and writer of the film's original story) batted them down. 'We became aware of that. But we didn't want the film to be perceived as a political statement. Because we'd started filming it before the Brexit referendum and we never saw it as an allegory.'[67] Park, who describes himself as 'tend[ing] to be on the Remain side', is of course correct to dismiss the associations the film might have with a supporting vote for Leave.[68] Indeed, Aardman's production and distribution support most recently comes from the French company StudioCanal (as I discuss in the final chapter), so Park's diplomatic support of cross-Channel cooperation is suitably on-message. Nevertheless, the fact that the film can facilitate such interpretations, even if contingent on subsequent and unforeseeable political contexts, is further suggestive of the ways in which cinematic myths of independence, self-reliance and victory have assumed currency in English cinema production. Even if their discussion as such rests on circumstance and ahistorical interpretation, we should still examine the ways such narratives and representations emerge, apparently free from any allegorical dimension.

Early Man's narrative is set up around a football match played between the lowly Stone-Age tribe and its more technologically proficient Bronze-Age invaders. The 2018 World Cup finals, held a few months after *Early Man*'s release, was a global event the film evidently hoped to ride (the UK DVD was released three weeks before the start of the tournament). The allusions to an England team that would, fortuitously, be competing in the 2018 tournament is evident, mostly in terms of the white shorts, red tops and comparatively weighty boots of the Stone-Age team led by the young hunter-gatherer Dug (voiced in the English-language version by Eddie Redmayne). This design evokes the kit worn in the 1966 World Cup final by the England team, the only English side to date to have won the trophy.

As a StudioCanal release, though, with its European production and distribution remit, the film is astute enough not to identify either of the teams in *explicitly* national terms. As I will touch upon in the final chapter, processes of dubbing in the mainland European context elide some of the more specific national connotations of language and accent. This means that the more self-evident Englishness on the part of Dug's team, in the English-language version, is in theory more susceptible to adaptation and different kinds of interpretation. It is possibly no accident, though, that the blonde-maned star striker of 'Real Bronzio' (as the team is called), shares some of the looks, and reputation for theatricality, of the great German and Tottenham Hotspur forward Jürgen Klinsmann, a player much derided by English fans

Figure 3.6 The connotations of the 'European' game: Dug's 'English' side faces 'Real Bronzio' in *Early Man*. Directed by Nick Park © StudioCanal UK 2018. All rights reserved.

for his skill at diving; or that this player, like so many of the Bronze-Age players, is sketched, with some reductive gender connotations, as investing narcissistically in long, *bouffant* hair-dos (Figure 3.6).

As has become a signature in Park's work, especially in the films he has made or co-directed featuring Wallace and Gromit, there is a usually ambiguous emphasis on the past as a nostalgic, pre-technological domain, associated with an 'idiosyncratic sense of Englishness'.[69] In *Early Man* this representational approach is reasserted by the further deferral of Park's imagined English North to the Stone Age: the introductory titles, deliciously, situate the film's desolate prehistoric location as 'near Manchester', with belching volcanoes standing in for the billowing factory chimneys of a rather less distant past. Yet even this ironic construction of English identity, aligned as it is with a particular context of time and place, becomes a potential narrative site of allegiance, in distinction to Real Bronzio's effete European connotations. Rather than in specific national terms, this rival team, overseen by the French-accented and unscrupulously avaricious Lord Nooth, is modelled more on the type of modern, international football squads, assembled with the financial clout of (foreign) billionaire investors, that increasingly dominate European football. The actual paradox here in an English context, though, is that negative images of the footballing 'other' can no longer be syphoned off onto wealthy, overachieving continental clubs like Spain's Real Madrid, Italy's AC Milan or Germany's Bayern Munich. This is because their most obvious manifestations are now in England's Premier League; be it the Roman Abramovich-owned Chelsea, or even more obviously – and more pointedly in respect of *Early Man* – Manchester City, owned since 2008 by a UAE-based private equity company, run by a member of the Abu Dhabi royal family (and also, since 2014, the dominant team in English football). Some reviewers of the film from outside Britain, in fact, less liable to link the references to England's victory in 1966, assumed that Dug's team colours evoked those not of the England team, but of City's historically more successful rivals, Manchester United. Nevertheless, inasmuch as the more venerable traditions of an 'old-fashioned' (albeit hugely wealthy) club like United might be contrasted to the new-moneyed, Arab-owned *arrivistes* from across town, the association with United over City is a similarly political viewing.

A willingness to take *Early Man* so seriously may seem to overstate the significance of a film peopled by animated Plasticine figures. As I have argued elsewhere, though, the formal properties of Park's work with Aardman, relying as it does mostly on older, pre-CGI animation techniques, informs their homely, 'local' quality in a way that strongly links a sense of place to an 'authentic' ethos of production. The artisanal effect of the company's stop-motion work, at the same time, offsets the films' actual status as high-budget, transnational commodities, produced for global sales with major studio backers: previously, Dreamworks Animation, and subsequently, StudioCanal (and Lionsgate for releases outside Europe).[70] There is a nuanced marriage, however, of the local and the global in the earlier *Wallace and Gromit* films, where the nostalgic past meets with Wallace's hyper-technologized inventions, and Northern-English reference points combine with detailed allusions to Hollywood's classical and more recent blockbuster history.[71] *Early Man*'s main contrast in this respect is to set up a narrative context of opposition that explicitly, and in a fairly Luddite way, contrasts its resolutely local, technologically less sophisticated English characters against a specifically foreign and more resourceful opposition.

In this regard, *Early Man*'s continuity is more firmly within a small tradition of British or Anglo-American sports films which celebrate the values of gutsy authenticity and honesty over the more advantaged, and consequently less authentic (or less honest), 'foreign' adversary. These are aspects we can see at work in films ranging from *Chariots of Fire* and *Escape to Victory* (1981), to more recent films such as *Wimbledon* (2005) and, albeit with a twist on the usual narrative, *Eddie the Eagle* (2016) – all of which, to varied levels, focus on 'underdog' English sportsmen overcoming the odds and adversity to achieve their respective goals. In *Wimbledon*, this involves a hapless English journeyman finding the form of his life to win the world's most famous tennis championship, beating the brash American number one in the process. As Tobias Hochscherf and James Leggott assert, situating *Wimbledon* within the broader output of its producers, Working Title, this particular film epitomizes the company's defining 'culture clash' motif, one that runs especially through their romantic comedy output: the conflict 'between a genteel, under-achieving or unassertive Britain' and 'a more demonstrative US culture'.[72] Yet if we replace the United States with any non-specific foreign other, this is a definition that could extend to several British films about sport: whether it be Michael Caine's prisoners-of-war team taking on the Germans in *Escape to Victory*; or Eddie 'The Eagle' Edwards facing down both his own fears of the ski-jumping hill, and the derision of a well-oiled and more professionalized Norwegian team. Though the trappings of the sporting context mean these narratives are sometimes delivered in a more humorous or self-effacing way than other films in the epic tradition, they nevertheless draw equally on the genre's tropes of resilience and resurgence, moral integrity, and its emphasis on individual or collective figures at odds with, and overcoming, the limitations of their times.

In two recent articles on the British sports biopic, Matthew Robinson has shown how national themes and narratives are constructed and reinforced in this process.[73] In *Eddie the Eagle*, about the English ski-jumper who became a household name in the late 1980s, it is Eddie's singular desire to be an Olympian, and the makeshift manner of his training, in spite of his evident limitations as a ski-jumper, that is the source of his unlikely heroism. Similarly, in *The Flying Scotsman* (2006), about the Scottish cyclist Graeme Obree, we witness Obree's 'make do and mend' approach, which sees him fabricating a bike – named 'Old Faithful' – using parts from a washing machine. Such amateur approaches distinguish him from both his closest (English) rivals and the bureaucracy of the international cycling authorities. As Robinson explores across both films, these narratives of individual amateur endeavour and resourcefulness are set up against opponents aligned with dominant power structures, along with superior economic and technological support. Hence, Eddie Edwards not only has to contend with the drilled efficiency of the Norwegians and Finns alongside whom he trains and competes; he also has to confront the stuffy resistance of the British Winter Olympic Selection Committee, who view Edwards, ironically, as too much of an amateur to compete for Britain in the Olympic Games.[74]

Eddie the Eagle is an interesting choice of subject for popular English cinema at this time, and in light of this chapter's discussion, a doubly nostalgic type of English film, given its emphasis on glorious under-achievement. Edwards, famously, in the 1988 Calgary Winter Olympics, came last in both his events, and a sizeable distance behind any other competitor. From the perspective already offered, *Eddie the Eagle* merely takes to an extreme the example set by earlier biographical films like *Scott of the Antarctic*. An important context here, though, is that this film is made and released within a period of hitherto unprecedented dominance on the part of British athletes in the Olympic Games, supported by high levels of financial investment in elite performers. The government policy of targeting potential medal-winners over other sports and competitors has, purely in terms of medals won, shown clear dividends. Olympic funding, drawn largely from income generated by the National Lottery, was substantially increased after the 1996 Games in Atlanta, where the British team returned with a solitary gold medal. This tally rose to 19 in 2008, to the 29 at the London Games and the 27 in Rio 2016, where Great Britain were second in the medal table, behind only the United States, but in front of historically more dominant Olympic nations such as China, Russia and Germany.

The period setting and mise-en-scène of *Eddie the Eagle*, which from its opening puts us within the domesticated contexts of English suburbia in the 1970s and 1980s, will revive memories, for some viewers, both of Edwards's televised exploits, and of a period before Britain's recent, policy-driven reinvention as an Olympic superpower. This consequently evokes a notionally more innocent and, somewhat ironically with regard to recent contexts, more 'familiar' era of English under-achievement. As a film about amateurism and 'failure', then, it is at once anachronistic in the contexts of the 2016 Olympic year into which it was released. But in its specific way, it is also an unusual and important film, in that it offers an implicit critique of Britain's current elite-driven system: a system that, having no real place for 'amateurs', would not encourage someone like Eddie Edwards to compete in the first place. Its fond celebration of failure may seem incongruous in contemporary contexts; but it is precisely the limits of these contexts, in terms of meaningful social inclusion, that underpins *Eddie the Eagle*'s own critical form of nostalgic mythology.

When we return to *Early Man* with these contexts in mind, it is not, then, just the disavowal of the film's more globally complex production origins that provides a sticking point. The film's narrative, that hinges around Dug's discovery of cave paintings revealing his footballing ancestors – and hence, the mythic inscription of football as *their* game – is aligned at a cultural level with the idea that England, where the rules of the game were originally drawn up, is the spiritual 'home' of football: a sentiment most famously echoed, literally, in the oft-chanted 'Three Lions' song, originally written for the Euro '96 championships, held in England.[75] But alongside this other form of origin myth, it is also the film's reiteration of a familiar underdog narrative that, especially in the contexts of 2018 – with England's economically dominant, globalized Premier League as backdrop – is problematically misrepresentative. As I have already noted, to what extent *Early Man* wishes to be taken seriously is a matter of opinion, and like all interpretations, a subjective matter. And yet, the film clearly invites this possible reading, because it so strongly harks back, mythically, to foundational narratives of nation; not just through the communal significance of sport, but in terms of the British islands' vaunted resistance to invasion: a myth that conveniently overlooks, of course, a millennium of French influence on English language and culture, following the Normans' successful invasion of 1066.

In its focus on the footballing 'arena' itself, *Early Man* also invokes the same narrative contexts of earlier epics such as *Gladiator*; while its emphasis on the resourceful, 'wild' tribe defeating technologically advanced invaders owes not a little to films such as *Braveheart* (1995), eliding even with the rough-hewn populism of *Legend of the Sword*. At a more obvious structural level, though, and even if the allusion may be both inadvertent and lost on many viewers, the main intertext here is with the hit Bollywood film *Lagaan* (2001). In both *Early Man* and *Lagaan*, a sports match (cricket in the latter instance) is set up as a contest for the future and livelihood of a community strangled by the presence of an imperial power (a British cantonment in *Lagaan*). While in *Lagaan* the price of defeat would be the tripling of an already punitive British tax, in *Early Man*, the tribe face being sent to do forced labour in Lord Nooth's mines.

Set as it is in 1893, and culminating in the serendipitous defeat of the unsportsmanlike British team, *Lagaan* looks forward, via a representation of the past, to Indian independence from Britain in 1947. In the process, it also uses the allegory of the sporting event (in which the colonized trump the colonizers at their own game) to symbolically bring together an otherwise disparate community of differentiated religions and castes.[76] *Early Man*'s notably multi-ethnic and mixed-gender tribe offers a similar envisioning of the future people, encapsulated in its historic, epic framework. As a collective image of a people-to-be, its appeal is inclusive and diverse. And yet, as I have discussed, such popular impressions find themselves running up against varied contexts of reception at the time of the film's release: be these the circumstances around the EU referendum and Britain's relationship with Europe; or the divergence between the film's persistent underdog myth, and the realities of Britain's sporting presence on the global stage. If anything, within these new political contexts, a triumphalism, fed by Britain's policy-led sporting successes, has fuelled and usurped broader popular myth-making. Occasionally, and inevitably, Britain's athletic prowess at this time becomes a means through which the nation's independence and resilience can be discursively upheld. Pointing to the dominance of the United States and Great Britain over Asian and European rivals, for instance, at the Rio Olympics (which took place only weeks after the EU referendum), a number of pro-Brexit commentators and politicians used the medal table to justify the superior model of a post-EU 'Anglosphere'.[77] These opinions may or may not be fringe cases, but whatever they are, they highlight the power of sport, and the myths constructed around it, to foster powerful feelings of national strength and self-sufficiency: who needs to be part of Europe when our little islands, all on their own, can do *this*?

Conclusion

Again, we can only really speculate why *Early Man* eventually proved a disappointment at the box office, under-performing especially outside the UK, despite its extensive distribution. Like *Legend of the Sword* and *The Kid Who Would Be King*, the film failed to recoup its budget costs through its theatrical release. We might again think about the limitations, within a global cinematic framework, of such inward-looking national myths; or what turned out to be the misassumption, underpinning the production of all three films, that both international and domestic audiences would embrace these actually very English stories.

Looking at the political representations at work in these films provides significant insight into the way popular English cinema constructs its identity, especially vis-à-vis Europe or the rest of the world. As I have highlighted, though, this remains only part of the issue. This chapter has pointed to the strategic appropriation of the epic form, and a particular focus on narratives of resilience and national-becoming, in a number of films, from established to aspiring franchise films, and from more tested genres (*Darkest Hour*) to less predictable ones (*The Kid Who Would Be King*; *Early Man*). In some instances, most notably in *Skyfall*, these films have capitalized on the local re-positioning of their global brands, turning such films into new forms of national myths. In the contexts of a post-referendum UK, though, and the discussion of the nation's post-EU status, the significance of many of these films may lie more in their expectations of England's global currency in political, cultural and above all cinematic terms. They offer a potent example of how, though the epic film as a form promotes or fosters mythic narratives of autonomy and resilience, *cinematic* and also *economic* self-sufficiency is a more illusory concept, exposed by the contingencies and vicissitudes of the market. In more ways than one, then, and only with some exception, the modern English epic film aspires to both a relevance and impact that appear largely optimistic and unsustainable within contemporary globalized contexts.

4

Genius of Britain: The English scientist film and other science fictions

Introduction: Brave old worlds

Genius of Britain was the name of a five-part series produced and screened on Channel 4 in 2010. Though its title suggested a brainier version of *Pop Idol*, the series proved to be a detailed and sober appraisal of the life and work of numerous British scientists, from the seventeenth century to the present day, with contributions from a range of British public intellectual figures. As the book accompanying the series noted, its aim was to show how 'the genius of British scientists has kept Britain at the forefront of scientific progress for four centuries'. In turn, the series would celebrate how such geniuses 'changed our world', giving us 'a history to be proud of – and an exciting future'.[1]

Statements from the same book, such as 'science has quite literally created the modern world', without contextualizing or evaluating what it has done for this modern world, effectively tell us nothing: the claim in itself is a circular description of the terms and conditions science has already shaped for itself.[2] This viewpoint exemplifies what some have called 'scientific realism': the idea that truth, or what can intrinsically be known about the world and the universe, proceeds from scientific enquiry: hence the potential tendency towards tautology in pronouncements about science's impact.[3] Modern science, the sceptical attitude suggests, creates its own criteria for judgement because it sees no higher authority. Beginning with Isaac Newton and his apple, scientific realism flips the Garden of Eden narrative around. As Yuval Noah Harari writes, in this new myth 'nobody punishes Newton – just the opposite. Thanks to his curiosity humankind gains a better understanding of the universe, becomes more powerful and takes another step towards the technological paradise'.[4]

Harari's broader point is that this revelation of scientific possibilities was fundamentally a *humanist* discovery. Where, though, does this trust in science's humanist basis reach a threshold? And more specifically, what definitions and boundaries shape our understanding and value of the human? The film *Never Let Me Go* (2010), adapted from British writer Kazuo Ishiguro's 2005 novel, carries scientific realism to disturbing yet, within the film itself, seemingly unquestioned lengths. The film posits an alternative history in which Britain, after the Second World War, experienced a technological breakthrough in genetic medicine. The outcome is that quantities of children cloned, it transpires, from the social 'underclass' – 'prostitutes and drug-addicts', as Keira Knightley's Ruth defines them in the film – are effectively farmed to serve as donors for the ill and ageing. When they reach adulthood, their vital organs are systematically removed until, in the Orwellian *newspeak* of the film, they 'complete'. The impact of this, as an inter-title at the film's beginning tells us, is that average life expectancy in Britain has reached 100 years. *Never Let Me Go* in this way sketches a hypothetical scenario of applied biotechnologies, and its use in the human pursuit of longevity, that is as much a discussion within contemporary scientific research as it is a scenario for future science fictions.[5]

What makes the film so unsettling is its willingness to frame this hypothetical scenario within a realist mise-en-scène barely distanced from everyday contexts, and evoking them in their banality. The donors, after leaving their schools, live in residential farmhouses and flats. Transit vans with the cheery 'National Donor Programme' logo on their doors ferry them around. Despite its narrative context of increased longevity, however, *Never Let Me Go*'s alternative England is not a crowded world of over-population: it is simply one that has got older. Beyond the school at which Ruth and her friends grow up, children are conspicuously absent from this scenario. When a group of donors go on a trip to a seaside town, hoping to find Ruth's original 'model', they sit conspicuously in a café deserted but for a cluster of aged customers. Later, when two of the donors try to meet the mistress of their former school, they find her in another seafront house, the promenade characterized by a spare scattering of the elderly. As the film hints in this way, the dystopian nation does not look like *1984* or a scene from *Blade Runner* (1982). Dystopia merely looks like the Bexhill-on-Sea, the southern seaside town where this scene from *Never Let Me Go* was filmed.

Never Let Me Go, in other words, offers a peculiar vision of the future as an idea of England *in the past*, maintained and preserved both through and for its ageing population – an image which also underlines the film's unnerving link to more recent cultural and political contexts. 'The England' of this film has the appearance of a sunny retirement home, enjoyed by the old and the affluent at the expense of any other social undesirables. By mostly erasing any non-white ethnicities, meanwhile, the film also removes the post-war history of immigration from its alternative past. The fact that the film narrates this through having the old literally harvest the young emphasizes, allegorically, its connections to broader present day issues; be these around social division and elitism, the modern slave economy or, indeed, around the function of schooling and the opportunities for younger generations, confronted with a diminishing job market, automation, absence of affordable housing, and the economic and social impacts of the ageing population.

Never Let Me Go is in this way an important inflection of science fiction cinema and its prevailing utopian and dystopian visions; especially so in an era of austerity, marked by disparities of opportunity not only between classes, but perhaps even more so by generation (a schism, as noted in my introduction, reflected in the EU referendum vote). In the case of this film, and the two main films discussed in this chapter, I am interested in the national or even *nationalistic* aspects of the way science is represented. As seen above, the critical inflection in *Never Let Me Go* is that scientific progress might shape an entirely selective and *nostalgic* utopian space. The alternate England of Ishiguro's novel may, from one perspective, be read as a purely hypothetical piece of 'what might have been' fiction, but this would be to ignore its understanding of British scientific history, especially with regard to the practices and philosophy of eugenics. Both Ishiguro's and the film's hypotheses are neither just rhetorical nor cautionary. The frozen post-war mise-en-scène of the film posits a country that has, in effect, realized some of the eugenicist dreams of an earlier and *actual* pre-war Britain – the same imaginary, for instance, that underpins Aldous Huxley's more overtly dystopian 1932 novel *Brave New World*. Huxley's book responded to a broader strain of thinking in British intellectual life in the early twentieth century, which saw eugenics – in essence, the programmatic management of breeding in the aim of social improvement – as a desirable policy.[6] In its most extreme form, realized in parts of the United States and, following this, Nazi Germany, such policy might extend to the sterilization of the 'mentally unfit' (an idea that Winston Churchill endorsed) or those deemed to be of poor 'genetic stock'.[7] If this did not actually happen in Britain, enforced segregation of such notional undesirables from the wider public by placing them in institutions, and the internal segregation of men from women (to prevent breeding) within these institutions, *was* put into policy action.[8] Prominent cultural figures like D.H. Lawrence and George Bernard Shaw, meanwhile, would make a claim for artificial breeding controls as part of an elite-minority response to the perceived threat of the 'high-breeding masses'.[9] But as *Nature* journal editor David Adam points out, alongside this anxious high-modernist British reaction to mass culture was also a form of ethnic anxiety, in response to the influx of European immigration following the First World War, and the misinformed perceptions that such immigrants had lower average IQs than the native population.[10]

Inevitably, there is a point at which selective and subjective ideas of what constitutes the socially desirable elide into ethnically informed notions of what society and culture should be. *Eugenics* literally means 'good breeding': behind the philosophy of selective birth control, then, one that ignores the significance of nurture and the structural impacts of wider living conditions on child development, is the idea that only certain children are 'well born'.[11] Britain's monarchical system, from this perspective, is eugenic, as is any social structure that privileges individuals according to birthplace or family. But when taken to its more extreme ethnically inflected and nativist lengths, the mythical idea of the nation itself – less the more diffuse idea of 'Britain', in this case, but the more specifically differentiated concept of England and 'the English' – is itself eugenic in its boundaries and exclusivity.

Never Let Me Go's subtlety as a film is in recognizing that the futuristic application of eugenic and genetic sciences might also be *backward-looking*, appealing to a regressive and enclosed form of English utopia. The possibility that the scientific imagination can be backward-looking is also relevant in terms of the other films I am looking at in this chapter. The key distinction here, I should highlight now, is between the practices of science, and these practices put to ends that are *nationalized*, or mobilized in the cause of a narrative of nation. As in the ambiguous title of *Genius of Britain*, the claim for national genius*es* drifts into the claim for an imagined kind of 'national genius' in itself. Why this *needs* to be asserted in and of itself is one question, but it also comes with historical problems. Can we disassociate this history of genius, for instance, from a long national history of rationalized colonialism and economic exploitation, one that the narrative of individual genius might prefer to avoid? To quote James Dyson, from the series' accompanying book, 'As a nation, we punch a long way above our weight – perhaps more so over the last 400 years than any other nation.'[12] Beyond asking what agenda informs such punchy assertions, this suggestion, that Britain's peculiar national genius lay in transforming a damp and resource-light island into a once-unchallenged global superpower, is an idea that both encompasses and disavows the UK's imperial history, and the latter's economic and logistical contribution to the nation's 'proud ... role in the history of science'.[13]

As I will indicate in this chapter, then, the significance or value of science itself is not what concerns me here. I actually lean strongly towards the view – one that Steven Pinker has forcefully argued in a recent study – that science does not just define the modern world, but has defined it very much for the better, in terms of its positive impact on the production of wealth, food, security and the eradication of disease.[14] The rationalist values of the Enlightenment, argues Pinker, continue to offer the best hopes for our future, just as they have helped make the world as a whole safer, healthier and more prosperous. There is a vital qualification here, though. Since these values are based on the principles of reason, they must by definition be universal rather than particular. A view of the world informed by what is universally *reasonable*, Pinker shows, naturally makes us sympathetic to the well-being and welfare of others. As he puts it, in a highly pertinent phrase for this present study: 'Nothing can prevent th[is] circle of sympathy from expanding from the family and tribe to embrace all of humankind, particularly as reason goads us into realizing that there can be nothing uniquely deserving about ourselves or any of the groups to which we belong.'[15]

Being critical, in this regard, about the claims made for British scientific achievement, is not at all to adopt what Pinker would call a 'progressophobic' or anti-scientific position; nor is it to question the wider significance or contribution to the world of such research, discoveries or inventions. Rather, it is to call into question their deployment within a narrative of national formation: a narrative that, in the process, becomes about something else other than the rational and universal value of science.[16] As already highlighted above, extolling the values of the nation as a form of collective group risks running counter to Enlightenment ideals, by valorizing one 'unique group' over another. Similarly, in its appeal to particular clusters of people, through calling on them to identify with specific national achievements, such narratives effectively reconstitute a random group of people as 'cells of a superorganism – a clan, tribe, ethnic group, religion, race, class, or nation'.[17] *Never Let Me Go*'s dark take on the eugenic utopian narrative, viewed from this perspective, is not in itself a rebuke of scientific progress. Instead, it is an imagined drama of what happens when science is applied, not *reasonably*, but for the benefit of the tribe – and in its focus on the wealthy or the ageing, for the subdivisions and hierarchies within these tribes, as well as the exclusion of socially or ethnically undesirable others.

In terms of its narrative construction of Britain, then, which is again here an English-centred construction, *Never Let Me Go* is astute as to the paradoxes of such nation-building: paradoxes, we have already seen, inherent within the EU referendum discourses and its subsequent results. On the one hand, the idea of the nation is founded on a partly illusory sense of prosperity and self-sufficiency, one which disavows the exclusion of the socially and economically underprivileged; the same constituency that is also, in part, mobilized by the populist appeal precisely around national prosperity and self-sufficiency – and the necessary exclusion of *another* set of undesirable others, in the form of non-nationals. It offers a vision of the future informed, essentially, by regression and erasure. Thinking about how the scientist film manages or avoids these potential contradictions, especially in its focus on the national value of science, will be a key aspect of this chapter.

The rationalist belief in the humanist value of science, rather than the limited perspective of the tribe, as Pinker suggests, 'force[s us] into cosmopolitanism'.[18] The latter, as I have discussed earlier, and as I will consider further in my final chapter, is both a main context and methodological aim for much of the work in this book. Looking especially at films about science and the scientist, then, the question that arises is what actually motivates the *national* image of science and the scientist? What exactly is at stake in the effort to construct an image of the scientific nation? Do such films contend with the cosmopolitan demands of scientific thinking, and how might they do so, if such films are bound within the industrial contexts and discourses around British or English cinema? This is the pertinent question, then, as we come to look at two recent, and in many respects, interlinking films: *The Theory of Everything* (2014), about the late cosmologist Stephen Hawking, and *The Imitation Game* (2014), which focuses on the life of mathematician and computer pioneer Alan Turing.

The biopic and genius: Exceptionality for everyone

Both of these biopics explore the particular figure of the genius. As I discuss here, the tendency not to think or act like others, the inclination towards eccentricity, and, in short, the idea of independence and originality are potent dramatic subjects for such films. Paradoxically, though, such difference in character can also be exploited as a discursive element in the construction of a collective, or national, archetype: uniqueness, in other words, as something that belongs to 'us all'. As I will explore, this slipperiness of genius as a property, its tendency to be appropriated into a national narrative in a way that overrides historical contexts, both serves and problematizes its use in and as a national cinema.

As biopics, both *The Theory of Everything* and *The Imitation Game* mine a rich vein of recent and older English cinema, important in terms of its popular potential and capacity for national myth-making. Such films exemplify a qualitative idea of England, and also of a kind of English cinema, reinforced by the cultural connotations of its subjects. Indeed, films such as the two main ones discussed in this chapter establish a connection with the forms of the classical Hollywood biopic, in terms of what we might call its historical and civic aims. As Belén Vidal suggests, the biopic has throughout its long history been exploited as a 'form of public history'. In its classical Hollywood development, the genre was often presented as a type of 'prestige' film for the studios that made them.[19] An important strand of the biopic in this classical period was made up of those films focusing on famous inventors or scientific innovators: *The Story of Louis Pasteur* (1936), *The Story of Alexander Graham Bell* (1939), *Edison, the Man* (1940) and *Madame Curie* (1943), to give just four examples.

It is not surprising that the scientist or technological innovator should be a suitable figure for a Hollywood industry dealing in mass cultural forms, and therefore, as Vidal notes, seeking to 'legitimise itself as an institution'.[20] The scientist as subject gives intellectual credibility to the movies and, in turn, the elusive figure of the scientist is given popular legitimacy as a cinematic figure. This is something of a paradox, to the extent that the actor him- or herself has to be at once the star *and* the figure they represent, in order for the biographical figure's exceptional life to be communicable to the mass audience. As George Custen puts it, as a popular genre form, the biopic has a narrative responsibility to 'render ... these different lives predictable and therefore mass producible ... The very novelty that makes a celebrated person famous, different from the viewer, must be packaged in a guise familiar to many viewers'.[21] For a number of reasons, since its classical-Hollywood heyday, the biopic has often been obliged to restrict complexity within classical narrative frameworks. It has also, to some extent experienced a historical transformation, from its more edificatory functions (films about scientists, inventors and political figures) to a more overtly 'popular' form of celebrity affirmation: films, for instance, about entertainers and sportsmen.[22] This was already happening during the classical period: as Custen suggests, drawing on the Frankfurt School critic Leo Lowenthal's terms, the change in subject reflected the cultural shift during and after the Second World War away from 'idols of production' towards 'idols of consumption'.[23]

We can in turn see how a specifically *English* engagement with the more notionally 'difficult' figure of the scientist serves as another means of projected cultural distinction (an idea, for example, of 'quality' English film), as well as product differentiation within globalized popular cinema. As already seen with relation to *Darkest Hour*, the biopic, with prestige performances at its centre, forms an important element of Working Title's cinematic brand, at least in this second decade of the twenty-first century. This was established by the success of *The Theory of Everything* (for which Eddie Redmayne, as Hawking, won an Academy Award), and the subsequent production, in 2015, of *The Danish Girl*: the period biopic in which Redmayne plays Einar Wegener, the transgender Danish painter.[24] But in terms of what we have considered so far, a question needs to be raised: if a popular English cinema turns to the exceptional intellectual figure of the scientist, yet explores this figure through the generic forms of the biopic, what are such films ultimately *about*? As noted above, the need for such films to be accessible in popular narrative terms means that the aspects of a life that make it exceptional are subordinated to classical narrative conventions and the logics of the star system. When this happens in the scientist biopic, as Christopher Frayling has suggested, such films are to an extent 'not really about science at all'.²⁵ This is especially pertinent in the case of Hawking and Turing, whose often highly theoretical work is fearsomely difficult for many viewers (in which I include myself) to understand. Both *The Theory of Everything* and *The Imitation Game*, in turn, focus on mostly impressionistic approaches to the work itself, alongside a narrative line emphasizing personal struggle, either against internal and bodily forces (Hawking's disability) or against cultural and political ones (for Turing, public-school bullying, British anti-homosexuality laws and government secrecy policies). But this shift *away from* science in both films raises the question of what science is being used for, strategically, in such productions.

To pick up on Vidal's point, there is an aspect of cultural legitimization at work in such films. As forms of culturally English production, moreover, both films can rely on the added market value of their historical English settings. The films also work through an appeal to history and the past, effectively re-making scientific research as an example of national 'heritage'. Such recourse to the past, beyond mere 'nostalgia', is also a potent means of packaging or disavowing a complex or problematic present. As I suggested previously, the *scientist* biopic contains the important added element of a contemporary technological, intellectual and economic relevance: the scientist as a form of esteemed national property. When it comes within the production frameworks of a popular English cinema, then, such films may also couch assertive narratives of national self-sufficiency and influence *within* the aesthetic trappings of nostalgia, heritage and period cinema.

A film such as *The Theory of Everything*, then, which recounts Hawking's emergence as a pioneering young researcher at Cambridge in the 1960s and 1970s, becomes as potent a film of 'Brand Britain' as any other, with its dual appeal to the significance of Hawking's work and to the venerable halls of learning in which it takes place. A critical success, the film topped the UK box-office the week of its release, going on to become the second most popular 'British' film of the year in the UK, and – as befits Working Title's remit and expectations – performing respectably across international markets. As I am suggesting here, then, films like *The Theory of Everything* are significant for the way that, in accord with much of the discourse around Brand Britain, they function within a very specific political and cultural context. As a manifestation of film policy (here, both in the appeal to a particular genre and also as an example of Working Title's production practices), the film promotes specific ideas of Britain (or England) and its cinema. At the same time, a film like *The Theory of Everything*, in its simplifications of science, works via its appeal to the past and to history, which it uses to construct an image of Englishness that is at once mythic, accommodating and *popular* in a broad sense. Such mythic constructions, as we will explore, work to efface some of the more difficult associations of nation, science and technology in this particular historical instance.

However, I will also argue that *The Imitation Game*, which focuses on Turing's code-breaking work on the German 'Enigma' machine in the Second World War, assumes a more nuanced and critical approach to these mythologizing tendencies. If these films work to generate myths of science and nation, then, they can also function as critical *revisions* of national history, working indeed to debunk reductive – and from an ideological point of view, convenient – narratives around Englishness and science. This is especially the case, as *The Imitation Game* explores, with regard to England's history and narrative of its own military application of technology and innovation. The capacity of popular English cinema to both allude to and disavow the national cultural propensity towards militarism, as I will consequently explore, is a revealing aspect of the work such cinema does to differentiate itself – from, in this case, a more overtly populist and militarist narrative cinema from which it is actually not so distant.

The solace of quantum: The science film as heritage film

Made at the higher end of the budgetary scale for 'independent' British films, and capitalizing on the rising profile of their young male stars, both *The Theory of Everything* and *The Imitation Game* were released within the optimal timeframe for the US awards season: an indicator of their pretensions towards 'quality' appeal and status. This aim is further underscored by both films' exploitation of historical and geographical contexts (wartime London and Bletchley Park in the case of *The Imitation Game*; Cambridge University in the 1960s in *The Theory of Everything*). As noted, we can even see these films as exploiting the 'heritage' aesthetics that still widely forms an important aspect of culturally English, and increasingly international, film production.[26]

At the time of their release, though, both these films suggested a quite novel departure from many of the more popular frameworks of popular English film. The idea of linking scientific narratives with a certain type of quality or 'middlebrow' taste has some precedent in the British context: there is, for instance, a BBC-produced television film *Life Story* (1987), which dramatized the race to identify DNA; or another television film, *Breaking the Code* (1996), based on Hugh Whitemore's 1986 stage play about Turing. *Life Story* (broadcast in the United States as *Race for the Double Helix*) was seen by some commentators at the time as representing a new level of engagement, on the part of the popular media, with scientific ideas.[27] This was a productive outcome of the increased visibility of scientific discussion, generated since the 1960s by new media forms such as television. Another factor here is the growth of popular scientific literature (Hawking's *Brief History of Time* [1988] being a key case in point), as well as the expansion of the higher education sector and, with it, a greater scientific literacy, during this same timeframe.[28]

Notably, though, even quite 'cinematic' productions such as *Life Story*, with its Cambridge University settings, and the presence of Tim Piggott-Smith and Jeff Goldblum as Francis Crick and James D. Watson, were still positioned within 'niche' broadcasting contexts, produced and screened as it was within the framework of the BBC's long-running science series *Horizon* (1964–). The more recent positioning of the scientific subject within the terms of a popular English *cinema* is therefore significant, as this indicates a shift in the perception and function of these films, from a more specifically scientific-interest focus, to the broader mythic tendencies of popular genre forms, such as heritage cinema.

So far as it has frequently been defined, the latter form makes use of a 'timeless' vision of the past, often by reference to specific locations and their architecture. In early formations of the term, this aesthetic was linked to films set in aristocratic or socially privileged contexts (country estates, boarding schools, elite universities): films like *Chariots of Fire* (1981), *Another Country* (1984), *Maurice* (1987) or *Howard's End* (1992), or prestige television mini-series such as *Brideshead Revisited* (Granada, 1982). Accordingly, this cinematic tendency was often linked to a conservative/Conservative politics of idealized stability and social order: an 'attempt to turn away from contemporary realities and seek an image of national stability in some golden age of the past'.[29] Early efforts to theorize heritage as a cinematic aesthetic, especially

Andrew Higson's early arguments on the subject, were perhaps overly eager, in a reflective and over-determined way, to link these representations with the prevailing political ideologies of Thatcherism.[30] Such aesthetics, in reality, both precede and exceed this political moment. Indeed, Higson's wider work on national myth-making in cinema identifies the importance of an idealized and pictorial aesthetic to British cinema as far back as the silent era.[31] Yet this itself underlines the persistence and embedded significance of such aesthetics within English film traditions.

As a way of understanding heritage cinema as a popular cinema, it is useful to identify the importance of a *continuity* with the past, as much as distance from it. Part of heritage cinema's presumed appeal links to the wider interest in heritage as a form of cultural industry.[32] In the forms of actual sites and properties that are open to visitors, its aesthetics connect present to history in a living embodiment of the past. The 'eternal' quality of medieval or early modern architecture, for example, is based as much on an identifiable sense of endurance and persistence across time: by inference, such architectural structures, and their endurance, convey an enduring image of idealized, even naturalized, *social* structures. In this light, the use of heritage aesthetics to engage here with *science* is somewhat paradoxical. Science and technology tend to be absent from earlier discussions of heritage culture, unless cited as reasons why people retreat into the past in the first place. For Patrick Wright, writing in the 1980s, science was part of the same rationalizing forces of capitalism that provided an impetus for the heritage imaginary itself. Science's claims to provide 'an abstract and universal form of knowledge' are precisely what distance it, for some, from the grounded experience of 'everyday life', yet science seems to preside over so many aspects of everyday life as a 'legitimating world-view'.[33] Unlike religion or the arts and the humanities, science offers 'a great increase in knowledge' but lacks the 'moral capacity [to] give meaningful sanction either to life or to the social order'.[34] Instead, science adds to the 'rationalized routine' of a society; one in which the 'ability to work within the terms of [its] institutions becomes a prerequisite of survival'.[35] This then begs the question what implications such arguments have for films like *The Theory of Everything* and *The Imitation Game*. What forms do such films take in order to negotiate the tensions between narrative and generic expectation and its 'abstract', 'rationalized' content? But also, why employ such heritage generic frameworks to encompass the figure of the scientist in the first place?

Stephen Hawking's self-presentation to the British and world publics already involved the use of technological interfaces rather than 'direct' communication (his special chair, his electronic 'voice'), lending itself to the greater public perception of the man as a kind of disembodied brain or 'pure intellect'. Hawking in fact was, and remains, something of a British cultural 'brand' in itself.[36] *The Theory of Everything* represents only the latest in a line of popular cultural representations of Hawking, including a 2004 BBC drama, *Hawking* (with Benedict Cumberbatch, the lead in *The Imitation Game*, here playing Hawking), numerous self-presented television series, and various live-action, virtual or animated cameo turns in popular US shows. *The Theory of Everything* represents something slightly different, however, in its efforts to situate its subject within the aesthetic contexts of its specifically English production values. James Marsh's film is, for instance, attentive to the wide spaces, and the shapes and textures of its Cambridge University settings, where Hawking studied for his PhD, and subsequently became Lucasian Professor of Mathematics. The early parts of the film combine this emphasis on the forms and tones of a pre-industrial architecture with the apparently quite relaxed pursuit of advanced knowledge (where beer-drinking and sleeping-in seem part of the scholarly process). If anything, such representations only reassert a quietly conservative vision of privileged social strata. This is reinforced by the fact that, until at least the intervention of Hawking's wife Jane (from whose memoir the screenplay is adapted), this academic enclave is the fiefdom entirely of young and older (white) men.

As already highlighted, one of the paradoxes of the scientist biopic, especially as a popular form, is that it is premised on specific achievements the film itself cannot properly articulate, but can at best only imply or suggest. *The Theory of Everything* contributes to the mythologizing of national science and innovation, but in doing so has to deal with the perceived, and to a large extent intractable, 'cognitive gap' operating between high-end scientific research and its lay perception.[37] The film, in light of this fact, tends to get around scientific explanation with an impressionistic and symbolic visual system that becomes a shorthand for the work itself. Our first sight of Hawking has the camera pan out of a bicycle wheel onto his riding figure, an image of circularity that is then reiterated at numerous points in the film: a swirl of cream in a coffee cup, fire from burning coal reflected across the pupil, the patterns on the carpet inside

Figure 4.1 'Heritage' space as the Futures of Britain: Jane Wilde, Stephen Hawking and Cambridge University in *The Theory of Everything*. Directed by James Marsh © Focus Features/Universal Pictures 2014. All rights reserved.

Buckingham Palace. Similarly, the mise-en-scène of a specifically antiquated and privileged academic life consequently stands, in part, for this endeavour itself. Tellingly, the film's producers chose on the whole not to shoot the film in Trinity Hall College, where Hawking studied, but in the more prepossessing grounds of its bigger neighbour, St John's, used for most of the exterior scenes (Figure 4.1). The potency of using such locations in the contexts of the *scientist* biopic is that they are not restricted to the frozen, pictorial and nostalgic connotations of the architectural past. In effect, these images of the past are presages of the future, already premised, retrospectively, by the film itself, as a coming-into-being of the intellectually dynamic scientist of the present day.

Within the broader concerns of Brexit and this book, the main point emerging here concerns the related notions of nostalgia and national 'decline' that frequently cohere around critical discussions of heritage (as per the title of Wright's book, *On Living in an Old Country*; or in the more pointed subtitle of Robert Hewison's book *The Heritage Industry: Britain in a Climate of Decline*). Such an aesthetic, this argument goes, serves as a cushion or comforter against the ravages of Britain's post-imperial, declining-influence present. Within the terms of the scientist film, though, this use is nuanced. As I have just suggested, as much as *The Theory of Everything* looks backward in a manner appealing to the heritage imaginary, it marries this to a *forward-*looking narrative. In drawing on the star qualities of Hawking as a scientific figure, *The Theory of Everything* links its subject to a continuing project of scientific innovation and, in particular, the centrality of *Britain* to this project, that is by its very nature a rebuff to the broader narrative of decline. There is a symbolic consecration of Hawking at the film's conclusion, when he receives the Order of the Companions of Honour award at Buckingham Palace. But the film also offers a lay celebration and veneration of sorts, in a sequence set after the publication of *A Brief History of Time*, where Hawking delivers a lecture on his life and work to an assembled public audience. The contrast here with an earlier talk witnessed by the younger Hawking, in which the physicist Roger Penrose addresses a cramped, chalky classroom of mostly male, racially homogenous students and specialists – or indeed, Hawking's first public presentation of his black hole thesis, to a sparsely filled lecture hall of ageing and largely incredulous academics – is marked and strategic. The modern university setting is here bright and informal, its audience drawing not merely on specialist colleagues, but on a mainly young, mixed-gender and mixed-ethnicity cluster of students and enthusiasts. This valedictory image of the cosmologist is one of a very public and popular figure.

It is in this mixture of the past with the present, or rather the present anticipated in the past, that the film achieves its most persuasive effects. The film's largely nostalgic aesthetic enables it to make its strong claim for national scientific influence within the gentle and *unassertive* generic form of the period film. *The Theory of Everything* becomes in this way another effective vehicle of national soft power, consistent also with what I would term the 'soft' patriotism evident in other examples of recent British culture. We have already seen in the previous chapter that *Skyfall* has the trappings of a 'declinist' Bond film, especially in its emphasis on the vulnerability of London and loss of Empire. Yet its inevitable vindication of 007, and in turn the whole Bond series itself, allows the film to have its post-imperial cake and eat it too. There is a sleight of hand here. To acknowledge decline is to lay bare the ideological project of heritage culture, which *disavows* decline in its return to the past; but this acknowledgement, in turn, becomes a cultural assertion of a nation that evidently does *not* see itself in decline – because it is not forcefully trying to assert the fact.

One further effect of reducing Hawking's story to a form of myth is that it mitigates the possibility of dissenting voices or competing discourses around scientific research (there is, for instance, no apparent *contemporary* opposition to Hawking's work or theories depicted in the film). As a cinematic product, then, *The Theory of Everything* proves doubly beneficial from a national perspective, not only in its significance as a distinctively 'English' cinematic product, but also in its tacit endorsement of a particular scientific and academic culture for which Hawking, until and beyond his death in early 2018, was a star attractor. The collaboration of Cambridge University in the making of the film is understandable here, underlining as it does the importance of such soft cultural influences on the global status and reputation of the country's oldest and wealthiest academic institutions. In line with prevailing heritage tendencies around the promotion and reception of popular English cinema, moreover, the various properties used in the making of the film are identified in several online contexts and guides to visiting movie locations.[38]

Notably, and perhaps not coincidentally, while *The Theory of Everything* was in post-production the green light was finally announced on another biopic, *The Man Who Knew Infinity* (2015), after the project had spent several years stalled in development.[39] This, the first film allowed to be shot in Cambridge's Trinity College, focused on the life of Srinivasa Ramanujan (played in the film by *Slumdog Millionaire* star Dev Patel), the Indian mathematician who became a Fellow of the college and of the Royal Society in 1918, before dying at the early age of thirty-two. Like *The Theory of Everything*, *The Man Who Knew Infinity* is an equally respectful treatment of a respected biographical subject, and one which can make cinematic use of its prestige, 'past' settings and contexts, while also linking these to the continuities of the college's and the wider university's traditions (Figure 4.2). It also provides the opportunity to critically address historical questions of race and privilege, and the historical shortcomings of these English institutions, while at the same time, serving a valedictory function, the making of the film itself an indication of historical revision and progress.[40] As *The Theory of Everything* did for Hawking, *The Man Who Knew Infinity* can provide a retrospective evaluation both of Ramanujan and of consequently his place of study, happily for the latter, despite Ramanujan's premature death. Both films, then, in similar ways, epitomize the synergy between old English institutions, the content strategies of English film production companies and the efforts to validate representations of the past through their continuity with the present: all in a form of combined promotional vehicle for the various stakeholders.

Whether or not universities such as Cambridge reap any obvious benefit from such films, or indeed need their help at all, is both debatable and, I expect, difficult to demonstrate. Yet the profile of these two films, and especially

Figure 4.2 Dev Patel as Srinivasa Ramanujan in *The Man Who Knew Infinity*: Critical history and institutional promotion combine. Directed by Matthew Brown © Warner Bros./IFC Films 2015. All rights reserved.

The Theory of Everything, tied as it is so closely with the global ubiquity of Hawking as a form of cultural icon, cannot help but re-inscribe the centrality of such institutions to a conception of English intellectual life, and to its global reputation, with obvious publicity benefits. Statistics offered earlier in 2018 by the *Times Higher Education*, indeed, show that Oxford and Cambridge, the anticipated impact of Brexit notwithstanding, had re-emerged on top of the *Times* world university rankings, displacing the California Institute of Technology as the previous leader, and inching above Harvard, MIT and London's Imperial College.[41] Such rankings are largely based on the research income that universities generate: the fact that the top of the list, as suggested above, is dominated by science- and technology-centred institutions suggests how significant research grants for scientific and technological innovations are to England's most ancient, and most photogenic, universities.

My broader argument here has been that the representational work in a film like *The Theory of Everything* does little to question this centrality, nor even much to explain it. Instead, complexity, contestation and context more broadly are smoothed over by a superficially architectural, impressionistic mise-en-scène, consolidating the scientist's status in the same process as failing to account for it. There is a similar confidence and universalist assumption around the film's narrative, as if it evidently speaks for all of us – something the shot of Hawking's most 'contemporary' public audience, in the scene I described above, works to underscore. As already noted at earlier points, this is precisely the kind of popular universalism that Working Title's production output has perennially looked to evoke, with evident commercial and critical results.

Once more, inasmuch as *The Theory of Everything*, as well as *The Man Who Knew Infinity*, are the products of particular filmmaking policies, they are also inherently political in their representations and, from the point of view of scientific research as a national business, their broadly informed aims. Debates around the EU referendum from this specific viewpoint would subsequently make this clear. The endorsement of the Remain camp on the part of the UK's scientific community, though not uncontested, was resounding. A cross-EU poll on the part of the leading science journal *Nature* indicated considerable support for Remain, with respondents highlighting the potential damage to research culture if Britain foregoes the economic funding infrastructure of the EU, the freedom of movement for researchers and, in turn, faces the draining of research expertise from outside the UK.[42] This was consistent with the overwhelming support for Remain on the part of UK university staff more broadly.[43]

As I know from personal academic experience, attracting undergraduate students, and especially post-graduate researchers and top-flight academics, is essential to the endurance of British universities in tables of world-leading institutions. Recruiting students and researchers from outside the UK, both for income and for prestige (which in turn generates more income), has become a vital part of university strategies, during a recent period in which academic institutions, supported less by government, have become more neoliberal and market-driven. Maintaining such levels of income and prestige has subsequently become an even greater anxiety for the country's top institutions in light of Brexit. It is little wonder, then, that cinema should be one of the means of bolstering institutional presence and reputation on cinema's global stage. As argued above, such cinema is never apolitical in its forms and goals. In the aftermath of the referendum, in fact, it has been striking how institutions like Oxford and Cambridge have been taken to task even by the mainly pro-EU sides of the British press. In a period of hiked student fees, alongside varied economic challenges to the public sector, the private wealth of Oxbridge colleges (Trinity alone has assets totalling £1.4bn), together with its perceived failure to diversify its student and staff bodies, has made the country's two most famous universities a target for anti-elitist discussion. Evidently, films like *The Theory of Everything* and *The Man Who Knew Infinity* are invested in either avoiding or gently refuting this perspective; and in this same gesture, we can recognize the more urgent agenda underpinning their production and representations.

The machine in the sitting room: Technology, mimesis and Englishness

The Theory of Everything exemplifies many of the qualities typifying a globally English cinema in the immediate pre-Brexit contexts: above all, its construction and celebration of a certain idea and iconography of Englishness, that also constructs a *mythic* contemporary England. On the surface, its close contemporary *The Imitation Game* seems a very similar sort of film. As we will see, though, the film is ultimately more reflexive and critical, especially in its uses of nostalgia. *The Theory of Everything* draws on the notionally 'declinist' contexts and aesthetics of heritage in order to make its contemporary, anti-declinist narrative even more amenable. Yet it is precisely this narrative of decline that *The Imitation Game* calls into question. In turn, the film offers an important reflection on the uses of genre in relation to national identity.

In the previous section of this chapter, I touched on the difficulties of broaching scientific ideas in popular cinematic form. Here, the difficulty and intractability of dealing with the scientific on film itself works as a mimetic strategy, a means of embodying the *irreconcilability* of scientific representation with generic cinematic norms. The relevant point here, which I will explore through an analysis of *The Imitation Game*, is that such representations stretch the limits of a *culturally* or *generically determined* construction of truth. If not unbelievable as such – and as a biographical film, its representation comes inevitably with some truth claims – it at least invites us to rethink the frameworks through which the cinematic 'real', and also in this case the representation of a nation or national culture, is constructed. Why, for example, do particular strains of a national cinema output take on particular generic or aesthetic forms? The idiosyncratic and difficult figure of Alan Turing becomes emblematic in this respect, as a figure at once not only associated with English technological innovation, but also one positioned so uncertainly with regard to historical narratives of nation.

These tensions inherent to *The Imitation Game* are illustrated by a sequence early on in the film, when two police officers, investigating a robbery in Alan Turing's Manchester home, are looking around his rooms. The inspector asks his sergeant what the Cambridge professor is doing in the North. 'Something with ... *machines*', he replies, the last quizzical word lingering as his attention is drawn left towards off-screen space. A shift of angle, now from this unseen space, shows us the inspector approaching, his expression in turn bemused and intrigued, as the camera rises slightly. From the reverse angle we now see the object of their gaze. It is also the object to which the extended initial sequence, with its teasing montage of slow tracking shots, and its glimpses of fragments – sketches, diagrams and various electronic debris – has been leading us: Turing's 'Universal Machine', the Computer. This early shot establishes the film's key aesthetic movement: on the one hand, the trappings of English period film, with its 1950s provincial *mise-en-scène* and on the other, the efforts to communicate an idea of the technologically new, and of the future.

As Steve Neale has pointed out, verisimilitude in film can be viewed in two distinct though inter-relating ways. On the one hand, the 'real-seeming' nature of a film relates to the consistency of its representations within the recognized conventions of cinematic genre.[44] The period or heritage drama, for instance, makes sense to us in terms of its use of historically contextual settings, an often restrained, static pictorial style, and certain ideas around casting and acting. Any deviations to these expectations would oblige us mentally to reconfigure our idea of the genre involved. Genre is in this respect an established contract between viewers and a body of films over time, and these genres can also become closely associated with the filmmaking contexts that produce them: such is the strong association with genres like the period drama, it effectively stands in for an idea of 'British cinema' itself. There is of course no imperative to take generic representations for the real itself. Yet the *political* issue of genre, Neale argues, is the point when this 'generic verisimilitude' elides into *cultural verisimilitude*: the point, in other words, when an arbitrary and constructed generic truth is taken for cultural or historical truth. Or, to pick up on my points at the beginning of this book, the point where the mythic aspects of a national cinema elide into presumed 'reflections' of the nation itself.

The opening scene of *The Imitation Game*, then, encapsulates some of the formal negotiations between generic and cultural verisimilitude. This early confrontation with Turing's machine is framed within the almost monochromatically washed-out tones of the house's wallpaper and furnishings. The policeman, as well as Turing himself on first appearance – hunched over on the kitchen floor, sweeping up spilled cyanide – inhabits the same naturalist mise-en-scène we might identify in, say, other recent representations of the Second World War – or post-war period, such as *Vera Drake* (2004), *Atonement* (2007) or *Their Finest* (2017). But the computer complicates this. It is not just the scale and material nature of the computer, with its structure of wires, valves and components, which situates it strangely within the setting. It is also its visual composition, the symmetry and frontality through which it occupies the widescreen cinematic space. Such framings more typically connote the other-worldly or rationalized spaces of science-fiction cinema.[45] In *2001: A Space Odyssey* (1968), for instance, frontality and symmetry dominate framing to particularly alien effect, precisely because such compositions break with the more unsymmetrical patterns of the 'natural' world, or the messiness and different levels of human interaction. It is a framing, though, to which *The Imitation Game* will return, when we see Christopher's predecessor, the Bletchley Park code-breaking machine, at work. The mise-en-scène here even goes to the extent of using overhead strip lights and desk-top lamps to create an impression of converging light moving towards its centre, as in the 'star-gate' sequence of *2001* (Figure 4.3).

Figure 4.3 The computer, situated futuristically within a 'natural' mise-en-scène, in *The Imitation Game*. Directed by Morten Tyldum © The Weinstein Company 2014. All rights reserved.

We have already seen how, in *The Theory of Everything*, there is an effort to integrate the visual representation of theoretical physics through a narratively associative and impressionistic mise-en-scène. Such aesthetic approaches work, in effect, to domesticate scientific otherness. The popular emergence of the computer in Western culture was precisely in the decades following the Second World War: this was at the point where Turing's vision of the Universal Machine was becoming realized in the research workshops of companies like Remington Rand and IBM, and where new technologies of computational power surfaced in the form of various acronymic machines: from the ENNIAC to the EDVAC, the BINAC and the UNIVAC.[46] As Andrew Utterson highlights, the otherness represented by these machines, and therefore its perceived *threat* to everyday working and cultural life, becomes a subject of narrative and aesthetic negotiation for popular fiction film. Early films that featured the new computers moved between a representational emphasis on the computer's incomprehensibility, through the 'proxy signification' of screens and blinking lights, and towards a form of anthropomorphism, in the use of more personifying acronyms and the establishing of an intrinsically human relationship with the technology.[47] Making the technology amenable to popular audiences was an important ploy in the promotion of these strange, though increasingly visible, machines.

In *The Imitation Game*, by contrast, the Machine occupies a deliberately strange position, cool and other-worldly within its domestic confines. The important difference here, then, between *The Imitation Game* and *The Theory of Everything*, is the former's resistance to consolidating the machine within what Higson calls the 'mythologising tendencies' common to popular English film.[48] Higson in fact suggests that the depiction of 'localized' or 'ordinary' Englishness in films is divergent enough from the more familiar generic frameworks of culturally English cinema to assume a 'democratic' dimension. Films such as *Vera Drake*, *Billy Elliot* and *The Land Girls* (1998), all of which focus on 'ordinary protagonists' in a recent or more distant past, depart in this sense from some of the more dominant conventions of popular national cinema. Since ideas of England and Englishness are frequently constructed *through* popular cinematic representation, such films 'effectively demythologise' these ideas.[49] This is the case too in *The Imitation Game*, though not entirely in the sense described by Higson. Higson's perspective here tends to set up the politics of representation, and an idea of realism, largely in terms of competing socio-economic or class-based, authenticated spaces. *The Imitation Game* invests instead in problematizing the issue of representation and mimesis more specifically: the limitations, in other words, of seeking to represent 'Englishness' only through the competing realisms of the national period drama. By situating the machine so prominently and conspicuously, in other words, it implicitly asks what is typically missing from prior representations.

The presence of the machine, in other words, calls into question what we mean by 'realistic' cinematic space itself in a national narrative context. If the machine is incongruous within generic frameworks, the presence of technology in the English period film invites us to think about its significance as a structuring *absence*, or repressed context, within this cinema. The American literary critic Leo Marx wrote about the 'Machine in the Garden' of American writing, especially in the nineteenth century.[50] Marx's discussion focused on the way the pastoral imagination of American romantic and transcendentalist writing, emerging at the same time as urbanization and the American railroad, was always and already shaped by the emerging technologies of an industrialized economy. Technology was in this respect the 'counterforce' to a form of American pastoral without which it would not have made sense. But it is also the thing that the pastoral has to disavow, in order to make sense at all. My point here, similarly, is that the machine's actual presence – not so much in the garden, but in the fusty sitting room or wartime bunkers of English film – underscores the idea that the 'ordinary' contexts it otherwise evokes, and from which it deviates, offered an incomplete version of reality. The generic vision of the English past, in other words, is its own 'counterforce' to a technological context that is disavowed. This, indeed, is part of *The Imitation Game*'s fixation with the covert and the secret; of truths buried, repressed and revealed.

The Imitation Game's formal character therefore draws attention to the unfamiliarity of this technological context, while at the same time establishing the machine's presence within a revisionist approach to representing the Second World War. *The Imitation Game*'s precedents in this regard are a sizeable line of mostly English films, whose own celebration of technological achievement is embedded within often backward-looking and conciliatory narratives of collective or individual technological endeavour. These are films, Robert Murphy suggests, poised between 'the pleasures of peace' and the desire to remember 'the drama and excitement of the war'.[51] War movies, he adds, 'were one of the few things that fathers [who had served in or lived through the war] could enthusiastically share with their sons'.[52] It is also an era of war films marked as much by the focus on everyday, working-class heroes as it is by films in which hegemonic class structures, of officers and ordinary soldiers, sought to reassert themselves through myth.[53] The post-war cinema was ideologically positioned to endorse the validity and aims of the preceding war, and also to reinforce the idea of national value(s) in the aftermath of victory, when the immediate material benefits of this victory – as Britain, rebuilding its economy and infrastructure, endured privation – were far from apparent. The ideological practices of a heritage cinema are in effect visible here, in a period of economic austerity and loss of global (imperial) influence – another link, albeit on distinct scales, between post-war contexts and those of the 2010s. As Frayling notes, the spate of 'boffin' films that emerged in the years after the Second World War, but which specifically looked back to the war for its narratives – *School for Secrets* (1946), *The Small Back Room* (1948), *The Dam Busters* (1955) and to a certain extent *The Bridge on the River Kwai* (1957) – makes cultural sense as 'play[ing] to Second World War nostalgia at a time of austerity and the perceived beginnings of national decline'.[54]

The emphasis on technology in some of these films is, however, far from arbitrary. Frayling's qualification here as to the *perceived* nature of British global decline is telling, reminding us as he does of Britain's emphasis on aircraft research and development during this same period (not to mention Britain's development of a nuclear bomb around this same time).[55] These technological contexts are underscored by the focus of contemporary films such as *The Sound Barrier* (1952) and *The Net* (1953), and in a slightly different way *The Dam Busters*, which all dealt with this same subject. The mystery in this respect is why we should talk about 'decline' at all, especially when it comes to scientific and technological research. C. P. Snow's polemical 1959 paper on the 'Two Cultures' charged the dominant British intellectual classes with being both ignorant and outdated with regard to scientific and technological ideas. But the suggestion that Britain was intellectually backward in this area overstates the case. US technological development and computer construction in the same post-war period are largely associated with the emergence of its military-industrial complex (the ENIAC, for instance, launched in 1946, was used mainly in the development of thermonuclear weapons). As the historian David Edgerton has shown, there is little obvious evidence of a similar narrative in histories of the British state; yet during this same period, the number of military personnel grew, university graduates and professional elites shifted more towards technical and scientific careers, and defence spending increased.[56] The claim that Britain was somehow scientifically lagging behind could in fact be strategically mobilized on both sides of the political fence. On one side, the nation's technological shortcomings are evoked in the call for a stronger military and higher defence spending; on the other, they are used to justify the importance of modernization. Both of these political emphases at once prove, but tactically disavow, Britain's more credible post-war identity as a 'warfare state'.

As Edgerton remarks, films such as the ones mentioned above focus on ingenious national *responses* to hostility, and therefore construct the idea of an England 'as it was thought to be': in other words, 'as a nation which is attacked, not a nation which attacks'.[57] Such narrative approaches tactically understate the actual nature of the country's military commitment, hostility and rationality (the Second World War programme of bombing, most notably, culminating in the destruction of Dresden); or the way that, after the war, the majority of existing research and development funding went into national defence.[58] It is in fact for Edgerton the *absence* of a technological narrative in British post-war history, and perhaps part of its developing tendency towards forms of 'soft' power, that is itself, 'paradoxically, a measure of the power of th[e technocratic] tradition in Britain'.[59] The certainty of national technological power is made evident by its undemonstrative assertion.

If popular English cinema, as is still the case in recent contexts, seems fated to reiterate versions or legacies of the Second World War, reinforcing its centrality in the same process as trying to question its narratives, it can nevertheless work to engage with the mode of representation itself. To return to my earlier point, any simplistic inclination either to paint these films with a generic broad brush or to take them for history itself can overlook the ways in which screen engagements with the past are at the same time about the *means* of representing the past. Screening the past can be a process, as Pam Cook argues, 'of contestation ... of collection and reassembly'.[60] Cook argues that the actuality of any period will always be elusive, relying on existent cultural impressions and reference points. The implication here is that 'there is no "real thing" when it comes to reconstructing history, just an endless series of replicas' – amongst which is cinema itself.[61]

Appropriately, then, *The Imitation Game* plays on its title's etymological ambiguity, since questions of imitation are also questions of *mimesis*. In turn, they become questions of filmic realism, and how this filmic realism elides into forms of cultural belief. Before we even get to the computer, in fact, *The Imitation Game* has already encouraged us to be on our guard. The opening sequence's combination of fragmented narrative, over-layered with Cumberbatch's cryptic voiceover instructions to 'pay attention', and its sense of visual movement towards its respective centres – the man at the desk, the machine itself – suggests that the film's secret, in a film about secrecy, is being conveyed by barely perceptible relays and channels. As a biopic, it should be noted, *The Imitation Game*'s broader focus is less on the breaking of the Enigma code, than it is on the machinations through which Turing's life story and legacy were kept for decades from the public eye, and his shameful mistreatment concealed. This involved, on the one hand, the secrecy preserved around Bletchley's Government Code and Cypher School, in the interests of national post-war security; and on the other, Turing's eventual prosecution for homosexuality, and the subsequent hormone treatment that may have contributed to his suicide in 1954.[62] In validating its subject retrospectively, against the grain of Turing's contemporary England, *The Imitation Game* fulfils many of the narrative generic demands of the biographical film: by their own nature, like the epic protagonist, the biopic subject is often an individual at odds with their time and place proved right by history. At the same time, in its narrative, the film also takes a critical aim at the same society that would otherwise appropriate Turing as 'their own'.

The film's stylistic departures from some of the erstwhile norms of the period film are, in a formal sense, aligned with this revisionist approach to historical narratives. As Higson writes of the heritage film genre, its aesthetic epitomizes the postmodern displacement of 'historical context' and its 'material dimensions' with a particularly nostalgic aesthetic, characterized primarily by a highly photographic and pictorial style that freezes and displaces the material contexts of history.[63] By contrast, the approach of director Morten Tyldum in *The Imitation Game* exemplifies a dynamic and far from static approach to form and narration. The opening displays a range of camera movements and quirky, non-realistically motivated framings, such as overhead shots; the editing, meanwhile, is more associative than respectful of classical continuity form, inviting us to work out the connections between the spaces and objects, rather than clearly indicate the spatial or narrative continuity between each image. Because *The Imitation Game* never settles into a clear generic shape, the film emphasizes how its historical representations are literally imitative, *playing at* being a certain 'type' of film – one that can never adequately contain its complex subject matter. 'Pay attention': this is the film's request to its immediate viewers concerning the film's story, but also a caution about genre cinema itself, and its constructions of national myth.

Conclusion: 'Think Different!' Science, Brexit and globalism

I have noted the congruity with which both *The Imitation Game* and *The Theory of Everything*, released within months of each other, combine to form something of an English genius-industry for cinematic export value. In 2015's *Steve Jobs*, directed by Danny Boyle, Turing's media status is further consecrated when his photograph is proposed by Jobs for one of Apple's 'Think Different' figures, to be used in the company's 1997 advertising campaign. In the film, Jobs decides not to use Turing's image as his former CEO has not heard of him: a neat scripting touch that retrospectively positions the Apple founder's appropriation of Turing well in advance of his more 'national' recognition (the formal apology for Turing's treatment on the part of the British government, for instance, was only issued in 2010). Andrew Hodges's 1985 biography of Turing, on which the screenplay for *The Imitation Game* is based, was itself already attentive throughout to the way Turing's achievements and character were both in line with the largely technocratic direction of society and power of the era, and *at the same time* out of step with the prevailing ideological and moral currents. The early phase of the war with Germany, as Hodges sees it, and as *The Imitation Game* depicts it, was a domestic conflict of ideas and organization: that between public school sporting values and 'patriotism', and the application of *'intelligence'*.[64]

As I have argued here, Turing's uneasy positioning within both the British establishment and twentieth-century history is projected through the situation of the film itself, in terms of its ambiguous relationship with both the national and global film cultures. Integrating its technological forms into an incongruous English cinematic context is to realign and reconfigure representational elements from the past, charging them in the process with new meanings gathered with the help of foresight. To this extent, *The Imitation Game* amply satisfies the period film's expectations of offering representations of the past, though it does this through the perspective of the technologized *present*. This reconfiguring of the past is conveyed through a visual approximation, in terms of both mise-en-scène and camera movement, of precisely the type of networked, electronic flows that would at once be ushered in and also accelerated by the revolution in computing technologies. As *The Imitation Game*'s narrative reminds or reveals to us, these were already being used covertly in the war effort, but were central to hastening its eventual end. The initial sequence in the film of relayed messages, through radio transmission, telephone and then printed words, shows us at once an intensified, spatially and temporally compressed vision of telecommunications in the immediate post-war era. At the same time, it is one that is almost parodically inefficient in its staggered processes, compared to the instantaneity of information access in the new cybernetic age. As a film, *The Imitation Game* is produced in the modern contexts of 'big data' practices, where masses of information are scanned in order to interpret and predict actions and events. Part of the film's contemporary relevance is that the Bletchley team's application of decrypted information, used in British naval strategy, was an early example of the latter. As if to highlight this fact, the film's opening conspicuously dwells on the period details of pre-digital communications, such as switchboard operators, short-wave radios and typists. Similarly, in the scene described earlier, where the office lamps converge on the central machine, the latter's incessant processing in the image's centre, reinforced aurally on the sound track, overwhelms the fruitless work of 'analogue' data-processing and individual manpower, carried out by pencil and paper in the foreground.

Given the wider aims of this book, all this discussion inevitably begs the big question: what is the significance of discussing *The Imitation Game*, along with its narrative and aesthetic approaches, in the contexts of Brexit?

The answer here relates to the importance of the Second World War both to the national self-image and to the domestic and global perception of British and, above all, English cinema. As noted earlier, the fact that popular English cinema in the years immediately following the EU referendum should turn so consistently to the Second World War, if largely coincidental, does have a correlative significance, as it reveals the expectations of an English popular cinema at this juncture – or indeed, at almost any juncture since 1945. The continued or even re-emergent potency of the Second World War as *the* myth of Englishness links to the heroic idea of self-reliance and self-sufficiency fostered by that particular event. The war's ceaseless re-enactment in film, literature and television in the post-war decades only consolidated this vision further in the post-war national imaginary.[65] A film such as *The Imitation Game*, in one respect, sits within these same national generic frameworks and traditions. Yet, on the basis of this chapter's argument, we might just as readily ask how, or indeed why, we should situate these films so readily within the contexts of 'English' filmmaking at all, so uneasily do they actually sit within its production or aesthetic parameters.

I have addressed in this chapter the ways in which some aspects of the national culture, less readily available to such popular discourses – the initially awkward fit, in this instance, between science and heritage – can still be co-opted to popular effect. As I have noted, the brand recognition of already transnational production companies like Working Title often relies on a strategic but effective 'underdog' tone. Many of their films – romantic comedies, sports movies or genre parodies – exploit the image of 'a genteel, under-achieving or unassertive Britain', but an image that is also assertive, as a form of product differentiation within the very same globalized cinematic framework Working Title has helped build.[66]

Superficially these films are 'English'; yet what we might think of as the *proprietorial* workings of biographical and period film, conflating the historical figure with the nation – the 'Genius of Britain' with which this chapter began – is problematized, as we have seen, in *The Imitation Game*. The film's Turing – and by extension, the film itself – operates less as a figure of uncontested national history and culture, and more as a contested and contesting figure appropriated by global and transnational cultural, political and economic constituencies. While hinting, like *The Theory of Everything*, at a revisionist positioning of national technological history and the narrative of decline, *The Imitation Game* ultimately calls into question the stability or integrity of such narratives. Beyond this, it even calls into question the coherence of 'the national' at all within the accelerated and intensified global flows of labour, economics and information. Explicit in the film's opening documentary footage of hungry Britons, and in its backdrop narrative of the Atlantic convoys, is of course the tacit acknowledgement that Britain could not go it alone, but was vitally dependent on the supply chain from both the United States and Britain's overseas colonies (something the more pugnacious *Darkest Hour*, despite some of its revisionist elements, mostly plays down). This is part of the film's critical historical context, yet *The Imitation Game* in this respect also uses its narrative, and difficult, estranged biographical subject, to figure for its own production circumstances: a film directed by a Norwegian, written by an American (Graham Moore) and sharing production credits between UK and US companies.[67] Ultimately, *The Imitation Game* is deft in its capacity to offer up a 'culturally English' film that at the same time reveals the problem of limiting such terms to exclusive and hemmed-in national boundaries. Not unlike *The Theory of Everything*, it is an 'English' film mostly dependent on the will and investment of others (I explore this idea further, in relation to Working Title films, in the following chapter).

It is not just, then, its willingness to engage critically with the histories of Britain's wartime and post-war character, or with national illusions of independent strength, that make *The Imitation Game* a key cinematic touchstone in the post-referendum contexts. While we can hardly call it prescient, the film works as an important narrative within many of the discourses around recent English film and its significance in the contexts of Brexit. Indeed, what stands out above all in this film, but also in *The Theory of Everything*, is the extent to which both scientists operate as English (cinematic) figures by virtue of their *international* appropriation and collaboration – even if, in *The Theory of Everything*, this is more implicit than obvious. In terms of his or her capacity to be corralled into mythic narratives of the nation, in fact, while actually operating within an international and collaborative model of production and distribution, the modern scientist becomes a supremely allegorical figure for the practices of 'independent' English filmmaking in a globalized economy. Speaking in the early 2000s, in his then position as Chair of the UK Film

Council, Working Title's Tim Bevan referred to the centrality of 'diverse teams' to innovation and creativity in the British film industry.[68] Just as we might properly understand a popular English cinema mainly in its capacity to attract global investors, creative partners and audiences, the 'national' character of both Hawking and Turing, but also of these two recent films about them, relies more on the idea of Britain as part of an international nexus – not a radiant hub, or shiningly self-sufficient island.

This is the same appeal to collaboration and the vitality of transnational working relationships that, as mentioned above, informed the wider scientific and academic community's opposition to Leave in the 2016 referendum. As I have argued in this chapter, these films might be seen to inform uncritically the persistent myths of Britain's genius and exceptional status. But in their complexity and ambiguities, they might also offer some direction for a culturally English cinema in the contexts of Brexit: one that is critically alert to the paradoxes and instabilities of the national, and the often-problematic role of cinema in the construction of history. It might also be a cinema attuned to the importance of international collaboration, and critical, in turn, of the myths of isolation and independence.

5

Through a screen, darkly: Austerity genres, Brexit topographies and the precarity of national cinema

Introduction

A persistent issue addressed in this book is the relevance of genre to questions of national cinematic identity. In itself, though, identifying the *types* of genre film at work in such contexts is only half the task, since we need to ask how a particular genre comes into being in the first place. Why, in this case, does it come into being *here* and *at a particular time*? Genres, as the study of films in cultural and industrial contexts shows, are the evolving result of an interrelationship between audiences and producers, often the fruits of filmmaking trial and error. Equally, the forms and content of genres are not etched immutably in stone but are subject to evolutions in form and content.[1] The reasons for this are hardly random and rarely just attributable to societal or cultural shifts. Rather, as I argue here, genres in a popular English context are contingent upon varied and wider economic and industrial forces. Continuing my discussion from the previous two chapters, then, this chapter considers the significance of global contexts to the production of a 'national' cinema.

This is an important inflection, as it reminds us what any given genre film 'reflects' is, to a large extent, the *film industry* circumstances in which it is produced and which precede the social and cultural contexts within which the films are, eventually, released. This is also important to bear in mind in the contexts of popular English cinema, as it reminds us that genres, especially in national contexts beyond Hollywood, are hardly ever autonomous: rather, they are vulnerable to evolving global circumstances and trends. We have already seen, in Chapter 3, how this plays out in relation to recent 'epic' forms such as the Arthurian film. In the last chapter, meanwhile, we saw how the scientist biopic, produced by transnationally operating companies like Working Title, is situated somewhere between global genre frameworks and the pursuit of national product differentiation.[2] But even the apparently totemic staples of inward investment 'British cinema' such as *Harry Potter* and the James Bond films, also discussed elsewhere in this book, are more contingent than inevitable. As I argued earlier, *Skyfall*, which had emerged out of precarious financial circumstances for its producing studios, represented a significant shift in the series' approach, partly in relation to what was happening in wider global cinema. Meanwhile, franchises such as the *Harry Potter* films, even if they do give impetus to certain established types of popular English cinema, such as 'YA', and other literary adaptations, are mainly outliers within the field. As I also noted in Chapter 3, though, other efforts to emulate the success of the Rowling series (including *Legend of the Sword*) have been much less successful: a point that gives the lie to any reductive idea that a culturally English cinema will always sell in a global, or even domestic, market.

As I argued in that earlier chapter, the fate of the epic English film at this historical juncture underscored the fragility of both English cinema as a brand and the potency of its national myths on a wider scale. These are also important reminders that popular cinema in a national context represents the efforts, on the part of a broader film industry, to compete on a global level. In itself, this inevitably suggests how contingent is the reliance on, or assumptions around, specific genres in the contexts of popular English film. Andrew Higson says as much when he argues that culturally English genres should be considered more 'in terms of production cycles'. They are, he suggests, 'loose bundles of attractions and ingredients that can be mobilised by filmmakers in different ways'.[3] Whether or not filmmakers will work in particular genres, Higson continues, 'will depend to some extent on what has proved successful on previous occasions'.[4] As noted above, this does not preclude the possibility that filmmakers and producers will take into account what they assume, or hope, will appeal to domestic audiences as well as (where relevant) international ones.

Part of the work in this chapter is therefore to define more precisely what we mean by the representation, or reflection, of socio-economic, cultural or political contexts in these films. It is important here to acknowledge the potentially leading way in which such analysis can be carried out. There is always the possibility, for instance, that our discussion of a national cinema, in terms of how it reflects broader contexts, is prescribed by the films that are successful – rather than, for example, the majority of films less widely seen and which may, taken together, tell us much more about the time and place they come from.[5] In the first chapter, I noted how Chris Smith's ebullient claims for British film in 1997, a key element in his *Creative Britain* agenda, were based on the impact of just four films: a small fraction of the total output of British films produced that year.[6] The mid-1990s to the early 2000s more broadly was a period that saw the domestic and international success of various mid-budget films, as topographically ranging as *Four Weddings and a Funeral* (1995), *Notting Hill* (1999), *Bean* (1997), *Love Actually* (2003), *Trainspotting* (1996), *The Full Monty* (1997) and *Billy Elliot* (2000). Exactly what such a cluster of films can tell us about the country in which they were produced is questionable: indeed, many of these films have been critically targeted precisely for their failure to engage with the more complex and contested social and economic contexts of their era.[7] If such films, as was indeed the case, contributed to a highly marketable image of England and other parts of Britain during this period – an image on which Smith drew in *Creative Britain* – does this suggest something unique, culturally, about this particular time? Or, from an empirical perspective at least, does it only tell us that, at this particular time, the international cinematic market was receptive to these types of films (and unreceptive to many others)?

Put bluntly, speaking of a national cinema in a globally focused cinema economy, how 'we' see 'ourselves' is, to a significant extent, dependent on what other people want, and also *don't* want, to see in us. If the national in this way is both *imagined* and *produced* through cinematic forms, it is vulnerable and fragile, shifting and fluid in relation to its anticipated or real audiences. This also has an impact on certain generic forms, which find themselves adapting to different, and in this case more austere, economic and industrial circumstances. As I argue here, some of the films produced in these contexts offer a sometimes unsettled and unsettling perspective on contemporary genre film within popular English cinema. This, I argue, is as much to do with the uncertain global place of a popular English cinema in the early 2010s. Up to this point, I have focused mainly on the ways a popular English cinema works to disavow or repudiate narratives of fragmentation and decline. Brexit as an imaginary works through this same process; in practical and political terms, it brings acutely into view Britain's more questionable global status and independence – and above all, the question of its self-sufficiency and sustainability as a nation within a globalized world system. The possibility of disavowing this codependency, then, is a frequent feature in popular English film. Yet this disavowal becomes problematic, and much less viable, when the same globalized system constrains and constricts the possibilities of such a cinema to operate in the first place.

The first part of this chapter, then, uses a genre case study to explore the limitations of self-sufficiency and independence, as far as claims to a national cinema are concerned. I draw attention to the ways that wider material contexts around genre and film production impact upon the content, and also the reception, of such films. Following this, the second part of the chapter focuses on two films that extend the parameters of national cinematic space while also highlighting, like the films discussed earlier in the chapter, an important, culturally resonant tonal shift in their uses of genre. As I discuss throughout, as much as these films can be said to refocus genre content to changing cultural or political contexts, ultimately, what we see in these films is their textual relationship to genre and to other earlier films. As this then suggests, in terms of some of the evolving forms and content in such genre films – and above all, in some of the diminished expectations they exhibit – we see a renegotiation of what a 'national cinema' means at this recent point in time.

Working Title and the challenges of independence

It is hardly surprising that in a book about popular English cinema, every chapter has so far has made reference to at least one film produced by Working Title. Formed in 1984, Working Title has, since the 1990s, been the most successful and well-known film production company working out of the UK. It has even become a cinematic brand in itself, conjuring up images of a certain type, and increasingly certain types, of film. It has worked to the tune of over $1 billion in UK box-office receipts alone – a small figure compared to the significant sums reaped through the films' international exports.[8]

More specifically, Working Title has developed brand-recognition through its association with key creative personnel, with whom the company has enjoyed a long-term relationship. These include, most prominently, screenwriter and director Richard Curtis, whose work across both his original screenplays and adaptations has shaped the company's core identity (through *Four Weddings and a Funeral*, *Love Actually*, *Bridget Jones's Diary* [2001] and more recently, *Yesterday* [2019]). We can also identify, alongside Curtis, actors associated with his films, such as Hugh Grant, Colin Firth and Rowan Atkinson (who, alongside his *Bean* films, also stars in Working Title's *Johnny English* series [2003–2018]). We should also highlight the director-star-writing team of Edgar Wright and Simon Pegg, who have made three films together for the company (*Shaun of the Dead* [2004], *Hot Fuzz* [2007] and *The World's End* [2013]). More recently, director Joe Wright has crafted a fruitful creative relationship with Working Title, mainly through his takes on the literary adaptation and the period drama (*Pride and Prejudice* [2005], *Atonement* [2007], *Anna Karenina* [2011] and *Darkest Hour* [2017]). As much as there is a Working Title 'signature', then, we can establish it around some of these frameworks. Firstly, comedies, based frequently around cultural clashes, and especially the clash between the UK and America, be this at the level of plot or, in the case of films like *Johnny English* or the Wright–Pegg parodies, of genre meeting English contexts.[9] Secondly, 'fish out of water' tales of British characters finding themselves out of their depths, yet usually winning the day. And thirdly, period and literary dramas, thriving on the notional appeal of English literary and historical figures to global cinematic markets.

Working Title is a 'British' success story, yet as analysts of their output have observed, the company's emblematic associations with British cinema need to be qualified in the light of its particular relationship with the United States and a still US-centric production and distribution context.[10] The success story of Working Title is often seen in light of a British production and distribution context dominated by the American major studios, one in which a minority number of American films takes in a substantial majority of the global theatrical box-office.[11] Within this context, the standard model for British production success is, as we have seen, inward investment, large-scale productions: blockbusters, to a large extent, that 'are for the most part too big to be initiated from the UK'.[12] In contrast to series such as *Harry Potter*,

Working Title is somewhat closer to the idea of 'a miniature British-based studio', one with more creative and financial control over its production slate and exemplified by the 'external development deals' it maintains with writers and directors like Curtis, Edgar Wright and Joe Wright.[13] Nevertheless, the actual circumstances of the company offer indication of the complex, and also precarious, nature of 'national' film industries in a globalized market.

Working Title's emergence in its first decade or so is linked with small-scale British films that found significant international notice and commercial success: films such as *My Beautiful Laundrette* (1985) and, especially, *Four Weddings and a Funeral*. It was their subsequent production and distribution deal with Universal, essentially an early development fund of $600m, moving up to $1.2bn in 2007, which gave them much of the reach they now enjoy.[14] As Nathan Townsend has noted, though, this deal has effectively made them an integral part of the parent company, with implications for its independence. Working Title officially operates not as an independent producer but as 'a directly owned subsidiary' of Universal.[15] As a working relationship with the Hollywood company, this makes the Working Title arrangement an exclusive one, yet one that involves certain negotiations. As Townsend explains, Working Title's autonomy extends only to films budgeted at under $25 million: any projects budgeted above that figure would be considered by the parent company on a 'case-by-case basis'.[16] Yet whether or not Working Title 'green-lights' a film also depends on whether or not the film is likely to be distributed – by Universal – or, in Fellner's words, it 'gets dumped'.[17] Whether or not any film will play, which often means play internationally, is a key part of the decision-making process. In reality, then, Working Title's deal with its Hollywood parent still relies substantially on 'consensus building and collective decision making'.[18]

Looking at things from this perspective, we are reminded how 'dominant versions of Britain and Britishness', such as those offered by Working Title's films, are not produced independently of globalized cultural and market forces.[19] In this respect these 'dominant versions' are at once variable and vulnerable to external factors. *Four Weddings and a Funeral*, produced within Working Title's previous deal with PolyGram (owned by the Dutch multinational Philips), was a surprise hit in the United States before anywhere else. It had in fact been released in such a way, strategically, in order to maximize its chances in the UK, which at the time were far from certain.[20] Its eventual and unexpected success owed something, as Geoffrey Macnab puts it, to 'luck'.[21] But more specifically, the film's success was rare in the wider contexts of PolyGram's output at that time and a film division that was actually losing money. As John Hill consequently argues, Working Title's emergence owed to the fact that it enjoyed 'the protection of a large multinational corporation that was prepared (and able) to sustain short-term losses'[22] until, that is, the company gets closed down, as PolyGram would be, by its owners in 1998.[23]

British cinema, as touched on at various points in this book, has a political function, in terms of its projection of certain versions or elements of the national that tally with broader agenda. This has implications, however, for what should or can be represented as such. As I have also noted, in a material sense, it is the health of the industry itself that serves as another marker of national well-being, in both cultural and economic terms. As I am suggesting here, though, such health is largely impermanent and cosmetic. Working Title has since the end of the 1990s been sheltered by its 'protection' deal with another multinational, in the form of Universal, but such a deal requires finding cinematic forms that work within a shifting, global cinematic economy. Such films have no obvious remit to reflect the 'real' contexts of British life at all, but rather what Townsend calls 'the versions of British and Britishness that persist … in the media ecology of the Hollywood studio system'.[24] This means that the potential impact of British film production is largely dependent upon this changing 'ecology' and, above all, on the broader capacity of 'Britishness' to maintain currency within it. The fortunes of a world-leading British company like Working Title, then, are inevitably linked both to the fortunes of its parent company and to the broader trends in Hollywood and the global film market. Working Title's main significance may be less, then, in terms of what it purports to show of British life than in the production decisions it makes, in terms of both what it thinks the rest of the world (such as the United States) wants and what it thinks the rest of the world thinks of Britain and its cinema. In other words, the particular spin we can put on Working Title is that it represents the circumstances of Britain first and foremost in a business-model and economic-dependency sense, and whatever the films themselves might offer us, in narrative or genre terms, is largely subordinate to this fact.

As argued in Chapter 1, Working Title's films, especially their London-based rom-coms, operate in a performative as much as representative way to construct a globally viable image of London ('Britain') as itself global.[25] Already globalized companies such as Working Title, therefore, represent less tangible and more ideological aspects of international cultural and economic relations. These are enacted, like the practices and processes of economic globalization itself, over the heads of many of the social constituencies the films cannot actually represent. A film like Working Title's *Darkest Hour*, meanwhile, is perhaps less telling as an allegory for Brexit (as I discussed in Chapter 3) and more telling as an analogy for the work of the company as a whole. *Darkest Hour* may intentionally or otherwise have tapped into a prevailing popular fascination with Churchill, promoting a potent narrative of a nation taking the offensive line in the face of external adversity.[26] But it also exists first and foremost as a *cinematic* offensive, in the fight to protect vested national interests, both cultural and economic. It is the Battle of Britain as one still being waged, on international cinema screens, at the impulse of film producers and film policy-makers. Yet in the broader contexts of Brexit, in terms of industry capital and the soft-power benefits of cinema, this is a significant battle. As I have argued throughout this book, the competition for cinematic prominence is in itself a struggle for international standing, prestige and cultural and economic power.

As J. D. Connor's study of late twentieth-century Hollywood has shown, what we frequently see in studio movies is the shifting industrial contexts, and even the struggles, in which they are made, to the extent that the films themselves become advertisements, self-serving product placements, for the studios that produce them. Similarly, the kinds of narrative tropes we might identify most predominantly with Working Title indicate how their films construct their own sense of place within a competitive global cinematic market. Theirs is a brand that is at once alert to the wider cultural expectations around Britishness (or/as Englishness), confident in its mobilization of such expectations, yet aware of the importance of the transatlantic, and also trans-European, cinematic relationship.[27] Nevertheless, Connor suggests that the taking up of Working Title by Universal in 1998 profoundly changed the relationship between Working Title and its now less easy-going parent. The 'parent' in this case was Seagram, the giant Canadian conglomerate that owned Universal, and had bought up PolyGram. As Connor explains: 'It had looked as though [Working Title] would be the launch point for a successful invasion of the major studios' ranks. But with PolyGram folded into Universal, Working Title found itself underwritten by an American, or, rather, Canadian company, one that was already desperate for cash.'[28]

Connor rather overstates the case when he suggests that the new contexts for Working Title meant that, from this point, 'there would be no more hymns to British nationalism like *Elizabeth* (1998)' or dirty, historical capers like *Plunkett and Macleane* (1999), 'where the baddies bear the names of Arsenal defenders' (they really do – and the film was a huge flop in both the UK and the United States).[29] Yet, in support of Connor's claim, a relative conservatism and pragmatism have crept into the company's roster of films since the 2000s. There would in fact be another film starring Cate Blanchett as the 'Virgin' Queen, *Elizabeth: The Golden Age* (2007), though this was a sequel rather than a new departure. And it is notably towards other tested formulae – the *Bridget Jones* series – to which the company was already rumoured to be returning just weeks after one of its biggest flops: Curtis's $50m *The Boat That Rocked* (*Pirate Radio* in the United States) (2009), which sank mostly without trace in UK and other international markets. *Bridget Jones's Baby*, as we have seen, was eventually released in 2016.

The example of the two period dramas released by Working Title at the end of 2017 – *Darkest Hour* and *Victoria and Abdul* – suggests an effort to galvanize the company's output around culturally English, yet internationally known historical and dramatic contexts, driven by the casting of equally distinctive British screen stars (given the continuity provided by its star, Judi Dench, *Victoria and Abdul* can also be seen as a sequel of sorts to the earlier *Mrs. Brown* [1998], also about Queen Victoria). Yet, as noted previously, it also indicates a coincidental, or simply pragmatic, confluence of production incentives across a short period of time. Both these films appeared not long after *Their Finest* (2017), another early Second World War drama (produced by the BBC), as well as Christopher Nolan's epic *Dunkirk* (2017), and on Netflix, the second season of Peter Morgan's epic take on the House of Windsor, *The Crown* (2016–).

Some of the Brexit-informed readings of these texts are problematic, as I have discussed at earlier points. But I have also argued that there is something disingenuous in Fellner's claim that as a world-leading production company, operating at mid-budget level within a globalized film economy, its only remit is to 'tell good stories'. This is because what constitutes 'good' in Working Title's terms, as we have seen here, is to a large degree contingent on what works for it at the box-office – if not, as already noted, reliant on ideas around Britishness and/or Englishness that 'most closely conform to the dominant representations of the nation already in circulation'.[30] But in terms of what works, Working Title is somewhat hostage to Hollywood fortune, in terms of changing fashions and industry economics. As Bevan and Fellner highlight in the aforementioned TIFF interview, they cannot, or at least can *no longer*, compete with contemporary Hollywood's superhero and franchise complex. This leads them to remark in the same interview that their output constituted their own smaller-scale version of the latter, only here with English history as their populated cinematic world and prime ministers, monarchs and literary characters as their superheroes.

But there is also a tacit acknowledgement in Fellner and Bevan's discussion that its previously defining films, and its romantic comedy cycle in particular, can no longer be relied on so easily in a contemporary cinematic climate dominated by the Hollywood franchise film: a climate, moreover, which has increasingly little confidence in 'standalone' movies like the ones that, in a more welcoming time, made the company's name.[31] 'Worldwide commercial appeal', as Townsend elaborates, has been the criterion for green-lighting production at Working Title.[32] We therefore need to acknowledge the extent to which a genre such as the rom-com lives or dies, not entirely by its relevance and appeal to the lives of its audiences but through the vicissitudes of global cinematic culture. The success of the Working Title rom-com has depended largely on the favour found by these mainly Anglo-American films in the competitive international, and above all American, marketplace.[33] There is in turn a reciprocal *cultural* impact from these films, in which the good fortune of these films in global terms feeds back into an increased perception of national global standing, albeit one which is, in all likelihood, a specious one – the notorious 'Cool Britannia', associated with the beginning of Blair's premiership, and his and Chris Smith's creative industries agenda, being just one example of this.[34] The key point here is that inasmuch as our ideas of the nation are imaginary, cinematic constructions, this 'nation' itself is a product of broader cinematic fortunes and investments.

We have already seen in the first chapter of this book the ambiguous way in which revenue figures, whether in terms of inward investment or domestic box-office returns, can be mobilized in the promotion of robust cultural and economic health, in a way that obviates more critical issues concerning the diversity or representative capacity of film production and reception. Significantly, the inward investment on the part of the Hollywood conglomerate film – like Disney-Lucasfilm's *Star Wars* saga or Heyday Films-Warner Bros.' *Harry Potter* and *Fantastic Beasts* series – helps shore up a now dominant global cinematic culture founded on the franchise: a 'tentpole' production logic that increasingly looks to mitigate risk, in a precarious cinematic environment, by investing huge amounts into limited but tested content, with the expectation of proportionally significant global returns.[35] This kind of logic, and its almost total dependency on the sequel or the remake, did not prevail twenty-five or even twenty years ago, when a low-budget Anglo-European comedy full of flapping, stuttering Brits – *Four Weddings and a Funeral* – could take in a quarter of a billion dollars worldwide and seemingly invent overnight the idea of Britain in the 1990s. Film- and policy-makers with vested interests in a buoyant national film industry may reasonably look back nostalgically, and enviously, to the days when small-budget films like *Billy Elliot* (made by Working Title's lower-budget subsidiary, WT² Productions) or genuinely independent films like Gurinder Chadha's *Bend It Like Beckham* (2002) could become worldwide hits. Yet, to suggest that 'we don't make them like that any more' is not wholly true. In some respects, the hope of making 'another *Four Weddings*', or even another *Full Monty*, whether we'd like to see one or not, has little or nothing to do with the talent, capacity or will of individual filmmakers and producers. Rather, its possibility is shaped by the wider industrial contexts of commercial cinema. These films may still be made in some form, but even if they are, it is often with a more negotiated sense of the global-local relationship or with diminished expectations of audiences and returns.[36] Most strikingly, as we see below with some recent iterations of established English genre film, we see a more reflexive engagement with a prior era and some of its most prominent cinematic texts and motifs. Made and released just after the century's first decade, it is also notable here how many of these films look back, often with a critically distant eye, to the same prior contexts of 'creative industries' Britain, and its buoyant metropolitan image, that we looked at earlier in this book.

Running out of time: Romance, revision and retrenchment in *One Day* and *About Time*

A film like the romantic drama *One Day* (2011), adapted from David Nicholls's 2010 novel, offers a useful illustration of the contemporary marketplace for a culturally English cinema shaped by globalized forces. As Higson has noted, the reliance on the British literary adaptation within the film industry complicates any straightforward notion of a 'national' cinema, given that many such adaptations are essentially 'literary properties exploited by the international film business ... [with] no UK production involvement'.[37] Moreover, the adaptation of the contemporary novel now operates as part of a controlled and frequently pre-emptive process of property acquisition and film development, which involves both publishing houses and film studios.[38] *One Day* exemplifies this synergy, being a venture on the part of publisher Random House's new film production unit. Random House (later to merge with Penguin) actually published the novel *after* shooting on the film, with a screenplay by Nichols, had already begun.

One Day already exists, then, in a nexus of global commercial interests and stakeholders and appropriates the model of transatlantic casting already familiar from Working Title productions: in this instance, with Anne Hathaway following Renee Zellweger's lead in the *Bridget Jones* series, partly concealing her American star status behind her character's Yorkshire accent and big glasses. In this respect, the film's production contexts underline the kind of cultural and industry negotiation that seems a constituent part of the contemporary globalized 'English' film. And yet, *One Day* also makes some striking narrative choices within these contexts – especially so, if we note that its synergistic production contexts make it less an adaptation as such than an original screenplay. The structure of the film shows what happens to its two protagonists on the same July day, over nearly twenty years, from their first awkward meeting, through their not-quite romantic relationship, to eventual marriage. It is in many senses a variation on the 'comedies of remarriage' Stanley Cavell identified in the Hollywood studio era.[39] Also, in its structural similarities to a film like *When Harry Met Sally* (1989), the film affords the pleasures of looking back, from a mature perspective, at its callow protagonists, as they contend with the various politics and fashions, sartorial or otherwise, of their times. Ultimately, though, *One Day*'s peculiarly dark take on this romance narrative suggests a wariness on its part towards such plots and comic motifs, offering in their place a less reassuring, and more politically oriented, representation of the recent past and one that seems wary of the illusions and consolations often proffered by the genre.

One Day, that said, is hardly immune to some of the formal imperatives of a kind of 'heritage' literary adaptation. It opens, for example, with inky shots of Edinburgh's old city centre silhouetted in the dawn light, as its young central characters, still in gowns and mortar boards, wind up their graduation party in 1988. For the most part, though, this opening seems ironic, as it offers an enchanted moment in time – with its vaguely *Brideshead Revisited* atmosphere of gilded youth – which the rest of the film cannot sustain. As just noted, reflection on both the foibles and the ravages of different times and ages is built into the premise of *One Day*. The allusion here to champagne-quaffing days of university life situates the film within the terms of nostalgia, yet it is a nostalgia that needs to be weighed against the changing contexts of the times. 1988 was the last year before student loans came in to replace grants and two decades before the hike in tuition fees made university life an exercise in attrition – the period, of course, in which the film came out. Moreover, while its story takes place in the final years of Conservative government and the first decade of New Labour, there is a significant interweaving of its initial action with the more contemporary contexts of recession, austerity politics and globalization. Emma's post-graduation rite of passage to London sees her shift-working in an ersatz Mexican restaurant and co-habiting cramped, rented accommodation. As if to stress this point, the film perennially shoots the usually glamorous Hathaway clothed in muted colours and patterns that literally blend into the drably coloured wallpaper, effectively flattening the space she is in (Figure 5.1). Only her eventual move upwards to professional life, as a secondary-school teacher, enables her to get some foothold on the property ladder, though only in the form of a slightly less cramped inner-city apartment.

The type of no-strings (and effectively no-job) income and property we see displayed by Hugh Grant's character in *Notting Hill* (on which more below) is pointedly out of reach to Hathaway's Emma, who as a lower-class provincial coming to the capital is positioned like a character from the novels she has read as an English undergraduate. Similarly, and in distinct contrast to the metropolitan topographies and demographics of the *Bridget Jones* films,

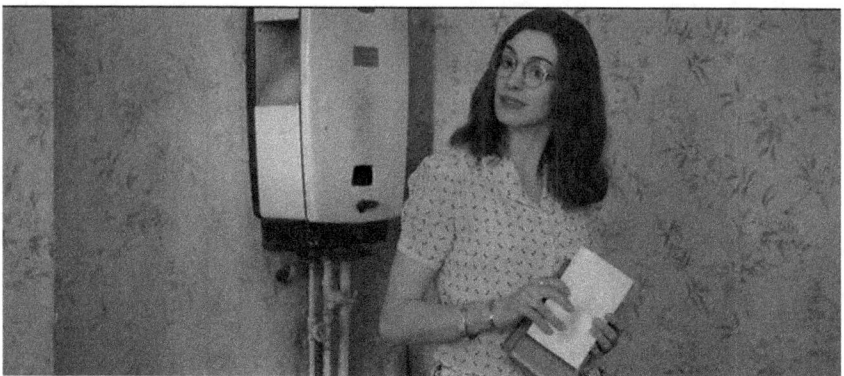

Figure 5.1 Continuity and revision: Transatlantic casting in austerity contexts – Anne Hathaway in *One Day*. Directed by Lone Sherfig © Focus Features 2011. All rights reserved.

Emma does not have free entry to the professional and lifestyle benefits of the 'creative classes' gravitating around London-based media providers. More to the point, Emma's Northern-ness and class situate her outside the perennial social demographics of romantic comedy in general, allying her more closely, in fact, with the female protagonists of English 'New Wave' dramas, played by actors like Rita Tushingham or Julie Christie, in *A Taste of Honey* (1959) or *Billy Liar* (1963). By contrast, for her friend Dexter, the passage to affluence is as apparently easy as it is unexplained. Our main indicator as to how Dexter has ascended through the ranks of metropolitan media life, culminating in him becoming a presenter for a derided but popular late-night 'youth' TV show, is that his elite and affluent background (wealthy home-counties parents; education at Winchester School) have made him sufficiently well connected to work in television in the first place. In fact, these are characteristics he shares precisely with Bridget Jones: like Bridget, Dexter is also academically underachieving, in distinction to Emma, whose first-class degree seems to offer her only very limited inroads into a metropolitan career.

One Day's most abrupt tactic is to reveal near its end that Emma died in 2006, when her bicycle was hit by a truck. The film here undermines the genre's usual capacity to provide reassurance, in the form of the 'happy' narrative resolution to which it otherwise seems to have been leading. There is a clear narrative trajectory in the film, moving towards equilibrium and a more mature idea of success, with Emma finally fulfilling her initial narrative promise and becoming a successful children's writer. Dexter, meanwhile, when his fleeting media career disintegrates, settles down to the responsibility and professional gratification of running an upmarket café and being a parent to the daughter from his previous marriage. In this qualified respect at least, the degree to which *One Day* transcends the genre's frequently conservative framework is debatable. And yet, it is ultimately the thread of disappointment and compromise, and the film's willingness to prick the bubble frequently cushioning the genre in its most culturally English contexts, which makes it a significant contribution to the form at its particular point in time. One of Hathaway's early starring roles was in the fairy-tale film *Ella Enchanted* (2004): *Emma Disenchanted* might be an alternative title for *One Day*, with its downbeat, less than eulogistic take on the previous twenty years and by association, some of the cinema connected with it.

When we similarly come to Working Title's *About Time* (2013), Curtis's return after a short hiatus to the rom-com genre, it is striking to see how the series' prevailing mood has shifted – or at least, in relation to the established format that reached its apogee in *Notting Hill* and *Love Actually*. As I suggested above, the image (and imaginary) of nation, especially in terms of Working Title films, operates in conjunction between cinematic fashions and sustainable production rosters. Genres that establish their narratives around present-day contexts, such as romantic comedies, cannot entirely forego their connections to the real world nor to prevailing cinematic styles (as noted previously in the discussion around *Skyfall*). As Richard Maltby has succinctly put it, the escapism offered by popular genre film needs realism as its anchor: the plausibility of setting and content provides a recognizable context from which, and through which, we might escape, via narratives of wish-fulfilment or compensation.[40] Both *About Time* and *One Day*, possibly for these reasons, suggest a revised approach to the prevailing types of representations and formal characteristics found in the earlier phase of English romance genre film. Stylistically, for instance, with its intimate, hand-held cinematography, and its use of largely low-key locations, *About Time* dispenses with some of the starrier and more spectacular set piece-driven aesthetics of Curtis's earlier films, where London's more touristically identifiable landmarks or most colourful quarters constitute a form of self-promoting 'city of delights'.[41] But *About Time* is also revealing in terms of its revised situation within the Working Title production scale, indicating a measure of economic retrenchment after the budgetary excesses and commercial failure of Curtis's previous *The Boat That Rocked*. Made for $12m, *About Time* was below the threshold for parent-company approval (as discussed above). There is the suggestion here, then, that expectations for this type of English film are no longer as high as they once were. Tellingly, *One Day* underperformed against expectations, possibly relating to its cooler treatment of the genre; and while *About Time* performed more favourably, it was far from matching the box-office precedents of Curtis's films up to and including *Love Actually*.

If anything else has changed in narrative terms by the time we get to *About Time*, most revealingly, it is that money suddenly matters. In *Love Actually*, almost everyone seems to be working in the forms of non-specified creative-industry jobs, making them at once perfect denizens of the post-industrial and metropolitan economy and exemplars for New Labour's vision of Creative Britain. The previous *Notting Hill*, by slight contrast, was in some ways quirky, in that its utopianism was founded on the *failures* of its main characters to live up to their Thatcherite entrepreneurial goals. Hugh Grant's Will Thacker, for example, runs a bookshop that he acknowledges is leaking money. The film's eventual resolution is plotted in a local restaurant, just opened by Will's friend Tony and which has abjectly failed; while the most economically prosperous member of the immediate group, Hugh Bonneville's Bernie, is a city broker – that ultimate symbol of Thatcherite Britain – who professes to be both unhappy and hopeless in his nevertheless lucrative career. The capacity for its cheerfully 'classless' protagonists nevertheless to endure the vicissitudes of free-market capitalism makes the film the target of much derision; yet the characters' failures, and more particularly the reluctance to compete, contains its own persuasive counter-narrative to the neoliberal orthodoxy of capitalism and success. As Charlotte Brunsdon comments, the failures of the characters in *Notting Hill* are not really failures at all, but rather markers of their specific locality, embedding them attractively within the 'village' of Notting Hill.[42] Such counter-narratives, as Higson persuasively suggests, are appealingly 'exotic' qualities onto which US audiences (just like Julia Roberts's harassed movie star in the film) can map fantasies of non-attainment and a decelerated lifestyle.[43]

Nevertheless, such fantasies are also and always predicated on an essentially aristocratic appeal, incarnated through Grant's familiar screen persona, acting as a safety net against the possibility of actual economic bankruptcy, ruin or homelessness. There is no apparent concern in *Notting Hill*, for instance, that Will or Tom might endure the trauma of home repossession. Perhaps because they are made within the contexts of inflated metropolitan housing prices, and also filmed in the aftermath of a global recession, both *One Day* and *About Time* allude at least to the idea that half-decent metropolitan property is not a given. In the latter film, Tim's (Domhnall Gleeson) point of anchoring in About Time is not the metropolis but a seafront family home in Cornwall, with his baby-boomer parents luxuriating in an effortless early retirement of parties, picnics and outdoor film screenings. In comparison to the earlier films in the cycle, though, what is most striking is not so much the retrenchment into this house as a consistent point of return, but the fact that Tim's security, and what locates him in class terms, is that he has a proper paying job (he is a solicitor in a London law firm). But *About Time* also hints that economic security, if not exactly under threat, at least involves compromises and negotiations – not to mention actual work. Tim identifies this when, a first child now in the picture, he and his American book-editor wife Mary – not a movie star in this film, though still played by one (Rachel McAdams) – move from their cramped but lively flat into a nice-but-dull house they confess they still 'can't afford'.

As David Bordwell has noted, Curtis's earlier *Love Actually* is a form of interweaving 'network narrative', in which the stories involving the various couples and other characters, in different parts of the city, intermittently cross paths and link up.[44] With its legacies in the Victorian novel, such narratives always aspire in some sense to evoke a contemporaneous social world, the network standing in figuratively for 'the city' or even 'the nation' more broadly. As Benedict Anderson has famously shown, such novels, in their efforts to depict interconnected individuals and constituencies, represented one early effort to represent the nation as an 'imagined community'.[45] In *Love Actually*, in fact, which is bookended by scenes at Heathrow Airport, and where London is a meeting point for an internationally diverse range of professionals, this imagined community is not limited by the nation space. Whatever we might think of this type of metropolitan world Curtis constructs in *Love Actually*, it is notable how in *About Time*, like in *One Day*, this world has been narrowed down and fragmented, focusing on single extended families, couples or even individuals. These films in effect turn away from a cross-sectional representational approach to the point where, in *About Time*, any sense of place has become atomized – the only identifiable and consistent locale now being the ex-urban family retreat. 'London' here exists in small, mostly non-located and monadic pockets of entirely private experience, in the form of rooms, bars or restaurants. This may well be shaped in part by budgetary factors and the declining global currency of this type of film; but this in effect underlines the point that the changing appearance of popular English film, and the idea of the nation it constructs, is in part a product of the material contexts and trends informing it.

If London at once shapes and is imaginarily shaped by Curtis's earlier films, then it is no longer clear in *About Time* where or what this place actually is. If *Notting Hill* was inadvertently prescient about the gentrification of London's former working- or lower-middle-class boroughs (or even served as its self-fulfilling prophecy), it now quaintly promotes the idea that financially floundering thirtysomethings once lived quite comfortably within the city's central transport zones. Will Thacker strolls to work in *Notting Hill*: in *About Time*, by contrast, Tim takes the Tube – something hitherto absent in the Curtis cycle – because he has been obliged to move to the dull anonymity of the urban margins.

About Time misses a trick here, though, reducing Tim's encounter with one of the city's most democratic and diverse spaces – a packed underground train – to a cheap vignette about a neighbouring passenger's noisy earphones. In the same sequence of everyday fragments we see Tim getting a smile from the young woman serving him his coffee in a franchise outlet; the previous camera position, from just behind the girl, is subsequently reversed to show her clearly in close-up. Are we supposed to assume that this girl is one of the thousands of EU and global economic migrants, or international students, fuelling the British service industries and handing exorbitantly priced coffee beverages to busy professionals like Tim? Where does the girl go, if not, like Tim, she too will take the long underground trip to accommodation in the further extremities of the global city? We never find out, as before we even have time to ponder on this potentially fertile encounter, the film has moved on.

Or more precisely, the film has moved *backwards*. If *About Time* was at this point Curtis's most socially and economically honest film, and in some respects his most political, it was also his most fantastical. *Notting Hill* and in a similar way *Love Actually* were always already fantastical in their efforts to fashion exotic cinematic spaces and cohesive communities out of the very rawest and sketchiest of the urban geographical material; yet they at least claimed some plausible basis in reality. *About Time*, for whatever its reasons, dismisses this form of community as unsustainable within the terms of its preferred narrative world. It instead elects to send its protagonists literally back in time: a magical genetic gift Tim has inherited from his father. While this is only once instanced as a journey to the distant past, it is consistently marked as a boyish act of wish-fulfilment, since it involves Tim retreating into dark enclosed spaces to carry it out. To reinforce the childhood associations, this is perennially done, with echoes of C.S. Lewis's Narnia novels, by having Tim climb into a wardrobe.

As Sean Redmond has argued, in much recent film and television time-travel narratives have become displaced from the future- or high-tech digital worlds of science fiction and have returned, in fact, back home. 'Home' in this context is not the present day, but a pre-digital, even pre-globalized, national moment: a time-travel 'built upon th[e] longing for a fixed point in time, where time, space, human relations, the working day … were all fixed and regular'.[46] It is one of the most notable aspects of *One Day*, in fact, that the globally outward-looking confidence of a film like *Love Actually* retracts here into forms of literal and figurative *isolation* from the ravages of the modern world. Texts like *About Time*, after this fashion, offer what Redmond calls a 'heterotopia of time': an imaginary suspension of temporal causality.[47] When the world in its relentless contingency can be stopped, and reversed like a DVD, anything can become tolerable. All of which begs the question what Curtis's hero cannot see or experience in his present world, or why. The simple answer would be that like the modern metropolitan subject Tim is, he just doesn't have the time.

About Time, then, seen within the wider contexts of Curtis's work with Working Title exemplifies a particular reluctance, or rather inability, for such cinema to deal head-on with the complexities of the present moment, just as it also suggests the limitations, at this point in time, in the types of metropolitan ensemble films that were the commercially buoyant hallmark of Working Title at the turn of the century. In terms of Curtis's transition to a kind of comic science fiction, we see the further shift away from more notionally representative narratives of the nation. Notably, Curtis's next screenplay, and his first film produced after the EU referendum, made in collaboration with director Danny Boyle, was *Yesterday* (2019): another fantasy, time-traveling film of sorts, in which a hapless English singer finds himself the only person alive on Earth who remembers The Beatles. I will return to this film at more length in the conclusion; but suffice it to say for now that like *About Time*, *Yesterday*, in its narrative premise, hints at its own complex, and perhaps compensatory, relationship to the present day. The fantastic premises of both films hint at the possibility that the fairy tales of a not-so distant era can now only be treated ironically; or, at least, if they can still be told, they are qualified by entirely obvious – and therefore equally ironic – fantastical generic frameworks.

Darkness on the edge of towns: *The World's End*, *Sightseers* and the cinema of suburbs

About Time and *Yesterday*, because rather than in spite of their nostalgic mode, are at heart despairing films, since they offer us contexts and characters within which the only way out is through fantasy. Similarly, Working Title's *The World's End* – the third in the loose trilogy of films made by Edgar Wright and co-written with its star, Simon Pegg – offers a troubled vision of ageing and working in the modern neoliberal economy, as well as being a disturbingly corrective fable about nostalgia, time-travel and the longing for 'home'. Like *About Time*, Wright's film is also a reflection on the desire for reverse time-travel as a contemporary condition. Looking backwards is at once the implied appeal of the film at the same time as being the catalyst for its drama. *The World's End*, in this way, offers something of a counter to the ebulliently playful Englishness and confidence on display in *Hot Fuzz*. Though also a genre parody of sorts, *The World's End* uses its formal juxtapositions of genre and setting to more critical effect, informed once more by the contexts of economic and cultural globalization.

Nostalgia permeates the film from its opening shots and the burst on the soundtrack of 'Summers Magic', a 1990 dance track that was *already* nostalgic, sampling as it does the theme from the children's TV show *The Magic Roundabout* (BBC, 1965–77). A silent montage designed to look like 8mm home-movie footage shows us the evening when the narrator, Pegg's Gary

King, unsuccessfully attempted with four schoolboy friends a crawl of their (fictional) suburban hometown's twelve pubs – 'The Golden Mile' – before winding up in a field, watching the sun rise. 'I said to myself', Pegg's voice-over recounts, 'that life would never feel this good again … And you know what?' Cut, after a brief fade-out to the adult Gary, now speaking from the present to other members of a counselling circle: 'It never did.'

The World's End, then, entices with the promise of a temporal retreat, only to reveal its illusions. The film is based around the prospect that the now dysfunctional and backward-looking King, still wearing a black trench coat and Sisters of Mercy tee shirt, could reunite his four mostly estranged and now affluent, professional friends to re-attempt the Golden Mile twenty years on, seemingly against all of their better judgement.

This ambivalence on the part of the film towards its own set-up, however, is the source of its particular tension. With its sequential narrative structure, orchestrated to the boozily repetitive montage of poured pints, *The World's End* delineates a ritual (doing the Golden Mile) within a ritual (watching/re-watching the film) that invites a specifically cultural, and also gendered, participation – one that is in many ways the same kind of narrow, re-performed ritual discussed earlier with regard to *The Inbetweeners*.[48] Like *About Time*, then, *The World's End* marks a trajectory of nostalgic and cultural enclosure around its limited and limiting national space. The structure of the film enacts a latent or overt desire for regression on the part of its upstanding males, one which they – and perhaps, in theory, we – are ultimately without power to resist. In this case, the contexts for this regression are played out and displayed during the beginning of the film. A composited lateral tracking shot during the main credits shows repetitive shots of the adult Gary getting dressed, intersected with images of his four friends in adulthood: Andy (Nick Frost) enters the wall-to-ceiling glass-panelled lawyer's firm, where he is a partner; estate agent Oliver (Martin Freeman) converses dramatically via his earpiece in a café; building contractor Steven (Paddy Considine) works out under the tutelage of his fitness-instructor girlfriend; and Pete (Eddie Marsan), heir to a prosperous car dealership, hides at the breakfast table behind his copy of the conservative *Daily Express*, its headline delightfully proclaiming 'New Survey Suggests Happier Britain' (Figure 5.2).

This is a different, more 'grown-up' set of characters from those of the earlier Wright-Pegg collaborations, though *The World's End* hardly suggests that this

Figure 5.2 'New Survey Suggests Happier Britain': A troubled view from Conservative England in *The World's End*. Directed by Edgar Wright © Focus Features/Universal Pictures 2013. All rights reserved.

professional advance represents any great personal development. In the same way that *About Time* hinted at the absence of true gratification in work, *The World's End* establishes in its opening scenes the idea that it is professional achievement and the things that come with it – family life, respectability, comforts, fitness routines – that distance its protagonists from the real, and real because repressed, goals of life. If we are to buy into the film's narrative premise, the real is in this case is the return to a fabled and irresponsible point of origin from twenty years previously and the desire to live out the at-once rebellious and infantile words sampled at the beginning of the 1990 Primal Scream song ('Loaded') playing over the sequence: 'We want to be free … to do what we want to do.'[49]

This is a peculiar aspect of the film's uncertain tone and narrative. It is, after all, the fact that their town of 'Newton Haven' has not changed, and is stuck in a version of 1990, that makes it so alienating to all of the group except Gary. Its now sterile and inert settings are a marked counter to the utopian moment evoked at the film's beginning and a reminder of the dangerous discrepancies between memory and actuality. The lure of memory forms a trap for the group, clearly visible once the film's generic premise is established: the moment we discover that Newton Haven is not just a boring provincial town but is, in fact, controlled by self-reconstructing androids, lubricated by an ink-like fluid and controlled via a centralized alien brain calling itself the Network. Aptly, it is at a 'School Days' club night – nostalgic throwback events appealing to the workings of actual social networks like Friends Reunited or Facebook groups – that the men are ensnared by the short-skirted and school tie-wearing sirens of their teenage past.

We might reasonably ask, then, where *The World's End* wants to lead us, since it appears to pull in antithetical directions. As I have argued elsewhere, this third film from the Wright–Pegg partnership deviates somewhat from its predecessor film's more celebratory negotiation of global and local impulses, by alluding to the more homogenizing impacts of cultural and economic globalization, and its potential erosion of an 'authentic' English life.[50] What we see as we move, in a series of matched shots, from pub to identical pub, is a simulacrum of the English public house modelled around standardized and entirely inauthentic forms of 'traditional' experience. Steven's contemptuous regard for what he calls the 'Starbucking' of contemporary culture, in this instance, in the form of the nationwide pub chains that have predominated in England since the 1990s, alerts us early on to the broader concern in *The World's End* with globalization, conformity and standardization.

The film in this sense extends the preoccupations in Wright and Pegg's earlier films with individuality and identity, either amid a pervasive and passive consumer culture (the zombiefied North London of *Shaun of the Dead*) or within the cultural constrictions of a conservative village community (in *Hot Fuzz*).[51] Yet while *The World's End*, like its predecessors, comfortably integrates global cinematic forms into its action and mise-en-scène, how it deploys global forces in *narrative* terms suggests a politically significant variation in its approach. The anxiety around homogenization in *The World's End* hints at a deeper concern in the film with the (im)possibility of reclaiming an 'authentic' past: one that is nevertheless problematized in the film as depthless and untrustworthy nostalgia. The film's ambiguities therefore reside in the way its characters' responses to contemporary contexts, but also its central 'quest' structure, appeal to a strong and almost folkloric sense of lost Englishness that it is in part the group's task to reclaim. Like *The Kid Who Would Be King* (discussed in Chapter 3), whose writer-director, Joe Cornish, is a frequent collaborator with Wright, *The World's End* is also conceived around a conception of Arthurian romance. This is conceptualized not just in terms of the pub crawl, here forming a type of ironic Grail quest, but also in terms of the characters' courtly naming – Andrew Knightley, Steven Prince,

Peter Page, Oliver Chamberlain, all congregating around Gary 'The Once and Future' King.[52] Indeed, the film's interest in linking (the) King's literal and spiritual 'return' with the reformation both of a chivalric band and with a form of national recovery – as they unite to confront the deadening forces of the Network – distils the climactic narrative themes of Malory's *Morte d'Arthur*, which sees King Arthur returning to an England darkened by Mordred's rule.

As with the other national 'epics' discussed earlier, it is ultimately this idea of return and national revival that shapes the narrative and tone of *The World's End*, when Gary, Andy and Steve combine to vanquish the Network. This is an action that, consequently, brings down the planet's energy and telecommunications systems: the latter, it transpires, having been sourced by the Network itself to sustain the androids slowly replacing the humans. It is another tonal quirk of the film that Gary repudiates the Network by quoting the same introductory dialogue from 'Loaded' that opened the film, locating resistance here in a moment of nostalgic, and childish, teenage rebellion. But by this point of the film, in fact, King's ideals of constructive irresponsibility have started to shape the film's dramatic and thematic oppositions. When the last-standing trio confront the Network in The World's End pub, their objections are not the stuff of reasoned debate but rather an outpouring of energized anti-rationality. The people of Earth, they claim – which in this respect effectively means the people of England – are just too stubborn and idiotic to follow programmes for social organization. 'We just don't like being told what to do', whines King, three years before the Conservative MP Michael Gove, on the referendum campaign trail for Leave, made his similar statement about the British public's attitude towards experts.[53] King then tells the Network to 'get back in [his] spaceship and fuck off back to Legoland'. Which it then does, mostly through apathy, triggering in turn the implosion that destroys the town and sets off a global blackout.

This conclusion to *The World's End* offers a perhaps unexpected critical take on our most recent economic contexts, as well as being unexpectedly tuned in, uncertainly, to populist ideas of anti-global nationalism. This film, like *About Time*, emphasizes at once the efforts to escape the frameworks of contemporary working life and the economic system, while never explicitly interrogating or critiquing these same frameworks. There is a peculiar note of apocalyptic despair in the film's final scenes, as the survivors of the Network's collapse eke out a living tilling meagre crops in a new, post-capitalist agrarian economy. 'We've all gone organic now', Andy quips in the concluding voice-over. But it is the film's insinuation that this global meltdown is caused, not by some near-earth object or natural disaster but by the dumb ecstasy of popular revolt, that eventually gives *The World's End* its peculiar and troubling resonance with subsequent times. As I have also noted here, like *About Time*, *The World's End* is also marked by a fascination with this same haven of nostalgia and a very localized form of retreat. As much as it engages with these ideas in a comic fashion, it is at the same time drawn inescapably to the pleasures of retrenchment and enclosure – all of which makes *The World's End*, along with *About Time*, highly ambiguous films for the contexts of Brexit soon to follow them.

As already hinted, *The World's End* is also significant within popular English cinema for its keenness to engage with suburban England as a narrative and thematic context. As David Forrest, Graeme Harper and Jonathan Rayner's recent book on the suburbs in cinema contends, this interest is sustained by a sense that suburbanites continue to make up the core market demographic for contemporary film.[54] As a cinematic narrative terrain, though, the suburbs have been an uncertain space in the English context. The English suburb as an idea, or its relative in the form of extra-metropolitan 'new towns' such as Stevenage, Hemel Hempstead or Letchworth Garden City, is premised on its relative amenability in comparison to the congestion and other demands of big city life. As an idea, it also appeals to a quasi-rural conception of the preferred life, offered up in the aftermath of the Second World War, but also in tandem with the aspirations and self-perceptions of an expanding middle class. Forrest and his co-writers point out that, in theory at least, this should render the suburbs less interesting as a cinematic space, plotted as they are between the more exciting or romantic spaces of the city and the countryside.[55] In practice, however, as these writers attest, the suburbs emerge by their very diverse and widespread nature as the dramatic site for all manner of conflicts, be they generational, gendered, racial or class-based.

A key point in this discussion is subsequently that just as there are multiple 'Londons' in cinema, there are also multiple suburbs. Addressing the diverse voices of both urban and suburban contexts has subsequently been a key recent concern of filmmakers and policy-makers, though sometimes with uncertain aims and results. As Clive Nwonka and Sarita Malik have shown, one of the notional aims of the UK Film Council, as a key driver of New Labour's Creative Britain agenda, was to 'promote social inclusion and cultural diversity', to 'challenge audiences' and to 'broaden the range of films on offer in the UK'.[56] Nwonka and Malik's critique of this policy, as implemented in some of the work funded by the Film Council, was that it often tended to exploit so-called 'multiculture' as just another commodity within the creative industries agenda. Diversity was in this respect another 'mechanism through which particular markets are opened out, in order to meet governmental objectives'.[57] Taking as their example the 2005 film *Bullet Boy*, a tale of gangland gun crime set in Hackney, Nwonka and Malik argue that the film exemplifies a naïve and stereotypical representation of black British life – one that tends to pay lip service to the idea of a diversified cinema culture rather than actually constitute one or help bring it into being. They consequently echo Robert Hewison's point that in seeking to make diversity a buzzword within the creative industries agenda, such works often suggested creativity in itself was a pathway out of social exclusion. In striving to promote inclusion and champion diversity, in other words, such an agenda ends up 'ignor[ing] the possibility that there are structural disadvantages produced by class, race, gender or sexuality'.[58]

Moreover, as Nwonka has explored elsewhere, films dealing with poverty and exclusion often show the individual protagonist breaking free of these contexts through artistic endeavour. They in turn end up reiterating the neoliberal view that any socio-economic situation can be transcended simply through talent and hard work.[59] Indeed, this idea that impoverished circumstances could be overcome through (creative) individual work and perseverance is central to the narratives of both *The Full Monty* and *Billy Elliot*: as already noted, two of the exemplary 'working class' films within the orbit of New Labour and its cultural-economic agenda.[60] In line with the discussion of my first chapter, then, Nwonka and Malik point to the ways in which narratives of inclusivity, within the creative industries agenda, may partly conceal or even reiterate the same structural disadvantages they notionally seek to correct. As in *Billy Elliot* – where value and meaning ultimately only come when Billy can leave the mining community of the North-East and become a dancer in London – such policy can end up confirming a limited view of success and inclusion, limited to metropolitan cultural existence and artistic achievement.

Sightseers (2012), in this respect, on which Edgar Wright worked as executive producer, is an important film, both for its willingness to engage more with the structural issues subtending social exclusion and in its efforts to find a different way of representing the socially excluded. It does this in a way that, ultimately, derides the recourse to neoliberal narratives of individual effort and creativity. Ben Wheatley's film is also notable for its focus on social disenfranchisement not, as is frequently the case, in the contexts of working-class life but in those of the suburban lower middle class.[61] As a film that specifically focuses on the economic and societal impacts of globalization and austerity within this previously under-represented class, *Sightseers* also seeks to expand the narrative of so-called 'broken Britain' beyond its more conventional (or stereotypical) locations in the sink-estates and gangland cultures of much British film.

Sightseers focuses on a caravan journey made by couple Chris and Tina (played by the film's writers, Steve Oram and Alice Lowe) around some of North-West England's national parks, stopping along the way at several 'heritage' sites and public attractions (such as the Critch Tramway Museum, Castleton's Blue John Mines, the Keswick Pencil Museum). Chris's stated plan is to use the trip to work on a book he has started. What begins as an apparently innocent trip between the young couple, though, quickly takes a darker turn, as Chris deliberately runs over and kills another visitor, after watching him litter one of the Tramway Museum's old vehicles. This provides a source of sexual and imaginative stimulation to the couple, and they subsequently embark on a killing spree, eliminating on their way various people viewed to be getting in their way or merely failing to conform to their shared worldview.

This axis of sex, death and the road is a familiar motif of numerous American films, from *Bonnie and Clyde* (1968) and *Badlands* (1973) to *Kalifornia* (1993) and *Natural Born Killers* (1994). It is in turn very easy to see *Sightseers* as offering a parodic example of the genre 'trans-contextualized' into an English setting.[62] In this sense, the more emblematically American contexts of the road movie, constituting a peculiar cinematic myth of the United States, find themselves relocated in caravan sites, genteel tourist attractions and in protagonists whose knitwear and hiking gear distance them from the more photogenic figures of Hollywood films. Yet the often graphically violent brutality of Chris and Tina's actions, as well as the film's efforts to make these killings comprehensible in narrative terms, unsettles any obvious parodic dimension. Their victims, meanwhile, are random and their murders horribly disproportionate: a self-satisfied though inoffensive travel writer; a middle-aged man complaining to Tina about her dog's mess; a passing cyclist, simply caught up in Tina's violent bid to make a point in an argument. It is nevertheless the peculiar justification for such killings on the couple's part, and the apparent motivations driving them, which becomes in fact the main point of the film.

What makes *Sightseers* more than just a formal exercise in dark comic incongruity, then, is its focus on the cultural and socio-economic contexts behind the trip. Chris claims to be taking a break from paid employment in order to write. The murder of the travel writer, taking place within a delirious dream-like sequence, seems to link to Chris's own fixation with trying, but failing, to write his own book. When in fact Tina secretly views Chris's 'work' towards the end of the film, she reveals nothing more than a series of childlike drawings, idealizing Chris and Tina's romantic journey, though also sketching Chris's 'happy ending': a suicide-pact jump from the top of the Ribblehead Viaduct. As part of this revelatory process throughout the film, we discover the true circumstances of Chris's situation: he has been made redundant, due either to an industrial buyout or production outsourcing (if, in this case, we correctly understand Chris's biting reference to China and 'five year plans'). Both his new caravan and the trip itself therefore represent a last, but unsustainable and nihilistic, grasp at happiness.

None of this, of course, makes Chris's actions any less acceptable, but it does position them within a context of economic precarity (to use Guy Standing's term), post-recessional malaise and social and political exclusion.[63] This is packaged within a vague sense of populist, anti-globalization sentiment, with sociopathic violence the troubled acting out of these circumstances. If there is a logic to Chris's actions, it is that they are directed towards representatives of the cultural or economic elites. For example, the older man Chris kills, after Tina has falsely accused him of sexual assault, admits after Chris's persistent questioning that he attended an English public school. Neither Chris nor Tina, by contrast, has any of the required economic, social or cultural capital to go beyond their limited contexts of mobility. The opening sequence shows Tina in the blandly furnished suburban house she shares with her mother: a certificate on the wall, identifying she has studied 'dog psychology', is the only indication of any educational or vocational qualifications, though it appears from the narrative contexts of the film that she has not put this to professional use.

Chris and Tina, whose accents mark them specifically as being from the West Midlands, consequently embody the marginalized non-metropolitan constituencies not just of economic globalization but of English class and regional division. Chris's exclusion is as much, then, an outcome of structural inequalities within the nation, linked to specific policy choices by a Conservative government – one whose most prominent figures at the time, and the main drivers of austerity policy, embodied the type of elite education and privilege Chris evidently despises.[64] And yet, structural inequalities are not the obvious target of Chris's anger but rather, as noted above, more generalized and demonized scapegoats linked to economic globalization, such as 'China'. Ironically, then, the protagonists' response to these circumstances of national division is to find solace and meaning through the enclosures of tourist spaces (and the film typically dwells on the entrances to these sights as forms of threshold points along the journey).[65]

Like the other films discussed in this chapter, then, the past, or its embodiment in sites of memory, becomes here a form of retrenchment and defence, more explicitly in the face of globalization and a post-industrial context seen to disenfranchise figures like Chris and Tina. *Sightseers* discloses what is already implicit though not always so forcefully articulated in earlier cultural uses of heritage: namely, its inherently nationalistic character, but also its specifically populist and even *nativist* potential. As subsequent commentators on the forms and functions of heritage would discuss, earlier analysts of the so-called 'heritage industry', whose views shaped the discourses around heritage cinema in the 1980s and 1990s, failed to account for the energy and complexity not so much of *British* nationalism but of the increasingly devolving *nationalisms* within Great Britain.[66] The recent devolution towards forms of specifically 'English nationalism' (which, by implication, distinguishes itself from any other regional British identities) implies a more essentialist notion of geography and race than the relatively inclusive, even multicultural tag of 'British'. Chris and Tina's trajectory in turn feels like an attempt to bolster a conception of local identity as a reinforcement against encroaching external forces, literalizing the trip into a self-defining inscription of self, history and space.

But we are also some distance here from the reductive attribution of 'heritage' merely to a conservative and nostalgic idealization of the past. *Sightseers* alludes to the paradoxical power of heritage culture to appeal beyond the class-based and economic inequalities that subtend it and to serve in the interests of a 'popular' imaginary that is at once a virulent response to, and rejection of, these same inequalities. Chris's anti-global imagination posits an entirely local response, which is in turn a markedly *English* response. But it is also one where the implicit rejection of economic and political elites, seen as the agents of globalization, can be smoothed out by those same agents through a localized idea of the 'common people' as a coherent and resistant body.[67] Indeed, this use of a populist imaginary mobilized against elites and globalization, precisely by a political elite who, in fact, embrace economic globalization (in the form of a neoliberal, free-market economy), underpinned much of the rhetoric of the Leave campaign at the time of the 2016 EU referendum.[68]

Sightseers' eventual significance, though, might be more in the way it confronts and challenges hitherto more culturally dominant forces of taste and judgement, especially in its intention to represent the previously unrepresented. The direct-to-camera shot of Chris and Tina moments before the culmination of their trip memorializes their journey and partnership in a potentially ironic fashion (it is scored by Frankie Goes to Hollywood's gaudy 1984 hit 'The Power of Love'); but the shot also insists that we as viewers take their lives and decisions into account. For the film's director, the potency of *Sightseers*' Northern landscape lies in its capacity to evoke a pre-industrial world in which, after living a hard and static life, 'you would have just died'.[69] In its generic allusions to the Hollywood road movie template *Sightseers* also offers the momentary pleasures of twenty-first-century mobility, where we can now 'bomb about the place ... and then go back to the city'.[70] Yet the film, and especially its conclusion, insists on the precarious illusions of that mobility and that we recognize that people still 'just die' in the geographic and economic environments that frame them.

In this respect the film eventually turns its scrutinizing gaze around, where the figures of comic derision, or the subjects of a culturally removed, almost anthropological gaze, look out at their judges (Figure 5.3). If we as viewers happen to be adopting the cultural high ground of distaste, then *Sightseers* at this point implicitly tells us where to go. But within the broader contexts

Figure 5.3 A laughing matter? Chris and Tina turn their gaze on the viewer towards the end of *Sightseers*. Directed by Ben Wheatley © StudioCanal UK 2012. All rights reserved.

of the film, it also insists that we recognize a complicity, through our own potential rejection or mockery of the couple, in the maintenance of the same social, cultural and economic hierarchies that work to entrap Chris and Tina in their dead-end life trajectories. Lowe, Oram and Wheatley's achievement in *Sightseers* is consequently to create a fractured film about post-recessional, pre-Brexit, Austerity Britain that speaks about and across division. While manifesting an excessively violent form of consequence, and sceptical of a populist ideology as a response to globalization, it also creates characters whose attitudes and predicament it is impossible merely to laugh off.

Conclusion

Like *The World's End*, then, *Sightseers* consolidates the aesthetic and thematic significance of situating narratives about national identity in the cinematically marginalized spaces of the suburbs. In doing so, films like these, and the others discussed in this chapter, rework the idea of locality in politically nuanced ways, challenging the erstwhile dominance of metropolitan narratives to 'speak for' a national cinema. By querying the supposed universality of popular English cinema, such films rethink the idea of the popular, and of the nation, for a more politically contested and, especially in film-industry terms, not so confident era. These kinds of cinematic conversations, and reflections on both traditional and alternative genre forms, rather than the metropolitan fairy tales of another, not so distant age, have already assumed a currency and a significance within the more recent contexts of Britain's EU referendum and the discourses around Brexit. As genre films continue to reconfigure themselves in line with transformations both in the film industry and broader society and in light of changing international attitudes to Great Britain and its role in the world, we should expect to see such films continue to play important representational roles in the coming years.

6

Just follow the bear? StudioCanal, transnational franchises and a European English cinema

In a conversation taking place shortly after the UK's EU referendum, Danny Perkins, the then CEO of StudioCanal UK, reflected on the recent past and possible futures both of his company, and of British cinema more generally. Discussing the success of StudioCanal's *Paddington* in 2014, a big hit internationally as well as in the UK, Perkins highlighted the significance of such culturally British material performing well across different territories. While acknowledging that the UK's vote for Brexit was like 'culturally … giv[ing] two fingers to the rest of Europe', Perkins notes *Paddington*'s irony, inasmuch as it 'counteracts the idea you have to put walls up'.[1]

The important detail here is that, in the case of the *Paddington* films, we are not simply referring to any supposed persistent appeal of British cinema abroad. My interest here in StudioCanal, and its popular *Paddington* series in particular (*Paddington 2* was released towards the end of 2017), relates to its distinctive position in the contexts of contemporary cinema and politics. At a moment when the UK has sought to distance itself politically from mainland Europe, StudioCanal, a French-based production and distribution company, has turned to English cultural content as a lynchpin in its creative and commercial strategies. In terms of Paddington, moreover, its key property is in the form of an immigrant bear in London. As this final chapter argues, viewing British cinema in 'European' terms is not only of cultural and political significance, but is also, as a bonus, strategically important in terms of a (so-called) 'national' industry.

As another mainly London-based, literary-derived film, *Paddington* is at first sight another example of the export-driven, metropolitan cinema that has to a large extent defined popular English cinema. The provenance of the films, though, as Anglo-French productions, complicates this idea. From one perspective, StudioCanal's recent turn towards English-language, family oriented films are a strategic attempt to consolidate presence in Anglophone markets. As noted in a previous chapter, alongside owning the Paddington IP, StudioCanal are also now the production and European distribution partners for the UK's Aardman Animations, overseeing recent titles such as *Early Man* (2018), *The Shaun the Sheep Movie* (2016) and its sequel, *Farmageddon* (2019).

As Christopher Meir has recently explored in his book on the company, this turn towards English-language content has come at a time of restructuring and expansion on the part of StudioCanal, as part of their aim to become a European 'major' studio.[2] As I explore in this chapter, while the company has looked to English-language content as one of its mainstays, it is important to note the ways the company's use of such properties conforms to its aims of becoming a specifically *European* cinematic force, with a distinctively continental view towards its content and its audiences.

As Meir has noted, a 'proximity to Hollywood' still persists on StudioCanal's part, with regard to what he calls the company's 'inclin[ation] to work within the Hollywood norms'.[3] We can see this in terms of StudioCanal's engagement with genre cinema (action and/or spy movies, such as *Unknown* [2011], *Tinker Tailor Soldier Spy* [2011] and *Non-Stop* [2014]); or their co-financing involvement with Working Title, in films like *Bridget Jones's Baby* (2016), as well as their 'concentration in the UK and the US' as far as production is concerned. Indeed, *Paddington* drew on the expertise of David Heyman's Heyday Films, the London-based production company behind the *Harry Potter* series. While acknowledging Meir's reservations, we can nevertheless make a strong case for the European peculiarity of the *Paddington* series; especially – in this instance – in terms of the films' content, but also, as I will go on to discuss, in terms of the way the films are released, promoted and viewed outside the UK.

The StudioCanal project is also a significant case study for the present book, since it invites us to reflect on possible limitations with regard to the concept of 'national cinema'; indeed, it invites us to question why we talk about a British or any other 'national cinema' at all. In a timely way, these films suggest that thinking European, and thinking of Britain *as* European, could be the fertile path for a 'British cinema' at this time; even if, to a significant degree, this means calling into question the identity and coherence of this national cinema in the first place. This potentially has significance for the ways, hitherto, we have often talked about, categorized and historicized film, and in turn, for what we might otherwise call 'British film studies'. As I mentioned in my introduction, one concern in this book is to question and challenge the forms of what Ulrich Beck calls 'methodological nationalism'.[4] This represents the critical tendency, sometimes inadvertent, to frame discussions and perspectives from a problematically, and for Beck, misleadingly limited viewpoint of the nation state. Such a perspective sees cultural production and representation predominantly in terms of what it says about 'the nation' or in its continuities with a 'national' tradition and history. For Beck, such approaches overlook the *cosmopolitan* contexts of contemporary identity and the political and representational obligations to think in these more hybrid and transnational terms.

British film production, often making use of transnational funding resources, has certainly not avoided the kinds of contexts Beck discusses. But the broader industrial, as well as political or identity-related question of a 'cosmopolitan' cinema has been less frequently addressed. While noting, as I discussed at the end of Chapter 1, that UK film policy has perennially been turned more towards the United States, Andrew Spicer, echoing Beck's terms, identifies the increasing tendency for more fragmented and polarized conceptions of cinematic taste and culture to be 'superseded by a "global cosmopolitanism"'.[5] This cosmopolitan sense, in spite of the broader Euroscepticism in the British film industry, has encouraged 'the particular attitude and alignment of UK producers towards "being European"'. Taking the same lead, this chapter therefore asks what benefits – commercial, as well as cultural – there might be for 'thinking European'. Is there a case, for example, for thinking of films such as *Paddington* not just as 'culturally English', to use Andrew Higson's term, but actually as *culturally European*?[6] Most importantly for the present study, why would such a way of understanding the films be important in the contexts of Brexit? Before answering these questions, however, it is useful to survey some of the recent contexts for British film production and the relationship to Europe within these contexts, before looking in more detail at what StudioCanal is doing as a European producer and distributor.

British cinema and the 'European Market'

As outlined in Chapter 2, in May 2018, the European Audiovisual Observatory published a document analysing the significance of UK film in the European market. Entitled *Brexit in Context*, the report highlighted both the recent and current status of British films amongst EU28 countries, and the potential impacts of Britain's withdrawal from the EU on this position. As we have already seen, the data, seen especially in the immediate contexts of the EU referendum, are revealing.[7] As a film-producing nation, between 2011 and 2016 the UK, out of all EU countries, led the way in terms of the amount of films made. Overall, 16 per cent of all films in the EU, it notes, are technically 'British'. In terms of these films' penetration in EU markets, moreover, the UK lies only behind France as the dominant exporter, providing 15 per cent of all non-national films screened in EU28 countries. These statistics on their own suggest at once a thriving domestic industry and healthy relationship with Europe. Such bare statistics alone only tell a partial story, though, not least because they do not address the *types* of films being exported. What is more, details regarding how the UK *receives* films from the wider EU are revealing in their contrast, indicating that the UK lags behind the EU average in terms of the EU non-national films it imports. Indeed, the UK is an outlier in the EU, inasmuch as other EU28 countries tend to watch a majority of non-native European films; the opposite of the case in the UK. Above all, though, these statistics in themselves do not address the question of co-production, which is, again, an area in which British cinema lags behind many EU counterparts.

This is a point taken up recently by Simon Perry, the veteran producer and former CEO of British Screen; the government-subsidized company that provided production loans for British films in the 1980s and 1990s, before being subsumed within the UK Film Council in 2000. Perry reiterates the point that British films are '[t]he one type of European film at the moment that crosses borders significantly', while also stressing how low a priority European co-production is for British producers.[8] In contrast to Perry's tenure at British Screen, the UK Film Council, as we have seen in Chapter 1, showed significantly more interest in larger-scale, inward investment films than in indigenous or European production: indeed, prominent voices from within either the UK Film Council or its progenitors specifically targeted British

Screen for its overly 'European' focus.⁹ For Perry, an irony here is that Britain, compared at least to some of its European neighbours, has got 'so much less money' to spend on film production, making European co-production, in fact, a more logical option as an industrial strategy.¹⁰

Research carried out for the recent Mediating Cultural Encounters through European Screens (MeCETES) project corroborates these findings, as well as identifying this export/co-production imbalance at a policy level. The 2012 *New Horizons for UK Film* plan, published by the BFI – since 2010, with the demise of the UK Film Council, the government-designated body responsible for the promotion of British cinema – makes no mention of European countries as potential production partners.¹¹ Indeed, as the *Brexit in Context* report highlighted, the significantly highest proportion of co-production investment in UK cinema (23 per cent of films) was from the United States. This is unsurprising, in terms of what we have already seen to be the UK's reliance on Hollywood inward investment. Yet at the same time, as Huw David Jones has shown, European investment in majority UK-produced films during a similar period seems to have benefited such productions. The wider distribution afforded to such films as co-productions encouraged higher audience presence across the EU than would otherwise be achieved by exclusively British productions. Yet the more successful films from this group, Jones notes – such as the period drama *The Duchess* (2008), or StudioCanal's John Le Carré adaptation *Tinker Tailor Soldier Spy* – were not ones that suggested any kind of *cultural* collaboration with co-producing nations, and could in fact 'pass as "culturally British"'.¹²

As Jones's research identifies, there are apparent benefits for British film working transnationally in production terms. But at the same time, the notion of British cinema as *part of* a broader 'European' cinema, such as it exists, is sketchy. In industry policy terms, the idea of Europe has been positioned uncertainly: between, on the one hand, a culture and market to which Britain belongs; or distinctly, as merely a captive external market for British films. In principle, as Philip Schlesinger notes in his work on the UK Film Council, the link to the wider continent was an inherent part of the latter's remit and practices.¹³ This 'European dimension' was a necessary aspect of the Council's brief, by simple virtue of the fact that the UK was a longstanding EU country when the UKFC was formed.¹⁴ This transnational remit on the part of the UKFC was borne out by its engagement with EU audiovisual policies, and its decision to set up a MEDIA Programme desk.[15] It remains questionable though how high the idea of developing a 'European' cinema, properly speaking, was on the agenda here: as Schlesinger suggests, even within the UKFC itself this was deemed by some a 'low priority'.[16] But how, though, could the ideas of a 'UK Film Council' and 'European cinema' ever be meaningfully reconciled? The operation of a *national* film-policy within the more federalist idea of the European Union is already, from one perspective, a contradiction in terms. As Schlesinger asks, 'how might film agencies such as the UKFC – expressly constituted as bastions of the national culture and economy, as state-created institutions in a world of states – relate to the international, the transnational and the global?'[17]

As part of an answer to this question, Schlesinger cites former film producer and executive David Puttnam, a key driver of New Labour film policy and the UKFC's formation, in terms of his appeal to cultural and economic struggle against US cinematic dominance. At the end of his 1997 book *The Undeclared War*, Puttnam's emphasis, notably, is as much on the continental as on the national:

> The roots of our strength in Europe go back a long way … The opportunities still beckon. Potentially, we possess a huge, if fragmented, domestic market right here on our doorstep. With over three hundred million consumers, the European Union has the largest fully developed audio-visual market in the world in terms of customers.[18]

As Meir argues, referring specifically to Puttnam's manifesto, the idea of a major European studio, while formerly 'posed in hypothetical terms … is now a reality'.[19] And yet, just as Meir queries the 'European' identity of StudioCanal, Puttnam's particular idea of a 'European' studio is here qualified by his own acknowledged location, shared with that of his implied British reader, of having 'Europe … on our doorstep'. There is consequently a tension at work between (as Schlesinger terms it) Puttnam's call 'to exploit Europe's cultural assets', and the sense that this is in actuality no more than a *British* 'domestic market' that just happens to be located in the European Union.[20]

These may seem like semantic quibbles. Yet on the one hand, they draw attention to the tendency to separate Britain from Europe in policy terms, rather than see Britain and its production as 'European'. They also raise the broader question of what 'British' film culture and industry might mean in 'European' terms, without just devolving the concept of European cinema to 'a simple aggregation of discrete national cinemas'.[21] As Andrew Higson and Richard Maltby have commented, historical efforts to think of a unified European cinema (or a 'Film Europe') as an industrial, competing counter-practice to Hollywood have inevitably been torn between irreconcilable agenda: the impulse, on the one hand, to be 'universally intelligible', while at the same time retaining 'local forms of cultural expression'.[22] What, indeed, could possibly constitute a 'European' cinema, given the tenuousness of the concept?

It is little wonder that so many aspirations to a transnational European film have had to contend with the complexities of accommodating varied personnel and languages. Or alternatively, as has perennially been the case since the 1980s, such films have aspired to wider significance precisely by *relinquishing* difference: the point Meir makes, similarly, in terms of StudioCanal's apparent concessions to 'Hollywood norms'. Typically, this means filming in the cinematic *lingua franca* of English, or at least in the 'global' audio-visual language of Hollywood narrative style. As Schlesinger persuasively suggests in an earlier essay, though, this 'problem' of European identity also has potentially transformative implications for how we understand so-called 'national cinemas' in the first place, especially with regard to ideas of representing national spaces and cultures in light of the impact of 'regional trade groupings', such as the EU.[23] In what ways, for instance, can 'discrete national cinemas' highlight and explore their own transformation within, say, these 'trade groupings', and to what effect? And what would be the broader benefits – political, cultural, commercial – of such an approach?

The internalist discourses of British cinema

Another point made by Schlesinger is that, inadvertently or otherwise, much of the discussion around UK film policy, both from an expansionist *or* protectionist perspective, in some ways amounts to the same inward-looking practice. Even when trying to reconcile cultural and economic questions, these discourses are typically 'internalist' in their preoccupation with 'the national', as an industry and an implied collective body represented in and through such films.[24] This is another example of the methodological nationalism critiqued by Beck, in the way its very methods and reference points work towards maintaining the coherence of the nation state, as well as naturalizing the idea of 'national' culture as a subject of history and of study. Film scholarship in the UK (or again, more accurately, English) context, my own included, has to some extent perpetuated this internalist framework without necessarily meaning to do so, as evidenced by the breadth of monographs or edited collections focusing on 'British cinema' or 'English cinema' as their object of study. Even when seeking, with good intentions, to distinguish a British national cinema within a global film industry dominated by Hollywood, such criticism can occasionally drift into an unabashedly internalist narrative of British cinema's struggles and triumphs. While alert to the UK's complex cinematic relationship to Europe, for instance, Geoffrey Macnab's recent history of the British film industry since the 1980s begins with ebullient but internally directed prefatory observations: '[In] 2018 ... business [for British cinema] appears to be booming as never before'; 'By 2018 ... [m]any of the biggest global box-office hits of the period were being made not in Hollywood but in Britain – a state of affairs that not even the most optimistic industry observers from 30 years before would ever have considered to be either likely or remotely possible.'[25]

This tendency to discuss British cinema mostly in isolation from European contexts, and alongside this, the peculiar situation of British cinema as operating at once within *and* outside the territories and discourses of the EU, is also highlighted by a recent high-profile volume, *The Europeanness of European Cinema*.[26] While both rich and comprehensive in its focus on national and above all transnational cinemas across the European continent, the volume happens not to devote any chapter to British films as a part of these contexts.[27] A number of the essays, nevertheless, touch on the recent dominance of English as a linguistic signifier in 'European' productions; whether this be in forms of 'prestige' co-productions, aspiring to universal appeal and UK/US audiences (*Goya's Ghosts* [2006]; *Perfume: The Story of a Murderer* [2006]), or from smaller producing countries, looking simply to 'broaden their potential markets, in the absence of ... higher production values'.[28] As Higson affirms elsewhere, in his analysis of the European box-office between 2005 and 2014, English-language 'heritage' dramas and literary adaptations enjoy a majority share: not just those dealing with specifically British subject matter (*Pride and Prejudice* [2005], *Elizabeth: The Golden Age* [2007], *Atonement* [2007]), but also those whose source material or reference points are from mainland European countries (*Perfume*; *The Three Musketeers* [2011]; *Les Misérables* [2012]; *Anna Karenina* [2012]).[29]

British cinema, in other words, either in a production or academic context, has until recently rarely been discussed *as* European; while the predominance of English-language productions in European cinema is often viewed as limited in its artistic reach, or again, a concession to dominant global norms. The productive possibilities of British cinema as a 'culturally European' entity are rarely broached, as recent UK film policy has underlined. In terms of the UKFC, the type of specifically cultural concerns relating to a 'shared European identity', a key focus of European Commission-driven film initiatives, were of markedly less concern to the inward-looking priorities of the Council.[30] Under its first chairman, the director Alan Parker, the UKFC was seen by many commentators to turn the industry 'away from Europe', together with its 'relationships and … support network', and in turn to pursue a Hollywood-style studio model.[31] Co-production support, moreover, was low on the financial support agenda, with just £45,000 per year being provided to help pursue European co-production agreements, compared, for example, to the £900,000 allocated annually to encourage (mostly United States) inward investment.[32] It is films made from this latter investment, of course, that constitute the 'biggest global box-office hits' mentioned above by Macnab.

When British Screen was dissolved to make way for the UKFC, this already marked a turn away from European concerns, as it also put an end to the European Co-Production Fund that British Screen had administered since 1991.[33] Indeed, as suggested by some of the most prominent figures behind the newly formed UKFC, such as Puttnam and Chief Executive John Woodward, to pursue 'European' cultural aspirations would only be a hindrance. For Puttnam, Simon Perry would have been unsuited to the leading Film Council role on the grounds that he was a 'film-maker's executive, not a business executive', and as a result too 'European-focused'.[34] Woodward, speaking to a French journalist in 2000, was even more pragmatic about the UKFC's role: 'We are certainly not prepared, nowadays, to support … European foreign-language films, which won't find a distributor in Britain.'[35]

One of the main suppositions emerging here is that adopting a more 'culturally European' approach to film production practices is incompatible with a commercial model. Certainly, as noted above, the UKFC's story is marked by the tension between pursuing more culturally driven schemes, such as Eurimages, that are more familiar in continental Europe, and the intention to 'turn the UK into the "Hollywood of Europe"'.[36] As former UKFC board member John Hill suggests, the 'pro-Hollywood position' of the Council's most powerful figures exerted a strong influence, and partly explained the resistance on the part of most board members to the UK re-joining Eurimages, which it had left in 1996.[37] What we should nevertheless note here, as a qualification, is that membership of Eurimages and participation in European co-production are not the same thing. The choice sometimes seems to be a straightforward and simplistic one between the economic advantages of an internalist, inward investment, exporting model and the (perhaps) culturally beneficial, though in principle economically inexpedient notion of making 'European' films. As already noted though, with reference to Jones's work, European co-production may offer economic benefits as well as cultural ones. For Spicer, moreover, one of the consequences of 'global cosmopolitanism' is the disruption of 'formerly polarized oppositions between Europe and Hollywood'.[38] In other words, the very contexts of global cosmopolitanism have opened up new ways of imagining national identity, with connotations and implications for film genre and style, beyond the schematic opposition between Hollywood and the rest of the world. As I will now discuss, this is very much evident as a view within StudioCanal's family oriented films, and just as specifically, the policies informing their production.

The 'family film' as culturally European film

I will focus here on the possibilities of the 'family' film, within which terms I discuss the *Paddington* movies, for a number of reasons. As Jones identifies, while the narrow cultural specificities of genres like comedy tend to travel badly, family film is a rare example of a film type that fares well across diverse European contexts. This is partly down to the fact that the family film – incorporating animations, fantasy and superhero franchises, and children's or Young Adult series like *Harry Potter* – is an increasingly comprehensive form that more or less 'transcends cinematic typology'.[39] As a relatively new phenomenon, though, the international significance of family cinema invites the question of why this form should work so persuasively across markets, and indeed, what such films actually *mean* across these different contexts.

The first two *Paddington* films might, on the surface, reiterate a similar production model to the *Harry Potter* movies (with which, as noted above, they share a producer). Both series make use of culturally English literary properties and locations, as well as drawing on an array of well-known English acting talent.[40] Yet the *Paddington* films also represent the fully developed outcome of several years of production strategy development on the part of StudioCanal. Significantly, coming as it does out of the more protectionist cinematic contexts of France, StudioCanal has, since the start of the 2010s, sought to shift its focus. Less interested now in financing Hollywood productions, its aim is to become a European distributor 'at the source': primarily, the major European markets of France, UK and Germany, where the company has sought to establish itself as 'the European leader in Europe'.[41] The language used by StudioCanal's French CEO Didier Lupfer is interesting in the way it echoes yet refines Puttnam's earlier vision for the role of Europe as a cinematic market. Rather than see Europe as a captive market just across the doorstep, Lupfer stresses StudioCanal's aim to make 'high-quality European films', using 'the biggest talent our continent has to offer'.[42]

Echoing these sentiments, a report on the French industry website *Le Film Français*, focusing on StudioCanal's presentation at the 2017 CineEurope convention, emphasized the company's reliance not only on family films, but on the specifically *international* diversity of family films they had to offer.[43] As Meir argues, StudioCanal's approach in this respect emulates the recent dominant Hollywood model, though it is at the same time an effort to capture this particular bit of the audience terrain from Hollywood.[44] As Meir and other industry commentators have argued, the transformation in StudioCanal's fortunes since the early 2000s owes much to its shift from mostly French-language content with a domestic slant, towards what is now a slate of around 70 per cent English-language films, with two thirds of revenues coming from international sales.[45] But in the CineEurope presentation there was also an implicitly political emphasis on the significance of sourcing production with a continental perspective. As Anna Marsh, its then vice-president of international marketing, put it, the support of diverse local talents was part of StudioCanal's 'vocation', from its standpoint as 'the premier European studio'. Notably, the previewed content and points of reference at the presentation centred on the company's British-made family offerings: *Paddington 2*, Aardman's *Early Man* and the second *Shaun the Sheep* movie.[46]

Paddington is in this respect seen, from its producers' viewpoint, not just as a Hollywood-style film 'made in Europe', but rather as a key aspect of StudioCanal's bid to identify and own 'big, resonant European cultural icons'.[47] It is, furthermore, an indication of Lupfer's belief in 'Europe's IP potential'; a potential which, Lupfer asserts, may be 'culturally, historically … even greater than in the US'.[48] It is worth pointing out that *Paddington* was only acquired by StudioCanal when it was dropped by Warner Bros., who have a first-look deal with Heyday Films (with whom they produced the *Harry Potter* films).[49] As Meir points out, initiatives such as the distribution deal with Working Title show that StudioCanal are capitalizing on 'European-themed projects': projects, in this instance 'that parent company Universal had passed over'.[50] Indeed, Aardman's current arrangement with StudioCanal followed the mixed results of their Hollywood major-studio production deals (with Dreamworks [1997–2007] and then Sony [2007–2013]).[51] In June 2016, to cement their investment, StudioCanal negotiated the rights to the Paddington Bear intellectual property, thereby opening up the possibility of a third and further films, in addition to other licensing opportunities.[52] In 2019, for example, the company announced it would be producing, with Heyday Films, an animated Paddington TV series for the children's network Nickelodeon.[53]

From a purely economic point of view, the *Paddington* films have added value as an Anglo-French property. As StudioCanal are also distributors in some territories, they can more easily access the markets seen as vital to their films' success. In these contexts, StudioCanal's management of distribution means that the films can be opened competitively against Hollywood films. Unsurprisingly, it is in France, as well as in Germany (where StudioCanal also manages distribution), that the *Paddington* films were released using a 'saturation' screening approach. *Paddington 2*, for instance, was released in France on the highest number of screens (631), and in the UK, the second highest number in its first week (607), and subsequently the highest for several weeks until the release of *Star Wars: The Last Jedi* (2017). Along with the similar release pattern for *Early Man*, there is clear indication here of the company's commitment to rivalling Hollywood: if not globally, then at least – and this is the key point – in its local European territories. One third of *Paddington 2*'s worldwide box-office receipts, in fact, came from Britain and France alone.[54]

But beyond these economic aspects, what about the films' cultural dimensions? In line with its recent production turn, as noted above, the *Paddington* films might confirm the view of StudioCanal as essentially an English-language 'content factory'.[55] To take such a sweeping view, though, would be to downplay some of the specific representational work the films perform. I do not refer simply to the fact that the two films deal with the adventures of an economic migrant in the UK; a point made widely in relation to the two films, emerging as they did, respectively, against the contexts of a rising support for Nigel Farage's UK Independence Party (UKIP), an emerging European refugee crisis, and subsequently, the UK's vote to leave the EU. To pick up on Spicer's point about the already 'cosmopolitan' contexts of contemporary 'national' culture, what is significant is the extent to which these already-European productions situate their narratives within English spaces re-worked and re-inscribed by layers of immigrant experience, and the traces of a cultural globalization that is identified and reflected upon. The films therefore address the question, posed above by Schlesinger, of what a 'national cinema' might look like when the national is revisioned through its placement within 'regional trade groupings' – or, in this instance, the impacts of economic and cultural globalization more broadly.

Resituating Michael Billig's notion of 'banal nationalism' within the contemporary contexts of globalization, Beck has argued for the prevalence, in major cities above all, of 'banal cosmopolitanism'. For Beck, cosmopolitanism is in many respects both a cause and product of consumerism; a hybrid, eclectic identity that permeates everyday culture and interactions. Like banal nationalism, which can be worn lightly, even unconsciously, banal cosmopolitanism is a 'badge' that many of us wear, 'whether willingly or unwillingly', merely by our immersion and interaction with diverse metropolitan identities and cultural forms.[56] This has important implications for films like *Paddington*, as the contexts of cosmopolitanism revise some of the erstwhile contexts of popular British cinema. I have argued elsewhere that certain tendencies of British film – specifically, parodic films such as *Wallace and Gromit: The Curse of the Were-Rabbit* (2005) or *Hot Fuzz* (2007) – are deft in the way they both appeal to, yet comically undermine, the stability of 'national' images and representations. In their uses of global inter-textual reference points, situated alongside traditional or stereotypical representations of Englishness, held in incongruous juxtaposition, such films highlight the already 'glocalized' nature of much contemporary English life, within a global cultural economy.[57] There are obviously points of continuity here with the *Paddington* films, yet there is some significant variation too. The purposeful strategy of a film like *Hot Fuzz* seems to destabilize, through ironic juxtaposition, the possibility of global and local forms operating in a coherent way. If the English parody film creates humour through its very incongruity, the *Paddington* series is slightly different, inasmuch as it takes this collision of identities within the modern metropolis as a fundamental and more *realist* aspect of its narrative and mise-en-scène. This is also what makes the films, arguably, more amenable to diverse audiences than, say, a film like *Hot Fuzz*, which is somewhat prescribed by its specific engagement with the peculiarities of modern English space and culture.

Within the terms of banal cosmopolitanism, cultural collisions take on different connotations, pointing less to impossible and ironized identities, but rather to a form of modern condition within globalization. As Beck puts it: 'What seems from a postmodern perspective to be [merely] "eclecticism" or "inauthenticity" (and from the perspective of critiques of culture as "lack of roots" or "lack of memory") can be understood in terms of a new reflexivity.'[58] Looked at from this perspective, in fact, the representational play at work in the *Paddington* films suggests as much a new form of *cosmopolitan realism*. Seen this way, the *Paddington* films also offer important perspectives for understanding contemporary cinematic style and content. Implicit in Beck's comment about 'critiques of culture', with its emphasis on 'lack of roots', is a perennial tension between the view of British film as a largely Hollywood-inflected industry, and its (in)capacity to represent the nation in terms of its politics, diversity and also social and economic disparities. As already noted in Chapter 1, this is a much-rehearsed issue across a range of outputs in the field of British film studies.[59] The transnational contexts and ambitions of the *Paddington* films, though, do not necessarily place them within the 'postnational'-type of cinema that, for many critics, replaces national specificities or distinctions with a 'global' (or, indeed, 'Hollywood') film style. At the same time, neither do the films collapse into a limiting or nostalgic view of the national. It is important, for example, to note the extent to which the first *Paddington* film builds the immigrant perspective not merely into its narrative but into its settings and mise-en-scène. The calypso band whose tunes play both extra-diegetically and, with the magical appearance of the band itself, diegetically, offer an audio-visual reiteration of Caribbean immigration, and its historical importance to the West London locations in which the film takes place. Specifically, this offers an implicit revision of the gentrified, predominantly white image of the area as seen in Working Title's *Notting Hill*.[60] *Paddington* director and co-writer Paul King has said he wanted to use this music because of its upbeat attitude to the realities of the immigrant experience, but also because it was, as he suggests, 'largely neglected'.[61] Moreover, the music's frequent plaintiveness, such as the song 'Blow Wind Blow', with its lyrics lamenting London's icy weather and less-than-warm welcome, combines with images of Paddington's temporary homelessness and rejection, bringing out the figurative 'coldness' of the capital city, especially for those living marginally within its rainy streets. There is a pleasant irony to the fact that the antagonist in *Paddington 2*, a faded and devious thespian named Phoenix Buchanan, is played by Hugh Grant, almost two decades after *Notting Hill* established a defining image of white, floppy-haired English masculinity. In a neat piece of self-effacement, which is also self-reflexive in its gesture, dozens of framed photos of Grant in his rom-com prime can be spotted around Phoenix's house: idealized images of another time, and by their allusions to Grant's earlier film work, another largely romanticized Notting Hill.

The *Paddington* films, it should be said, are not without their own contradictions and tensions. It is a stretch to suggest that the revision of the Notting Hill area here seriously redresses decades of occlusion in British film: the nod to history, for instance, cannot cover the fact that the films' main roles are almost exclusively played by white actors. Yet as a film about a particular kind of immigrant perspective, albeit refracted through the figure of a talking bear, it is not unreasonable here to evoke Hamid Naficy's concept of an 'accented cinema' to describe the series. 'Accented' films, for Naficy, which narrate the experience of displaced or diasporic peoples, tend to be 'simultaneously local and global … commenting upon, and critiquing the home and host societies and cultures' in which they are made and set'.[62] As well as evocations of metropolitan harshness and rejection, though, 'critique' can also take the softer form of ironic or parodied representations, viewed from a marginal perspective. For example, when the film plays Aldwyn Roberts' song 'London is the Place for Me' over a montage of the city, viewed from Paddington's taxi window, the already-accented, over-the-top lyrics allow the song's upbeat tone to be gently offset with wry humour.

As Meir has argued, StudioCanal's increased global prominence and ambition has impacted, in a reductive fashion, on its approach to geographical representation. As he puts it, the company has increasingly tended in its films 'to picture Europe via a catalog of capitals and clichés'.[63] In particular, argues Meir, films like *Paddington* 'make use of what Charlotte Brunsdon has dubbed "Landmark London" … and as such visually run through a litany of familiar sites'.[64] As Brunsdon highlights in her study of London on film, the montage sequence, such as we see in the taxi ride in *Paddington*, is a familiar means of introducing the cinematic city. Meir nevertheless underestimates the way that, in *Paddington*, the uses of musical soundtrack, but also a more parodic use of the montage device, offer an accented reading. In this instance, the taxi ride takes in the 'litany of familiar sites' that includes Piccadilly Circus and other West End landmarks. Though the joke may be largely for the benefit of those familiar with London geography, the specific gag here is that this is a nonsensical route from Paddington Station. This is underscored when, at the end of the taxi ride, the fastidious Mr Brown questions the driver's diversion, motivated mainly by the generic demands of the film (as the driver himself comments, he wanted Paddington to 'see the city'). There is a tacit acknowledgement here that this sort of introductory 'landscape montage' rarely makes any strict geographical sense, but rather forms part of the 'impossible geographies' constituted aesthetically and virtually by film.[65]

This negotiation of global genre expectations, while also introducing variation, humour and ambiguity, is key to the aesthetic strategies of the *Paddington* films. True to their global commercial remit, the films allow for types of exoticized or touristic Englishness, with *Paddington* briefly visiting Buckingham Palace, and its sequel staging sequences at both Tower Bridge and Saint Paul's Cathedral. Yet it is also *through* the use of its 'typically English' settings that the films underscore the way national space, and especially *metropolitan* space, is already transnational, and predominantly *European*, constructed via decades of immigrant and refugee experience: contexts that informed Michael Bond's original books.[66] Mr Gruber's Portobello Road shop, for instance, with its toy trains and fine china cups, also accumulates wall-to-wall paintings and bric-a-brac, which along with its old furniture and knitted throws is a nostalgic bubble of an English past constructed by the proprietor (sent to England, as he narrates, on the *Kindertransport* during World War Two). Similarly, the travelling funfair that plays an important narrative role in *Paddington 2*, in its itinerant status already a liminal space of sorts, is owned by a Polish woman, Madame Kozlova. As the author of the pop-up book of London that, in the film's narrative, provides the key to hidden treasure, Madame Kozlova's 'accented' view of the city adroitly allows the film to showcase a series of preferred tourist locations. Yet at the same time, it can filter these through an outsider's idealizing gaze: an early scene in the film, in fact, shows these sights literally unfolding and rising in book form, the film's characters imaginarily projecting themselves inside. Like this book, the toy train that daily brings Mr Gruber his eleven o'clock cup of tea in *Paddington* is an overtly fabricated view of an idealized city, but its framing as such allows such images to work in a form of suspension between the actual and the imagined (Figure 6.1). The fact that this is the same train used to recall Mr Gruber's childhood flight from the Nazis, in fact, indicates how the film neatly and poignantly bridges these two worlds: a fantasy it may be, but one highlighted as a form of refuge from terrible realities.

Figure 6.1 London's European city as a port in a storm: Mr Gruber remembers the *Kindertransport* in *Paddington*. Directed by Paul King © StudioCanal 2014. All rights reserved.

This supports King's point that his film, rather than one targeting contemporary British immigration policies, is a universal story, referring to a much longer history of economic migration and broader political intolerance.[67] Yet these are also important aspects of the Paddington stories', and the films', particular appeal to an aspect of British history, one threaded through so much of its wider children's fiction. The review of *Paddington* in the left-wing French daily *Libération* underscores, in this regard, the almost ambassadorial and wider European identity of such films, as indeed their economic *and* cultural commitment to a particular kind of European cinema. In this instance, the paper's critic highlights 'the way in which British identity serves as a backdrop, even the stage, for a whole range of literary or cinematic output aimed at children'.[68] As the review concludes, *Paddington* is 'a lesson in tolerance … and a welcome invitation, in the charitable post-war British tradition, to all of life's shipwrecked'.[69]

As astutely noted in a later French article, a production feature on *Paddington 2* in *Première* magazine, it is actually the introduction of these outside elements that, both in this same British tradition and in the *Paddington* films themselves, makes the domestic more hospitable. It is the stuffy refinement and rigid stability associated with more hierarchical English culture that, in fact, contains its own barbarism: one that consequently needs to be challenged and transformed by 'the difference of others'.[70] The subsequent significance of *Paddington 2* to the emerging contexts of Brexit was, unsurprisingly, not lost on that particular writer. It is telling, though, that the same critic saw the *Paddington* series as a means of confronting Britain's complex but also rich past and present situation vis-à-vis these foreign 'others' – and not simply a means of avoiding them via nostalgic idealizations.

Accenting animation: The family film across European contexts

Additionally – and significantly, in terms of these films' intended markets – this 'accented' element has an added layer in international distribution, because of the spoken languages used in dubbed versions. In some cases, in fact – as in Aardman's *Shaun the Sheep* films, which barely use dialogue at all – StudioCanal's investment in family film enables them to bypass national specificity and language altogether. These films are therefore more easily able 'to transcend linguistic borders', as well as incur less production expense for foreign language versions: a significant addition, in other cases, to films' bottom-line costs.[71] It would seem, nevertheless, that *Paddington* is a different proposition: as Noel Brown remarks, for instance, while the company's investment in films like *Shaun the Sheep* shows economic pragmatism, StudioCanal's investment in English-language productions like *Paddington* is 'telling', indicating again the perceived dominance of English-language cinema in the global market.

There is, certainly, a distinction between the Anglo-French *Paddington* series and earlier efforts to construct a European family franchise; a key example being the long-running French-language *Astérix* films (1999–), which have enjoyed a fair amount of success on the European mainland, but are barely seen or discussed in Anglophone countries.[72] A key reason for this, we would surmise, would be less a familiarity or otherwise with the source material (Astérix is as familiar to many British readers as Paddington is to those across the Channel), but rather the difficulty that foreign-language film has in making a major impact in the subtitle- and dubbing-resistant British and American markets. By contrast, in the more flexible viewing contexts of France and other mainland European countries, 'English-language productions' are more amenable to audiences, meaning such production strategies have less obvious negative impact.

Yet also, as full or partial animations, films like the Aardman productions or the *Paddington* series offer additional benefits in European contexts. A quick look at box-office statistics for films in France offers an indication of how 'English-language films', but above all English-language *animations*, comfortably transcend national and (notional) linguistic barriers. While France's strong production and exhibition culture help an uncommon amount of domestically produced films to reach wide audiences, French films jostle alongside a number of franchise works familiar from the British or US lists. Notably, Hollywood animated films – Disney-Pixar's *Toy Story 4* (2019), *Coco* (2017) and *Inside Out* (2015), Disney's *Moana* (2016) and *Zootopia* (2016), or Universal's *Despicable Me 3* (2017) and *Minions* (2015) – have figured highly in these lists over the last few years. Of course, with animation, the attribution of 'language' becomes hazier: *all* animation, in contrast to live-action film, is technically 'dubbed', in terms of the lack of precise synchronization between vocal track and 'speaking' character. This enables animation in particular to adapt to varied linguistic contexts. As Rayna Denison has observed, for example, in her work on the transnational distribution processes underpinning Studio Ghibli's animation *Spirited Away* (2001), the 'Japanese' aspects of the latter film in French versions are to a large extent played down. This is partly through the effort in the French dialogue to rewrite Japanese specificities into French idioms or concepts; but mostly, it is through an accented delivery that imposes a form of 'linguistic naturalisation' on the text.[73]

Though live-action films, the *Paddington* series exploits the fact that its central protagonist is rendered in CGI, which allows the flexibility and more realistic voice synchronization otherwise available to animated characters. As in other markets, French publicity material for both *Paddington* and, subsequently, *Early Man* would highlight the familiar voice actors performing on the French-language versions.[74] But the amenability of non-UK and non-US audiences to subtitles is also advantageous, from an economic *and* cultural viewpoint, as it facilitates varied points of access to the films. As Denison points out, there were two versions of *Spirited Away* available to French 'audio-viewers': either the French-language *Le Voyage de Chihiro*, as it was more literally called, or the Japanese-language film *Sen to Chihiro no kamikakushi*. If the first version could effectively pass for a slightly accented form of 'French' film, the other could be enjoyed for its appeal to niche audiences and fans, distinguished in the process from the mainstream of cinematic exhibition.

Following a similar pattern, the original English-language version of *Paddington 2* opened alongside a dubbed version in fourteen out of twenty-two cinemas in the central Paris area: similarly, StudioCanal's 2018 release of *Early Man* in the same metropolitan concentration of screens offered fifteen subtitled versions out of twenty cinemas. In its opening week, cinemas showing both versions showed a fractionally higher audience average per screen than for those cinemas showing only dubbed versions (995 entries compared to 955).[75] This suggests that there is a benefit to exhibiting in the original English, while also hinting that the mainstay of exhibition – especially outside the metropolitan centre, where original-language versions were scarce – remains the French version. *Paddington* is in turn able to play in non-Anglophone markets both as a 'foreign' film for an audience amenable to subtitling, and yet predominantly, as a more 'mainstream' example of 'European' family film entertainment.

In this instance, the specific address within the family film, and above all in its animated form, to *children*, is an important inflection. As Jonathan Bignell has shown with reference mainly to television, the history of European children's animations, especially in the later decades of the twentieth century and beyond, is largely one of transnational cooperation: one in which TV series might have multiple points of production origin, and then exist in diverse forms according to the post-production editing and dubbing carried out prior to broadcast. The resulting products, including shows such as *The Magic Roundabout* and *The Moomins*, 'exemplif[ied] and instantiate[d] a transnational form of modernity', even if still perceived potentially as 'national' works.[76] Most pertinently for the aims of this chapter, Bignell's conclusions point towards our more contemporary moment and its possibilities for screen media more broadly, in terms of its capacity to signify and communicate across borders, especially within the terms of an expanding and more porous European Union:

> The kinds of hybridity, migration and exchange that were evident [through these animated series], but which went virtually unnoticed, point towards a contemporary moment in which a potential European audience of about 550 million people is open to stronger film and television co-production, format trading, reversioning and personnel exchange across national borders because of the changes in technology and political configuration that mark the early twenty-first century.[77]

In its bid to engage this sizeable 'European audience', StudioCanal's investment in both the *Paddington* brand and Aardman Animations is not surprising, underpinned as it is by the already-transnational status of these properties. *Shaun the Sheep*, for instance, was already a popular long-running television series across the world, and therefore had significant pre-awareness ahead of the 2016 movie, which consequently performed well in StudioCanal's key European markets (UK, France and Germany) as well as internationally (China, Japan, Australia and the United States). The *political* point to which Bignell gives voice, though, relates more specifically to the particular idea of 'the child' that views such shows and films. As Bignell concludes, the European child audience 'was thought of as a transnational entity that could be addressed and provided for by transnational programming'.[78] Bignell's argument, as noted above, focuses on the way that the perceived *national* significance of children's television texts, which in its own discursive terms connoted a sense of distinction from the hegemony of American television, belied the hybrid, already transnational nature of these children's shows.[79] The question of address, and in turn how the viewing subject is 'shaped' by the text, inevitably comes into play here, in terms of how or to what extent the child *in the audience*, rather than the demographic 'child audience', is itself constituted as 'a transnational entity'.

While it is impossible to answer such a broad question without wider audience study, we can offer some perspectives based on the examples presented in this chapter. As I have discussed, and as is implicit in Bignell's discussion of European television, particular forms of family film, along with the international exhibition practices that go with them, encourage a far less fixed and determined representation of space and place. These practices work further to produce and support an understanding of the film text as already reflexive; reasserting, especially in the case of the *Paddington* films, the form of cosmopolitan realism that, for Beck, is central to the representational stakes of contemporary globalization. Indeed, what is significant about the *Paddington* project is that, contrary to some of the critical expectations of British cinema as mainly an export commodity, such films perform parallel roles. Higson has argued, for instance, that globalization, though in theory bringing about a weakening or blurring of 'self-consciously national identity' in film, in fact generates the opposite outcome. Referring in fact to *Notting Hill*, Higson suggests that 'often the most traditional and stereotypical manifestations of ... national identity are reproduced ... for films intended for transnational circulation'.[80] I would not argue against this as a general point; but there is a risk that in looking at such films entirely from a national export perspective, we reduce the discussion of British film in Europe to a mostly Anglo-centric commercial strategy, established around deceptively or self-consciously inauthentic visions of the nation; or at least (in, say, *Notting Hill*, *Love Actually* or the *Bridget Jones* series), to limited articulations of the nation from a narrow perspective. In contrast, what is at work in films such as the *Paddington* series, *especially* once it circulates in a non-Anglophone context, is a destabilization of this 'national identity', constituting and representing its own expression and formation of a hybrid, cosmopolitan identity.

As concluding thoughts, we might also consider the significance of such films within, or rather against, the forms of 'internalist' critical and industrial frameworks discussed earlier in this chapter. As Brown suggests in his work on children's cinema, the discourses around such film, especially in the era of globalized cinema, frequently deal with the 'felt incompatibility' between national cultural and social expectations, and the 'economic necessity for [the family film] to transcend regional specificities … and reach a larger, transnational market'. This, Brown adds, 'is a perennial point of tension in concepts of "national" cinema'.[81] In relation to *children's* cinema, more particularly, the apparently aggressive and commercially protectionist policies of Hollywood studios in terms of content creation have been seen as a threat to children's cultural education and identity.[82] It is one of the ironies in this discussion, then, that films deemed to challenge this economic and cultural hegemony may themselves reiterate a similarly protectionist, but also an internalist and nationalist message. Brown, for instance, cites the popularity of the first *Asterix* installment, *Asterix and Obelisk vs.Caesar* (1999), which made $100m worldwide – though most of this, it should be noted, in France, where *Le Monde* described it rather grandly as 'the image of resistance to American cinematographic imperialism'.[83] Brown is alert to the fact that, in actuality, the *Asterix* films reflect a pan-European production ethos, in part demanded by the films' relatively high expense: the 1999 film, for instance, found its $45m budget through a three-way co-production deal with companies in France, Germany and Italy.[84] Such a transnational means of producing 'national' content underlines how in many cases (*Asterix*'s French example above all) models of 'resistant', 'national' cinema disavow their own links to broader cinematic practices and funding sources; while at the same time, they rely generically and stylistically on a demonized form of 'cultural globalization … crudely reified in the vision of Hollywood hegemony'.[85]

What might be more assertively stated, though, is the extent to which transnational practices of filmmaking are not merely semi-ironic, practical realities for the production of 'national' family movies. Rather, and especially in a time of resurgent populism and its threat to the European idea, the very transnational aspect of the family film, when foregrounded and celebrated, might work as a counter to the prevailing, protectionist binaries of 'Hollywood hegemony' versus national 'resistance'. And notably, such an idea would reposition and rethink 'conglomerate' production sources such as StudioCanal, especially if held up against the more internalist attitudes and practices on the part of more non-commercial national production infrastructures.

Conclusion: Waving the flag(s)

This chapter started with Danny Perkins's assessment regarding the ironies of *Paddington*'s success, in light of the UK's EU referendum. The deeper post-referendum irony is that this successfully 'British' series is born of the very European co-operation that the Brexit ideology wishes to reject – and that withdrawal from the EU would most likely jeopardize. Perkins' damning prognosis for Brexit, explicitly reworking the 'take back control' rhetoric of Leave, was that it risked privileging more inward investment from opportunistic studios over and above creative opportunity for smaller, independent companies. Brexit, he argues, 'feeds into having less control and putting things in the hands of big international companies who can exploit the fluctuations in the currency'.[86] It is again ironic that one of Britain's foremost cinematic ambassadors (Paddington, in this case, rather than Perkins) is threatened by the same forces that might, potentially, seek to defend him as a symbol of venerable, self-sufficient British traditions. But it is also notable that Paddington's continued rude health in the future would most likely result from the protection afforded not by the UK government or by those opportunistic 'big international companies', but rather by his French production parent, bolstered against the regulatory and economic vicissitudes of EU withdrawal. Paddington waves a flag that is red, white and blue, but whether this is the Union Jack or the *Tricolore* is a moot point. Personally, I prefer one of each in either hand: this, in any case, is a more accurate reflection not just of the films' production contexts, but also its European cultural affinities.

As Simon Perry comments, a potential irony of Brexit is that it reminds producers and film-policymakers of the importance of a European market, and area for co-production, they may have hitherto overlooked. Qualifying as EU product, Perry notes, holds significant benefits for films, giving them 'bigger value on the European market'.[87] Though Perry does not explain this point in detail, his meaning is made clear in some of the industry briefings commissioned in the wake of the EU referendum. As identified in Chapter 1, this relates to a combination of potential negative impacts; from the increased expense and logistical difficulty of production, to the lost added value of EU funding channels, to the added costs of distributing non-EU commodities across EU countries.[88] The cultural impact aside, Perry's conclusion is that, as a consistently popular export across European territories, British cinema would miss out if it failed to build contingencies for Brexit.

The homely but outward-looking lesson offered by the *Paddington*'s community-oriented stories is that we are less effective, and less happy, when working in isolation. But in terms of its localized global aesthetics, and its industrial production model, the same is true for the films themselves, as examples of European *and* English popular film. If these films suggest anything, then, it is that the opportunities for a thriving popular English cinema, and one that makes a cultural, political but also economic difference, will not be forthcoming if it merely looks inward, and contains its cinematic horizons within island shores. To borrow a slogan from 2016's Remain campaign, a message from the *Paddington* films is that we are 'stronger in Europe', in more ways than one.

Conclusion: Longing for yesterday?

One of the main observations emerging from this book is that the past maintains an imaginative grip on popular English cinema. A similar view emerged from a YouGov poll carried out in the spring of 2019. 'For each of the following times in history', the survey asked, 'do you think life was better then than it is now, or better now than it was then?'[1] Amongst those responding, there was perhaps surprisingly little idealism about the earlier decades of the twentieth century, up to the 1940s and 1950s. This did not simply reflect, however, the age of the respondents, since many found in favour of periods for which they could have no actual memory. Over a quarter of 18–29-year-olds, for example, believed that life was better in the 1980s than it is now, with the same number making the same claim for the present day. Identical figures were produced in the 30–39 bracket with reference to the 1960s. By their own nature, then, such data suggest the potency of popular cultural output from those eras, in terms of sustaining a favourable and attractive impression of a time and place.

Above all, though, the poll reflected the tendency to see 'better times' in relation to youth, while at the same time, highlighting the possible impact of recent political and economic contexts across specific demographics. Respondents between eighteen and forty-nine, for instance, overwhelmingly viewed the previous decade as better than the present one – the most contented age group being the over-60s. Over half of 30–39-year-olds and 40–49-year-olds, meanwhile, said that life was better in the 1990s, with only one in six saying the same thing for the present decade. On the whole, 48 per cent of over-60s, similarly, saw the 1960s as their decade of choice. Notably, economic affluence or social status seemed to make little difference in terms of view. Only slightly more respondents in the 'working class' C2DE grade than in the 'higher' ABC1 grade took the view, overall, that the past was better than the present. Nostalgia has a powerful hold on the British imagination, across the board.

As the journalist Simon Kuper remarks, in response to this survey, the British perspective of its past – which, as he nuances, is in majority terms an *English* view and lacks the historical antagonisms of other national perspectives within the UK – is a remarkably secure one, and also one with significance to the production of popular film.² Though Britain endured the Blitz, the loss of civilian life, and the death of servicemen and servicewomen, unlike other European countries, it was not invaded. Britain (with considerable help) was also spared the national trauma of surrender, occupation or collaboration. As already argued in this book, the capacity of popular English cinema to turn so readily and frequently to the Second World War, even when accommodating more revisionist details, is a remarkable indication of the cultural hold this event has on the national imaginary (or, at least, an expectation of this imaginary on the part of filmmakers and producers). Even the British Empire, and its colonial relationship to South Asia in particular, can become the stuff of light-hearted historical comedy (*Victoria and Abdul*), while the traumas of Indian Partition can still be negotiated within popular forms of historical drama with 'heritage' trappings, as in *Viceroy's House* (2017). The bustling activities of a stately home between the wars, meanwhile, preparing to meet the king and queen, are the subject of *Downton Abbey* (2019), the feature-film based on the hugely popular ITV series. Scripted as usual by the show's creator, Julian Fellowes (known to his fellow Conservative peers as Lord Fellowes of West Stafford), the film's upstairs–downstairs view suggests the past wasn't *all* forelock-tugging obsequiousness – even if, as the film's very existence demonstrates, this most exportable of English screen properties perpetuates a popular cultural deference to historical, upper-class life and history.

This is old news as far as British or English film studies is concerned. As I have discussed in this book, though, some of the erstwhile connotations of a 'heritage' cinema and its nostalgic work have shifted towards other forms, less obviously reducible to heritage culture's more conservative aesthetics and ideologies. As I argued in Chapter 4, we can see this in the move to appropriate more 'progressive', technologically modern contexts, such as science. As touched on in Chapter 5, in films like *One Day*, *About Time* and *The World's End* (and to some extent, especially given its 1980s soundtrack, *Sightseers*), we see at work the appeal of the *recent* past as a site of imaginative retrenchment. As we saw in this book's first chapter, when we looked at the 2012 Olympic ceremony, it is the presumed value of a recent cultural history – most accurately, a *pop-cultural* history, and the figures associated with it – that sustains England's preferred version of itself and how it sells itself to the world. On more recent evidence, this idea of pop-cultural ambassadorship has continued to inform popular English cinema as both a domestic and exportable commodity.

The Elton John biopic *Rocketman*, for instance, is something of a lynchpin film in our aims to fathom popular English cinema at this point. This musical film reunites the director (Dexter Fletcher), star (Taron Egerton) and producer (Matthew Vaughn) of *Eddie the Eagle*, the 1980s-set sports biopic discussed in Chapter 3. Fletcher had also come in to replace director Bryan Singer on another culturally English pop biopic from 2018, *Bohemian Rhapsody*. *Rocketman* was scripted by Lee Hall, most widely known as the writer of *Billy Elliot*, itself a key musical of sorts from the very beginnings of the 2000s, and itself an oddly nostalgic, feelgood film about its otherwise politically traumatic and contested past (the Miners' Strike of 1984–5). Indeed, one of the more curious legacies of *Billy Elliot* is that, like *The Full Monty* a few years previously, it eventually became a fully fledged hit musical – with music by Elton John – opening in London's West End in 2005.

There is something very curious at work when, in this case, stories set in the disenfranchised, economically traumatized backdrops of *Billy Elliot* or *The Full Monty* can so transcend these contexts, not just to become feelgood films, but hit stage shows. We have already seen how, from the viewpoint of the incoming UK Film Council at the end of the 1990s, which shaped many ideas around national film production into the next two decades, such films epitomized the model for successful British film. Their experience in part as films themselves, and especially as subsequent stage musicals, involves a palimpsestic layering and deferral of experience and memory. As the above-mentioned survey suggests, it is memory produced above all in and through cultural products that British respondents hold up favourably against the experience of the present: a memory of a memory, in other words. This is the point at which already 'lost' industrial contexts, implied and partly disavowed within films like *Billy Elliott* or *The Full Monty*, now find themselves in the newly mediated form of the stage musical, which now engages with the memory of the films themselves as much as their supposed contexts. Indeed, in the case of *Billy Elliot*, we have a West End show about a boy who, in the end, makes it in a West End show. As was foretold, show business supersedes industry.

Even if this is what popular English film is doing now, I would like, as some concluding thoughts, to add some nuance to this view. As Richard Dyer has explored, the musical has an essentially *utopian* form and function, yet one that is deeply linked to the 'realist' contexts within which musicals often take place. There is always, in other words, a more *dystopian* context within which many of these films function. The musical, Dyer argues, 'offers the image of "something better" to escape into, or something we want deeply that our day-to-day lives don't provide'.[3] Paradoxically, in order to allow viewers to escape through the musical form, it must 'take off from the real experiences of the audience. Yet to do this, [it must] draw attention to the gap between what is and what could be.'[4] In *Billy Elliot*, Billy's dances, though choreographed and edited as if they were musical numbers, are always shaped by the environment – walls, back-to-back terraces, railings, boarded-up streets – in which he is effectively contained. His escape, and the idea of 'what could be', is always counter-pointed by the hard knowledge of 'what is'.

To use a term generally applied to musicals in their developed narrative form, a film and musical like *Billy Elliot* 'integrates' its numbers into the narrative. The songs are rarely 'just' songs; rather, they reveal, or reflect on, what is happening. What, though, do we make of the rise, on stage and more recently on screen, of so-called 'jukebox' musicals, like the very successful *Mamma Mia!* films (2008, 2018), or in a slightly different way, *Rocketman*? By their own nature, while such films contrive to integrate their songs into a narrative context, they are obviously premised on the expectations of, and memories of, the film's songs in and of themselves. We can hardly discount the utopian and compensatory functions of such musicals; but do such films, as both *Billy Elliot* and *The Full Monty* did, 'take off from the real experiences of the audience'? Or do they simply avoid them or displace them?

Working Title's *Yesterday*, written by Richard Curtis, is a similar case in point, and in many respects – in its form, narrative and production contexts – exemplifies the type of films I have discussed in this book. It is not just that *Yesterday* was directed by Danny Boyle, the main orchestrator of the 2012 Olympic ceremony, that gives this concluding discussion a sense of return. As we have just recalled, that ceremony was both informed by and fed into a wider cultural, economic and in some respects political project, in terms of its projection of 'soft power', formed around cinematic, literary and other forms of popular creative output as signifiers of the nation. In mining the song catalogue of the country's most internationally celebrated pop band (and the rights to these songs alone formed a substantial part of the film's budget), *Yesterday* was able to exploit Britain's renowned pop-cultural heritage, which required little introduction to its global audience.

Yesterday, in this way, is another film to draw on the somewhat intangible benefits of popular English culture, in a way that has seemingly very little to do with the wider national culture it purports to represent. Indeed, how could it? *Yesterday* is a fantasy, by its own nature a purely cinematic confection. It is also, on the surface, an obviously nostalgic piece. When The Beatles are mysteriously wiped from the world's memory and historical record, Jack, a hapless singer-songwriter from Suffolk, more or less alone in remembering the Fab Four, gets to re-record their back catalogue in his mega solo-album. Like this record itself, the film works as a form of karaoke movie for the songs it subsequently also advertises. This much is obvious. But to assume it is a nostalgia piece really begs the question: for *what* exactly is it nostalgic?

The Capra-esque hypothesis offered by the film has dramatic and comic potency because, unlike almost everyone in the film, *we* can't forget the past or its culture. In turn, we are aligned with Himesh Patel's Jack, at once able to remember, yet obliged to witness the collective amnesia around him. From one perspective, the 'event' behind *Yesterday* is not that distant from the type of statistical wipeout scenarios familiar from science-fiction or superhero movies: the random erasure of half the global population at the beginning of *Avengers: Endgame* (2019); the mass infertility and absent generation that sets up *Children of Men* (2006). *Yesterday* is ultimately quite different, though, as by its own nature, this is not a loss that anyone, bar Jack and a few other 'survivors', can actually mourn, since no one knows what he is talking about.

Yesterday is therefore a film in which an implied and profound cultural loss is neither noticed nor acknowledged. In *Yesterday* everyone just gets on with it – and remarkably, even at the end of the film, nothing changes. When Jack, days after the global blackout that eradicated The Beatles, tries out 'Yesterday' to his friends in a pub garden, Boyle cuts to a shot of a dad playing by the beach with his son, and other images of the banal everyday. The poignancy of the loss is only accentuated here by its incapacity to affect. Life, slightly boringly, carries on. The real traumatic event in the film, in fact, is not the loss of The

Beatles at all: it is the fact that no one notices or cares. When Jack sings, then, in the context of the film, we are made acutely aware of 'the gap between what is and what could be'. Or more precisely, and in a more melancholy sense: between what is and *what once was*.

The point around which the film turns, in this way, and the place to which it wants to return, is not the 1960s at all. If Curtis and Boyle really wanted to make a nostalgic film about the 1960s, they probably wouldn't have called it *Yesterday*. It would also, more logically, take place in the 1960s, rather than just refer to that decade obliquely. The film's title is in this respect a pointed one. Paul McCartney's lyrics do not express the glib desire to go back in time: they speak of a desire to redeem a terrible recent mistake, with drastic implications for the present day. It is for a better *now*, rather than a preferred past, that is the song's hopeless lament. *Yesterday*, like the song from which it gets its title, does not hark back to some idea of the good old days. The film simply longs for things to go back to how they were; but Jack, like everyone else, cannot go home again.

From one perspective, then, Boyle and Curtis's hymn to England's cultural treasure is also a tale of collective stupidity. This 'Feelgood Film of the Year!' – another advert viewed on the side of my local number 25 bus – was, for this viewer at least, also one of its most disturbing. As the carnival of EU withdrawal dragged on past its original planned date of March 2019, bringing with it a new (unelected) prime minister, the (unlawful) prorogation of Parliament, and the increased likelihood of a No Deal (that was, in truth, never part of the deal), myself and many others in England and the rest of the UK went to see *Yesterday*, though not, necessarily, to 'escape' from this real world. The film's harking back to a past musical reference point, certainly, indicates its more conservative location within the contexts of recent English cinema. In many respects, as demonstrated by its international box-office success (matched by *Rocketman*), *Yesterday* was pretty much what we might expect a contemporary popular English film to be. And yet, there is also something genuinely dystopian at work in the film: its depiction of an unnoticed, seemingly untroubling, national brain-death.

At this late point in the book, I am hardly going to fall into the interpretive trap of bending *Yesterday*'s fantastical narrative into a Brexit-shaped hole, especially since, like many of the films I have discussed, it had been several years in gestation (the original treatment for the film surfaced in 2013).⁵ Boyle and Curtis's film is clearly as much or as little about Brexit as you want it to be. As an example of contemporary popular English film, following the arguments in this book, it is always going to be ambiguously positioned: on the one hand, using English myths and motifs for both domestic and international appeal and, on the other, inadvertently or deliberately revealing, and possibly exploring, the contradictions and tensions in those same myths. Indeed, while Curtis has not discussed his film explicitly in relation to Brexit, its implications are there, in terms of what he sees The Beatles representing – and in turn, what their absence also represents:

> There is a [potential] version of this film where the world is much more drab. The Beatles really did revolutionize social structure. Before The Beatles, everything was about respect. The prime minister was always a 60-year-old man. We were obsessed with the First and Second World War. It was a place where you knew your place and you respected age and culture. The Beatles said that, actually, young people are more interesting, and we've all got a right to really enjoy our lives. We don't have to go on in a world of rations and worry.⁶

For a film supposedly about the past, *Yesterday*'s conclusion, while involving a 50-year-old song, asserts Curtis's investment in the future and the young, and a rejection of more traditional hierarchical structures. We are notably far away here from the more glamorous, buoyant send-offs familiar from 'Curtisland': the white, upper-middle-class Metropolitan fairytale space of earlier romantic comedies such as *Notting Hill* and *Love Actually*.⁷ Jack returns to Suffolk, to married life and a family, and to state-school teaching. The ending, eventually, sees him in work shirt and tie, perched on the edge of a school-hall stage, leading children in an acoustic rendition of McCartney's ska-influenced, jokey 'Ob-La-Di Ob-La-Da'. '*La La how the life goes on*', Jack and the assembled school sing: an ending that is as fatalistic as it is drily optimistic about the future to come.

Yesterday in this respect epitomizes so many of the things explored in this book. In many ways – in its address to the past, to pop-cultural heritage, to global expectations of Englishness – it typifies the form of soft-power promotional value familiar in popular English film and, in turn, encapsulates many of the limitations in such cinema's efforts to address or represent

present-day contexts and concerns. Yet the film also does so much more. As a soundtrack to the British summer of 2019, the tension and uncertainty within the film are note-perfect; and as a fable about the effects of happy ignorance, its tone, even if caged in allegory, is acutely political. *What are we singing now*, the film seems to ask, *and why*? As a film that celebrates, commemorates, laments and looks forward all in the same gesture, *Yesterday* encapsulates not only the troubled circumstances, but also the dramatic possibilities, for popular English film at this time and place.

Notes

Introduction: Film through the looking glass

1. It is one of the further serendipities of movie releasing patterns that the major Hollywood release on 24 June 2016, presumably to the delight of Nigel Farage and the Leave-supporting British press, was the sequel to *Independence Day*.
2. Andrew Higson, *Film England: Culturally English Filmmaking since the 1990s* (London and New York: I.B. Tauris, 2011), 28.
3. Ibid., 29.
4. See, for example *Brexit, Trump and the Media*, ed. John Mair, Tor Clark, Neal Fowler, Raymond Snoddy and Richard Tait (Bury St. Edmunds: Arima, 2017); *Reporting the Road to Brexit*, ed. Anthony Ridge-Newman, Fernando León-Solís and Hugh O'Donnell (Basingstoke: Palgrave Macmillan, 2018).
5. This at least is the conclusion of Thiemo Fetzer's comprehensive study on the subject: Thiemo Fetzer, 'Did Austerity Cause Brexit?', *American Economic Review* 109, no. 11 (2019): 3849–86.
6. Gideon Skinner and Glen Gottfried, 'How Britain Voted in the EU Referendum', Ipsos MORI, 5 September (2016), https://www.ipsos.com/ipsos-mori/en-uk/how-britain-voted-2016-eu-referendum; Lorenza Antonucci, Laszlo Horvath and André Krouwel, 'Brexit Was Not the Voice of the Working Class Nor of the Uneducated – It Was of the Squeezed Middle', LSE British Politics and Policy blog, 13 October (2017), http://blogs.lse.ac.uk/politicsandpolicy/brexit-and-the-squeezed-middle/; Harold D. Clarke, Matthew Goodwin and Paul Whiteley, *Brexit: Why Britain Voted to Leave the European Union* (Cambridge: Cambridge University Press, 2017), 153–7.
7. Andrew Higson, 'The Concept of National Cinema', *Screen* 30, no. 4 (1989): 36–47; Andrew Higson, *Waving the Flag: Constructing a National Cinema in Britain* (Oxford: Clarendon, 1995); Andrew Higson, 'The Limiting Imagination of National Cinemas', in *Cinema and Nation*, ed. Mette Hjort and Scott Mackenzie (London and New York: Routledge, 2000), 63–74.
8. Higson, 'The Concept of National Cinema', 37.
9. Ibid.
10. Richard Dyer and Ginette Vincendeau, eds., *Popular European Cinema* (London and New York: Routledge, 1992), 4.

11 See, for example, Huw David Jones, 'UK/European Co-productions: The Case of Ken Loach', *Journal of British Cinema and Television* 13, no. 3 (2016): 368–89.
12 Dyer and Vincendeau, *Popular European Cinema*, 2; Theodor W. Adorno and Max Horkheimer, *Dialectic of Enlightenment* (London and New York: Verso, 1997); see also Theodor W. Adorno, *The Culture Industry: Selected Essays on Mass Culture* (London and New York: Routledge, 1991).
13 Dyer and Vincendeau, *Popular European Cinema*, 3.
14 At the 2016 European Screens Conference in York, 5–7 September, organized as part of the trans-European MeCETES project (Mediating Cultural Encounters through European Screens), a debate was held entitled 'Brexit and Beyond: The UK Film Industry and Europe'. The panellists were Working Title's Tim Bevan, BFI CEO Amanda Nevill, and Screen Yorkshire's Hugo Heppel. A video of the debate can be found at https://www.youtube.com/watch?v=wmZfOTfk3TQ. A Research Workshop was also held at Keele University on 4 April 2017, entitled *Film and Television Studies after Brexit*, which included contributions from myself, Owen Evans, Beth Johnson, James Leggott, Jonathan Murray and Julian Petley.
15 See *Impacts of Leaving the EU on the UK's Screen Sector* (2017), prepared by Oxera.com for the BFI's Screen Sector Task Force: https://www.bfi.org.uk/sites/bfi.org.uk/files/downloads/bfi-impact-leaving-eu-uk-screen-sector-2017-v1.pdf; also *BFI2022*: https://www.bfi.org.uk/2022/
16 Jones, 'UK/European Co-productions'.
17 Neil Archer, *Beyond a Joke: Parody in English Film and Television Comedy* (London and New York: I.B. Tauris, 2017), 151–3.
18 Ibid., 189–94.
19 Ibid., 70.
20 For an excellent introduction to heuristics, see Daniel Kahnemann, *Thinking, Fast and Slow* (London: Penguin, 2011).
21 Clarke et al, *Brexit*, 86.
22 Ian Jack, '*Dunkirk* and *Darkest Hour* Fuel Brexit Fantasies – Even if They Weren't Meant To', *The Guardian*, 27 January 2018, https://www.theguardian.com/commentisfree/2018/jan/27/brexit-britain-myths-wartime-darkest-hour-dunkirk-nationalist-fantasies
23 David Bordwell, *Poetics of Cinema* (London and New York: Routledge, 2012), 30.
24 Ibid., 31.
25 'The *Guardian* at Tiff 2017: *Darkest Hour* Producers on Brexit and Churchill – Video', *The Guardian*, 25 September 2017, https://www.theguardian.com/film/video/2017/sep/25/the-guardian-at-tiff-2017-darkest-hour-producers-on-brexit-and-churchill-video

26 See, for example, Jack, '*Dunkirk* and *Darkest Hour*'.
27 Bordwell, *Poetics of Cinema*, 30.
28 Jack, '*Dunkirk* and *Darkest Hour*'.
29 On Working Title's production and decision-making processes, see Nathan Townsend, 'Working Title Films and Universal: The Integration of a British Production Company into a Hollywood Studio', *Journal of British Cinema and Television* 15, no. 2 (2018): 179–203.
30 Tobias Hochscherf and James Leggott, 'Working Title Films: From Mid-Atlantic to the Heart of Europe?', *Film International* 48 (2010): 11.
31 Higson, *Film England*, 97–123.
32 Geoffrey Macnab, *Stairways to Heaven: Rebuilding the British Film Industry* (London and New York: I.B. Tauris, 2018), xiii.
33 Higson, *Film England*, 12.
34 Ibid.
35 Nick Roddick, 'If the United States Spoke Spanish, We Would Have a Film Industry', in *British Cinema Now*, ed. Martin Auty and Nick Roddick (London: BFI, 1985), 5.
36 Higson, *Film England*, 25.
37 The quote is in ibid., 41.
38 Andy Medhurst, *A National Joke: Popular Comedy and English Cultural Identities* (London and New York: Routledge, 2007), 187–203.
39 Ibid., 190.
40 We might take as a point of reference here the recently televised show *Stewart Lee: Content Provider* (BBC, 28 July 2018), in which, discussing Leave voters, the avowedly left-liberal comedian suggested it was not fair simply to call them 'racists'. They were also, he added, 'fucking cunts'.
41 Julian Petley, 'The Englishness of British Cinema: Beyond the Valley of the Corn Dollies', in *A Companion to British and Irish Cinema*, ed. John Hill (Chichester and Hoboken: Wiley-Blackwell, 2019), 461–89.
42 Richard Weight, *Patriots: National Identity in Britain 1940–2000* (Basingstoke: Macmillan, 2002), 711–22.
43 The quotation – using an Australian vernacular phrase – is from Boris Johnson in 2004; quoted in Petley, 'The Englishness of British Cinema', 468.
44 Ibid., 465.
45 Raymond Durgnat, *A Mirror for England: British Movies from Austerity to Affluence* (London: BFI, 2012).
46 Alexander Walker, *Hollywood, England: The British Film Industry in the 1960s* (London: Michael Joseph, 1974).

47 Petley, 'The Englishness of British Cinema', 482–3. The quotation is from Claire Monk, 'Film England: Culturally English Filmmaking since the 1990s', *Sight & Sound* 21, no. 9 (2011): 92.
48 Monk, 'Film England', 92.
49 For a specific engagement, for instance, with the recent contexts and possibilities of Scottish cinema, see Jonathan Murray, *The New Scottish Cinema* (London and New York: I.B. Tauris, 2014); also Jonathan Murray, 'Blurring Borders: Scottish Cinema in the Twenty-First Century', *Journal of British Cinema and Television* 9, no. 3 (2012): 400–18.
50 As examples, I would draw the reader's attention to two monographs: Clive James Nwonka, *The Aesthetics of British Urban Cinema* (London and New York: Bloomsbury, 2020), and David Forrest, *New Realism: Contemporary British Cinema* (Edinburgh: Edinburgh University Press, 2020). The recent AHRC-funded project *Beyond the Multiplex*, meanwhile, a collaboration between the universities of Glasgow, Sheffield, York and Liverpool, has offered an important look at the exhibition and reception of 'specialized' (non-mainstream) filmmaking across regional UK contexts (https://www.beyondthemultiplex.net/).
51 See Murray, *The New Scottish Cinema*, 78–110; also Murray, 'Blurring Borders'.
52 Greta Thunberg, *No One Is Too Small to Make a Difference* (London: Penguin, 2019), 50.
53 Ulrich Beck, *Cosmopolitan Vision* (Cambridge: Polity, 2006), 27.
54 The terminology is borrowed here from Christopher Frayling, *Mad, Bad and Dangerous? The Scientist and the Cinema* (London: Reaktion, 2005).
55 The phrase, as I elaborate in Chapter 4, is from David Edgerton, *Warfare State: Britain, 1920–1970* (Cambridge: Cambridge University Press, 2006).

Chapter 1

1 Andrew Higson, *Waving the Flag: Constructing a National Cinema in Britain* (Oxford: Clarendon, 1995), 6.
2 John Hill, '"This Is for the Batmans as well as the Vera Drakes": Economics, Culture and UK Government Film Production Policy in the 2000s', *Journal of British Cinema and Television* 9, no. 3 (2012): 333–56.
3 See especially Andrew Higson, *Film England: Culturally English Filmmaking since the 1990s* (London and New York: I.B. Tauris, 2011), 39–65.

4 Hill, '"This Is for the Batmans as Well as the Vera Drakes": Economics, Culture and UK Government Film Production Policy in the 2000s', 333–56; Clive James Nwonka, 'Diversity Pie: Rethinking Social Exclusion and Diversity Policy in the British Film Industry', *Journal of Media Practice* 16, no. 1 (2015): 73–90; Jack Newsinger, 'British Film Policy in an Age of Austerity', *Journal of British Cinema and Television* 9, no. 1 (2012): 133–44.
5 Hill, 'This Is for the Batmans', 337.
6 Ibid.
7 Newsinger, 'British Film Policy', 142.
8 See Higson, *Film England*; also Belén Vidal, *Heritage Film: Nature, Genre and Representation* (London and New York: Wallflower, 2012), 15–16.
9 Shelley Anne Galpin, 'Harry Potter and the Hidden Heritage Films: Genre Hybridity and the Power of the Past in the Harry Potter Film Cycle', *Journal of British Cinema and Television* 13, no. 3 (2016): 447–8.
10 On the Paddington trail, see https://www.visitlondon.com/things-to-do/family-activities/paddington-bear-itinerary
11 Culture, Media and Sport Committee, *Third Report from the Culture, Media and Sport Committee: Session 2010–2011, HC 464-II* (2010–2011), 24.
12 Newsinger, 'British Film Policy', 133.
13 Christopher McMillan, 'Broken Bond: *Skyfall* and the British Identity Crisis', *Journal of British Cinema and Television* 12, no. 2 (2012): 194–5.
14 Newsinger, 'British Film Policy', 133–4.
15 McMillan, 'Broken Bond', 194.
16 David Bordwell, *Poetics of Cinema* (London and New York: Routledge, 2008), 31.
17 Paul Dave, 'Film Policy and England: The Politics of Creativity', in *The Routledge Companion to Cinema and Politics*, ed. Yannis Tzioumakis and Claire Molloy (London and New York: Routledge, 2019), 189.
18 Chris Arning, 'Soft Power, Ideology and Symbolic Manipulation in Summer Olympic Games Opening Ceremonies: A Semiotic Analysis', *Social Semiotics* 23, no. 4 (2013): 540.
19 Gary Whannel, *Fields in Vision: Television Sport and Cultural Transformation* (London and New York: Routledge, 1992), 174.
20 See Robert Hewison, *Cultural Capital: The Rise and Fall of Creative Britain* (London and New York: Verso, 2014), 173–4.
21 Gov.uk, Department for Digital, Culture, Media and Sport, https://www.gov.uk/government/organisations/department-for-digital-culture-media-sport
22 GREAT Britain campaign, http://greatbritaincampaign.com/#!/about

23 McMillan, 'Broken Bond', 195; '007 Bond – Visit Britain, TV Commercial – Unravel Travel TV', https://www.youtube.com/watch?v=JBgpAij4X98
24 Arning, 'Soft Power, Ideology and Symbolic Manipulation', 536.
25 Neil Archer, *Beyond a Joke: Parody in English Film and Television Comedy* (London and New York: I.B. Tauris, 2017), 214.
26 Ibid., 215.
27 Thomas Elsaesser, *European Cinema: Face to Face with Hollywood* (Amsterdam: Amsterdam University Press, 2005), 71–2.
28 Ibid., 78.
29 Dan Harries, *Film Parody* (London: British Film Institute, 2000); Dan Harries, 'Film Parody and the Resuscitation of Genre', in *Genre and Contemporary Hollywood*, ed. Steve Neale (London: British Film Institute, 2002), 281–93.
30 Higson, *Film England*, 10.
31 Hewison, *Cultural Capital*, 194–5.
32 Ibid.
33 Maximos Malfas, Barrie Houlihan, and Eleni Theodoraki. 'Impacts of the Olympic Games as Mega-Events', *Proceedings of the Institution of Civil Engineers* 157, ME3 (2004): 213.
34 See ibid; also See Jonathan Grix and Barrie Houlihan, 'Sports Mega-Events as Part of a Nation's Soft Power Strategy: The Cases of Germany (2006) and the UK (2012)', *The British Journal of Politics and International Relations* 16, no. 4 (2014): 572–96.
35 James Chapman, *Past and Present: National Identity and the British Historical Film* (London and New York: I.B. Tauris, 2005), 286.
36 Ibid.
37 Margaret Dickinson and Sarah Street, *Cinema and State: The Film Industry and the Government, 1927–84* (London: British Film Institute, 1985), 248.
38 Hill, 'This Is for the Batmans', 349.
39 Culture, Media and Sport Committee, *Third Report*, 25–6.
40 Ibid., 348.
41 See Hewison, *Cultural Capital*; Dave, 'Film Policy and England'; also Andy C. Pratt, 'Cultural Industries and Public Policy: An Oxymoron?', *International Journal of Cultural Policy* 11, no. 1 (2005): 31–44.
42 Chris Smith, *Creative Britain* (London: Faber & Faber, 1998), 12.
43 Ibid., 87.
44 Department for Culture, Media and Sport Film Policy Review Group, 'A Bigger Picture': *The Report of the Film Policy Review Group* (1998), 4.

45 Ibid., 32.
46 Ibid.
47 Nick Roddick, 'Show Me the Culture!', *Sight & Sound* 8, no. 12 (1998): 24.
48 James Leggott, 'Travels in Curtisland: Richard Curtis and British Comedy Cinema', in *British Comedy Cinema*, ed. I. Q. Hunter and Laraine Porter (London and New York: Routledge, 2012), 186; Tobias Hochscherf and James Leggott, 'Working Title Films: From Mid-Atlantic to the Heart of Europe?', *Film International* 48 (2010): 8–20.
49 Joseph Nye, *Soft Power: The Means to Success in World Politics* (New York: Public Affairs, 2004).
50 Portlandcommunications.com, *The Soft Power 30: A Global Ranking of Soft Power*, https://portland-communications.com/pdf/The-Soft-Power_30.pdf (Accessed 7 December 2017).
51 Grix and Houlihan, 'Sports Mega-Events as Part of a Nation's Soft Power Strategy', 583.
52 Ibid., 586.
53 Matthew Syed, 'Higher, Faster, Yes. More Meritocratic, No', in *The Sport and Society Reader*, ed. David Karen and Robert E. Washington (London and New York: Routledge, 2010), 88–9.
54 See Richard Gruneau and James Compton, 'Media Events, Mega-Events and Social Theory: From Durkheim to Marx', in *Sport, Media and Mega-Events*, ed. Lawrence A. Wenner and Andrew C. Billings (London and New York: Routledge, 2017), 37.
55 Gerben Bakker, *Soft Power: The Media Industries in Britain since 1870*, London School of Economics, Economic History Working Papers 200 (2014), 4.
56 Ibid., 4–5.
57 Ibid., 5.
58 Ibid., 36.
59 Ulrich Beck, *Cosmopolitan Vision* (Cambridge: Polity, 2006).
60 Thomas Elsaesser, 'In the City but Not Bounded by It: Cinema in the Global, the Generic and the Cluster City', in *Global Cinematic Cities: New Landscapes of Film and Media*, ed. Johan Andersson and Lawrence Webb (London and New York: Wallflower, 2016), 20. On the 'global' city see Saskia Sassen, *The Global City: New York, London, Tokyo* (Princeton, NJ: Princeton University Press, 1991).
61 Johan Andersson and Lawrence Webb, 'Introduction: Decentring the Cinematic City – Film and Media in the Digital Age', in Andersson and Webb, eds., *Global Cinematic Cities*, 6.

62 David W. Kearn, 'The Hard Truths about Soft Power', *Journal of Political Power* 4, no. 1 (2011): 76.

63 John Hill, 'The Issue of National Cinema and British Film Production', in *New Questions of British Cinema*, ed. Duncan Petrie (London: British Film Institute, 1992), 18.

64 Andrew Higson, 'The Limiting Imagination of National Cinemas', in *Cinema and Nation*, ed. Mette Hjort and Scott Mackenzie (London and New York: Routledge, 2000), 63–74 (71).

65 British Film Institute, 'New BFI Statistics Show Robust Year for Film in the UK in 2016', 26 January 2017, http://www.bfi.org.uk/news-opinion/news-bfi/announcements/highest-grossing-films-uk-box-office-2016

66 British Film Institute, 'The Wide Angle: The BFI's International Strategy', http://www.bfi.org.uk/sites/bfi.org.uk/files/downloads/bfi-wide-angle-international-strategy-2013-v2.pdf, 4

67 Ibid., 2.

68 Ibid., 3.

69 British Film Commission, *UK in Focus 2016*, https://issuu.com/britishfilmcommission/docs/ukinfocus_lr__1_

70 Bfi.org, 'New BFI Statistics Show Robust Year' (emphases added).

71 See the design case study at https://www.thecreativeindustries.co.uk/industries/design/design-case-studies/design-case-great-campaign

72 Higson, *Film England*, 28.

73 Andrew Howard Spicer, '"Being European": UK Production Companies and Europe', *Studies in European Cinema* 16, no. 1 (2019): 56.

74 In ibid., 58.

75 Andrew Higson, 'British Cinema, Europe and the Global Reach for Audiences', in *European Cinema and Television: Cultural Policy and Everyday Life*, ed. Ib. Bondebjerg, Eva Novrup Redvall and Andrew Higson (Basingstoke: Palgrave Macmillan, 2015), 131.

76 Dave, 'Film Policy and England', 189.

77 European Audiovisual Observatory, *Brexit in Context: The UK in the EU28 Audiovisual Market* (2018), https://rm.coe.int/brexit-in-context/16808b868c

78 Oxera.com, *Impacts of Leaving the EU on the UK's Screen Sector* (Screen Sector Task Force, 2017), https://www.bfi.org.uk/sites/bfi.org.uk/files/downloads/bfi-impact-leaving-eu-uk-screen-sector-2017-v2.pdf

79 Stephen Follows, 'The Effect of Brexit on the UK Film Industry', *Stephenfollows.com* 26 June (2017), https://stephenfollows.com/effect-brexit-uk-film-industry/

80. BFI, *BFI2022: Supporting UK Film* (2017), 3, https://www.bfi.org.uk/2022/downloads/bfi2022_EN.pdf
81. Ibid., 23.
82. Ibid., 3, 5.
83. Ibid., 19.
84. Ibid., 24.
85. Spicer, 'Being European', 58–9.

Chapter 2

1. Alan O'Leary, 'On the Complexity of the *Cinepanettone*', in *Popular Italian Cinema*, ed. Louis Bayman and Sergio Rigoletto (London: Palgrave Macmillan, 2013), 200–13.
2. Noël Carroll, *Humour: A Very Short Introduction* (London and New York: Routledge, 2014), 77.
3. Ibid., 83–4.
4. Andrew Stott, *Comedy* (London and New York: Routledge, 2014), 105.
5. Ibid. (emphasis added).
6. Dominic Sandbrook, *Seasons in the Sun: The Battle for Britain, 1974–1979* (London: Penguin, 2012), 331–2.
7. Ibid.
8. Hugo Young, *This Blessed Plot: Britain and Europe from Churchill to Blair* (New York: Overlook, 1998).
9. Dominic Sandbrook, *State of Emergency: Britain 1970–1974* (London: Penguin, 2010), 140–1.
10. John Urry and Jonas Larsen, *The Tourist Gaze 3.0* (London: Sage, 2011), 55.
11. Ibid., 56.
12. Sandbrook, *State of Emergency*, 144.
13. ABTA, *Holiday Habits Report 2017* (2017), 9, https://www.abta.com/sites/default/files/media/document/uploads/Holiday_Habits_Report_2017_0.pdf
14. Anon., 'Daily Chart – Where Britons Go on Holiday', *Economist*, 15 August 2017, https://www.economist.com/graphic-detail/2017/08/15/where-britons-go-on-holiday
15. Andrew Higson, 'British Cinema, Europe and the Global Reach for Audiences', in *European Cinema and Television: Cultural Policy and Everyday Life*, ed. Ib Bondebjerg, Eva Novrup Redvall and Andrew Higson (Basingstoke: Palgrave Macmillan, 2015), 129.

16　Gareth Shaw, Sheela Agarwal and Paul Bull, 'Tourism Consumption and Tourist Behaviour: A British Perspective', *Tourism Geographies* 2, no. 3 (2000): 277.

17　Hazel Andrews, 'Feeling at Home: Embodying Britishness in a Spanish Charter Tourist Resort', *Tourist Studies* 5, no. 3 (2005): 252.

18　Ibid.

19　Ibid., 262.

20　Ibid., 252.

21　Miriam Akhtar and Steve Humphries, *Some Liked It Hot: The British on Holiday at Home and Abroad* (London: Virgin, 2000), 111–14.

22　Steve Gerrard, 'What a Carry On! The Decline and Fall of a Great British Institution', in *Seventies British Cinema*, ed. Robert Shail (London: Palgrave, 2008), 42.

23　See, for example, Leo Barraclough, '"Carry On" Comedy Movie Franchise to Be Revived', *Variety*, 16 May 2016, https://variety.com/2016/film/global/carry-on-comedy-movie-revived-1201775752/; Stuart Heritage, 'Ooh, Matron! Why Carry On Films Refuse to Remain Dead', *The Guardian*, 2 July 2019, https://www.theguardian.com/film/2019/jul/02/carry-on-films-return

24　Geoff King, *Film Comedy* (London: Wallflower, 2002), 39.

25　Ibid., 37.

26　Ibid., 37–8.

27　Ibid., 38.

28　See Neil Archer, *Hot Fuzz* (Leighton Buzzard: Auteur, 2015).

29　Andy Medhurst, *A National Joke: Popular Comedy and English Cultural Identities* (London and New York: Routledge, 2007), 133.

30　King, *Film Comedy*, 39.

31　Brett Mills, *The Sitcom* (Edinburgh: Edinburgh University Press, 2009), 23. Thanks to my PhD student Daniel Skentelbery for drawing my attention to this fact.

32　Medhurst, *A National Joke*, 140.

33　Ibid.

34　Ibid., 19.

35　Ibid.

36　Karen O'Reilly, 'Hosts and Guests, Guests and Hosts: British Residential Tourism in the Costa del Sol', in *Cultures of Mass Tourism: Doing the Mediterranean in the Age of Banal Mobilities*, ed. Pau Obrador Pons, Mike Crang and Penny Travlou (Farnham and Burlington: Ashgate, 2009), 136.

37　Shaw et al., 'Tourism Consumption', 273.

38　Ibid., 275.

39 King, *Film Comedy*, 38.
40 Stott, *Comedy*, 81.
41 Robert and Isabelle Tombs, *That Sweet Enemy: Britain and France, the History of a Love-Hate Relationship* (London: Pimlico, 2006), 654.
42 Ibid., 657.
43 On this scheme, see the page on the Film France website: https://www.filmfrance.net/v2/gb/home.cfm?choixmenu=taxrebate
44 Urry and Larsen, *The Tourist Gaze*, 24.
45 Mariana Liz, *Euro-Visions: Europe in Contemporary Cinema* (London: Bloomsbury, 2016), 116.
46 Ibid., 116–21.
47 European Audiovisual Observatory, *Brexit in Context: The UK in the EU28 Audiovisual Market* (2018), https://rm.coe.int/brexit-in-context/16808b868c
48 Kieron Corless and Chris Darke, *Cannes: Inside the World's Premier Film Festival* (London: Faber and Faber, 2007), 1.
49 In ibid., 52.
50 Ibid., 58.
51 Ibid., 67.
52 Mary Harrod, Mariana Liz and Alissa Timoshkina, 'The Europeanness of European Cinema: An Overview', in *The Europeanness of European Cinema: Identity, Meaning, Globalization*, ed. Mary Harrod, Mariana Liz and Alissa Timoshkina (London and New York: I.B. Tauris, 2015), 4; Liz, *Euro-Visions*, 23.
53 Lucy Mazdon and Catherine Wheatley, 'Introduction. Franco-British Cinematic Relations: An Overview', in *Je t'aime … Moi Non Plus: Franco-British Cinematic Relations*, ed. Lucy Mazdon and Catherine Wheatley (New York and Oxford: Berghahn, 2010), 1–15 (9).
54 Corless and Darke, *Cannes*, 147.
55 Ibid., 148.
56 Patrick Fahy, 'Mr. Bean's Holiday', *Sight & Sound* 17, no. 5 (2007): 72.
57 Tobias Hochscherf and James Leggott, 'Working Title Films: From Mid-Atlantic to the Heart of Europe?', *Film International* 48 (2010): 8–20 (16).
58 Ibid., 10–11.
59 Corless and Darke, *Cannes*, 207.
60 Cannes Festival director Thierry Frémaux, quoted in ibid.
61 See Nicole Vulser, 'Mister Bean aux Marches du Palais', *Le Monde*, 28–29 May 2006, https://www.lemonde.fr/festival-de-cannes/article/2006/05/27/mister-bean-aux-marches-du-palais_776799_766360.html

62 *The Trip to Italy* was screened on the BBC in 2014 in six thirty-minute episodes; an edited feature-film had a limited theatrical release in the same year. For the purposes of the discussion, I refer to episodes from the TV series, as this was more widely seen in the UK. Given the manner of its production, though, I still opt to refer to this series as a 'film'.

63 David Laderman, *Driving Visions: Exploring the Road Movie* (Austin: University of Texas Press, 2002), 132.

64 Bruce Bennett, *The Cinema of Michael Winterbottom: Borders, Terror, Intimacy* (London and New York: Wallflower, 2014), 136.

65 Young, *This Blessed Plot*, 502.

66 Anon., 'Boris Johnson's Brexit Victory Speech: Full Transcript', *Newsweek*, 24 June 2016, http://www.newsweek.com/boris-johnsons-brexit-victory-speech-full-transcript-474086 (Accessed 5 December 2017).

67 Ginette Vincendeau, 'The French Resistance through British Eyes: From *'Allo 'Allo!* to *Charlotte Gray*', in Mazdon and Wheatley, *Je t'aime ... Moi Non Plus* (New York and Oxford: Berghahn), 247.

68 Ibid.

Chapter 3

1 See Robert Murphy, *British Cinema and the Second World War* (London and New York: Continuum, 2000).

2 James Chapman, *Past and Present: National Identity and the British Historical Film* (London and New York: I.B. Tauris, 2005), 7.

3 Ibid.

4 Notably, *Mary Queen of Scots* was scripted by American screenwriter and *House of Cards* showrunner Beau Willimon.

5 Paul Innes, *Epic* (London and New York: Routledge, 2013), 19.

6 Vivian Sobchack, '"Surge and Splendor": A Phenomenology of the Hollywood Historical Epic', *Representations* 29, no. 1 (1990): 24–49.

7 Robert Burgoyne, 'Introduction', in *The Epic Film in World Culture*, ed. Robert Burgoyne (London and New York: Routledge, 2011), 2.

8 Dina Iordanova, 'Rise of the Rest: Globalizing Epic Cinema', in *The Epic Film*, ed. Burgoyne (London and New York: Routledge, 2011), 101–23.

9 Robert Burgoyne, 'Bare Life and Sovereignty in *Gladiator*', in *The Epic Film*, ed. Burgoyne (London and New York: Routledge, 2011), 82–3.

10 Ian Jack, '*Dunkirk* and *Darkest Hour* Fuel Brexit Fantasies – Even if They Weren't Meant To', *The Guardian*, 27 January 2018, https://www.theguardian.com/commentisfree/2018/jan/27/brexit-britain-myths-wartime-darkest-hour-dunkirk-nationalist-fantasies
11 Alan Bennett, *Keeping On Keeping On* (London: Faber & Faber/Profile, 2016), 376.
12 Iordanova, 'Rise of the Rest'.
13 Christopher McMillan, 'Broken Bond: *Skyfall* and the British Identity Crisis', *Journal of British Cinema and Television* 12, no. 2 (2015): 191–206 (195).
14 Klaus Dodds, 'Shaking and Stirring James Bond: Age, Gender, and Resilience in *Skyfall* (2012)', *Journal of Popular Film and Television* 42, no. 3 (2014): 120.
15 Ibid., 118.
16 Marouf Hasian, Jr., '*Skyfall*, James Bond's Resurrection, and 21st-Century Anglo-American Imperial Nostalgia', *Communication Quarterly* 62, no. 5 (2014): 578.
17 Terence McSweeney, *The 'War on Terror' and American Film: 9/11 Frames Per Second* (Edinburgh: Edinburgh University Press, 2014), 104.
18 On the 'darkest moment' in screenplay design, see David Bordwell, *The Way Hollywood Tells It: Story and Style in Modern Movies* (Berkeley: University of California Press, 2006), 29.
19 Dodds, 'Shaking and Stirring James Bond', 119.
20 Sally Faulkner, 'Introduction. Approaching the Middlebrow: Audience, Text, Institution', in *Middlebrow Cinema*, ed. Sally Faulkner (London and New York: Routledge, 2016), 6–7.
21 Ibid., 7.
22 Tim Bergfelder, 'Popular European Cinema in the 2000s: Cinephilia, Genre and Heritage', in *The Europeanness of European Cinema: Identity, Meaning, Globalization*, ed. Mary Harrod, Mariana Liz and Alissa Timoshkina (London and New York, 2015), 33–57 (44); quoted in Faulkner, 'Approaching the Middlebrow', 7.
23 Jim Collins, *Bring on the Books for Everybody: How Literary Culture Became Popular Culture* (Durham and London: Duke University Press, 2010), 131–40; Bergfelder, 'Popular European Cinema in the 2000s', 42–5.
24 See Tom Brown and Belén Vidal, eds. *The Biopic in Contemporary Film Culture* (London and New York: Routledge, 2014); Robert Burgoyne, ed., *The Epic Film in World Culture* (London and New York: Routledge, 2010).
25 Statistics here are taken from the BFI *Statistical Yearbook 2013* (https://www.bfi.org.uk/sites/bfi.org.uk/files/downloads/bfi-statistical-yearbook-2013.pdf), and the BFI *Research and Statistics 2016: Audiences* document (https://

www.bfi.org.uk/sites/bfi.org.uk/files/downloads/bfi-statistical-yearbook-audiences-2015-2016-08-25.pdf).

26. Tobias Hochscherf, 'Bond for the Age of Global Crises: 007 in the Daniel Craig Era', *Journal of British Cinema and Television* 10, no. 2 (2013): 306.
27. Dodds, 'Shaking and Stirring James Bond', 120.
28. McMillan, 'Broken Bond', 197.
29. See, for example, Jack, '*Dunkirk* and *Darkest Hour*'.
30. See Chapman, *Past and Present*, 161.
31. Iordanova, 'Rise of the Rest', 102.
32. In Dan Hassler-Forest, *Capitalist Superheroes: Caped Crusaders in the Neoliberal Age* (Winchester: Zero, 2012), 44 (emphasis added).
33. Andrew Higson, 'Re-Presenting the National Past: Nostalgia and Pastiche in the Heritage Film', in *Fires Were Started: British Cinema and Thatcherism*, ed. Lester D. Friedman (London and New York: Wallflower Press, 2006), 91–109 (95).
34. Will Higbee, 'Counter-Heritage, Middlebrow and the *Fiction Patrimoniale*: Reframing "Middleness" in the Contemporary French Historical Film', in *Middlebrow Cinema*, ed. Sally Faulkner (London and New York: Routledge, 2016), 140.
35. Luc Chessel, '"*Les Heures sombres*": Winston Churchill Sans Filtre', *Libération*, 2 January 2018, https://next.liberation.fr/cinema/2018/01/02/les-heures-sombres-winston-churchill-sans-filtre_1619988 (emphasis in the original).
36. Ibid.
37. Nicolas Azalbert, '*Les Heures sombres*', *Cahiers du cinéma* 740 (2018): 51.
38. Chapman, *Past and Present*, 161.
39. In the French, '*un épisode méconnu de la Seconde Guerre mondiale*'. Stéphanie Belpeche, '"Dunkerque", le Dixième Film de Christopher Nolan, est Exceptionnel', *Journal du dimanche*, 18 July 2017, https://www.lejdd.fr/Culture/Cinema/dunkerque-le-dixieme-film-de-christopher-nolan-est-exceptionnel-3391967
40. Alexandre Buyukodabas, '"Dunkerque": Christopher Nolan Signe Son Film le Plus Intense', *Les Inrockuptibles*, 17 July 2017, https://www.lesinrocks.com/cinema/films-a-l-affiche/dunkerque/. The quotation in French, '*chaque anglais*', could also be translated as 'every English person': Nolan's educational experience was, though, at what was then an all-boys school, which explains my translation here.
41. Burgoyne, 'Introduction', 1–2.
42. Burgoyne, 'Bare Life and Sovereignty', 74.
43. Chapman, *Past and Present*, 161.
44. J. B. Priestly, quoted in ibid., 161–2.
45. Andrew Higson, *Film England: Culturally English Filmmaking since the 1990s* (London and New York: I.B. Tauris, 2011), 81.

46 Burgoyne, 'Bare Life and Sovereignty', 94.
47 Ibid., 89.
48 Ibid., 94.
49 Ibid., 85.
50 Higson, *Film England*, 219.
51 Burgoyne, 'Bare Life and Sovereignty', 86.
52 Higson, *Film England*, 219.
53 Ibid., 216.
54 Thomas Malory, *Le Morte D'Arthur: Volume 1* (London: Penguin, 1969), 167–93; Simon Armitage, *The Death of King Arthur* (London: Faber and Faber, 2012).
55 Alex Ritman, 'Joe Cornish on "The Kid Who Would Be King," Rejecting Hollywood Franchises', *Hollywood Reporter*, 24 January 2019, https://www.hollywoodreporter.com/news/joe-cornish-kid-who-would-be-king-rejecting-major-franchises-1178767
56 In ibid.
57 We can allude here to the contexts of the Brexit vote, which as already noted, was driven to a large extent by older voters, and which of course did not consider the voices of under-18s. The subsequent 2017 general election, which saw Jeremy Corbyn's Labour make gains from the previous election in 2015, saw the highest turn-out (67 per cent) of 18–24-year-olds for 25 years. These voters are predominantly in support of Labour or other opposition parties, and the 2017 turnout was seen in part as a reaction to the EU referendum's vote to Leave: see John Burn-Murdoch, 'Youth Turnout at General Election Highest in 25 Years, Data Show', *Financial Times*, 20 June 2017, https://www.ft.com/content/6734cdde-550b-11e7-9fed-c19e2700005f. Climate activism initiatives, meanwhile, such as School Strike 4 Climate, have mobilized under-18s globally since 2018, with its instigator, the teenage activist Greta Thunberg, the most visible public face.
58 Rebecca Rubin, '"The Kid Who Would Be King" Could Lose $50 Million at Box Office', *Variety*, 29 January 2019, https://variety.com/2019/film/box-office/the-kid-who-would-be-king-box-office-flop-1203119724/
59 Gwilym Mumford, 'Epic Fail: Why Has *King Arthur* Flopped So Badly?', *The Guardian*, 16 May 2017, https://www.theguardian.com/film/2017/may/16/epic-fail-why-has-king-arthur-flopped-so-badly
60 Peter Krämer, '"The Best Disney Film Never Made": Children's Films and the Family Audience in American Cinema since the 1960s', in *Genre and Contemporary Hollywood*, ed. Steve Neale (London: BFI, 2002), 185–200; Noel Brown, '"Family" Entertainment and Contemporary Hollywood Cinema', *Scope: An Online Journal of Film and Television Studies* 25 (2013): 1–21; Elissa Nelson,

'The New Old Face of a Genre: The Franchise Teen Film as Industry Strategy', *Cinema Journal* 57, no. 1 (2017): 125–33.

61. Brown, '"Family" Entertainment', 2.
62. See Nelson, 'The New Old Face of a Genre'.
63. Brown, '"Family" Entertainment', 3.
64. For a more detailed summary of these discussions see Neil Archer, *Twenty-First-Century Hollywood: Rebooting the System* (London and New York: Wallflower, 2019), 82–8.
65. Higson, *Film England*, 97–100.
66. Steve Rose, '*Early Man* Review – Aardman Claymation Comedy Brings Brexit to the Bronze Age', *The Guardian*, 14 January 2018, https://www.theguardian.com/film/2018/jan/14/early-man-review-aardman-animations
67. In Nigel Andrews, 'Nick Park on Why He "Refused" to Sell Wallace and Gromit', *Financial Times*, 26 January 2018, https://www.ft.com/content/10922a92-00f2-11e8-9650-9c0ad2d7c5b5
68. In ibid.
69. John Fitzgerald, *Studying British Cinema: 1999–2009* (Leighton Buzzard: Auteur, 2010), 29.
70. Neil Archer, *Beyond a Joke: Parody in English Film and Television Comedy* (London and New York: I.B. Tauris, 2017), 44–51.
71. See ibid.
72. Tobias Hochscherf and James Leggott, 'Working Title Films: From Mid-Atlantic to the Heart of Europe?', *Film International* 48 (2010): 12.
73. Matthew Robinson, '"Make Do and Mend': Crafting a Scottish Underdog in *The Flying Scotsman* (2006)', *Open Screens* 1, no. 1 (2018); Matthew Robinson, 'It's Spiritual, Man': *Eddie the Eagle* and English Amateurism', *Journal of British Cinema and Television* 16, no. 2 (2019): 170–90.
74. Robinson, 'It's Spiritual, Man', 181–2.
75. Written and performed by the band The Lightning Seeds, along with comedians David Baddiel and Frank Skinner, the song ends with the repeated refrain 'It's coming home/It's coming home/It's coming/Football's coming home': a familiar sound from the stands during England matches (when they are winning).
76. For a detailed analysis of *Lagaan* see Seán Crosson, *Sport and Film* (London and New York: Routledge, 2013), 150–6.
77. Chris York, 'Rio 2016 Medal Table: Brexit Voters Claim Credit for Team GB Olympic Games Success', *HuffPost*, 15 August 2016, https://www.huffingtonpost.co.uk/entry/brexit-team-gb-olympics_uk_57b162b9e4b01f97d8f2eab3?guccounter=1

Chapter 4

1. Robert Uhlig, *Genius of Britain: The Scientists Who Changed the World* (London and New York: HarperCollins, 2010), 317–18.
2. The quotation is from the inventor James Dyson, in ibid., x.
3. On scientific realism, see Tim Lewens, *The Meaning of Science* (London: Penguin, 2015), 107.
4. Noah Yuval Harari, *Homo Deus: A Brief History of Tomorrow* (London: Harvill Secker, 2016), 114.
5. Michio Kaku, *Physics of the Future: The Inventions That Will Transform Our Lives* (London: Penguin, 2011), 139–47.
6. See Dan Stone, *Breeding Superman: Nietzsche, Race and Eugenics in Edwardian and Interwar Britain* (Liverpool: Liverpool University Press, 2002).
7. David Adam, *The Genius Within: Smart Pills, Brain Hacks and Adventures in Intelligence* (London: Picador, 2018), 128.
8. Ibid., 128–9.
9. Bryan Appleyard, *Brave New Worlds: Genetics and the Human Experience* (London: HarperCollins, 1999), 60.
10. Adam, *The Genius Within*, 126–7.
11. Appleyard, *Brave New Worlds*, 50.
12. In Uhlig, *Genius of Britain*, x.
13. Ibid.
14. Steven Pinker, *Enlightenment Now: The Case for Reason, Science, Humanism and Progress* (London: Penguin, 2018).
15. Ibid., 11.
16. Pinker quotes Anton Chekhov to this effect: 'There is no national science just as there is no national multiplication table.' In ibid., 387.
17. Ibid., 31.
18. Ibid., 11.
19. Belén Vidal, 'Introduction: The Biopic and Its Critical Contexts', in *The Biopic in Contemporary Film Culture*, ed. Tom Brown and Belén Vidal (London and New York: Routledge, 2013), 4.
20. Ibid., 5.
21. George Custen, *Bio/Pics: How Hollywood Constructed Public History* (New Brunswick, NJ: Rutgers University Press, 1992), 18.
22. Vidal, 'The Biopic and Its Critical Contexts', 5.
23. Custen, *Bio/Pics*, 32–4.

24 The screenplay for *The Theory of Everything* was by *Darkest Hour* writer Anthony McCarten.
25 Christopher Frayling, *Mad, Bad and Dangerous? The Scientist and the Cinema* (London: Reaktion, 2005), 132.
26 Andrew Higson, *Film England: Culturally English Filmmaking since the 1990s* (London and New York: I.B. Tauris, 2011); Belén Vidal, *Heritage Film: Nature, Genre and Representation* (London and New York: Wallflower, 2012).
27 Frayling, *Mad, Bad and Dangerous*, 176–8.
28 Peter J. Bowler, *Science for All: The Popularization of Science in Early Twentieth-Century Britain* (Chicago and London: University of Chicago Press, 2009), 264–77.
29 Andrew Higson, *Waving the Flag: Constructing a National Cinema in Britain* (Oxford: Clarendon, 1995), 273.
30 See especially Andrew Higson, 'Re-Presenting the National Past: Nostalgia and Pastiche in the Heritage Film', in *Fires Were Started: British Cinema and Thatcherism*, ed. Lester D. Friedman (London and New York, 2006), 91–109.
31 Higson, *Waving the Flag*.
32 Robert Hewison, *The Heritage Industry: Britain in a Climate of Decline* (London: Methuen, 1987).
33 Patrick Wright, *On Living in an Old Country: The National Past in Contemporary Britain* (Oxford: Oxford University Press, 2009), 18.
34 Ibid.
35 Ibid., 19.
36 Frayling, *Mad, Bad and Dangerous*, 31.
37 Nicholas Russell, *Communicating Science: Professional, Popular, Literary* (Cambridge: Cambridge University Press, 2010), 117–18.
38 See, for example, http://www.movie-locations.com/movies/t/Theory-Of-Everything.php; https://www.radiotimes.com/news/2015-02-11/the-theory-of-everything-travel-guide-to-cambridge/
39 https://variety.com/2014/film/news/dev-patels-the-man-who-knew-infinity-moves-to-production-after-8-years-in-development-1201262436/
40 There is something of a dialogue here with a film like *Chariots of Fire*, the narrative of which shows significantly more criticism of Cambridge University and its racial politics. Notably, it was on this basis that the university did not permit filming to be carried out in its grounds: see James Chapman, *Past and Present: National Identity and the British Historical Film* (London and New York: I.B. Tauris, 2005), 277.

41 Judith Burns, 'Oxford and Cambridge Top World University Rankings', *BBC News*, 5 September 2017, https://www.bbc.co.uk/news/education-41160914
42 Daniel Cressey, 'Scientists Say "No" to UK Exit from Europe in *Nature* Poll', *Nature*, 30 March 2016, https://www.nature.com/news/scientists-say-no-to-uk-exit-from-europe-in-nature-poll-1.19636
43 John Morgan, 'EU referendum: Nine out of 10 University Staff Back Remain', *Times Higher Education*, 16 June 2016, https://www.timeshighereducation.com/news/european-union-referendum-nine-out-of-ten-university-staff-back-remain.
44 See Steve Neale, *Genre and Hollywood* (London and New York: Routledge, 2000).
45 See especially Christine Cornea, *Science Fiction Cinema* (Edinburgh: Edinburgh University Press, 2007).
46 Andrew Utterson, *From IBM to MGM: Cinema at the Dawn of the Digital Age* (London: BFI, 2011), 65.
47 Ibid., 19.
48 Higson, *Film England*, 244.
49 Ibid., 243–4.
50 Leo Marx, *The Machine in the Garden: Technology and the Pastoral Ideal in America* (Oxford and New York: Oxford University Press, 1964).
51 Robert Murphy, *British Cinema and the Second World War* (London and New York: Continuum, 2000), 204.
52 Ibid., 205.
53 Ibid.
54 Frayling, *Mad, Bad and Dangerous*, 186.
55 Ibid., 187; see also David Edgerton, *England and the Aeroplane: An Essay on a Militant and Technological Nation* (Basingstoke: Macmillan, 1991).
56 David Edgerton, *Warfare State: Britain 1920–1970* (Cambridge and New York: Cambridge University Press, 2006).
57 Edgerton, *England and the Aeroplane*, 56, 61.
58 Ibid., 85.
59 Edgerton, *Warfare State*, 193.
60 Pam Cook, *Screening the Past: Memory and Nostalgia in Cinema* (London and New York: Routledge, 2005), 221.
61 Ibid., 226.
62 On Turing, see Andrew Hodges, *Alan Turing: The Enigma* (London: Vintage, 2012).
63 Higson, 'Re-Presenting the National Past', 95.
64 Hodges, *Alan Turing*, 239 (emphasis in the original).

65 As Dominic Sandbrook notes, between 1945 and 1960, over 100 war films were produced in Britain, admittedly to varied levels of success: Dominic Sandbrook, *Never Had It So Good* (London: Abacus, 2006), 202–3.
66 The quotation is from Tobias Hochscherf and James Leggott, 'Working Title Films: From Mid-Atlantic to the Heart of Europe?', *Film International* 48 (2010): 12.
67 On the international funding contexts of *The Imitation Game*, see Andreas Wiseman, 'Crack the Code', *Screen International*, 1782 (2014): 24–7.
68 In Jack Newsinger, 'British Film Policy in an Age of Austerity', *Journal of British Cinema and Television* 9, no. 1 (2012): 142.

Chapter 5

1 On the development and evolution of genres, see especially Rick Altman, *Film/Genre* (London: BFI, 1999).
2 Andrew Higson, *Film England: Culturally English Filmmaking since the 1990s* (London and New York: I.B. Tauris, 2011), 29.
3 Higson, *Film England*, 29–30.
4 Ibid., 30.
5 The work of Franco Moretti, for instance, which has involved studying literature as vast data sets – such as the many thousands of (mostly unknown) novels published throughout the decades – has drawn attention to the highly prescribed ways we use 'canonical' books to explain or historicize social, economic and cultural contexts, not to mention 'literary history'. See Franco Moretti, *Distant Reading* (London and New York: Verso, 2013).
6 The precise number of 'British' releases in 1997 depends in part on criteria. An acknowledged 'incomplete' list on Wikipedia puts the total at 44 (https://en.wikipedia.org/wiki/List_of_British_films_of_1997), while a similar list on IMDb shows 139 titles (https://www.imdb.com/search/title/?title_type=feature&year=1997-01-01,1997-12-31&countries=gb&sort=alpha,asc&start=101&ref_=adv_nxt).
7 See, for example, Paul Dave, *Visions of England* (Oxford: Berg, 2006); also Robert Murphy, 'City Life: Urban Fairytales in Late 90s British Cinema', in *The British Cinema Book*, ed. Robert Murphy, 2nd ed. (London: BFI, 2001), 292–300.
8 See Geoffrey Macnab, *Stairways to Heaven: Rebuilding the British Film Industry* (London and New York: I.B. Tauris, 2018), 93.

9 Tobias Hochscherf and James Leggott, 'Working Title Films: From Mid-Atlantic to the Heart of Europe?', *Film International* 48 (2010): 8–20.
10 See especially Michael Wayne, 'Working Title Mark II: A Critique of the Atlanticist Paradigm for British Cinema', *International Journal of Media and Cultural Politics* 2, no. 1 (2006): 59–73; Higson, *Film England*.
11 Johanne Brunet and Galina Gornostaeva, 'Company Profile: Working Title Films, Independent Producer: Internationalization of the Film Industry', *International Journal of Arts Management* 9, no. 1 (2006): 61–2.
12 Higson, *Film England*, 22.
13 Nathan Townsend, 'Working Title Films and Universal: The Integration of a British Production Company into a Hollywood Studio', *Journal of British Cinema and Television* 15, no. 2 (2018): 185.
14 Higson, *Film England*, 26; Hochscherf and Leggott, 'Working Title Films', 9.
15 Townsend, 'Working Title Films and Universal', 184.
16 Ibid., 183.
17 Ibid., 188.
18 Ibid., 187.
19 Ibid., 201.
20 Macnab, *Stairways to Heaven*, 84–5.
21 Ibid., 85.
22 John Hill, *British Cinema in the 1980s* (Oxford: Clarendon, 1999), 45–6.
23 Macnab, *Stairways to Heaven*, 89–92.
24 Townsend, 'Working Title Films and Universal', 201.
25 Charlotte Brunsdon, *London in Cinema: The Cinematic City since 1945* (London: BFI, 2007), 113.
26 Ian Jack, "*Dunkirk* and *Darkest Hour* Fuel Brexit Fantasies – Even If They Weren't Meant to" *Guardian* 27 January 2018, https://www.theguardian.com/commentisfree/2018/jan/27/brexit-britain-myths-wartime-darkest-hour-dunkirk-nationalist-fantasies
27 As Hochscherf and Leggott note, a key strategy in Working Title's production remit involves the casting of (mainland) European star actors alongside its more familiar transatlantic casting strategies (see Hochscherf and Leggott, 'Working Title Films'). It is also useful to add that the company also has a distribution deal in Europe with StudioCanal (see Chapter 6).
28 J. D. Connor, *The Studios after the Studios: Neoclassical Hollywood (1970–2010)* (Stanford: Stanford University Press, 2015), 253.
29 Ibid., 253.

30. Townsend, 'Working Title Films and Universal', 201.
31. On franchise logic, and the problem of the 'standalone' film, see Neil Archer, *Twenty-First-Century Hollywood: Rebooting the System* (London and New York: Wallflower, 2019), 13–26.
32. Ibid., 190.
33. Hochscherf and Leggott, 'Working Title Films'.
34. See Robert Hewison, *Cultural Capital: The Rise and Fall of Creative Britain* (London and New York: Verso, 2014).
35. Archer, *Twenty-First-Century Hollywood*, 13–26.
36. Just to take one example, in its narrative structural premise, Chadha's *Blinded by the Light* (2019) about a young British Pakistani obsessed with Bruce Springsteen, is a remake of *Bend It Like Beckham*. Both films are about young lower-middle-class British Asians going against parental and cultural wishes, in pursuit of personal creative ambitions (to be a footballer in *Bend It Like Beckham*; a writer in *Blinded by the Light*); while both also draw by association – or in the latter film's case, through the use of Springsteen's songs – on globally identifiable popular figures. Despite favourable reviews, though, *Blinded by the Light* has barely recouped its $15m production costs; *Bend It Like Beckham*, by contrast, was at the time of its release the highest-grossing independent British film domestically and also a hit in the United States.
37. Higson, *Film England*, 100.
38. Ibid., 111–12. See also Simone Murray, *The Adaptation Industry: The Cultural Economy of Contemporary Literary Adaptation* (London and New York: Routledge, 2012).
39. Stanley Cavell, *Pursuits of Happiness: The Hollywood Comedy of Remarriage* (Cambridge and London: Harvard University Press, 1981).
40. Richard Maltby, *Hollywood Cinema* (Malden and Oxford: Blackwell, 2003), 269.
41. See Murphy, 'City Life'.
42. Brunsdon, *London in Cinema*, 116.
43. Higson, *Film England*, 79–81.
44. David Bordwell, *The Way Hollywood Tells It: Story and Style in Modern Movies* (Berkeley: University of California Press, 2006), 100–2.
45. Benedict Anderson, *Imagined Communities: Reflections on the Origin and Spread of Nationalism* (London and New York: Verso, 1991), 25.
46. Sean Redmond, *Liquid Space: Science Fiction Film and Television in the Digital Age* (London and New York: I.B. Tauris, 2017), 35–6. Ibid., 36.
47. Ibid., 25.

48 Predictably, entering 'The World's End drinking game' on Google throws up a sizeable number of entries on how to emulate the action of the film.
49 This is a quotation within a quotation: the words are spoken by Peter Fonda, in the Roger Corman biker film *The Wild Angels* (1966).
50 Neil Archer, *Hot Fuzz* (Leighton Buzzard: Auteur, 2015), 107.
51 Neil Archer, *Beyond a Joke: Parody in English Film and Television Comedy* (London and New York: I.B. Tauris, 2017), 116–44.
52 As discussed in the director's commentary on the UK DVD.
53 Gove's exact statement, during a Sky News interview with Faisal Islam (3 June 2016), was that 'the people of this country have had enough of experts'. See the YouTube video, 'Gove – Britons "Have Had Enough of Experts"', https://www.youtube.com/watch?v=GGgiGtJk7MA
54 David Forrest, Graeme Harper and Jonathan Rayner, 'Introduction. Filmurbia: Cinema and the Suburbs', in *Filmurbia: Screening the Suburbs*, ed. David Forrest, Graeme Harper and Jonathan Rayner (London: Palgrave Macmillan, 2017), 4.
55 Ibid., 3.
56 Quotation from the UKFC's policy brief *Towards a Sustainable UK Film Industry* (2000), quoted in Clive James Nwonka and Sarita Malik, 'Cultural Discourses and Practices of Institutionalised Diversity in the UK Film Sector: "Just get something black made"', *The Sociological Review* 66, no. 6 (2018): 1116.
57 Ibid., 1113–14.
58 Hewison, *Cultural Capital*, 71.
59 The quotation is from Tony Blair; in Clive James Nwonka, 'Estate of the Nation: Social Housing as Cultural Verisimilitude in British Social Realism', in *Filmurbia*, ed. Forest et al. (2017), 68.
60 On the politics of these films, in the contexts of New Labour, see especially Paul Dave, *Visions of England* (Oxford and New York: Berg, 2006), 61–82; also Steve Blandford, *Film, Drama and the Break-Up of Britain* (Bristol and Chicago: Intellect, 2007), 19–47.
61 Inasmuch then as we might understand Wheatley as a 'realist' director, he is closer to Mike Leigh's more stylized takes on the English lower middle classes than, say, to Ken Loach's work. The similarity between *Sightseers* and Leigh's TV film *Nuts in May* (1976) is highlighted by Ben Walters, 'Psycho Geography', *Sight & Sound* 22, no. 11 (2012): 30–3.
62 The phrase is from Linda Hutcheon, *A Theory of Parody: The Teachings of Twentieth-Century Art Forms* (London: Methuen, 1985).

63 Guy Standing, *The Precariat: The New Dangerous Class* (London and New York: Bloomsbury, 2011).

64 If it needs reiterating, both former Prime Minister David Cameron and his Chancellor, George Osborne, were public school- and Oxford-educated; both were also members, along with future Prime Minister Boris Johnson, of Oxford's exclusive Bullingdon Club.

65 Manfred Steger, *Globalization: A Very Short Introduction* (Oxford: Oxford University Press, 2013), 117–25. For more on this aspect of the film, see Neil Archer, '*Et in Arcadia Ego*: Precarious Romanticism and the English Road Movie', in *The Global Road Movie: Alternative Journeys around the World*, ed. José Duarte and Timothy Corrigan (Bristol: Intellect, 2018), 203–16.

66 See, for example, Richard Weight, *Patriots: National Identity in Britain 1940–2000* (Basingstoke: Macmillan, 2002); also Julian Petley, 'The Englishness of British Cinema: Beyond the Valley of the Corn Dollies', in *A Companion to British and Irish Cinema*, ed. John Hill (Chichester and Hoboken: Wiley-Blackwell, 2019), 461–89.

67 Cas Mudde and Cristóbal Rovira Kaltwasser, *Populism: A Very Short Introduction* (Oxford: Oxford University Press, 2017), 9–11.

68 Thanks to Dr Simon Weaver at Brunel University for drawing my attention to this irony.

69 Quoted in Walters, 'Psycho Geography', 32.

70 Quoted in ibid.

Chapter 6

1 In Andrew Pulver, 'Disaster Looms if British Film Disconnects from Europe, Says Studio Head', *Guardian* 9 July 2016, https://www.theguardian.com/film/2016/jul/09/disaster-looms-if-british-film-disconnects-from-europe-says-studio-head.

2 Christopher Meir, *Mass-Producing European Cinema: Studiocanal and Its Works* (London and New York: Bloomsbury, 2019); also Christopher Meir, 'European Cinema in an Era of Studio-Building: Some Artistic and Industrial Tendencies in Studiocanal's Output, 2006–Present', *Studies in European Cinema* 16, no. 1 (2019): 5–21.

3 Meir, 'European Cinema in an Era of Studio-Building', 17.

4 Ulrich Beck, *Cosmopolitan Vision* (Cambridge: Polity, 2006).

5 Andrew Howard Spicer, '"Being European": UK Production Companies and Europe', *Studies in European Cinema* 16, no. 1 (2019): 56.

6   Andrew Higson, *Film England: Culturally English Filmmaking since the 1990s* (London and New York: I.B. Tauris, 2011).
7   European Audiovisual Observatory, *Brexit in Context: The UK in the EU28 Audiovisual Market* (2018), https://rm.coe.int/brexit-in-context/16808b868c.
8   In Andrew Spicer, 'The European Producer: Simon Perry', *Journal of British Cinema and Television* 15, no. 4 (2018): 605.
9   See, for example, the opinions of David Puttnam and UKFC CEO John Woodward, cited at length in Geoffrey Macnab, *Stairways to Heaven: Rebuilding the British Film Industry* (London and New York: I.B. Tauris, 2018), 144–5.
10 In Spicer, 'The European Producer', 604.
11 Andrew Higson, 'British Cinema, Europe and the Global Reach for Audiences', in *European Cinema and Television: Cultural Policy and Everyday Life*, ed. Ib. Bondebjerg, Eva Novrup Redvall, Andrew Higson (Basingstoke: Palgrave Macmillan, 2015), 131.
12 Huw David Jones, 'The Cultural and Economic Implications of UK/European Co-Production', *Transnational Cinemas* 7, no. 1 (2016): 13.
13 Philip Schlesinger, 'Transnational Framings of British Film Policy: The Case of the UK Film Council', In *Transnational Mediations: Negotiating Popular Culture between Europe and the United States*, ed. Christof Decker and Astrid Böger (Heidelbeg: Universitatätsverlag, 2015). Sourced from Enlighten: University of Glasgow Research Publications, http://eprints.gla.ac.uk/114438/.
14 Ibid., 12.
15 Ibid., 29.
16 Ibid.
17 Ibid., 10.
18 David Puttnam, *The Undeclared War* (London: HarperCollins, 1997), 346.
19 Meir, 'European Cinema in an Era of Studio-Building', 6.
20 Schlesinger, 'Transnational Framings', 18.
21 Ibid., 7.
22 Andrew Higson and Richard Maltby, '"Film Europe" and "Film America": An Introduction', in *'"Film Europe" and "Film America": Cinema, Commerce and Cultural Exchange*, ed. Andrew Higson and Richard Maltby (Exeter: University of Exeter Press, 2006), 18.
23 Philip Schlesinger, 'The Sociological Scope of "National Cinema"', in *Cinema and Nation*, ed. Mette Hjort and Scott MacKenzie (London and New York: Routledge, 2000), 27.
24 Ibid., 24.

25 Macnab, *Stairways to Heaven*, xiii, xviii.
26 Mary Harrod, Mariana Liz and Alissa Timoshkina, eds. *The Europeanness of European Cinema: Identity, Meaning, Globalization* (London and New York: I.B. Tauris, 2015). For the record, I contributed a chapter to this volume, though evidently not on British film.
27 The essays in that particular volume derive from the one-day conference (which I attended) called *The Europeanness of European Cinema* held at King's College, London, 4 June 2010. The wider programme did not feature any papers discussing British films, though there was, interestingly, one paper on Irish cinema. Any omission of British subject matter in the volume, it is reasonable to suggest, reflects the absence of contributors offering papers on the topic, rather than an editorial viewpoint; but this still supports my wider view that British cinema seems a subject apart in terms of European cinema studies.
28 Mariana Liz, 'From European Co-Productions to the Euro-Pudding', in Harrod et al., *The Europeanness of European Cinema*, 76–7; Laëtitia Kulyk, 'The Use of English in European Feature Films: Unity in Diversity', in Harrod et al., *The Europeanness of European Cinema* (London and New York: Routledge, 2011), 176.
29 Andrew Higson, 'Historical Films in Europe: The Transnational Production, Circulation and Reception of "National" Heritage Drama', in *Screening European Heritage: Creating and Consuming History on Film*, ed. Paul Cooke and Rob Stone (Basingstoke: Palgrave Macmillan, 2016), 191.
30 Gillian Doyle, Philip Schlesinger, Raymond Boyle and Lisa W. Kelly, *The Rise and Fall of the UK Film Council* (Edinburgh: Edinburgh University Press, 2015), 12.
31 Producer Peter Watson in ibid., 83.
32 Ibid., 137–8.
33 Macnab, *Stairways to Heaven*, 141.
34 In ibid., 144.
35 In ibid., 145.
36 Doyle et al., *Rise and Fall*, 81.
37 In ibid.
38 Spicer, 'Being European', 56.
39 Noel Brown, '"Family" Entertainment and Contemporary Hollywood Cinema', *Scope: An Online Journal of Film and Television Studies* 25 (2013): 3.
40 The *Paddington* films make use of actors already recognized from their work on the *Harry Potter* films, such as Jim Broadbent and Julie Walters. Mr Brown is played by Hugh Bonneville, internationally recognized through his role as the

presiding Earl of Grantham in *Downton Abbey* (ITV, 2010–2015); *Paddington 2* casts Hugh Grant as the villainous thespian Phoenix Buchanan.

41 Former StudioCanal CEO Olivier Courson, in Mike Goodridge, 'Studio Building', *Screen International* 1721 (2010): 40.
42 In Melanie Goodfellow, 'Studiocanal Adds Production Exec, Expands Role of UK CEO Danny Perkins', *Screen Daily*, 30 March 2016, https://www.screendaily.com/news/studiocanal-adds-production-exec-expands-role-of-uk-ceo-danny-perkins/5102041.article.
43 Anon., 'StudioCanal s'appuie sur ses pilliers', *Le Film français*, 20 June 2017, http://www.lefilmfrancais.com/cinema/132902/cineeurope-2017-studiocanal-snappuie-sur-ses-piliers.
44 Meir, *Mass-Producing European Cinema*, 191–2.
45 John Hopewell, 'Creative Punch Meets Biz Savvy', *Variety* 427, no. 1 (2012): 79.
46 Anon., 'StudioCanal s'appuie sur ses pilliers'.
47 In John Hopewell and Elsa Keslassy, 'StudioCanal Acquires Paddington Bear Brand, Plans Third Paddington Movie', *Variety* 20 June 2016, https://variety.com/2016/film/global/studiocanal-acquires-paddington-brand-third-movie-1201799112/.
48 In ibid.
49 Charles Gant, 'Development Tale: *Paddington*', *Sight & Sound* 24, no. 12 (2014): 14.
50 Meir, 'European Cinema in an Era of Studio-Building', 16.
51 Ibid., 16–17.
52 Hopewell and Keslassy, 'StudioCanal Acquires Paddington Bear Brand'.
53 John Hopewell, 'Mipcom: Studiocanal to Launch Paddington Animated TV Series', *Variety*, 9 October 2017, https://variety.com/2017/tv/news/mipcom-studiocanal-paddington-animated-tv-series-1202584183/.
54 Data from boxofficemojo.com.
55 Matt Mueller, 'Studiocanal UK: 10 Years in the Making', *Screen Daily*, 5 July 2016, https://www.screendaily.com/distribution/studiocanal-uk-10-years-in-the-making/5106455.article.
56 Beck, *Cosmopolitan Vision*, 41.
57 Neil Archer, *Beyond a Joke: Parody in English Film and Television Comedy* (London and New York: I.B. Tauris, 2017), 141.
58 Beck, *Cosmopolitan Vision*, 41.
59 See, for instance, Paul Dave, *Visions of England* (Oxford: Berg, 2006); Paul Dave, 'Film Policy and England: The Politics of Creativity', in *The Routledge Companion to Cinema and Politics*, ed. Yannis Tzioumakis and Claire Molloy (London and New York: Routledge, 2019), 186–96; Steve Blandford, *Film, Drama and*

the Break-Up of Britain (Bristol: Intellect, 2007),19–45; John Hill, 'The Issue of National Cinema and British Film Production', in *New Questions of British Cinema*, ed. Duncan Petrie (London: BFI, 1992), 10–21.

60 See Higson, *Film England*, 75–81.
61 In Tim Masters, 'The Story behind *Paddington*'s Calypso Songs', *BBC News*, 28 November 2014, https://www.bbc.co.uk/news/entertainment-arts-30196290.
62 Hamid Naficy, *An Accented Cinema: Exilic and Diasporic Filmmaking* (Princeton and Oxford: Princeton University Press, 2001), 4.
63 Meir, *Mass-Producing European Cinema*, 194.
64 Ibid., 193; Charlotte Brunsdon, *London in Cinema: The Cinematic City since 1945* (London: BFI, 2007).
65 Brunsdon, *London in Cinema*, 1–16.
66 Michelle Pauli, 'Michael Bond: 'Paddington Stands Up for Things, He's Not Afraid of Going to the Top and Giving Them a Hard Stare', *Guardian*, 28 November 2014, https://www.theguardian.com/books/2014/nov/28/michael-bond-author-paddington-bear-interview-books-television-film.
67 In Catherine Shoard, 'How *Paddington* Took Paul King from *Mighty Boosh* to Almighty Blockbuster', *Guardian*, 23 March 2015, https://www.theguardian.com/film/2015/mar/23/paddington-mighty-boosh-paul-king-garth-marenghi.
68 Clément Ghys, 'Peluche de Parfait', *Libération*, 2 December 2014, https://next.liberation.fr/cinema/2014/12/02/peluche-que-parfait_1155218.
69 Ibid.
70 Gaël Golhen, 'La Peau de l'ours', *Première* 480 (2017), 27.
71 Noel Brown, *The Children's Film: Genre, Nation and Narrative* (London and New York: Wallflower, 2017), 92.
72 Ibid., 89–90.
73 Rayna Denison, 'The Global Markets for Anime: Miyazaki Hayao's Spirited Away (2001)', in *Japanese Cinema: Texts and Contexts*, ed. Alastair Phillips and Julian Stringer (London and New York: Routledge, 2007), 315.
74 Respectively, the French stage-and-screen stars Guillaume Gallienne and Pierre Niney.
75 Data here taken from the professional web magazine Lefilmfrancais.com.
76 Jonathan Bignell, 'Migration, Translation and Hybridity: European Animation on British Television', unpublished paper presented at the 'Continental Connections' conference, De Montfort University, 10–11 July 2007, 10. Transcript accessed at https://s3.amazonaws.com/academia.edu.documents/38108386/BignellEuroAnimation.pdf?response-content-disposition=inline%3B%20

filename%3DMigration_Translation_and_Hybridity_Euro.pdf&X-Amz-Algorithm=AWS4-HMAC-SHA256&X-Amz-Credential=AKIAIWOWY YGZ2Y53UL3A%2F20190926%2Fus-east-1%2Fs3%2Faws4_request&X-Amz-Date=20190926T104106Z&X-Amz-Expires=3600&X-Amz-SignedHeaders=host&X-Amz-Signature=76a7328e983de546153ec17d0c1f33a95 3ccf9cf86ae93d40124eb26041642bb.

77 Ibid.
78 Ibid.
79 Ibid.
80 Higson, *Film England*, 71.
81 Brown, *The Children's Film*, 86.
82 Ibid., 87.
83 Ibid., 89–90.
84 Ibid., 89.
85 Ibid.
86 In Joe Utichi, 'British Indies Face "Less Control" Post-Brexit, Warns StudioCanal UK CEO', *Deadline Hollywood*, 16 October 2016, https://deadline.com/2016/10/brexit-warning-british-indies-danny-perkins-studiocanal-vivendi-1201835141/.
87 In Spicer, 'The European Producer', 604.
88 For details, see Oxera.com, *Impacts of Leaving the EU on the UK's Screen Sector* (Screen Sector Task Force, 2017), https://www.bfi.org.uk/sites/bfi.org.uk/files/downloads/bfi-impact-leaving-eu-uk-screen-sector-2017-v2.pdf

Conclusion: Longing for yesterday?

1 A link to the breakdown of results can be found in Matthew Smith, 'When, Exactly, Were the "Good Old Days"?', *YouGov*, 6 June 2019, https://yougov.co.uk/topics/lifestyle/articles-reports/2019/06/05/when-exactly-were-good-old-days
2 Simon Kuper, 'Boris, Corbyn and Other English Archetypes', *Financial Times*, 27 June 2019, https://www.ft.com/content/5e4e0094-9796-11e9-9573-ee5cbb98ed36
3 Richard Dyer, *Only Entertainment* (London and New York: Routledge, 2002), 20.
4 Ibid., 26–7.
5 Tom Grater, 'The Story behind Beatles Film "Yesterday": Richard Curtis, Danny Boyle, Working Title and a Rising UK Producer', *Screen Daily*, 3 May 2019, https://www.screendaily.com/features/the-story-behind-beatles-film-yesterday-richard-curtis-danny-boyle-working-title-and-a-rising-uk-producer/5138875.article

6   In Matt Patches, 'Unraveling the Romantic Spacetime Continuum of Richard Curtis', *Polygon*, 26 June 2019, https://www.polygon.com/2019/6/26/18759706/yesterday-movie-richard-curtis-interview-douglas-adams-mamma-mia-3
7   See James Leggott, 'Travels in Curtisland: Richard Curtis and British Comedy Cinema', in *British Comedy Cinema*, ed. I. Q. Hunter and Laraine Porter (London and New York: Routledge, 2012), 196–207.

Bibliography

ABTA, *Holiday Habits Report 2017* (2017), https://www.abta.com/sites/default/files/media/document/uploads/Holiday_Habits_Report_2017_0.pdf (Accessed 17 October 2019).

Adorno, Theodor W., *The Culture Industry: Selected Essays on Mass Culture*. London and New York: Routledge, 1991.

Adorno, Theodor W. and Max Horkheimer, *Dialectic of Enlightenment*. London and New York: Verso, 1997.

Akhtar, Miriam and Steve Humphries, *Some Liked It Hot: The British on Holiday at Home and Abroad*. London: Virgin, 2000.

Altman, Rick, *Film/Genre*. London: BFI, 1999.

Anderson, Benedict, *Imagined Communities: Reflections on the Origin and Spread of Nationalism*. London and New York: Verso, 1991.

Andersson, Johan and Lawrence Webb, 'Introduction: Decentring the Cinematic City – Film and Media in the Digital Age'. In *Global Cinematic Cities: New Landscapes of Film and Media*, edited by Johan Andersson and Lawrence Webb, 1–16. London and New York: Wallflower, 2016.

Andrews, Hazel, 'Feeling at Home: Embodying Britishness in a Spanish Charter Tourist Resort', *Tourist Studies* 5, no. 3 (2005): 247–66.

Andrews, Nigel, 'Nick Park on Why He "Refused" to Sell Wallace and Gromit', *Financial Times*, 26 January 2018, https://www.ft.com/content/10922a92-00f2-11e8-9650-9c0ad2d7c5b5 (Accessed 17 October 2019).

Anon., 'Boris Johnson's Brexit Victory Speech: Full Transcript', *Newsweek*, 24 June 2016, http://www.newsweek.com/boris-johnsons-brexit-victory-speech-full-transcript-474086 (Accessed 17 October 2019).

Anon., 'StudioCanal s'appuie sur ses pilliers', *Le Film français*, 20 June 2017, http://www.lefilmfrancais.com/cinema/132902/cineeurope-2017-studiocanal-snappuie-sur-ses-piliers (Accessed 17 October 2019).

Anon., 'Daily Chart – Where Britons Go on Holiday', *Economist*, 15 August 2017, https://www.economist.com/graphic-detail/2017/08/15/where-britons-go-on-holiday (Accessed 17 October 2019).

Antonucci, Lorenza, Laszlo Horvath and André Krouwel, 'Brexit Was Not the Voice of the Working Class Nor of the Uneducated – It Was of the Squeezed Middle', *LSE British Politics and Policy Blog*, 13 October 2017, http://blogs.lse.ac.uk/politicsandpolicy/brexit-and-the-squeezed-middle/ (Accessed 17 October 2019).

Archer, Neil, *Hot Fuzz*. Leighton Buzzard: Auteur, 2015.

Archer, Neil, *Beyond a Joke: Parody in English Film and Television Comedy*. London and New York: Bloomsbury, 2017.

Archer, Neil, '*Et in Arcadia Ego*: Precarious Romanticism and the English Road Movie', in *The Global Road Movie: Alternative Journeys around the World*, ed. José Duarte and Timothy Corrigan, 203–16. Bristol: Intellect, 2018.

Archer, Neil, *Twenty-First Century Hollywood: Rebooting the System*. London and New York: Wallflower, 2019.

Armitage, Simon, *The Death of King Arthur*. London: Faber and Faber, 2012.

Arning, Chris, 'Soft Power, Ideology and Symbolic Manipulation in Summer Olympic Games Opening Ceremonies: A Semiotic Analysis', *Social Semiotics* 23, no. 4 (2013): 523–44.

Azalbert, Nicolas, '*Les Heures sombres*', *Cahiers du cinéma* 740 (2018), 51.

Bakker, Gerben, 'Soft Power: The Media Industries in Britain since 1870', *London School of Economics, Economic History Working Papers* 200 (2014).

Barraclough, Leo, '"Carry On" Comedy Movie Franchise to Be Revived', *Variety*, 16 May 2016, https://variety.com/2016/film/global/carry-on-comedy-movie-revived-1201775752/ (Accessed 17 October 2019).

Beck, Ulrich, *Cosmopolitan Vision*. Cambridge: Polity, 2006.

Belpeche, Stéphanie, '"Dunkerque", le Dixième Film de Christopher Nolan, est Exceptionnel', *Journal du dimanche*, 18 July 2017, https://www.lejdd.fr/Culture/Cinema/dunkerque-le-dixieme-film-de-christopher-nolan-est-exceptionnel-3391967 (Accessed 17 October 2019).

Bennett, Alan, *Keeping On Keeping On*. London: Faber & Faber/ Profile, 2016.

Bennett, Bruce, *The Cinema of Michael Winterbottom: Borders, Terror, Intimacy*. London and New York: Wallflower, 2014.

Bergfelder, Tim, 'Popular European Cinema in the 2000s: Cinephilia, Genre and Heritage', in *The Europeanness of European Cinema: Identity, Meaning, Globalization*, ed. Mary Harrod, Mariana Liz and Alissa Timoshkina, 33–57. London and New York: I.B. Tauris, 2015.

Bignell, Jonathan, 'Migration, Translation and Hybridity: European Animation on British Television', unpublished paper presented at the 'Continental Connections' conference, De Montfort University, 10–11 July 2007, 1–11. Transcript accessed at https://s3.amazonaws.com/academia.edu.documents/38108386/BignellEuroAnimation.pdf?response-content-disposition=inline%3B%20filename%3DMigration_Translation_and_Hybridity_Euro.pdf&X-Amz-Algorithm=AWS4-HMAC-SHA256&X-Amz-Credential=AKIAIWOWYYGZ2Y53UL3A%2F20191017%2Fus-east-1%2Fs3%2Faws4_request&X-

Amz-Date=20191017T084341Z&X-Amz-Expires=3600&X-Amz-SignedHeaders=host&X-Amz-Signature=75f0f180c0558358719363af6a0fd299368bdf5265451a8bfdffc8b4cf4140ba (Accessed 17 October 2019).

Blandford, Steve, *Film, Drama and the Break-Up of Britain*. Bristol and Chicago: Intellect, 2007.

Bordwell, David, *Narration in the Fiction Film*. London: Methuen, 1985.

Bordwell, David, *The Way Hollywood Tells It: Story and Style in Modern Movies*. Berkeley: University of California Press, 2006.

Bordwell, David, *Poetics of Cinema*. London and New York: Routledge, 2012.

Bowler, Peter J., *Science for All: The Popularization of Science in Early Twentieth-Century Britain*. Chicago and London: University of Chicago Press, 2009.

British Film Commission, *UK in Focus 2016*. 2016, https://issuu.com/britishfilmcommission/docs/ukinfocus_lr__1_ (Accessed 17 October 2019).

British Film Institute, *Statistical Yearbook 2013*. 2013, https://www.bfi.org.uk/sites/bfi.org.uk/files/downloads/bfi-statistical-yearbook-2013.pdf (Accessed 17 October 2019).

British Film Institute, *The Wide Angle: The BFI's International Strategy*. 2013, http://www.bfi.org.uk/sites/bfi.org.uk/files/downloads/bfi-wide-angle-international-strategy-2013-v2.pdf (Accessed 17 October 2019).

British Film Institute, *Research and Statistics 2016: Audiences*. 2016, https://www.bfi.org.uk/sites/bfi.org.uk/files/downloads/bfi-statistical-yearbook-audiences-2015-2016-08-25.pdf (Accessed 17 October 2019).

British Film Institute, 'New BFI Statistics Show Robust Year for Film in the UK in 2016', 26 January 2017, http://www.bfi.org.uk/news-opinion/news-bfi/announcements/highest-grossing-films-uk-box-office-2016 (Accessed 17 October 2019).

British Film Institute, *BFI2022: Supporting UK Film*. 2017, https://www.bfi.org.uk/2022/ (Accessed 17 October 2019).

Brown, Noel, '"Family" Entertainment and Contemporary Hollywood Cinema', *Scope: An Online Journal of Film and Television Studies* 25 (2013): 1–21.

Brown, Noel, *The Children's Film: Genre, Nation and Narrative*. London and New York: Wallflower, 2017.

Brown, Tom and Belén Vidal, eds. *The Biopic in Contemporary Film Culture*. London and New York: Routledge, 2014.

Brunet, Johanne and Galina Gornostaeva, 'Company Profile: Working Title Films, Independent Producer: Internationalization of the Film Industry', *International Journal of Arts Management* 9, no. 1 (2006): 60–9.

Brunsdon, *London in Cinema: The Cinematic City since 1945*. London: BFI, 2007.

Burgoyne, Robert, 'Bare Life and Sovereignty in *Gladiator*', in *The Epic Film in World Culture*, ed. Robert Burgoyne, 82–97. London and New York: Routledge, 2011.

Burgoyne, Robert, ed. *The Epic Film in World Culture*. London and New York: Routledge, 2011.

Burgoyne, Robert, 'Introduction', in *The Epic Film in World Culture*, ed. Robert Burgoyne, 1–15. London and New York: Routledge, 2011.

Burn-Murdoch, John, 'Youth Turnout at General Election Highest in 25 Years, Data Show', *Financial Times*, 20 June 2017, https://www.ft.com/content/6734cdde-550b-11e7-9fed-c19e2700005f (Accessed 17 October 2019).

Burns, Judith, 'Oxford and Cambridge Top World University Rankings', *BBC News*, 5 September 2017, https://www.bbc.co.uk/news/education-41160914 (Accessed 17 October 2019).

Buyukodabas, Alexandre, '"Dunkerque": Christopher Nolan Signe Son Film le Plus Intense', *Les Inrockuptibles*, 17 July 2017, https://www.lesinrocks.com/cinema/films-a-l-affiche/dunkerque/ (Accessed 17 October 2019).

Carroll, Noël, *Humour: A Very Short Introduction*. London and New York: Routledge, 2014.

Cavell, Stanley, *Pursuits of Happiness: The Hollywood Comedy of Remarriage*. Cambridge and London: Harvard University Press, 1981.

Chapman, James, *Past and Present: National Identity and the British Historical Film*. London and New York: I.B. Tauris, 2005.

Chessel, Luc, '"*Les Heures sombres*": Winston Churchill Sans Filtre', *Libération*, 2 January 2018, https://next.liberation.fr/cinema/2018/01/02/les-heures-sombres-winston-churchill-sans-filtre_1619988 (Accessed 17 October 2019).

Clarke, Harold D., Matthew Goodwin and Paul Whiteley, *Brexit: Why Britain Voted to Leave the European Union*. Cambridge: Cambridge University Press, 2017.

Collins, Jim, *Bring on the Books for Everybody: How Literary Culture Became Popular Culture*. Durham and London: Duke University Press, 2010.

Connor, J.D., *The Studios after the Studios: Neoclassical Hollywood (1970–2010)*. Stanford: Stanford University Press, 2015.

Cook, Pam, *Screening the Past: Memory and Nostalgia in Cinema*. London and New York: Routledge, 2005.

Corless, Kieron and Chris Darke, *Cannes: Inside the World's Premier Film Festival*. London: Faber and Faber, 2007.

Cornea, Christine, *Science Fiction Cinema*. Edinburgh: Edinburgh University Press, 2007.

Cressey, Daniel, 'Scientists Say "No" to UK Exit from Europe in *Nature* Poll', *Nature* 30 March 2016, https://www.nature.com/news/scientists-say-no-to-uk-exit-from-europe-in-nature-poll-1.19636 (Accessed 17 October 2019).

Crosson, Seán, *Sport and Film*. London and New York: Routledge, 2013.

Culture, Media and Sport Committee, *Third Report from the Culture, Media and Sport Committee: Session 2010–2011, HC 464-II*. London: The Stationary Office, 2011.

Custen, George, *Bio/Pics: How Hollywood Constructed Public History*. New Brunswick: Rutgers University Press, 1992.

Dave, Paul, *Visions of England*. Oxford: Berg, 2006.

Dave, Paul, 'Film Policy and England: The Politics of Creativity', in *The Routledge Companion to Cinema and Politics*, ed. Yannis Tzioumakis and Claire Molloy, 186–96. London and New York: Routledge, 2019.

Denison, Rayna, 'The Global Markets for Anime: Miyazaki Hayao's Spirited Away (2001)', in *Japanese Cinema: Texts and Contexts*, ed. Alastair Phillips and Julian Stringer, 308–21. London and New York: Routledge, 2007.

Department for Culture, Media and Sport Film Policy Review Group, '*A Bigger Picture*': *The Report of the Film Policy Review Group*. 1998.

Dickinson, Margaret and Sarah Street, *Cinema and State: The Film Industry and the Government, 1927–84*. London: BFI, 1985.

Dodds, Klaus, 'Shaking and Stirring James Bond: Age, Gender, and Resilience in Skyfall (2012)', *Journal of Popular Film and Television* 42, no. 3 (2014): 116–30.

Doyle, Gillian, Philip Schlesinger, Raymond Boyle and Lisa W. Kelly, *The Rise and Fall of the UK Film Council*. Edinburgh: Edinburgh University Press, 2015.

Durgnat, Raymond, *A Mirror for England: British Movies from Austerity to Affluence*. London: BFI, 2012.

Dyer, Richard and Ginette Vincendeau, eds., *Popular European Cinema*. London and New York: Routledge, 1992.

Edgerton, David, *England and the Aeroplane: An Essay on a Militant and Technological Nation*. Basingstoke: Macmillan, 1991.

Edgerton, David, *Warfare State: Britain, 1920–1970*. Cambridge: Cambridge University Press, 2006.

Elsaesser, Thomas, *European Cinema: Face to Face with Hollywood*. Amsterdam: Amsterdam University Press, 2005.

Elsaesser, Thomas, 'In the City but Not Bounded by It: Cinema in the Global, the Generic and the Cluster City', in *Global Cinematic Cities: New Landscapes of Film and Media*, ed. Johan Andersson and Lawrence Webb, 19–35. London and New York: Wallflower, 2016.

European Audiovisual Observatory, *Brexit in Context: The UK in the EU28 Audiovisual Market*. 2018, https://rm.coe.int/brexit-in-context/16808b868c (Accessed 17 October 2019).

Fahy, Patrick, 'Mr. Bean's Holiday', *Sight & Sound* 17, no. 5 (2007): 72.

Faulkner, Sally, 'Introduction. Approaching the Middlebrow: Audience, Text, Institution', in *Middlebrow Cinema*, ed. Sally Faulkner, 1–12. London and New York: Routledge, 2016.

Fetzer, Thiemo, 'Did Austerity Cause Brexit?', *CESifo Working Paper Series* 7159 (2018), https://papers.ssrn.com/sol3/papers.cfm?abstract_id=3251187 (Accessed 17 October 2019).

Fitzgerald, John, *Studying British Cinema: 1999–2009*. Leighton Buzzard: Auteur, 2010.

Follows, Stephen, 'The Effect of Brexit on the UK Film Industry', *Stephenfollows.com*, 26 June 2017, https://stephenfollows.com/effect-brexit-uk-film-industry/ (Accessed 17 October 2019).

Forrest, David, *New Realism: Contemporary British Cinema*. Edinburgh: Edinburgh University Press, 2020.

Forrest, David, Graeme Harper and Jonathan Rayner, 'Introduction. Filmurbia: Cinema and the Suburbs', in *Filmurbia: Screening the Suburbs*, ed. David Forrest, Graeme Harper and Jonathan Rayner, 1–10. London: Palgrave Macmillan, 2017.

Frayling, Christopher, *Mad, Bad and Dangerous? The Scientist and the Cinema*. London: Reaktion, 2005.

Galpin, Shelley Anne, 'Harry Potter and the Hidden Heritage Films: Genre Hybridity and the Power of the Past in the Harry Potter Film Cycle', *Journal of British Cinema and Television* 13, no. 3 (2016): 430–49.

Gant, Charles, 'Development Tale: *Paddington*', *Sight & Sound* 24, no. 12 (2014): 14.

Gerrard, Steve, 'What a Carry On! The Decline and Fall of a Great British Institution', in *Seventies British Cinema*, ed. Robert Shail, 36–45. London: Palgrave, 2008.

Ghys, Clément, 'Peluche de Parfait', *Libération*, 2 December 2014, https://next.liberation.fr/cinema/2014/12/02/peluche-que-parfait_1155218 (Accessed 17 October 2019).

Golhen, Gaël, 'La Peau de l'ours', *Première* 480 (2017): 26–7.

Goodfellow, Melanie, 'Studiocanal Adds Production Exec, Expands Role of UK CEO Danny Perkins', *Screen Daily*, 30 March 2016, https://www.screendaily.com/news/studiocanal-adds-production-exec-expands-role-of-uk-ceo-danny-perkins/5102041.article (Accessed 17 October 2019).

Goodridge, Mike, 'Studio Building', *Screen International* 1721 (2010): 40.

Grix, Jonathan and Barrie Houlihan, 'Sports Mega-Events as Part of a Nation's Soft Power Strategy: The Cases of Germany (2006) and the UK (2012)', *The British Journal of Politics and International Relations* 16, no. 4 (2014): 572–96.

Gruneau, Richard and James Compton, 'Media Events, Mega-Events and Social Theory: From Durkheim to Marx', in *Sport, Media and Mega-Events*, ed. Lawrence A. Wenner and Andrew C. Billings, 33–47. London and New York: Routledge, 2017.

Harari, Noah Yuval, *Homo Deus: A Brief History of Tomorrow*. London: Harvill Secker, 2016.

Harries, Dan, *Film Parody*. London: British Film Institute, 2000.

Harries, Dan, 'Film Parody and the Resuscitation of Genre', in *Genre and Contemporary Hollywood*, ed. Steve Neale, 281–93. London: British Film Institute, 2002.

Harrod, Mary, Mariana Liz and Alissa Timoshkina, 'The Europeanness of European Cinema: An Overview', in *The Europeanness of European Cinema: Identity, Meaning, Globalization*, ed. Mary Harrod, Mariana Liz and Alissa Timoshkina, 1–13. London and New York: I.B. Tauris, 2015.

Hasian, Jr., Marouf, '*Skyfall*, James Bond's Resurrection, and 21st-Century Anglo-American Imperial Nostalgia', *Communication Quarterly* 62, no. 5 (2014): 569–88.

Hassler-Forest, Dan, *Capitalist Superheroes: Caped Crusaders in the Neoliberal Age*. Winchester: Zero, 2012.

Heritage, Stuart, 'Ooh, Matron! Why Carry On Films Refuse to Remain Dead', *Guardian*, 2 July 2019, https://www.theguardian.com/film/2019/jul/02/carry-on-films-return. (Accessed 1 October 2019).

Hewison, Robert, *The Heritage Industry: Britain in a Climate of Decline*. London: Methuen, 1987.

Hewison, Robert, *Cultural Capital: The Rise and Fall of Creative Britain*. London and New York: Verso, 2014.

Higbee, Will, 'Counter-Heritage, Middlebrow and the *Fiction Patrimoniale*: Reframing "Middleness" in the Contemporary French Historical Film', in *Middlebrow Cinema*, ed. Sally Faulkner, 139–55. London and New York: Routledge, 2016.

Higson, Andrew, 'The Concept of National Cinema', *Screen* 30, no. 4 (1989): 36–47.

Higson, Andrew, *Waving the Flag: Constructing a National Cinema in Britain*. Oxford: Clarendon, 1995.

Higson, Andrew, 'The Limiting Imagination of National Cinemas', in *Cinema and Nation*, ed. Mette Hjort and Scott Mackenzie, 63–74. London and New York: Routledge, 2000.

Higson, Andrew, 'Re-Presenting the National Past: Nostalgia and Pastiche in the Heritage Film', in *Fires Were Started: British Cinema and Thatcherism*, ed. Lester D. Friedman, 91–109. London and New York: Wallflower, 2006.

Higson, Andrew *Film England: Culturally English Filmmaking since the 1990s*. London and New York: I.B. Tauris, 2011.

Higson, Andrew, 'British Cinema, Europe and the Global Reach for Audiences', in *European Cinema and Television: Cultural Policy and Everyday Life*, ed. Ib. Bondebjerg, Eva Novrup Redvall and Andrew Higson, 127–50. Basingstoke: Palgrave Macmillan, 2015.

Higson, Andrew, 'Historical Films in Europe: The Transnational Production, Circulation and Reception of "National" Heritage Drama', in *Screening European Heritage: Creating and Consuming History on Film*, ed. Paul Cooke and Rob Stone, 183–208. Basingstoke: Palgrave Macmillan, 2016.

Higson, Andrew and Richard Maltby, '"Film Europe" and "Film America": An Introduction', in *'Film Europe' and 'Film America': Cinema, Commerce and Cultural Exchange*, ed. Andrew Higson and Richard Maltby, 1–31. Exeter: University of Exeter Press, 2006.

Hill, John, 'The Issue of National Cinema and British Film Production', in *New Questions of British Cinema*, ed. Duncan Petrie, 10–21. London: BFI, 1992.

Hill, John, *British Cinema in the 1980s*. Oxford: Clarendon, 1999.

Hill, John, '"This Is for the Batmans as Well as the Vera Drakes": Economics, Culture and UK Government Film Production Policy in the 2000s', *Journal of British Cinema and Television* 9, no. 3 (2012): 333–56.

Hochscherf, Tobias, 'Bond for the Age of Global Crises: 007 in the Daniel Craig Era', *Journal of British Cinema and Television* 10, no. 2 (2013): 298–320.

Hochscherf, Tobias and James Leggott, 'Working Title Films: From Mid-Atlantic to the Heart of Europe?', *Film International* 48 (2010): 8–20.

Hodges, Andrew, *Alan Turing: The Enigma*. London: Vintage, 2012.

Hopewell, John, 'Creative Punch Meets Biz Savvy', *Variety* 427, no. 1 (2012): 79.

Hopewell, John, 'Mipcom: Studiocanal to Launch Paddington Animated TV Series', *Variety*, 9 October 2017, https://variety.com/2017/tv/news/mipcom-studiocanal-paddington-animated-tv-series-1202584183/ (Accessed 1 October 2019).

Hopewell, John and Elsa Keslassy, 'StudioCanal Acquires Paddington Bear Brand, Plans Third Paddington Movie', *Variety*, 20 June 2016, https://variety.com/2016/film/global/studiocanal-acquires-paddington-brand-third-movie-1201799112/ (Accessed 1 October 2019).

Hutcheon, Linda, *A Theory of Parody: The Teachings of Twentieth-Century Art Forms*. London: Methuen, 1985.

Innes, Paul, *Epic*. London and New York: Routledge, 2013.

Iordanova, Dina, 'Rise of the Rest: Globalizing Epic Cinema', in *The Epic Film in World Culture*, ed. Robert Burgoyne, 101–23. London and New York: Routledge, 2011.

Jack, Ian, 'Dunkirk and Darkest Hour Fuel Brexit Fantasies – Even if They Weren't Meant To', *Guardian*, 27 January 2018, https://www.theguardian.com/commentisfree/2018/jan/27/brexit-britain-myths-wartime-darkest-hour-dunkirk-nationalist-fantasies (Accessed 1 October 2019).

Jones, Huw David, 'The Cultural and Economic Implications of UK/European Co-Production', *Transnational Cinemas* 7, no. 1 (2016): 1–20.

Jones, Huw David, 'UK/European Co-productions: The Case of Ken Loach', *Journal of British Cinema and Television* 13, no. 3 (2016): 368–89.

Kahnemann, Daniel, *Thinking, Fast and Slow*. London: Penguin, 2011.

Kaku, Michio, *Physics of the Future: The Inventions That Will Transform Our Lives*. London: Penguin, 2011.

Kearn, David W., 'The Hard Truths about Soft Power', *Journal of Political Power*, 4, no. 1 (2011): 65–85.

King, Geoff, *Film Comedy*. London: Wallflower, 2002.

Krämer, Peter, '"The Best Disney Film Never Made": Children's Films and the Family Audience in American Cinema since the 1960s', in *Genre and Contemporary Hollywood*, ed. Steve Neale, 185–200. London: BFI, 2002.

Kulyk, Laëtitia, 'The Use of English in European Feature Films: Unity in Diversity', in *The Europeanness of European Cinema: Identity, Meaning, Globalization*, ed. Mary Harrod, Mariana Liz and Alissa Timoshkina, 173–81. London and New York: I.B. Tauris, 2015.

Laderman, David, *Driving Visions: Exploring the Road Movie*. Austin: University of Texas Press, 2002.

Leggott, James, 'Travels in Curtisland: Richard Curtis and British Comedy Cinema', in *British Comedy Cinema*, ed. I. Q. Hunter and Laraine Porter, 184–95. London and New York: Routledge, 2012.

Lewens, Tim, *The Meaning of Science*. London: Penguin, 2015.

Liz, Mariana, 'From European Co-Productions to the Euro-Pudding', in *The Europeanness of European Cinema: Identity, Meaning, Globalization*, ed. Mary Harrod, Mariana Liz and Alissa Timoshkina, 73–85. London and New York: I.B. Tauris, 2015.

Liz, Mariana, *Euro-Visions: Europe in Contemporary Cinema*. London and New York: Bloomsbury, 2016.

Macnab, Geoffrey, *Stairways to Heaven: Rebuilding the British Film Industry*. London and New York: I.B. Tauris, 2018.

Mair, John, Tor Clark, Neal Fowler, Raymond Snoddy and Richard Tait, eds. *Brexit, Trump and the Media*. Bury St. Edmunds: Arima, 2017.

Malfas, Maximos, Barrie Houlihan, and Eleni Theodoraki. 'Impacts of the Olympic Games as Mega-Events', *Proceedings of the Institution of Civil Engineers* 157, ME3 (2004): 209–20.

Malory, Thomas, *Le Morte D'Arthur: Volume 1*. London: Penguin, 1969.

Marx, Leo, *The Machine in the Garden: Technology and the Pastoral Ideal in America*. Oxford and New York: Oxford University Press, 1964.

Masters, Tim, 'The Story behind *Paddington*'s Calypso Songs', *BBC News*, 28 November 2014, https://www.bbc.co.uk/news/entertainment-arts-30196290 (Accessed 1 October 2019).

Mazdon, Lucy and Catherine Wheatley, 'Introduction. Franco-British Cinematic Relations: An Overview', in *Je t'aime … Moi Non Plus: Franco-British Cinematic Relations*, ed. Lucy Mazdon and Catherine Wheatley, 1–15. New York and Oxford: Berghahn, 2010.

McMillan, Christopher, 'Broken Bond: *Skyfall* and the British Identity Crisis', *Journal of British Cinema and Television* 12, no. 2 (2012): 191–206.
McSweeney, Terence, *The 'War on Terror' and American Film: 9/11 Frames Per Second*. Edinburgh: Edinburgh University Press, 2014.
Medhurst, Andy, *A National Joke: Popular Comedy and English Cultural Identities*. London and New York: Routledge, 2007.
Meir, Christopher, 'European Cinema in an Era of Studio-Building: Some Artistic and Industrial Tendencies in Studiocanal's Output, 2006-Present', *Studies in European Cinema* 16, no. 1 (2019): 5–21.
Meir, Christopher, *Mass-Producing European Cinema: Studiocanal and its Works*. London and New York: Bloomsbury, 2019.
Mills, Brett, *The Sitcom*. Edinburgh: Edinburgh University Press, 2009.
Monk, Claire, 'Film England: Culturally English Filmmaking since the 1990s', *Sight & Sound* 21, no. 9 (2011): 92.
Moretti, Franco, *Distant Reading*. London and New York: Verso, 2013.
Morgan, John, 'EU Referendum: Nine Out of 10 University Staff Back Remain', *Times Higher Education* 16 June 2016, https://www.timeshighereducation.com/news/european-union-referendum-nine-out-of-ten-university-staff-back-remain. (Accessed 1 October 2019).
Mudde, Cas and Cristóbal Rovira Kaltwasser, *Populism: A Very Short Introduction*. Oxford: Oxford University Press, 2017.
Mueller, Matt, 'Studiocanal UK: 10 Years in the Making', *Screen Daily*, 5 July 2016, https://www.screendaily.com/distribution/studiocanal-uk-10-years-in-the-making/5106455.article (Accessed 1 October 2019).
Mumford, Gwilym, 'Epic Fail: Why Has *King Arthur* Flopped So Badly?', *Guardian*, 16 May 2017, https://www.theguardian.com/film/2017/may/16/epic-fail-why-has-king-arthur-flopped-so-badly (Accessed 1 October 2019).
Murphy, Robert, *British Cinema and the Second World War*. London and New York: Continuum, 2000.
Murphy, Robert, 'City Life: Urban Fairytales in late 90s British Cinema', in *The British Cinema Book*, ed. Robert Murphy, 2nd ed. 292–300. London: BFI, 2001.
Murray, Jonathan, 'Blurring Borders: Scottish Cinema in the Twenty-First Century', *Journal of British Cinema and Television* 9, no. 3 (2012): 400–18.
Murray, Jonathan, *The New Scottish Cinema*. London and New York: I.B. Tauris, 2014.
Murray, Simone, *The Adaptation Industry: The Cultural Economy of Contemporary Literary Adaptation*. London and New York: Routledge, 2012.
Naficy, Hamid, *An Accented Cinema: Exilic and Diasporic Filmmaking*. Princeton and Oxford: Princeton University Press, 2001.

Neale, Steve, *Genre and Hollywood*. London and New York: Routledge, 2000.

Nelson, Elissa, 'The New Old Face of a Genre: The Franchise Teen Film as Industry Strategy', *Cinema Journal* 57, no. 1 (2017): 125–33.

Newsinger, Jack, 'British Film Policy in an Age of Austerity', *Journal of British Cinema and Television* 9, no. 1 (2012): 133–44.

Nwonka, Clive James, 'Diversity Pie: Rethinking Social Exclusion and Diversity Policy in the British Film Industry', *Journal of Media Practice* 16, no. 1 (2015): 73–90.

Nwonka, Clive James, 'Estate of the Nation: Social Housing as Cultural Verisimilitude in British Social Realism', in *Filmurbia: Screening the Suburbs*, ed. David Forrest, Graeme Harper and Jonathan Rayner, 65–78. London: Palgrave Macmillan, 2017.

Nwonka, Clive James, *The Aesthetics of British Urban Cinema*. London and New York: Bloomsbury, 2020.

Nwonka, Clive James and Sarita Malik, 'Cultural Discourses and Practices of Institutionalised Diversity in the UK Film Sector: "Just get something black made"', *The Sociological Review* 66, no. 6 (2018): 1111–27.

Nye, Joseph, *Soft Power: The Means to Success in World Politics*. New York: Public Affairs, 2004.

O'Leary, Alan, 'On the Complexity of the *Cinepanettone*', in *Popular Italian Cinema*, ed. Louis Bayman and Sergio Rigoletto, 200–13. London: Palgrave Macmillan, 2013.

O'Reilly, Karen, 'Hosts and Guests, Guests and Hosts: British Residential Tourism in the Costa del Sol', in *Cultures of Mass Tourism: Doing the Mediterranean in the Age of Banal Mobilities*, ed. Pau Obrador Pons, Mike Crang and Penny Travlou, 129–42. Farnham and Burlington: Ashgate, 2009.

Oxera.com, *Impacts of Leaving the EU on the UK's Screen Sector*. 2017, https://www.bfi.org.uk/sites/bfi.org.uk/files/downloads/bfi-impact-leaving-eu-uk-screen-sector-2017-v1.pdf (Accessed 1 October 2019).

Pauli, Michelle, 'Michael Bond: 'Paddington Stands Up for Things, He's Not Afraid of Going to the Top and Giving Them a Hard Stare', *Guardian*, 28 November 2014, https://www.theguardian.com/books/2014/nov/28/michael-bond-author-paddington-bear-interview-books-television-film (Accessed 1 October 2019).

Petley, Julian, 'The Englishness of British Cinema: Beyond the Valley of the Corn Dollies', in *A Companion to British and Irish Cinema*, ed. John Hill, 461–89. Chichester and Hoboken: Wiley-Blackwell, 2019.

Pinker, Steven, *Enlightenment Now: The Case for Reason, Science, Humanism and Progress*. London: Penguin, 2018.

Portland Communications, *The Soft Power 30: A Global Ranking of Soft Power*. 2015, https://portland-communications.com/pdf/The-Soft-Power_30.pdf (Accessed 1 October 2019).

Pratt, Andy C., 'Cultural Industries and Public Policy: An Oxymoron?', *International Journal of Cultural Policy* 11, no. 1 (2005): 31–44.

Pulver, Andrew, 'Disaster Looms if British Film Disconnects from Europe, Says Studio Head', *Guardian*, 9 July 2016, https://www.theguardian.com/film/2016/jul/09/disaster-looms-if-british-film-disconnects-from-europe-says-studio-head (Accessed 1 October 2019).

Puttnam, David, *The Undeclared War*. London: HarperCollins, 1997.

Redmond, Sean, *Liquid Space: Science Fiction Film and Television in the Digital Age*. London and New York: I.B. Tauris, 2017.

Ridge-Newman, Anthony, Fernando León-Solís and Hugh O'Donnell, eds. *Reporting the Road to Brexit*. Basingstoke: Palgrave Macmillan, 2018.

Ritman, Alex, 'Joe Cornish on "The Kid Who Would Be King," Rejecting Hollywood Franchises', *Hollywood Reporter*, 24 January 2019, https://www.hollywoodreporter.com/news/joe-cornish-kid-who-would-be-king-rejecting-major-franchises-1178767 (Accessed 1 October 2019).

Robinson, Matthew, '"Make Do and Mend": Crafting a Scottish Underdog in *The Flying Scotsman* (2006)', *Open Screens* 1, no. 1 (2018): n/p.

Robinson, Matthew, '"It's Spiritual, Man": *Eddie the Eagle* and English Amateurism', *Journal of British Cinema and Television* 16, no. 2 (2019): 170–90.

Roddick, Nick, 'If the United States Spoke Spanish, We Would Have a Film Industry', in *British Cinema Now*, ed. Martin Auty and Nick Roddick, 3–18. London: BFI, 1985.

Roddick, Nick, 'Show Me the Culture!', *Sight & Sound* 8, no. 12 (1998): 22–6.

Rose, Steve, '*Early Man* Review – Aardman Claymation Comedy Brings Brexit to the Bronze Age', *Guardian*, 14 January 2018, https://www.theguardian.com/film/2018/jan/14/early-man-review-aardman-animations (Accessed 1 October 2019).

Rubin, Rebecca, '"The Kid Who Would Be King" Could Lose $50 Million at Box Office', *Variety*, 29 January 2019, https://variety.com/2019/film/box-office/the-kid-who-would-be-king-box-office-flop-1203119724/ (Accessed 1 October 2019).

Russell, Nicholas, *Communicating Science: Professional, Popular, Literary*. Cambridge: Cambridge University Press, 2010.

Sandbrook, Dominic, *Never Had It So Good: A History of Britain from Suez to the Beatles*. London: Abacus, 2005.

Sandbrook, Dominic, *State of Emergency: Britain 1970–1974*. London: Penguin, 2010.

Sandbrook, Dominic, *Seasons in the Sun: The Battle for Britain, 1974–1979*. London: Penguin, 2012.

Sassen, Saskia, *The Global City: New York, London, Tokyo*. Princeton: Princeton University Press, 1991.

Schlesinger, Philip, 'The Sociological Scope of "National Cinema"', in *Cinema and Nation*, ed. Mette Hjort and Scott MacKenzie, 19–31. London and New York: Routledge, 2000.

Schlesinger, Philip, 'Transnational Framings of British Film Policy: The Case of the UK Film Council', in *Transnational Mediations: Negotiating Popular Culture between Europe and the United States*, ed. Christof Decker and Astrid Böger, 191–208. Heidelbeg: Universitatätsverlag, 2015. Digital copy sourced from Enlighten: University of Glasgow Research Publications, 1–37, http://eprints.gla.ac.uk/114438/13/114438.pdf (Accessed 1 October 2019).

Shaw, Gareth, Sheela Agarwal and Paul Bull, 'Tourism Consumption and Tourist Behaviour: A British Perspective', *Tourism Geographies* 2, no. 3 (2000): 264–89.

Shoard, Catherine, 'How *Paddington* Took Paul King from *Mighty Boosh* to Almighty Blockbuster', *Guardian*, 23 March 2015, https://www.theguardian.com/film/2015/mar/23/paddington-mighty-boosh-paul-king-garth-marenghi (Accessed 1 October 2019).

Skinner, Gideon and Glen Gottfried, 'How Britain Voted in the EU Referendum', *Ipsos MORI*, 5 September 2016, https://www.ipsos.com/ipsos-mori/en-uk/how-britain-voted-2016-eu-referendum (Accessed 1 October 2019).

Smith, Chris, *Creative Britain*. London: Faber & Faber, 1998.

Sobchack, Vivian, '"Surge and Splendor": A Phenomenology of the Hollywood Historical Epic', *Representations* 29, no. 1 (1990): 24–49.

Spicer, Andrew, 'The European Producer: Simon Perry', *Journal of British Cinema and Television* 15, no. 4 (2018): 589–608.

Spicer, Andrew Howard, '"Being European": UK production companies and Europe', *Studies in European Cinema* 16, no. 1 (2019): 55–72.

Standing, Guy, *The Precariat: The New Dangerous Class*. London and New York: Bloomsbury, 2011.

Steger, Manfred, *Globalization: A Very Short Introduction*. Oxford: Oxford University Press, 2013.

Stone, Dan, *Breeding Superman: Nietzsche, Race and Eugenics in Edwardian and Interwar Britain*. Liverpool: Liverpool University Press, 2002.

Stott, Andrew, *Comedy*. London and New York: Routledge, 2014.

Syed, Matthew, 'Higher, Faster, Yes. More Meritocratic, No', in *The Sport and Society Reader*, ed. David Karen and Robert E. Washington, 88–9. London and New York: Routledge, 2010.

Thunberg, Greta, *No One Is Too Small to Make a Difference*. London: Penguin, 2019.

Tombs, Robert and Isabelle Tombs, *That Sweet Enemy: Britain and France, the History of a Love-Hate Relationship*. London: Pimlico, 2006.

Townsend, Nathan 'Working Title Films and Universal: The Integration of a British Production Company into a Hollywood Studio', *Journal of British Cinema and Television* 15, no. 2 (2018): 179–203.

Uhlig, Robert, *Genius of Britain: The Scientists Who Changed the World*. London and New York: HarperCollins, 2010.

Urry, John and Jonas Larsen, *The Tourist Gaze 3.0*. London: Sage, 2011.

Utichi, Joe, 'British Indies Face "Less Control" Post-Brexit, Warns StudioCanal UK CEO', *Deadline Hollywood*, 16 October 2016, https://deadline.com/2016/10/brexit-warning-british-indies-danny-perkins-studiocanal-vivendi-1201835141/ (Accessed 1 October 2019).

Utterson, Andrew, *From IBM to MGM: Cinema at the Dawn of the Digital Age*. London: BFI, 2011.

Vidal, Belén, *Heritage Film: Nature, Genre and Representation*. London and New York: Wallflower, 2012.

Vidal, Belen, 'Introduction: The Biopic and Its Critical Contexts', in *The Biopic in Contemporary Film Culture*, ed. Tom Brown and Belén Vidal, 1–32. London and New York: Routledge, 2013.

Vincendeau, Ginette, 'The French Resistance through British Eyes: From *'Allo 'Allo!* to *Charlotte Gray*', in *Je t'aime ... Moi Non Plus: Franco-British Cinematic Relations*, eds. Lucy Mazdon and Catherine Wheatley, 237–53. New York and Oxford: Berghahn, 2010.

Vulser, Nicole, 'Mister Bean aux Marches du Palais', *Le Monde*, 28–29 May 2006, https://www.lemonde.fr/festival-de-cannes/article/2006/05/27/mister-bean-aux-marches-du-palais_776799_766360.html (Accessed 1 October 2019).

Walker, Alexander, *Hollywood, England: The British Film Industry in the 1960s*. London: Michael Joseph, 1974.

Walters, Ben, 'Psycho Geography', *Sight & Sound* 22, no. 11 (2012): 30–3.

Wayne, Michael, 'Working Title Mark II: A Critique of the Atlanticist Paradigm for British Cinema', *International Journal of Media and Cultural Politics* 2, no. 1 (2006): 59–73.

Weight, Richard, *Patriots: National Identity in Britain 1940–2000*. Basingstoke: Macmillan, 2002.

Whannel, Gary, *Fields in Vision: Television Sport and Cultural Transformation*. London and New York: Routledge, 1992.

Wiseman, Andreas, 'Crack the Code', *Screen International* 1782 (2014): 24–7.

Wright, Patrick, *On Living in an Old Country: The National Past in Contemporary Britain*. Oxford: Oxford University Press, 2009.

York, Chris, 'Rio 2016 Medal Table: Brexit Voters Claim Credit for Team GB Olympic Games Success', *Huffington Post*, 15 August 2016, https://www.huffingtonpost.co.uk/entry/brexit-team-gb-olympics_uk_57b162b9e4b01f97d8f2eab3?_guc_consent_skip=1569939765 (Accessed 1 October 2019).

Young, Hugo, *This Blessed Plot: Britain and Europe from Churchill to Blair*. New York: Overlook, 1998.

Index

About Time 185–90, 192, 195, 230
Absolutely Fabulous (TV series) 73–4
Absolutely Fabulous: The Movie 1–2, 10, 12, 13–14, 20, 61–2, 66–7, 72–7, 80, 91, 94, 95–6
animated film 221–4
Atonement 99, 159, 175, 210–11
Attack the Block 126, 127,
austerity 6, 141, 162, 183–4, 197, 199

'banal cosmopolitanism' (Beck) 215–16
'banal nationalism' (Billig) 65, 215
Beck, Ulrich 30, 205, 210, 215–16, 224
Bend It Like Beckham 181
Bergfelder, Tim 109
Bevan, Tim (*see also* Working Title) 18, 47, 168–9, 180
Bignell, Jonathan 223–4
A Bigger Picture (Film Policy Review Group report) 48
Billy Elliot 160, 173, 181, 196, 231–2
Biopics 21, 108, 109, 119, 134, 145–7, 151–2, 164, 231
Blair, Tony 6, 63, 92, 180
    (*see also* New Labour)
blockbusters,
    and British film 1–2, 107–10, 117–18, 120, 175
The Boat that Rocked (*Pirate Radio*) 179, 186
'boffin' films 162
Bordwell, David 18–19, 40, 187
Boyle, Danny 189–90, 232, 234
'Brand Britain' 23–4, 32, 38, 44, 48
Braveheart 136
Breaking the Code 149
Brexit,
    as majority English vote 26
    possible causes of 6–8,
    potential impact on cinema production 54, 55–8, 203, 206–7, 226–7
    voting preferences for 7–8, 26

Bridget Jones's Baby 2, 50–1, 53, 179
Bridget Jones series 50, 175, 179, 182–3, 224
British film industry,
    and Europe 79, 86, 205–9
    and Hollywood 9–11, 14, 22, 27, 28, 40, 54, 56, 79, 94, 99, 127–30, 176–81, 207, 209–12, 216–17
    as 'internalist' 209–10
British Film Institute (BFI) 13, 53–4, 55–8, 207
    and Europe 57, 207
    response to Brexit of 56–7
British Empire 31, 39, 43–5, 92, 113–14, 116–17, 143, 152–3, 230
    as national imaginary 45
British Screen 55, 206, 211
Brown, Noel 128, 221
Brunsdon, Charlotte 186, 218
Burgoyne, Robert 102, 120, 123, 124

Cambridge (University) 148, 149, 151–2, 154–5, 156
Cameron, David 6, 18
Cannes festival 2, 79–85
Carroll, Noël 60–61
Carry on Abroad 32, 65–6, 70, 71
Chapman, James 46–7, 99–100, 113–14, 119, 121
Chariots of Fire 42, 45, 46, 100, 134, 149
Churchill, Winston 18, 45, 103, 104–5, 106, 107, 111, 113, 114, 115, 178
Cinepanettone ('Christmas-cake film') 60
comedians,
    and Englishness 67–9
comedy,
    and ambivalence 61, 93, 98
    and 'bilateralism' 95–8
    and exclusion 24–5, 60–1
    and ideology 69
Connor, J.D. 178–79

Index

Cook, Pam 163-4
Corless, Kieron and Chris Darke, *Cannes* 80, 82-3
cosmopolitanism 96, 144, 205, 212, 215-16
Creative Europe scheme 56, 57
creative industries 24, 47, 57, 180, 181, 196
The Crown 18, 45, 179
'culturally English filmmaking' (Higson) 2-3, 22, 23, 28-9, 33, 44, 108, 129-30, 147, 168-9, 172, 179, 182, 185, 205, 213, 231
'culturally European' film 205, 211-12
Curtis, Richard 175, 176, 185-9, 234-5
Custen, George 146

Darkest Hour 9-10, 17-22, 33, 45, 99, 103-5, 106, 108, 111-12, 113-14, 115, 118-20, 121, 138, 146, 168, 178, 179
Dave, Paul 40
Denison, Rayna 222
Dickinson, Margaret 47, 52
Diversity 14, 53, 57, 114, 181, 195-6, 216
Dodds, Klaus 107
Downton Abbey 230
Dunkirk 9-10, 17-20, 45, 99, 104, 106, 119, 179
Dunkirk evacuation
 As Brexit 'myth' 17, 104
 As British 'myth' 119-20
Dyer, Richard 12-13, 232

Early Man 20, 33, 99, 101, 130-4, 136-8, 204, 214, 215, 222
Eddie the Eagle 134-6, 231
Edgerton, David 163,
Elizabeth 100, 101, 179
Elizabeth: The Golden Age 101, 179
Elsaesser, Thomas 44
English film
 as brand 21, 23-4, 37, 38, 44, 48, 138, 146, 167, 172, 174-5, 178
 as 'British' film 27-8
 as European 203, 204-5, 209, 215, 216, 218-19, 220
 and 'managed contradiction' 14, 22
 and myth 15-17, 20, 22, 23, 33, 34, 40, 100-1, 103, 105, 114, 116, 118, 119, 121, 130, 131, 136-8, 145, 148, 149-50, 157, 160, 162, 165, 168, 172, 235
 as 'propaganda' 39, 50
Englishness 7, 10, 15, 23, 26-31
 as 'Britishness' 26-9
 versus 'Britishness' 26-7
epic film 15, 99-138, 194
 globalized tendencies of 101, 102-3, 115, 127-9, 138
 and nation-building 32-3, 101-2, 122-5, 136-8
Erasmus scheme 77-8
Escape to Victory 134
eugenics 141-2
 and idea of nation 142
Eurimages scheme 21, 55, 57, 80, 212
Europe,
 English attitudes towards 5, 6, 11, 15-16, 17, 24-5, 47-8, 59-98
 as holiday destination 63-7, 71-7, 89-90
European cinema,
 English attitudes towards 77-91
 as part of European project 77, 92
European Union,
 and UK film policy 47-8, 55-8, 80, 85-6, 206-11
'Europeanization' of 222-223

family film 126-8, 212-6
 'Europeanness' of 214, 216-17, 218-26
Fantastic Beasts and Where to Find Them 10, 53, 127, 181
Farage, Nigel 6, 16, 215
Faulkner, Sally 108-9
Fellner, Eric (*see also* Working Title) 18-19, 21, 176, 179-80
'film politics' 17-24
The Flying Scotsman 134-5
football 131-4, 136
 as 'English game' 136
Forrest, David, Graeme Harper and Jonathan Rayner, *Filmurbia* 195
Four Weddings and a Funeral 48, 173, 175, 176, 181
France,
 British relationship with 72-3, 74-5, 81-2, 85-6, 94-6

Frayling, Christopher 146–7, 162
The Full Monty 47, 173, 181, 196, 231

genres,
    as shaped by film industry contexts 19, 21, 102, 109, 120, 127–30, 158, 171–3, 180, 204 (*see also individual entries*)
Gladiator 122–5
Globalization 4, 6, 11–13, 15, 17, 44, 66, 75, 117–18, 178, 180, 182–3, 190, 193, 197, 198–9, 200–1, 215, 224–5
    and anti-globalization 6, 197, 198–9, 200–1
GREAT Britain campaign 41–3, 49, 53–5

Harari, Yuval Noah 139–40
Harry Potter series 3, 10, 39, 53, 54–5, 127, 128, 129–30, 172, 175–6, 181, 204, 213,
    studio tours for 39
    use in GREAT Britain campaign 54–5
Hassler-Forest, Dan 116
Hawking 151
Hawking, Stephen 147, 149, 151–5, 169
    as 'brand' 151, 153–5 (*see also* The Theory of Everything)
Heath, Edward 62–3
heritage culture
    and film 38–9, 42, 109, 116–17, 147, 148–50, 152–4, 157, 158, 162, 164, 167, 183, 197, 199–200, 210–11, 230
    and globalization 199–200
    and populism 200
Hewison, Robert 41, 45, 152, 196
Heyday Films 10, 181, 204, 214
Higson, Andrew 2–3, 9, 22–3, 27–8, 45, 53, 54–6, 116–17, 123–4, 129, 150, 160–1, 172, 182, 186, 209, 210–11, 224
Hill, John 23, 38, 47, 52, 177, 212
The Hitchhiker's Guide to the Galaxy 14, 15
Hochscherf, Tobias 83, 84, 111, 134
holiday films 59–98
    and ambivalence towards Europe 61, 62
    and comedians 67–9
    and sitcoms 68–9

holidays,
    as 'banal nationalism' (Billig) 65
    Europe as English destination 62–7
    as heterotopia 62, 72, 75
Hot Fuzz 14–15, 190, 193, 216
Huxley, Aldous, *Brave New World* 141

I, Daniel Blake 2, 3, 12
The Imitation Game 145, 147–8, 157–169
The Inbetweeners Movie 67, 70–2, 75, 76, 77, 78, 94
'Inward investment' films 10, 21, 47–8, 53–6, 58, 94, 111, 175, 181, 207, 212, 226
Iordanova, Dina 115
Ishiguro, Kazuo, *Never Let Me Go* 140

Jack, Ian 17
James Bond series 31, 41, 42, 44, 97, 103, 105–8, 109–18, 153, 172 (*see also* Skyfall)
Johnson, Boris 5, 22, 92–3, 104–5
    and Churchill narrative 104–5

The Kid Who Would Be King 33, 99, 125–30, 138, 193
King, Geoff 67
King, Paul 217, 220
King Arthur legend 113, 124–5, 193–4
    in films 32–3, 99–100, 120–30
King Arthur: Legend of the Sword 33, 99, 120–7, 129–30, 136, 138, 172
The King's Speech 39–40, 41

Lagaan 136–7
Leggott, James 83, 84, 134
Life Story (*Race for the Double Helix*) 149
Liz, Mariana 77, 82
Loach, Ken 2, 12
London,
    centrality to English cinema of 42, 48, 50–1, 54–5, 57, 77, 177–8, 203
    changing representation of 107, 109, 121, 153, 183–8, 218–19
    as 'global city' 41, 49, 51–2, 177–8
London 2012 Olympic Games 6, 41, 42, 45–6
    legacy of 46
    and media 42, 56

opening ceremony of 41, 42
policies behind 45–6, 48–50
as soft power 48–9, 52
Love Actually 48, 173, 185, 186, 187–9, 235

Macnab, Geoffrey 22, 176–7, 210, 211
McMillan, Christopher 39, 42, 105–6, 107, 113
McSweeney, Terence 106, 107
Malik, Sarita 195–6
Mamma Mia! series 79, 232
The Man Who Knew Infinity 154–5, 156–7
Marx, Leo 161
Mary, Queen of Scots 101
Mayle, Peter, *A Year in Provence* 74, 94
Medhurst, Andy 25, 68, 69
MEDIA scheme; *see* Creative Europe scheme
Meir, Christopher 204, 208, 209, 213–14, 218
'methodological nationalism' (Beck) 30, 205, 210
middlebrow cinema 108–10
militarism,
    national disavowal of 148, 162–3
    (*see also* warfare state)
Monk, Claire 27–8
Mr. Bean,
    as national media figure 31, 42, 44, 46
Mr. Bean (TV series) 42–3
Mr. Bean's Holiday 67, 80–6, 91, 94–5, 96–7
Murphy, Robert 161–2
Murray, Jonathan 29
musicals 231–2
    as 'jukebox' musicals 232

Naficy, Hamid 217–18
Neale, Steve 158
neoliberalism 6, 156, 186, 190, 196, 197, 200
Never Let Me Go 140–2
Nevill, Amanda 39, 47, 54
New Labour 6, 31, 34, 38, 41, 43–4, 47, 50, 56, 84, 183, 186, 195–6, 208
    and 'creative industries' agenda 47, 186, 196
Newsinger, Jack 38, 39
Nolan, Christopher 10, 119

nostalgia, uses of 18–19, 34, 39, 42, 50, 128, 132, 135–136, 141, 147, 152–3, 157, 162, 164, 183, 190–5, 219, 220, 230, 231, 233–4
Notting Hill 48, 173, 183, 185, 186–7, 188, 217, 224, 235
Nwonka, Clive 195–6

O'Leary, Alan 60
One Day 182–6, 187, 189, 230
Osborne, George 6, 49
Oxford (University) 155, 156

Paddington 203–4, 213–16, 217–20, 221–4, 226–7
Paddington 2 10, 20, 203, 214–17, 219, 220, 221–4, 226–7
Paddington Trail 39
Park, Nick 130–1
Parker, Alan 211
parody, uses of 15, 16, 43, 44, 45, 60, 77, 85, 190, 216
Perry, Simon 55, 206–7, 211, 226–7
Petley, Julian 26–7, 29
Pinker, Steven 143, 144
Plunkett and Macleane 179
popular cinema,
    definitions of 8–15
populism 4, 6, 16–17, 25, 122, 126, 136, 144, 148, 194, 199–200, 201, 225
precarity (Standing) 198
Pride and Prejudice 175
Puttnam, David 208, 211, 213

'quality' film 47, 108–9, 148–9
    as national product differentiation 47, 108, 149

Redmond, Sean 189
road movies 3, 87, 197–8, 200
Robinson, Matthew 134–5
Rocketman 231, 232
Roddick, Nick 22, 48
romantic comedies/'rom-coms' 2, 3, 48, 134, 167, 177–8, 180, 182, 184, 185

Sandbrook, Dominic 62, 63
Sassen, Saskia 52
Schlesinger, Philip 207–8, 209–10, 215

science,
    and Brexit 166-7
    cinematic representation of 145-7, 151-2
    and globalization 167-9
    as 'heritage' 147, 148-50, 152-4, 157, 158, 162, 164-5, 167
    and mimesis/verisimilitude 158-9, 160-1, 164
    and nationalism 142-4
    and 'scientific realism' 139-40
    as 'soft power' 153
    and 'Two Cultures' debate 162-3
Scott of the Antarctic 99, 115, 121, 135
Scottish cinema 28, 29
Scottishness 26-7, 28
Second World War,
    in film 45, 99, 119, 159, 161-162, 163, 167, 179
    as national 'myth' 45, 107-8, 119, 167, 230
Shaun of the Dead 67, 175, 193
Shaun the Sheep (TV series) 223
Shaun the Sheep series 204, 214, 220-1
Sightseers 197-201, 230
Skyfall 19, 33, 40, 41, 42, 100, 101, 103-18, 120, 121, 123, 138, 153, 172, 185
Smith, Chris, *Creative Britain* 47-8, 173
Sobchack, Vivian 102
soft power 24, 32, 48-50, 51-2, 54, 96, 118, 153, 232-3
Spicer, Andrew 55, 57, 205, 212, 215
sport,
    and Brexit 137
    in British film 133-4
Stott, Andrew 61, 73
Street, Sarah 47
StudioCanal 10, 82, 84, 131, 133, 203-5, 208-9, 212-15, 218, 220-3, 225-6
suburbia 195, 197, 201

T2 Trainspotting 28-9
Tennyson, Alfred (Lord), *Ulysses* 112-13, 115
That Riviera Touch 67, 68-9, 95, 96
The Theory of Everything 21, 103, 145, 146-8, 150-7, 160, 167, 168
Their Finest 18, 45, 159, 179

Thunberg, Greta 30
time-travel,
    as motif in recent cinema 188-90
Tinker Tailor Soldier Spy 204, 207
tourism,
    films as promotion of 38-9, 54-5, 75, 77, 185, 218-19
'tourist gaze', the (Urry) 72-3, 77
The Trip 87
The Trip to Italy 87-91, 97-8
Turing, Alan 145, 147, 148, 157, 160, 164, 165-6 (*see also* The Imitation Game)
Turner, J. M. W., *The Fighting Temeraire* 114-15
Townsend, Nathan 176, 177, 180

UK Film Council 38, 40, 47, 55-6, 168-9, 206-207, 207-8, 231
    policies toward Europe of 55-6, 206-7, 207-8
UKIP (UK Independence Party) 6, 215
Urry, John and Jonas Larsen, *The Tourist Gaze 3.0* 64, 75
Utterson, Andrew 160

Vera Drake 159, 160
Viceroy's House 230
Victoria and Abdul 18, 21, 45, 179, 230
Vidal, Belén 145
Vincendeau, Ginette 12-13, 94-5

Wallace and Gromit series 14, 132, 133, 216
'warfare state' (Edgerton),
    Britain as 163
Weight, Richard 27
Wilson, Harold 62
Wimbledon 134
Woodward, John 212
Working Title,
    autonomy of 174-80
    defining films and genres of 34, 43, 48, 84, 85, 101, 134, 146, 147-8, 155-6, 167, 175, 179, 182, 185-6
    and PolyGram 48, 176-7, 178-9
    and StudioCanal 82, 84, 204, 214
    and Universal 46, 84, 103, 147-8,

175–6, 177, 178–9 (*see also individual titles*)
The World's End 190–5, 230
Wright, Patrick 150, 152

Yesterday 175, 189–90, 232–6
Young, Hugo 63
young adult (YA) film 128, 129, 172, 213

www.ingramcontent.com/pod-product-compliance
Lightning Source LLC
Chambersburg PA
CBHW072125290426
44111CB00012B/1786